Social Policy Expansion in Latin America

Throughout the twentieth century, much of the population in Latin America lacked social protections, as social benefits and services primarily reached formal-sector workers. Since the 1990s, however, several countries have initiated a dramatic expansion of social policy for millions of outsiders – rural, informal, and unemployed workers and their dependents. *Social Policy Expansion in Latin America* shows that the critical factors driving expansion are electoral competition for the votes of outsiders and social mobilization for policy change, both of which are more likely to emerge in democratic regimes. The balance of partisan power and the involvement of social movements in policy design explain cross-national variation in policy models, in terms of benefit levels, coverage, and civil society participation. This book draws on in-depth case studies of policy making in Argentina, Brazil, Chile, and Mexico over several administrations and across three policy areas: health care, pensions, and income support. Secondary case studies illustrate how the theory applies to other developing countries.

Candelaria Garay is an associate professor of public policy at the Kennedy School of Government, Harvard University. She received a PhD in political science from the University of California, Berkeley, and a BA in sociology from the University of Buenos Aires, Argentina.

Social Policy Expansion
in Latin America

CANDELARIA GARAY

Kennedy School of Government, Harvard University

CAMBRIDGE
UNIVERSITY PRESS

CAMBRIDGE
UNIVERSITY PRESS

One Liberty Plaza, New York, NY 10006, USA

Cambridge University Press is part of the University of Cambridge.

It furthers the University's mission by disseminating knowledge in the pursuit of education, learning, and research at the highest international levels of excellence.

www.cambridge.org
Information on this title: www.cambridge.org/9781316606407
10.1017/9781316585405

© Candelaria Garay 2016

This publication is in copyright. Subject to statutory exception and to the provisions of relevant collective licensing agreements, no reproduction of any part may take place without the written permission of Cambridge University Press.

First published 2016

Printed in the United States of America by Sheridan Books, Inc.

A catalogue record for this publication is available from the British Library.

ISBN 978-1-107-15222-9 Hardback
ISBN 978-1-316-60640-7 Paperback

Cambridge University Press has no responsibility for the persistence or accuracy of URLs for external or third-party Internet Web sites referred to in this publication and does not guarantee that any content on such Web sites is, or will remain, accurate or appropriate.

Contents

Figures

Tables

Acknowledgments

It is a pleasure to express my gratitude to the many people and institutions that supported me as I worked on this book. Although my concern for social policy began long before I became a graduate student, the first version of this project was written as doctoral dissertation and I would like to especially thank my advisors and mentors at the University of California, Berkeley, for their encouragement and support. Ruth Berins Collier provided invaluable guidance and intellectual inspiration. I am grateful for all that I learned from her, for her enthusiasm and encouragement to pursue the issues that seem interesting, and for our conversations. Jonah Levy taught me how to think about social policy in his stimulating class on the welfare state and in countless office hours, and my work has been greatly enhanced by his advice and generosity. David Collier has been a major source of motivation and guidance over the years. At the later stages of writing this book, David's encouragement reminded me I was not alone in the solitude of writing. Paul Pierson led the workshop where I first developed this project. His intellectual clarity and his comments have been extremely helpful, and his work a constant source of inspiration. Peter Evans helped me think about what ideas to pursue further as I began my research.

At Berkeley I also had the opportunity to learn from Margaret Weir and Nick Ziegler, and I was fortunate to discuss the early versions of this project at the Latin American politics seminar. I am grateful to colleagues and friends Mauricio Benítez-Iturbe, Taylor Boas, Sebastián Etchemendy, Tasha Fairfield, Natalia Ferreti, Sam Handlin, Danny Hidalgo, Maiah Jaskoski, Simeon Nichter, Wendy Sinek and Rodrigo Zarazaga for their feedback.

Fieldwork in four countries would not have been possible without the generosity of many interviewees and colleagues or the support of many institutions. In the first place, I would like to thank the public officials, social movement activists, politicians, businesspeople, and labor leaders I was fortunate to interview for their openness and time in sharing their ideas with me. These hundreds of interviews have provided an invaluable amount of information and enriched my understanding of politics immensely. The debt to these many interviewees has been a strong source of encouragement in writing this book.

Many colleagues and friends kindly helped me during my fieldwork. In Mexico, I was lucky to stay with Jenny Dyer, who taught me about everyday life in her country. I especially thank Xóchitl Castañeda, Dwight Dyer, Daniel Hernández, Asa Cristina Laurell, Leonardo Lomelí, Miguel Székely, Arturo Vargas-Bustamante, Gustavo Verduzco, Pablo Yankelevich, and Alicia Ziccardi for providing invaluable help during my fieldwork and for answering many questions on Mexico's politics and social policy. I also thank the staff at the Library of Congress for their help and hospitality. In Brazil, several people kindly helped me with my fieldwork. I would like to thank Vera Schattan P. Coelho, Telinha Grossi, Renato Martins, Rômulo Paes de Sousa, and André Urani for helping me better understand Brazil's politics and contact busy public officials and civil society activists. I would also like to thank the staff at the library of the Ministério da Previdência Social, at the Biblioteca do Senado, and at the Central Única dos Trabalhadores (CUT), for their time and hospitality. In Argentina, I enjoyed the friendship of Inés González Bombal, Laura Golbert, and Mario Roitter, my former colleagues at the Centro de Estudios de Estado y Sociedad (CEDES), where I began my life as a researcher before coming to the United States. It is always a great pleasure to get together to discuss Argentine politics. Many other people helped during my fieldwork in Argentina. I especially thank Silvina Ramos, Daniel Maceira, and Julián Gadano, who put me in touch with numerous policy makers and movement activists. In Chile, I am grateful to Marcela Jiménez, who opened the doors of MIDEPLAN to me, and to Alejandra Matus for talking with me about Chilean politics.

Support from an SSRC International Dissertation Fieldwork Grant, a Simpson Fellowship from the Institute for International Studies at Berkeley, and a Social Policy Grant from the Horowitz Foundation allowed me to pursue fieldwork for this project in Argentina, Brazil,

Chile, and Mexico. Funding from the Kennedy School, especially from the Ash Center for Democratic Governance and Innovation allowed me to pursue additional work for this book and fund a workshop for my manuscript.

The Kennedy School provided an ideal environment for turning this project into a book. I especially thank Matt Baum, Archon Fung, Merilee Grindel, Alex Keyssar, Jenny Mansbridge, Tarek Masoud, Quinton Mayne, Tony Saich, and Moshik Temkin for their invaluable support. Steve Levitsky, Jorge Dominguez, and Frances Hagopian have also provided vital feedback and support since I came to Harvard, and have offered venues to present and discuss this project. I am also grateful to Matt Amengual and Danny Hidalgo, and to Lant Pritchett and Dani Rodrik, who provided opportunities for me to present this project at MIT and at Harvard. Many research assistants have provided indispensable help: Belén Fernández Milmanda, Francisco Iglesias, María Marta Maroto, Luke Raffin, Facundo Salles Kobilanski, Agustina Schijman, and Hannah Taber. I would also like to thank the students at the Kennedy School who read chapters of the manuscript and made insightful comments.

Different parts of this book were presented at conferences and workshops. I would like to thank participants and discussants at the meetings of the American Political Science Association (APSA), the Latin American Studies Association (LASA) and at seminars and talks at Brown University, Columbia University, Cornell University, Di Tella University (Argentina), Harvard University, MIT, University of New Mexico, University of California, Berkeley, the University of Chicago, the University of Pennsylvania, the University of São Paulo (Brazil) and the Red Latinoamericana de Economía Política (REPAL).

Several friends and colleagues have read chapters of this book at different stages of its development. I am grateful to Alejandro Bonvecchi, Ruth Berins Collier, David Collier, Cosette Creamer, Jorge Domínguez, Tasha Fairfield, Tulia Falleti, Belén Fernández Milmanda, Yanilda González, Frances Hagopian, Alisha Holland, Jonah Levy, Jenny Mansbridge, María Marta Maroto, and Brian Palmer-Rubin for their helpful comments. I would like to especially thank Ben Ross Schneider, who kindly gave me comments on parts of this book and organized presentations at MIT and REPAL to discuss the manuscript; Steve Levitsky, who insisted on my thinking critically about Peru, which helped me refine the argument on electoral competition; and Vicky Murillo, who has been an extremely generous and supportive colleague, providing feedback, and opening up space for me to present this and other research projects.

Lew Bateman at Cambridge University Press was an invaluable source of support as the manuscript became a book. I will always be grateful for his enthusiasm for this project. Sara Doskow took over the task of finalizing this project as the new editor at Cambridge and has been fantastic to work with. I would also like to thank Joshua Penney at Cambridge University Press and the production team for their support. Two anonymous reviewers provided insightful comments and suggestions that helped me improve the book.

Maria Gould provided wonderful editorial support to improve my writing, and I am extremely grateful for her dedicated work. I would also like to thank Kathleen Schnaidt for helping me put together a book workshop and Sarah McLain for providing wonderful support in the process of finalizing this book.

Deep gratitude goes to the Garay and Pérez Leirós families. In particular, my mother, Margarita Rübsaamen, has been a source of understanding and inspiration to me. Both my mother and my mother-in-law, Susana Motti, have been in many ways sources of solidarity, encouragement, and love. I also thank Daniela Garay for her support, and Mabel Casimiro for her enormous help and high spirits. Claudia Pérez Leirós became a role model of academic and family life when I was a college student and continues to be a source of inspiration to me.

I dedicate this book to my family: Fernando, Gonzalo, and Camila Pérez Leirós. My deep gratitude for them is hard to express. I would not have been able to pursue this project without their immense kindness and encouragement. I am especially grateful for Fernando's understanding, and for my family's unfaltering belief that writing this book was worth the sacrifices it sometimes imposed on them. Over the years, they saw this project evolve and contributed to it in many ways, reading sections of this book, revising the data, and asking questions about the implications of this research. After this long journey, I am sure they know how happy I am to now dedicate this book to them.

Acronyms and Abbreviations

ANSES	Administración Nacional de la Seguridad Social (National Social Security Agency)
ARENA	Aliança Nacional Renovadora (National Renewal Alliance)
AUGE	Acceso Universal de Garantías Explícitas (Access to Guaranteed Treaments)
AUH	Asignación Universal por Hijo (Universal Child Allowance)
BPC	Benefício de Prestação Continuada (Non-contributory pension, Brazil)
CA	Assambleia Constituinte (Constituent Assembly)
CGT	Confederación General del Trabajo (General Confederation of Labor)
CNBB	Conferência Nacional dos Bispos do Brasil (National Conference of Bishops of Brazil)
CONSEA	Conselho Nacional de Segurança Alimentar (National Food Security Council)
CONTAG	Confederação Nacional dos Trabalhadores da Agricultura (National Confederation of Agricultural Workers)
COSATU	Congress of South African Trade Unions
CPMF	Contribuição Provisória sobre a Movimentação Financeira (Temporary Tax on Financial Transactions)
CS	Comunidade Solidária (Solidary Community)

CTA	Central de los Trabajadores de la Argentina (Argentine Workers' Central)
CTM	Confederación de Trabajadores de Mexico (Confederation of Mexican Workers)
CUT	Central Única dos Trabalhadores (Unified Workers' Central)
CUT	Central Unitaria de Trabajadores de Chile (Unified Workers' Central of Chile)
DA	Diálogo Argentino (Argentine Dialogue)
DC	Partido Demócrata Cristiano (Christian Democratic Party)
FA	Frente Amplio (Broad Front)
FBH	Federação Brasileira de Hospitais (Brazilian Federation of Hospitals)
FONASA	Fondo Nacional de Salud (National Health Fund)
FREPASO	Frente País Solidario (Party for a Country with Solidarity)
FRENAPO	Frente Nacional contra la Pobreza (National Front against Poverty)
FV	Frente para la Victoria (Victory Front)
FZ	Fome Zero (Zero Hunger)
IBASE	Instituto Brasileiro de Análises Sociais e Econômicas (Brazilian Institute of Social and Economic Analysis)
IFE	Instituto Federal Electoral (Electoral Federal Institute)
IMSS	Instituto Mexicano del Seguro Social (Mexican Institute of Social Security)
MEP	Movimento Ética na Política (Movement for Ethics in Politics)
MIDEPLAN	Ministerio de Planificación (Ministry of Planning)
MST	Movimento dos Trabalhadores Sem-terra (Landless Workers' Movement)
PAN	Partido Acción Nacional (National Action Party)
PDS	Partido Democrático Social (Social Democratic Party)

PFL	Partido da Frente Liberal (Liberal Front Party)
PJ	Partido Justicialista (Peronist Party)
PMDB	Partido do Movimento Democrático Brasilero (Brazilian Democratic Movement Party)
PPD	Partido por la Democracia (Party for Democracy)
PRD	Partido de la Revolución Democrática (Party of the Democratic Revolution)
PRI	Partido Revolucionario Institucional (Institutional Revolutionary Party)
PROGRESA	Programa de Educación, Salud y Alimentación (Education, Health and Nutrition Program)
PRONASOL	Programa Nacional de Solidaridad (National Solidarity Program)
PS	Partido Socialista Chileno (Socialist Party of Chile)
PSDB	Partido da Social Democracia Brasileira (Brazilian Social Democracy Party)
PT	Partido dos Trabalhadores (Workers' Party)
RN	Partido Renovación Nacional (National Renewal Party)
SP	Seguro Popular de Salud (Health Insurance for All)
SUDS	Sistema Único Decentralizado de Saúde (National Descentralized Health System)
SUS	Sistema Único de Saúde (National Health System)
SUF	Subsidio Único Familiar (Family Subsidy System)
UCR	Unión Cívica Radical (Civic Radical Union)
UDI	Unión Democrática Independiente (Independent Democratic Union)
UHHP	Programa Jefas y Jefes de Hogar Desocupados (Unemployed Heads-of-Household Program)
UNT	Unión Nacional de Trabajadores (National Workers' Union)

I

Including Outsiders in Latin America

1.1 INTRODUCTION

Throughout the twentieth century, much of the population of Latin America lacked access to health care services, stable income, and pensions. Although states introduced social protections for workers in the formal sector (those with labor contracts), workers outside the formal labor market and their dependents, whom I call "outsiders," remained unprotected or underserved by social policy. Outsiders include the urban informal sector – the self-employed, street vendors, and employees hired off the books – as well as rural workers and the unemployed. In the last decade of the twentieth century, outsiders represented between 40 percent and 80 percent of the population in the middle-income countries of the region, and a large share of them lived in poverty.[1]

Two macro-level transformations that occurred in the last decades of the twentieth century – the adoption of democratic regimes and economic liberalization – raised contradictory expectations about the likelihood that Latin American states would extend social protections to outsiders. Democracies institutionalized electoral participation and opened channels for the expression of interests and demands, which seemed to augur well for initiatives to reduce the welfare gap. Yet the debt crisis of the early 1980s and the implementation of market-oriented reforms gave rise to a period of state retrenchment marked by the remarkable spread of pension privatization in the 1990s and the extension of small-scale, targeted, and often clientelistic benefits to the very poor. In light of these

---

[1] Estimates with government data (see Appendix 1). See also Portes and Hoffman (2003: 49, 53).

changes, a broad academic consensus maintained that despite the wide-spread adoption of democracy, Latin America had entered a new era of market expansion and limited state involvement in social protection.[2]

Contrary to this picture of state retreat, a dramatic expansion of social policy for outsiders took shape in several middle-income countries of Latin America during the 1990s and 2000s, when governments began to extend pensions, cash transfers, and health care services to millions of previously unprotected outsiders. Consider these examples. Following a constitutional reform in the late 1980s, Brazil adopted a universal health care system as well as broad-reaching pension programs for outsiders, both of which began implementation in the early 1990s. Cash transfers initiated in 2001 reached 11 million low-income households by 2006. In the 2000s, Mexico, which had been historically characterized by modest social expenditures, launched a health insurance system for outsiders, cash transfers for 5 million children, and pensions for outsiders that by 2010 reached a similar share of people 65 and older than the preexisting program for formal workers.[3] With some exceptions, by 2010, several middle-income countries in the region had expanded cash transfers, pensions, and health care services for at least 35 percent of the outsider population.[4]

As demonstrated in Figure 1.1, the magnitude of social policy change is striking. By 2010 pensions in select countries reached between 48 percent and 100 percent of outsiders aged sixty-five and older, and transfers were provided to school-age children on a massive scale.[5] At the same time, these benefits are costly. Although cash transfers are able to reach many individuals with relatively smaller investments, representing between 0.2 percent and about 1 percent of the GDP – comparable to family allowances for formal-sector workers – health care services and some pension programs demand more significant investments.

[2] See, for example, Haggard and Kaufman (2008); Kaufman and Segura-Ubiergo (2001); Rudra (2002); on pension reform, see Brooks (2001; 2009); Huber and Stephens (2000); Kay (1998); Madrid (2002; 2003); Mesa-Lago (1994); on clientelism, see Cornelius et al. (1994); Dresser (1994); Kurtz (2004a); Magaloni (2006); Roberts (1995); Weyland (1996a).

[3] Calculated with data on formal-sector pension coverage for people 65 and older in 2011 and benefits for outsiders in 2010 from SEDESOL.

[4] In South America, exceptions include Paraguay, Peru, and Venezuela. The latter two cases are discussed in Chapter 8. As discussed in Chapter 2, I use the threshold of 35 percent to operationalize expansion.

[5] Author's estimate with government data of pensions, cash transfers and population. For more information and sources, see Appendix 1.

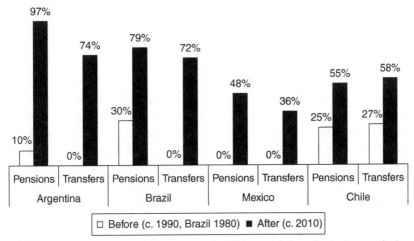

FIGURE I.I Share of outsider seniors and children with benefits before and after expansion, selected countries.
Note: Outsider seniors 65+ (60+ Brazil, 1980).
Source: Author's calculations with government sources (see Appendix 1).

These social policy innovations for outsiders are puzzling for a number of reasons. First, not only did social policy expansion take place at a time of state retreat, but these benefits also reached the most vulnerable and disempowered sectors of the population. This outcome runs counter to the widely held assumption that outsiders lack the capacity to exert political influence and attain meaningful policy responses in Latin America's nascent democracies. According to the literature, outsiders face formidable obstacles to collective action because they have heterogeneous interests stemming from their diverse and often individualistic economic activities (e.g., working as street vendors), which limit their ability to coordinate around common goals and demands and develop organizations to represent their interests (see Cross 1998; Kurtz 2004a). At the same time, if organizations form among outsiders, these are seen as having scarce resources. This prevents these organizations from having a meaningful influence on state policy and often leads them to succumb to co-optation and clientelism.[6] Furthermore, scholars argue that in the context of scarcity produced by the debt crisis and market reforms, powerful insiders prioritized the protection of their own benefits over

---

[6] See particularly Kurtz (2004a). For a critique and discussion of this literature, see Arce and Bellinger (2007); essays in Collier and Handlin (2009); Garay (2007); Holland and Palmer-Rubin (2015).

the establishment of insider–outsider coalitions that could have improved outsiders' political organization (see Etchemendy 2011; Oxhorn 1998; Weyland 1996a).

Social policy expansion is also intriguing because it involves nondiscretionary benefits. Existing research often characterizes most middle-income countries of Latin America as having patronage-based bureaucracies and clientelistic parties,[7] both of which hinder the creation of nondiscretionary policies for the most vulnerable sectors of the population (Kitschelt and Wilkinson 2007; Rothstein 2011), as such benefits are expected to loosen voters from clientelistic arrangements, and thus undermine the power of clientelist machines. Yet, as we see in the following chapters, political parties considered exemplars of clientelism, such as the Peronist or Justicialista Party (PJ) in Argentina, sponsored nondiscretionary social policy innovations for millions of low-income outsiders, revealing more complex relationships between political parties and poor voters.[8]

Finally, new social policies for outsiders display remarkable cross-national variation. Two distinct models of social policy, which I call *inclusive* and *restrictive*, can be identified. Inclusive policies provide relatively generous benefits to all or a large pool of outsiders and tend to involve some level of social participation in policy implementation. Restrictive policies, by contrast, provide smaller benefits to a more limited pool of outsiders and are implemented in a nonparticipatory way. Although there is variation within each of these broad categories, sharp contrasts distinguish the two models.

This book seeks to explain the circumstances under which incumbents in Latin America extended large-scale, nondiscretionary social policies to outsiders, the most vulnerable and disempowered sector of the population, and why we observe remarkable differences in the policy models that have taken shape. More specifically, why have some incumbents embarked on the expansion of nondiscretionary social policies for outsiders while others have not? Why have some governments created more generous, broad-reaching policies than others? Why do some allow social organizations and movements to participate in policy implementation while others reach out to beneficiaries in a top-down manner?

To address these questions, this study draws on a comparative historical analysis of social policy development in three areas that have

---

[7] On bureaucracies, see Calvo and Murillo (2004) and Luna and Mardones (2014). On party systems, see Hagopian (2014); Kitschelt et al. (2010); Mainwaring (1999); Roberts (2014). On clientelistic linkages, see Luna (2014).

[8] Levitsky (2003); for the recent period, see Etchemendy and Garay (2011).

exhibited a marked social policy divide separating insiders from outsiders – pensions, income support, and health care – in four of the most industrialized countries of Latin America – Argentina, Brazil, Mexico, and Chile – since democratization in the 1980s and 1990s. In an effort to better understand the circumstances under which expansion occurred, this study examines all democratic administrations in these countries within this period, some of which did embark on expanding social policy while others did not. Furthermore, it assesses the leverage of the analytical argument through a longitudinal analysis of these same cases since the establishment of benefits for insiders in the first half of the twentieth century, and conducts a broader comparison with four middle-income countries in Latin America and beyond, discussing the applicability of the argument to Peru, Venezuela, Uruguay, and South Africa.

As presented later in this chapter and laid out in Chapter 2, this study finds that expansion occurred in democratic regimes with (a) high electoral competition for outsiders and/or (b) large-scale social mobilization from below. Each of these two dynamics compelled incumbents to expand nondiscretionary social policy and temper the existing divide separating insiders and outsiders. At the same time, contrasting models of social protection resulted from the negotiations involved in policy design, the preferences of those engaged in the design process, and their institutional power. Restrictive models were built when conservatives had strong institutional power and social movements were not involved in policy design; inclusive models were adopted when social movements demanding policy change participated in negotiations around expansion, either because they had propelled that process in the first place, or because they could influence policy design through an allied party in government. To preview the outcomes documented and analyzed in this book, social policy expansion in Argentina and Brazil produced inclusive social policy, while in Chile and Mexico, a restrictive model took shape.

1.2 WHY STUDY SOCIAL POLICY EXPANSION AND POLICY MODELS?

Mapping and understanding these social policy innovations is critical for comparativists interested in the sources of welfare development and variation in social policy models in developing countries, and in their political and welfare effects. The cases discussed in this book illuminate the challenges of extending benefits in societies with deep insider-outsider divides, where some sectors are protected and others are not.

The adoption of broad-reaching benefits for outsiders has been largely unanticipated and initially overlooked by scholars of social policy in the region. In fact the comparative literature has emphasized obstacles towards expansion, stressing in particular financial impediments to social policy adoption.[9] Yet, as analyzed in this book, financial considerations are not the critical factor determining adoption of social policy innovations in middle-income countries. Governments have embarked on expansion under particular circumstances, and then employed different strategies to raise the necessary resources for implementation. At the same time, even if some programs may seem relatively inexpensive, expansion has often taken place across different policy areas requiring substantial investments.

Understanding these expansions is important because they target outsider populations who have received much less attention within the social policy – and political science – literature despite their numerical relevance in a region characterized by massive labor informality, segmented labor markets, and unemployment. Most of the comparative social policy literature has instead focused on the well-protected labor force and on social programs for insiders. Even the health care initiatives that reached outsiders and were created before the third wave of democracy have remained largely unaddressed by comparativists, with the exception of James McGuire's seminal work on the evolution of infant mortality rates (2010). The focus on formal-sector programs has overshadowed important aspects of the historical evolution of social policy in the region within the comparative literature. Understanding the conditions of social policy expansion for outsiders may shed new light on broader political dynamics that require deeper exploration. This book seeks to contribute to this pursuit.

A focus on the features of the new social programs also helps advance our understanding of social policy dynamics. Unlike the literature on the welfare state in industrial democracies, which has paid significant attention to the characteristics of social programs and explored the political underpinnings of variation in social policy models, research on programs for low-income populations in Latin America (e.g., conditional cash transfers) has tended to treat these programs as a homogenous group, thereby hiding significant variation that remains unexplained. This is particularly the case also in studies of clientelism that have focused primarily

---

[9] Haggard and Kaufaman's book on Latin America, East Asia, and Eastern Europe reaches this conclusion (2008).

on the method of distribution of social programs, rather than also examining the different types of benefits that have been extended, and in studies of social expenditure, which do not separate investments across policy areas with precision, identify what kinds of programs are funded, and indicate whether beneficiaries are insiders, outsiders, or both.[10] Knowing the features of different policies, how consistent they are across policy areas, and how they interact with benefits for insiders is fundamental for informing policy making and advancing our understanding of the politics of social policy. More generally, learning more about these benefits for outsiders will allow us to better understand the shape of welfare systems in the region, which include programs for insiders and outsiders, and to comprehend the ways in which these benefits interact. These are fundamental concerns for those seeking to improve welfare and labor markets in developing countries, and they are critical aspects of social policy dynamics that connect with themes of inequality, redistribution, and government responsiveness.

More broadly, the expansion of social programs for outsiders has important political and normative implications. First, these benefits have created new and stronger connections between the state and citizens who previously lacked access to many programs. At least in the language in which social programs are framed, these benefits are presented as linking the fate and prosperity of the larger political community to individual improvement, access to services, and transfers for the most vulnerable – and often marginal – populations. At the same time, some of these initiatives – as discussed in this book – have included participatory arrangements for implementation, which have opened up spaces of interaction between beneficiaries and the state, providing new opportunities for citizens to have a "voice" and participate in policy making. Secondly, the adoption of some of these programs has contributed to reducing inequality, improving infant mortality rates, and increasing school enrollment and completion.[11] These are all historically difficult accomplishments for developing countries. At the same time, these expansions have mainly benefited women, who have been generally less able to access social security protections in the formal labor market, and who now constitute the main beneficiaries of pensions for outsiders and transfers for low-income households in several countries. How this

---

[10] Haggard and Kaufman (2008); Huber, Mustillo, and Stephens (2008); Rudra (2002); Rudra and Haggard (2005); Segura-Ubiergo (2007).

[11] See Appendix 1 for further reference.

connection between welfare and women unfolds and what its ramifications are across different models of social policy for outsiders constitutes a fundamental topic of research, as gender inequality has been associated with many pernicious social dynamics worldwide.

A key political question, then, is why outsiders matter in some countries, to the point of becoming the target of large-scale policy innovations. The next section discusses alternative explanations for social policy expansion, and the following sections present the argument advanced in this book.

1.3 ALTERNATIVE EXPLANATIONS

Three different arguments have emerged within popular discourse and in academic debates as potential explanations to account for incumbents' decisions to launch social policies for outsiders and for variation in the resulting policies. The first account focuses on economic change and emphasizes the abundance of agricultural and mineral revenues in the 2000s to explain social policy innovations and the amount of benefits distributed. The second highlights the arrival of left-wing coalitions to power, while the final argument references the diffusion of policy models to explain the increased popularity of social programs for outsiders and the models adopted.

Economic Abundance and the Commodity Boom

At first glance, the timing of recent social policy innovations suggests that increased state revenue from the agricultural and mineral commodity boom of the early twenty-first century has provided incumbents with the resources needed for social policy expansion, fueling or making possible the adoption of large-scale social programs across the region.[12] According to this view, fiscal constraints in the 1980s and 1990s precluded politicians from expanding, but in the 2000s the rise in commodity prices and the GDP growth it propelled allowed commodity exporters to extend social policy to the excluded. Expanding the logic of this argument, one should then expect the amount of revenue from the boom or the share of resources controlled by the state to be related to the social

---

[12] Contrasts in average regional rates of economic growth are not particularly marked between the 1990s, when Latin America grew on average 2.6 percent, and the 2000s, when the region's average growth rate was 3.2 percent (GDP rates of growth from ECLAC; CEPALSTAT).

policy model adopted – restrictive or inclusive – with more generous and broad-reaching benefits made possible by higher export-led growth.

Several studies have argued that export-led growth has allowed left-wing governments in the region to implement their redistributive agendas (see Campello 2015; Levisky and Roberts 2011; Weyland 2011). Without denying the importance of the commodity boom and the broader economic context in which it unfolded, proving its centrality to social policy expansion and the resulting models of social policy adopted faces major empirical and theoretical challenges.

Empirically, a close examination reveals that the occurrence and the timing of expansion – understood as the creation of broad-reaching nondiscretionary programs in selected policy areas – do not coincide neatly with the timing of the boom, as governments adopted new benefits both before and during the boom or did not expand nondiscretionary benefits across selected social policy areas despite growing export-led revenue. At the same time, countries that are not primarily commodity exporters did embark on expansion, as illustrated by Mexico.[13] Second, GDP growth does not explain cross-national variation in the magnitude of new benefits. In other words, incumbents with larger commodity earnings are not necessarily more enthusiastic providers of benefits for outsiders.

With respect to the timing and occurrence of expansion, incumbents adopted new social policies for outsiders at times of both economic strain and abundance since the late 1980s (see Figure 1.2). For example, facing a severe economic crisis in 1998, Ecuadoran president Jamil Mahuad (1998–2000) established a massive transfer program reaching 1 million outsiders to contain the political and social ramifications of his fiscal adjustment program (personal communication, Mahuad; Banco Central de Ecuador 2010). By the time Ecuador achieved economic growth – fueled in part by rising oil prices – after a dramatic drop in GDP in 1999, 40 percent of the country's households were already receiving income transfers on a regular basis. In Brazil, social policy expansion began in the late 1980s, propelled by coalitions of social movements and labor unions that actively mobilized during the democratic transition. Implementation

---

[13] Data from Cepalstat (www.cepal.org, accessed March, 2015), shows that in 2010, Mexico's primary exports represented 24 percent of total exports while in the middle-income economies of South America, primary exports represented between 62.9 percent and 95.7 percent of total exports. Between 2002 and 2013, the average share of primary exports was 23.4 percent in Mexico and it ranged from 55.3 to 92.5 percent in the countries of South America.

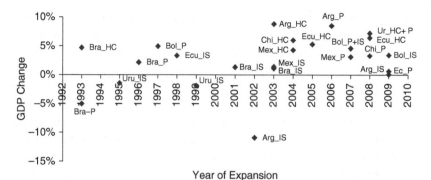

FIGURE 1.2 Timing of expansion and GDP change, selected countries, 1992–2010.
Note: IS: Income Support (cash transfer programs); P: Pensions; HC (health care).
Sources: Author's estimates of timing of expansion, GDP from World Bank
Development Indicators and ECLAC.

started at a time of economic hardship and inflation in the early 1990s,
which anteceded the successful stabilization accomplished by Itamar
Franco's finance minister, Fernando Henrique Cardoso, in 1994, well
before the commodities boom.

Other episodes of expansion coincide with buoyant international markets and favorable macroeconomic conditions, such as the extension of
pension benefits in Argentina beginning in 2006. Still other policy innovations, such as Mexico's policy expansion between 2001 and 2007, took
shape at a time of modest growth and in the absence of windfalls from
agricultural, oil, or mineral exports.

Finally, the expansion of nondiscretionary, large-scale benefits did not
take shape consistently across selected policy areas in Peru, Paraguay,
or Venezuela, three countries that benefited from the commodity boom
(see Figure 1.3). Even though Peru experienced a massive increase in
GDP driven by mineral exports, it only expanded health services gradually, achieving some meaningful coverage by 2010 (see Cameron 2011).
In Venezuela under Hugo Chávez (1998–2012), an undeniable case of
export boom and state control of oil revenues and social policy innovations did not include broad-reaching, nondiscretionary transfers for
children or seniors.[14]

The level of GDP growth is not a good predictor of the model adopted.
Focusing on the four countries under examination, we see that Brazil
adopted and implemented inclusive health care and pension benefits at

---

[14] I discuss the cases of Peru and Venezuela in Chapter 8.

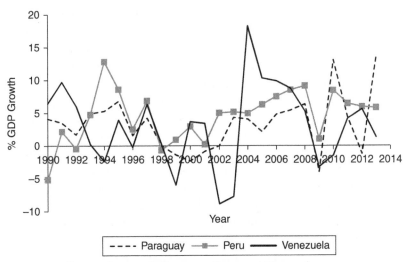

FIGURE 1.3 Economic growth, Paraguay, Peru, and Venezuela, 1990–2014.
Sources: GDP from World Bank Development Indicators.

times of low GDP growth (late 1980s–90s), while Bolsa Família, a famous cash transfer that was not costlier than prior innovations, was adopted in 2003 before the commodity boom that benefited Brazil beginning in 2004. Argentina also adopted the inclusive model with expansions occurring at times of both severe economic decline (2002) and growth (2005–7). On the other hand, in Chile, during times of economic growth bolstered by growing copper exports, incumbents did not adopt an inclusive model but rather a restrictive one (2003–4, 2008), as they did in Mexico, where incumbents faced overall modest growth (2001–3, 2006).

At a theoretical level, a critical weakness of an explanation of expansion based on the commodity boom is that new economic resources in and of themselves do not provide a straightforward explanation for why incumbents would want to devote part of those resources for social programs for outsiders. Undoubtedly states that benefited from the commodity boom had more room to maneuver financially (see Campello 2015). Yet governments faced competing demands for funding from various economic and social actors. In the context of economic growth, powerful businesses and producers often demanded funding for infrastructure, transportation, energy projects or subsidies while labor unions expected better salaries and pension benefits for insiders, which had deteriorated in several countries in the 1980s and 1990s (see Etchemendy and Collier

2007). In cases in which the state did not control revenues from commodities directly but captured them via export taxes or royalties, businesses and producers also pressured to avoid taxation (see Fairfield 2015).

Understanding why governments paid so much attention to outsiders beginning in the 1990s, in the context of state retreat, economic crisis, or high levels of growth, requires an explanation that goes beyond the availability of increased resources. Resources in and of themselves do not tell us why governments were willing to reach out to outsiders, historically the poorest and most politically vulnerable sectors of the population, and why they chose to allocate resources through social policy transfers and services instead of prioritizing other initiatives such as food subsidies or employment-creation programs. This book argues that specific political factors are fundamental to understanding governments' social policy decisions and the incentives that led incumbents – regardless of having windfall revenue or not – to embark on expansion.

Partisan Politics: The Left Turn

Another potential explanation for social policy adoption emphasizes the rise of left-wing governments in Latin America since the early 2000s. This "left turn" by which "nearly two-thirds of Latin Americans lived under some form of left-leaning national government" (Levitsky and Roberts 2011: 1), seems to lend credence to a theory of expansion based on left-party power.[15]

In their most recent book, Huber and Stephens argue that in twenty-first-century Latin America, "the longevity of democracy and the strength of parties to the left of center" have produced a departure from the historic trend of poverty and inequality and help explain differences in redistributive outcomes across countries (2012: 240). Although this book shares the view that partisanship matters for the social policy model adopted, it challenges the centrality of left-party strength in the executive branch or in congress in accounting for *why* large-scale social policies for outsiders were adopted in the first place. First, political parties in Latin America face a highly divided social structure and left and left-populist parties have generally prioritized the interests of labor union allies over those of outsiders (see, for example, Collier and Collier 1991; Levitsky 2003). The preference of left parties toward labor unions and insiders is also found in Western Europe (see Rueda 2005, 2007; Lindavall and Rueda

---

[15] See Levitsky and Roberts (2011); Weyland, Madrid, and Hunter (2010).

2013), where unionized workers are more numerous. In Latin America, left and left-populist governments only launched policies for outsiders under specific circumstances. The goal of this book is to identify these circumstances and explain when and why left parties embarked on large-scale expansion.

Second, the episodes of expansion analyzed herein demonstrate that incumbents on both the left and the right of the political spectrum launched significant policy innovations for outsiders. A focus on the left as the driver of social policy change leaves unanswered the question of why right-wing incumbents pursued expansion as well. For example, the creation of massive income transfers and health insurance occurred under the right-leaning presidency of Vicente Fox (2000–6) of Mexico's National Action Party (PAN), at a time when the left held only a small share of seats in Congress. Likewise, some episodes of policy adoption in Brazil took place under the administrations of José Sarney (1985–90) and Itamar Franco (1992–5), neither of whom belonged to a popular-based party or faced more than a minor left-wing party presence in the Constituent Assembly and in Congress, the bodies that effectively passed some of these innovations into law.

As shown in subsequent chapters, partisanship does help account for different preferences regarding policy design that may affect policy outcomes, as left or center-left politicians typically favor broader benefits, and center-right or conservative parties prefer more modest ones (see also Huber and Stephens 2012; Pribble 2013). However, left party strength, understood as the arrival of left-wing candidates to office or the growth of the share of left-party seats in Congress, does not in and of itself explain the adoption of broad-reaching social programs for outsiders in the cases under investigation.

Diffusion of Policy Models

A final potential explanation for the expansion of social policy and the models adopted is based on the diffusion of policy models. The scholarly literature on market reforms does emphasize diffusion as an important factor contributing to the adoption of social policy change, particularly privatization, in Latin America's nascent democracies. As discussed by Weyland (2006; 2004), theories of diffusion contend that policy change results from the spread of policy *principles* (such as universality) or policy *models* (such as social security) in temporal waves across geographically proximate countries (see Weyland 2006: 19–21). Despite background differences, policy blueprints disseminated across borders influence governments into adopting similar policies, producing policy convergence. Models typically spread through two mechanisms: (a) a strong international actor that pressures or provides strong incentives for governments to adopt a particular policy blueprint; or (b) policy makers' decisions to emulate policy models they find prestigious, appropriate, or legitimate to solve a specific problem.[16]

As subsequent chapters show in greater detail, diffusion provides an inadequate account for social policy expansion in the cases under investigation, for three main reasons: (a) the lack of evidence that the mechanisms of diffusion – imposition or incentives granted by a powerful actor, and emulation – play significant roles in policy adoption, (b) the absence of policy convergence across countries, and relatedly, (c) the challenge posed to the diffusion argument by cases of non-adoption despite expansion in other cases.

Powerful international actors with the capacity to pressure or provide strong incentives for countries to adopt new policy models or principles did not play key roles in expansion. The World Bank (and associated agencies) was a key player in pension privatization and social development debates in the region (Brooks 2009, 2001; Madrid 2003; Weyland 2004, 2006), yet the process tracing for this project showed that multilateral agencies have not been relevant actors behind recent expansions in Argentina, Brazil, Chile and Mexico. Acknowledging that countries such as Brazil and Mexico, rather than international agencies, were the first movers in the design of conditional cash transfers for outsiders, an interviewed World Bank official suggested that the agency "has trailed behind governments in the region."[17]

Concerning emulation, scholars have often suggested that diffusion is facilitated by the existence of a coherent, simple model (see Weyland 2004, 2006). In the 1990s, there was no consistent single model of health care services (Kaufman and Nelson 2004; Weyland 2006: 7), pensions, or even cash transfers for outsiders that multilateral institutions promoted or sought to impose on developing countries. At the same time, early initiatives such as Brazil's social assistance pensions or the universal health system (SUS) were not a source of inspiration for policy makers in the other countries under investigation. Proponents of social programs generally paid attention to benefits for insiders within their own countries

---

[16] On these mechanisms, see the classic literature on diffusion: Heclo (1974); Meyer and Rowan (1977).

[17] Author's interview, World Bank office, Buenos Aires.

only, or to multiple initiatives rather than to a particular model of social policy for outsiders.

Regarding the policy outcome, this study found no evidence of convergence around a common model of expansion. There is remarkable variation in the scope of coverage, benefit levels, and the form of implementation of social programs across cases. Funding mechanisms also diverge sharply across countries, with some programs being tax-financed and others funded by cross-subsidies from social security benefits. New income support programs, which have become highly visible interventions cross-nationally, are a good example; they generally employ similar tools in the form of cash transfers. Yet these cash transfer programs also vary significantly across critical features of social policy that are relevant to this study. Some transfers are conditional on school attendance while others are not; some are temporary while others are permanent; and, as detailed in subsequent chapters, these programs vary in scope, benefit level, and funding mechanism.[18] Aside from the specific tool used, these programmatic features are important definitional elements of social policy models, and they imply different welfare and political effects. The absence of convergence in these key policy features undermines the explanatory power of a theory based on diffusion.

Finally, theories of diffusion have a hard time explaining instances of non-adoption. Why did Venezuela not adopt broad-reaching transfers despite political rhetoric favoring the poor and despite available economic resources to launch large-scale policies? Given that technocrats constitute important "carriers" of best practices and models lauded by epistemic (knowledge-based) communities and are critical sources of expertise and advice for governments and parties (Murillo 2009: 35–6; Weyland 2006: 46–7),[19] why did Peru not launch large-scale social policy expansion in the twenty-first century despite high levels of economic growth and the power of technocrats within the national government (Dargent 2011)?

With respect to policy principles, it is difficult to attribute expansionary decisions to the spread of a particular principle such as universality or fairness. In the cases analyzed in this book, debates and consensus about fairness, universality, and the need to provide social policy benefits to the excluded existed among policy experts and some policy makers

---

[18] On variation in income transfers, see Garay (2016).

[19] On the classic literature on diffusion and emulation, see Heclo (1974); Meyer and Rowan (1977); on sociological institutionalism, see Thelen (1999). For diffusion in Latin America, see Collier and Messick (1975).

long before the expansion of social policies occurred, without resulting in policy adoption.[20]

More generally, ideas do matter for policy making. Several studies have addressed the way in which ideas favoring innovation influence the policy process (Hall 1992, 1997; Weir 1992). Empirical cases in this book demonstrate that program features are informed by ideas advocated by social movements or technocrats and experts linked to political parties. In some cases, these ideas are influenced by existing policy arrangements for insiders, which inspire the demands of social movements who often press for benefits similar to those received by these sectors. Ideas may also be imported through technical assistance, technocrats' training, or emulation. However, though these factors are important for informing the availability and technical soundness of specific initiatives, they have not been sufficient on their own to drive policy makers to embark on costly policy innovations or determine why broader or leaner benefits, or participatory rather than direct state implementation, were adopted.

1.4 OUTSIDERS: POLITICAL RELEVANCE AND SOCIAL POLICY NEGLECT

The comparative political economy literature on Western Europe defines outsiders as workers who – unlike insiders – lack secure employment (Esping-Andersen 1999; Rueda 2007: 20). In Latin America, throughout most of the twentieth century, outsiders not only lacked secure, formal employment, but they and their dependents were also excluded from social security protections (e.g., health insurance and pensions) that were historically and systematically extended in the region to formal workers only.[21] Outsiders represent a large share of the workforce in Latin America, including urban informal workers (e.g., street vendors or the self-employed), employees hired off the books, rural workers, and the unemployed.

The size and composition of the outsider population has evolved since the first half of the twentieth century, when labor and social legislation was first established. As Chapter 3 shows, several categories of workers were formalized between the 1920s and 1940s with the creation of labor regulations and social security (or social insurance) systems funded mainly with payroll contributions by employers and employees. If we measure outsiders as the share of the total population that is not affiliated

---

[20] See Chapter 3 for further reference.
[21] See Chapter 3 for full discussion.

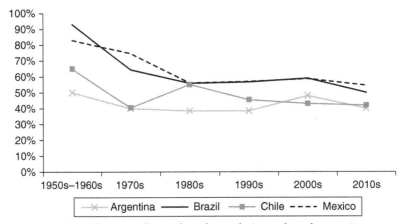

FIGURE 1.4 Outsiders as a share of total population, selected countries, 1950s–2010.

Note: In Chile and Brazil, the share of outsider workers out of economically active population; Argentina and Mexico, the share of outsider population out of total population.

Source: Author's estimates with government sources and secondary literature (Appendix 1).

to social security, we see that this share declined at different rates with industrialization and the growth of public-sector employment between the 1950s and 1980s. By the early 1980s or 1990s, it reached a plateau, making up between 40 percent and 60 percent of the total population – including both workers and their dependents – in the cases under investigation (Figure 1.4). The size of the outsider population did grow at different moments during crises, but usually on a temporary basis. Within the workforce, informal and rural workers are the groups that generally fall into the ranks of the unemployed during economic shocks, recessions, and times of high inflation.[22]

At the same time that the relative size of the outsider population stagnated – growing during crises – the political relevance of outsiders increased significantly in the last quarter of the twentieth century. Beginning in the late 1970s, Latin America witnessed the longest, broadest, and deepest wave of democratization in the region's history, which afforded outsiders political weight in different ways. First, compared to previous episodes of democratic rule, outsiders gained often unprecedented

[22] On the informal economy, see Beccaria and Maurizio (2003); Schijman and Dorna (2012); Portes and Hoffman (2003).

access to the vote, made possible by the elimination of prior restrictions on suffrage in countries in which these restrictions existed (e.g., literacy requirements). Second, democratic politics also created a more favorable environment for political organization and participation in protests, and raised the cost for incumbents to repress social movements.[23] These two conditions made the outsider population electorally more attractive and consequential for party leaders, and created incentives for social activism and organization among outsiders to emerge and endure.

Following the democratic transitions in each country, outsiders displayed two fundamental features that under particular circumstances incentivized governments to reach out to them with large-scale social policies: *political relevance* and *social policy neglect*. The argument introduced next and fully developed in Chapter 2 explains why, when, and how within this environment incumbents decided to "include outsiders," that is, to provide them with nondiscretionary benefits across social policy areas characterized by deep divides separating insiders from outsiders.

1.5 THE ARGUMENT IN BRIEF

In explaining the two questions of why, after decades of neglect, some incumbents expanded nondiscretionary provisions to outsiders while others did not, and why there is remarkable variation in the shape of social policies that were adopted, this study provides an analytical framework that emphasizes the role of factors likely to emerge within democratic politics. Regarding the first question, I argue that incumbents expanded social policy when faced with high levels of electoral competition for the vote of outsiders and/or with large-scale social mobilization by coalitions of social movements and labor unions that pushed for social policy expansion through the use of protest, institutional channels, or alliances with the governing party. In the face of these pressures, incumbents considered social policy expansion (a) a powerful instrument to elicit outsiders' electoral support when a credible challenger threatened to defeat the incumbent party by courting outsider voters, and (b) necessary to mitigate intense social mobilization. When democracies lack the incentives created by these two conditions – electoral competition for outsiders and social mobilization from below – incumbents are less likely to embark on the expansion of large-scale nondiscretionary social benefits.

---

[23] See, for example, Houtzager (1998), Huneeus (2000), and Novaes (1991), and references in Chapter 3.

Dynamics of expansion therefore feature two politically driven processes: one "from above," motivated by electoral competition for outsider voters that credibly threatens incumbents' continuity, as exemplified by the episodes of expansion in Chile and Mexico in the late 1990s and 2000s and Brazil in the 2000s; and one "from below," propelled by social mobilization, characteristic of Argentina in the 2000s as well as the episodes of policy expansion in Brazil in the late 1980s and early 1990s. Absent these conditions, large-scale nondiscretionary social policy expansion is less likely to take place, despite the fact that outsiders make up a large electorate and are relatively excluded from social policy.

Regarding the second question of why there is striking variation in the policy models adopted (considering the scope of coverage, benefit levels, and the presence of participatory or state-centric implementation), I argue that negotiations over policy design, considering those involved in negotiations, their preferences, and their institutional power, yielded distinct models of social policy. Schematically, incumbents may negotiate policy design either (a) exclusively with the parties in Congress, or (b) with social movements in addition to, or instead of, parties in Congress. In the presence of social movements pushing for expansion, it is likely that incumbents negotiate with them or respond strategically to their demands.

When expansion is negotiated among parties in Congress, those negotiations are likely to produce policy outcomes that accommodate the preferences of different parties regarding social policy. Parties' influence in turn is shaped by their institutional power. When conservative and center-right parties are strong (that is, parties that represent higher-income sectors, as discussed in Chapter 2), resultant policies are generally restrictive; in consonance with the preferences of elites, and often with these parties' programs as well, they provide relatively small or moderate coverage through direct state implementation and do not protect the full outsider population. In Mexico and Chile, the processes of social policy design occurred in the context of high electoral competition (without social mobilization from below); they included negotiations among congressional parties and were shaped by the balance of partisan power. Given the power of conservative parties in both cases, these negotiations resulted in restrictive models.

If incumbents negotiate expansion with social movements or respond strategically to these movements' demands, policy outcomes tend to result in inclusive benefits, with broad coverage and participatory implementation. Large-scale coalitions of social movements and union allies, which, as discussed previously, were the coalitions driving incumbents to launch expansion in some cases, generally demand both broad benefits – similar to those received by low-income insiders – and participation in policy implementation.

Social movements generally gain access to the policy design process when they have catalyzed expansion through protest or pressure in institutional arenas (e.g., via lobbying or public opinion campaigns), or when they are allied to the governing coalition and exercise influence over policy choices from within the government (even if they are not able to propel on their own the initial decision to launch massive benefits). As long as powerful social movement coalitions that push for expansion are involved in the process of design, resultant policies are more likely to take on inclusive features. In Argentina, social movements and labor allies have engaged in social policy making by pushing their social policy proposals through protest and – sometimes also – through institutional channels and negotiating with policy makers over policy design. In Brazil, social movements and labor allies primarily used institutional channels to advance their social policy agenda for expansion and/or to influence policy design. As a result, inclusive policies were adopted in these two country cases.

1.6 RESEARCH DESIGN, CASES, AND DATA

This study provides the first comprehensive analysis of social policy expansion in four of the largest and most industrialized economies of Latin America – Argentina, Brazil, Mexico, and Chile – in three policy areas: pensions, health care, and income support since the beginning of the democratic transitions in the 1980s until 2010. To identify the factors and mechanisms driving social policy change, I have conducted process tracing of social policy making across all different administrations in each case, covering a total of twenty-one administrations, analyzing instances of successful social policy expansion as well as failed attempts to create large-scale nondiscretionary benefits for outsiders.[24] The empirical analysis is based on original measures of outsiders and social benefits and new data sets of electoral dynamics and social mobilization constructed for this project, as well as archival research and extensive interviews with key informants, as detailed later.

---

[24] On process tracing, see Bennett and Checkel (2015) and Seawright and Collier (2004).

Comparative Approach and Cases

Recent comparative studies of social policy in Latin America have focused generally on a single social policy across countries, on the evolution of social policy in a single country, or on large-N cross-national comparisons of aggregate spending.[25] To better address the questions raised in this book, I conducted a small-N comparative study of four countries across several administrations and three policy areas in each country. Given the absence of substantial research on this topic, this combination of longitudinal within-case and cross-country perspectives enables a comprehensive assessment of different theoretical insights and of potential explanatory factors underlying policy change, and allows for substantial theory development.

Within each country case, I employ process-tracing analysis of the policy-making process for each episode of policy expansion as well as for instances of unsuccessful attempts to expand social policy. Careful process tracing of policy making enables both identifying the factors and the specific causal mechanisms shaping expansion and assessing alternative explanations by presenting detailed evidence on their role in policy processes. Process tracing also facilitates the generation of credible and detailed information on social policy, which is notably absent in large-N studies of social spending in Latin America.[26]

This comparative design involving cross-country and within-country comparisons across different administrations and policy areas also allows for an exploration of the effects of alternative national-level and policy-specific conditions that may be driving observed outcomes. Moreover, a longitudinal analysis explicitly takes into account temporal dynamics that affect expansion – especially time lags between policy adoption and implementation – and avoids "excessive causal proximity" in the analysis of processes that may unfold over longer periods of time (see Grzymala-Busse 2002: 16).

---

[25] On single-country studies, see Díaz-Cayeros, Estévez, and Magaloni (forthcoming). On large-N analysis using social expenditure see Huber, Mustillo, and Stephens (2008); Rudra (2002); Rudra and Haggard (2005); Segura-Ubiergo (2007).

[26] Several studies of social expenditure use IMF expenditure data that a) only capture direct national-level spending and thus severely underestimate social service expenditure in federal systems, and that b) group spending by theme into two categories – social services, and social security and welfare – which prevents students from observing variations across individual policy areas. See, for example, Carnes and Mares (2009); Haggard and Kaufman (2008); Kaufman and Segura-Ubiergo (2001); Segura-Ubiergo (2007).

Main Cases: Argentina, Brazil, Chile, and Mexico
This case selection maximizes variation in potential explanatory factors while holding constant certain background conditions. In terms of similarities, Argentina, Brazil, Chile, and Mexico are among the most industrialized countries in Latin America, and together with Colombia, Uruguay, and Venezuela, they have the highest income per capita in the region.[27] In the 1990s, all four countries adopted market-oriented reforms associated with neoliberal ideas of social protection.[28] These four countries, moreover, had experienced extensive periods of authoritarianism and/or limited democratic competition since the 1920s, when social security systems for formal-sector workers were first adopted in some of these countries. Finally, following the creation of labor market regulations and social benefits for insiders, labor movements in all four countries were among the most powerful in the region (see Collier and Collier 1991).

Despite these similarities, there is theoretically relevant variation in potential explanatory factors across cases and over time throughout the period under examination, from the 1980s through 2010. First, the cases differ in terms of the presence of social movement coalitions (SMCs) – alliances of social movements and labor unions demanding social policy for outsiders – in the policy areas under investigation. These SMCs emerged in Brazil and Argentina but not in Chile and Mexico. Second, the composition and level of institutionalization of party systems vary across countries and over time. Though still fluid, since the third wave of democracy and until 2010, the party systems in Chile and Mexico, and increasingly in Brazil, became more institutionalized, with rather stable partisan coalition options at the national level, whereas the party system in Argentina experienced a partial collapse in the early 2000s (see Lupu 2014; Roberts 2014). Third, partisan competition for the votes of outsiders took place in Chile and Mexico since 1999 and 2000, respectively, but occurred in Argentina and Brazil only in 1999 and 2002, respectively.

Economic conditions, such as financial stability, unemployment, and the existence of a major economic crisis or windfall economic resources, also vary across cases and over time, which allows for assessment of their weight on decisions to expand. There are contradictory expectations in

[27] The most industrialized countries in the region are Argentina, Brazil, Chile, Mexico, Uruguay, and Venezuela. These are also the countries with the highest GDP per capita, and the ones that have developed systems of social protection for insiders since the first half of the twentieth century. At the same time, they comprise close to 75 percent of the population in the region (see CEPAL 2009).
[28] See Brooks (2001); Madrid (2003); Weyland (2004).

the literature regarding these economic indicators. While economic crises may affect a government's ability to fund new benefits, they may also produce more need and demand. As shown in the chapters that follow, when combined with electoral competition or mobilization, crises may intensify the level of mobilization or increase the chances of a challenger seeking to win office.

Furthermore, variation in the size of the outsider population across the four cases provides a two-pair comparison displaying relatively lower and higher levels of exclusion. Between 1990 and 2010, Argentina and Chile had outsider populations of similar – and relatively smaller – sizes, ranging from 40 percent to less than 50 percent of the total population. Mexico and Brazil, by contrast, had relatively larger outsider populations, ranging from more than 50 percent to 60 percent of the total population, an important share of which resided in rural areas. This two-pair comparison permits assessment of the effect of structural conditions on social policy change. Did the countries with smaller outsider populations build more generous and broad-reaching benefits? As we see in the following chapters, resulting social policy models do not map onto preexisting structural and socioeconomic characteristics, with Argentina and Brazil, and Mexico and Chile, respectively, building systems more similar to each other.

Broader Comparisons

In Chapters 3 and 8, the main findings of this book are further assessed against two additional comparison sets of cases: (a) a longitudinal analysis of the four cases under investigation since the establishment of benefits for insiders in the 1920s and 1940s, and (b) a broader cross-country comparison within and beyond Latin America.

Longitudinal Comparison. In Chapter 3, I examine the period that starts with the creation of benefits for insiders in the 1920s and 1940s and that ends with the recent adoption of large policies for outsiders. This comparison has two main goals. First, I seek to assess the explanatory power of this study's framework against a period in which most benefits were extended to insiders and outsiders were largely neglected. Second, this longitudinal comparison also permits the analysis of variation in social policy provisions incumbents extended to outsiders under nondemocratic political regimes and different economic circumstances. Specifically, I investigate why incumbents in some authoritarian regimes provided some benefits to outsiders while others did not introduce social policy innovations, and I analyze the specific features of those provisions (e.g., scope, benefit levels, nondiscretionary access) and why they were adopted.

Cross-country Comparison. The second broader comparison involves three additional middle-income countries in the region – Peru, Uruguay, and Venezuela – as well as South Africa, a middle-income country with high levels of economic inequality, which has been analyzed in comparative political economy and public policy studies together with middle-income countries of Latin America (see Lieberman 2003, 2009; Seidman 1994). These four cases display broad variation across both explanatory factors and outcomes. Venezuela and Peru allow us to assess social policy dynamics in cases without significant expansion of large-scale nondiscretionary benefits, and without a strong presence of the key factors propelling incumbents to expand. Uruguay in turn exemplifies dynamics of expansion propelled by electoral competition for outsiders and exhibits intertemporal variation in the process of policy design, with conservatives dominating policy making in the early expansions and social movements engaging in the process of expansion through an allied party at a later stage. Finally, South Africa provides an excellent case for assessing the applicability of the argument in a context of no electoral competition for outsider voters. In this particular case, social movements allied to a dominant party played a prominent role in prompting adoption and shaping policy in specific areas.

Data Sources and Analysis

This book's comparative analysis of social policy processes relied on original data from multiple sources gathered for this project. I collected social policy data from policy documents and public archives in all four of the main country cases, and used them to create new measures of social policy. I conducted interviews with approximately 265 key informants. These included leaders of social movements, labor unions and rural organizations, policy makers who were directly involved in policy expansion (including secretaries, ministers, and former presidents), legislators, party leaders, politicians and candidates involved in presidential campaigns, representatives of employers' associations, pension funds, and private providers in the health care sector. These interviews helped to reconstruct the process of policy expansion and policy design, its underlying motivations, and the goals and policy preferences of the different actors involved. Transcripts of congressional sessions, party documents and campaign platforms, as well as petitions and documents produced by social movements and congresses of labor confederations, further contributed to understanding the motivations, demands, and expectations regarding expansion, the coalitions or alliances they formed to achieve or oppose expansion, and the negotiations over the shape of social programs.

In addition, I constructed a database of episodes of social policy making based on content analysis of newspaper articles referring to policies for outsiders from 1989 through 2011 in Argentina, 1987 through 2006 in Brazil, 2002 through 2008 in Chile, and 1988 through 2007 in Mexico. For each country, I surveyed at least one national newspaper: *Clarín* in Argentina, *El Mercurio* in Chile, and *La Jornada* in Mexico. For Brazil, I worked with an index built by the Library of the Brazilian Senate with seven national newspapers.[29] For the cases of Mexico and Argentina, I also consulted *Reforma* and *La Nación*, respectively, for parts of the period under investigation. Finally, I created a Data Set of Protest for Argentina that maps the evolution of social mobilization for social benefits, which was led primarily by unemployed workers and their labor union allies from 1996 through 2010. This data set includes close to 2,000 protest events, as well as information on these events concerning their duration, location, participants, demands, state responses, and violence.

Collecting data systematically from different sources afforded the opportunity for triangulating information, a fundamental aspect of process tracing in qualitative research. The database of policy-making events further helped inform the examination of government documents and the conducting of interviews, and ultimately produced more detailed and accurate chronologies of social policy processes – another critical aspect of process tracing.

To characterize the evolution of electoral competition for outsiders, I used available quantitative data, especially electoral surveys (from survey firms and academic institutions), as well as ecological data. With poll data I identified outsider and insider voters and mapped their voting patterns in Brazil, Chile, and Mexico since the first democratic election (comparable national data were not available for Argentina). To complement these measures, I constructed measures of electoral competition for outsiders for each selected country since the first democratic presidential elections until about 2010–11, identifying districts in which outsiders

---

[29] *Folha de São Paulo, O Estado de São Paulo, Jornal do Brasil, Jornal da Tarde, Jornal de Brasília, Correio Brasiliense*, and *O Globo*. Some articles from other newspapers have also been used.

are the majority of the population, and measuring levels of competition in presidential elections in those districts. For some countries and years I relied on existing election data sets constructed by other researchers, while for others, I used government documents and archival research to construct new data sets of elections (see Appendix 3 for further information on these data sets).

1.7 STRUCTURE OF THIS BOOK

This book is organized into eight chapters. Chapter 2 presents this book's analytical argument, which accounts for the expansion of social policy for outsiders and for the different models these policies took. It introduces the conditions that lead incumbents to expand nondiscretionary social policy and the factors that shape policy design along restrictive and inclusive models. It also considers the strategies incumbents use to overcome opponents and to obtain funding for new programs. Chapter 3 adopts a longer historical perspective, drawing on the analytical framework to understand why large-scale, nondiscretionary social programs were not expanded to outsiders prior to the expansions documented here. It further analyzes the kinds of policies created for outsiders in previous decades and identifies the conditions under which governments: (a) did not expand any benefits for outsiders, (b) expanded large, discretionary (often temporary) benefits, or (c) created small benefits for outsiders. The time period begins with the creation of the first large-scale social programs for the formal workforce in the 1920s and 1940s through the 1980s or 1990s, depending on when large-scale expansion began in each country. In this chapter, I demonstrate that governments provided little social protection for outsiders during this period because of the few instances of democracies that had mobilization from below or electoral competition for outsiders. The two cases in which social protection was extended to outsiders – the inauguration of health care services in Argentina in the late 1940s and in Chile in the 1960s – occurred in the context of electoral competition for outsiders.

Chapters 4 through 7 draw on this analytical framework to explain social policy expansion and the adoption of inclusive social policy for outsiders in Argentina and Brazil, and restrictive social policy in Mexico and Chile. Through an in-depth analysis of social policy making in each administration since democratization, I show that incumbents, irrespective of partisan affiliation, were likely to expand social policy in response to high electoral competition for outsiders and/or mobilization from below pressing for social benefits. I further show that governments adopted different models of social policy depending on whether incumbents negotiated policy design with the congressional opposition or whether they (also) responded to social mobilization and granted social movements access to the process of policy design. The concluding chapter extends the argument to a broader comparison of middle-income countries and assesses the social and political effects and theoretical implications of these social policy transformations.

2

Explaining Social Policy Expansion and Policy Models

Despite the remarkable expansion of social policy for outsiders in several Latin American countries and the emergence of distinct social policy models in the region, the comparative politics literature has not yet systematically documented or explained these phenomena. This chapter presents a theoretical framework to account for the large-scale expansion of nondiscretionary social benefits for outsiders and for variation in resultant models of social policy in Argentina, Brazil, Chile, and Mexico. Two models are distinguished: a *restrictive model*, which provides relatively modest coverage and entails nonparticipatory implementation; and an *inclusive model*, which provides universal or broad coverage for outsiders and involves some level of social participation in program implementation.

The next sections organize the presentation of this book's argument around its two central questions. First I focus on why some incumbents embarked on social policy expansion and why others did not, within democracies featuring a deep social policy divide between insiders and outsiders. To that end, I conceptualize the critical factors motivating expansion: (a) electoral competition for the vote of outsiders and (b) social mobilization from below, and the mechanisms by which they are likely to compel incumbents to respond with large-scale nondiscretionary provisions.

The following section addresses the second key question in the theoretical framework by explaining variation in policy choice within cases of large-scale expansion, a neglected issue in the social policy scholarship in the region.[1] I focus on the critical negotiations that unfold around policy design, showing how different policy outcomes occur depending on the actors involved, these actors' preferences, and their institutional power.

Given that policy expansion is a popular but complex and costly endeavor, the final section of this chapter identifies critical challenges to expansion and lays out the strategies incumbents have employed to overcome funding constraints and to neutralize, compensate, or bring opponents on board.

2.2 THE OUTCOMES: SOCIAL POLICY EXPANSION AND POLICY MODELS

Social Policy Expansion

I define social policy expansion as the creation of new social benefits or the extension of preexisting ones to a significant share – at least 35 percent – of the outsider population. This threshold for what constitutes "expansion" is based on the theoretical assumption that large-scale policies and smaller-scale initiatives are driven by different political dynamics.[2] The critical issue I explore is the inauguration of provisions that reach a significant threshold of beneficiaries against the historical backdrop of exclusion within these policy areas.

Social policy comprises social transfers and services for individuals and households, such as pensions and income support programs (e.g., family allowances, workfare benefits, food stamps), as well as health care and social assistance services (e.g., food assistance and services for people with special needs). Within this universe of policies, I focus on policy areas that share two critical features. The first feature is the presence of a stark divide between insiders and outsiders regarding access to policy

---

[1] An exception within the social policy literature is the comparison of Chile and Uruguay in Pribble and Huber (2011), and Pribble (2013). On cash transfers, see Diaz-Cayeros, Estévez, and Magaloni (forthcoming).

[2] This refers to 35 percent of the relevant population reached by a program. For example, in the case of old-age pensions, expansion should entail the protection of at least 35 percent of the population aged sixty-five and older. Most of the cases studied here consist of expansions in which some people are already covered, e.g., a preexisting pension benefit reaches 5 percent of outsiders, and governments then create one that reaches 50 percent or 80 percent. In a few cases, however, a prior administration would cover 20 percent of outsiders and a new government would extend the benefit to reach 35 percent. In those

benefits and services. This condition excludes policy areas in which benefits are provided for the entire population irrespective of employment situation, such as basic education, as well as those erratically provided for both insiders and outsiders, such as housing. Within the policy areas addressed here, by contrast, an unmistakable legal and actual difference in access between insiders and outsiders has existed since benefits for insiders were first extended in the region.

With this feature in mind, I choose to analyze three policy areas: pensions (including old-age and disability benefits for seniors), income-support programs for households (such as family allowances and other cash transfers), and health care services (including primary care as well as hospital services). These policy areas moreover allow for assessing the processes of expansion with regard to both transfers and services.

Second, I further restrict the social policies analyzed here to those provisions that have institutional features similar to those governing policies for insiders. Such policies are included in national laws, decrees, or ministerial resolutions; are distributed nationwide – rather than implemented in a single region; are governed by clear eligibility rules; and, unlike temporary emergency relief measures for the poor, such as short-term workfare provisions, they provide permanent benefits. Scholars argue that central state authority and clear eligibility criteria are fundamental for social policies to be nondiscretionary, meaning that they treat similarly situated individuals in identical terms (see Lieberman 1998: 16). This is particularly relevant in countries with weak policy enforcement by local-level actors,[3] and scant bureaucratic capacity on the ground – especially in low-income districts in which outsiders often reside. Clear eligibility rules reduce biases in decision making, and the presence of a national-level implementation agency precludes the determination of access by local agencies with weak bureaucratic capacity or that are captured by local political interests. In addition to examining institutional features to determine whether a program is nondiscretionary, I also focus on the transparency of the implementation, identifying whether governments employ measures to increase public awareness about benefits and to prevent bias in beneficiary selection. If these features are not present, and/or if secondary literature, interviews,

---

cases, I consider expansions innovations that reach 35 percent. See Chapters 4 and 5 in particular.
[3] On weak institutions, see Levitsky and Murillo (2009); on enforcement, see Holland (2016).

and newspaper sources document systematic biases in implementation, I then characterize a program as discretionary.

This universe of social policies therefore excludes temporary schemes and highly targeted programs that protect a small portion of the outsider population.[4] Analytically, as discussed in the explanatory framework, the incentives to create temporary, small, and discretionary benefits differ sharply from those encouraging incumbents to launch nondiscretionary, large, and permanent policies.

To measure the occurrence of expansion, I use two indicators: (a) the adoption of the policy with the features just described through the enactment of legislation or resolutions involving the legal creation of benefits, and (b) the implementation of these benefits, understood solely in terms of the actual launching of the programs and accomplishment of their proposed reach, not in terms of their evolution over time.

Looking at both adoption and implementation addresses the fact that there may be time lags – temporal disjunctures – between the creation of the policy and its actual launching that should be analyzed to gain a comprehensive understanding of the process of expansion. Although we might expect policies to be launched immediately after their adoption, the empirical chapters in this book show that governments often fail to start implementation, establish a phased implementation that takes place over the course of a number of years, or delay implementation for different reasons. A close examination of both indicators – adoption and implementation – is analytically important because time lags may result from challenges that incumbents or proponents of social policies may encounter after the adoption of a program, including resistance from vested interests – even from new incumbents – or lack of adequate funding, as discussed in this book's case studies. This is particularly relevant concerning the first innovations in Brazil.

The timing of social policy expansion varied across cases. In Brazil, the adoption of new provisions occurred at the beginning of the new democracy with the inclusion of new rights in the 1988 constitution, followed by implementation in the early 1990s and a new phase of innovations surrounding the 2002 elections. In Argentina and Chile, social policy innovations were introduced in the early 2000s after several years of democratic rule. In Mexico, social policy innovations began in 2001 with the first democratic administration after a prolonged transition from decades of nondemocratic politics.

---

[4] See Appendix 1 for further clarification.

Restrictive versus Inclusive Policies

The social policies resulting from these processes of expansion exhibit striking variation along three dimensions of critical welfare and political importance: (a) the scope of policy coverage, (b) the generosity of benefits, and (c) the participation of beneficiary organizations in policy implementation.[5] The first two features reflect the core concerns of social policy beneficiaries: who gets covered and how. The scope of coverage refers to the proportion of the relevant outsider population receiving benefits (seniors, children, or when it comes to health care services, the entire outsider population); the benefit level refers to the amount of the transfer or service provided compared to the benefits granted to insiders.[6] The scope of coverage ranges from universal to barely covering 35 percent of the outsiders. Benefit levels range from levels comparable to significantly lower than those received by low-income formal-sector workers (see Appendix 1 for measures and categories).

Aside from their effect on welfare, the scope of coverage and benefit levels affect the formation of coalitions that support social policies.[7] Scholarship on advanced industrialized democracies has found that broad-reaching egalitarian benefits generate common interests among beneficiaries and facilitate the formation of large social policy coalitions, while narrower and more segmented benefits typically hinder the formation of common interests and alliances (see Esping-Andersen 1990; Esping-Andersen and Korpi 1984). This is consequential for the perceptions that beneficiaries develop about social policies and about their own political efficacy (see Soss 1999), as well as their ability to defend these policies from future cutbacks (Pierson 1994).

The final dimension, participation in implementation, concerns the inclusion of social organizations representing outsiders in policy councils or similar units. These organizations perform several tasks, such as overseeing policy implementation, deliberating about policy improvements, performing consultative roles by advising the state on policy implementation, and participating in information and outreach campaigns.[8] The policy councils considered here are created through ministerial resolution,

---

[5] About the features of welfare programs in industrialized democracies, see Mares (2003); Pierson (1994).

[6] Different parameters are used to measure the level of income transfers (the minimum wage, poverty line, and – when available – similar benefits for insiders). See Appendix 1.

[7] See, for example, Anderson (2001); Esping-Andersen (1990); Lynch (2006); Mares (2003); Pierson (1994); Rothstein (1992).

[8] On different types of social policy councils, see particularly Arvitzer (2009).

law, or decree, or may be more informal arrangements involving social organizations taking on specific tasks in implementation, particularly outreach and information campaigns, in combination with state agencies.

Participatory arrangements are subject to varying treatments in the literature. Scholars and analysts often consider participatory arrangements valuable spaces for social involvement in policy making, deliberation, and for the empowerment of citizens and social organizations (see Fung and Wright 2003; Baiocchi 2005). Yet others have pointed to the risk of participatory institutions becoming potential grounds for state co-optation of social organizations or state capture by social actors.[9] Scholars and activists further highlight concerns of participatory arrangements becoming ceremonial or "ossified," thereby reducing their impact on citizen engagement, transparency, and deliberation.[10] And yet others have documented positive welfare effects resulting from participatory arrangements (Touchstone and Wampler 2014).

I include participatory arrangements in the analysis to highlight their potential for facilitating policy deliberation and learning, circulation of information, and implementation oversight. Where policy design empowers organizations to interact regularly with the state around policy-specific issues affecting outsiders, the policy may stand a better chance of effectively delivering benefits to the most needy, marginalized populations. Policy inclusion through participatory arrangements may also affect the fate of these policies by entrenching them. The impact of participation in turn depends on these arrangements' institutional features and on whether they are effectively implemented.

With this in mind, the key questions I address regarding participatory arrangements include (a) whether social organizations engage in any of the following activities: oversight, deliberation, consultation, and/ or information and outreach campaigns, as these are critical ways of contributing to policy improvement as well as key tasks activists seek to carry out in participatory spaces; and (b) the level of participation in each policy area. More specifically, I view arrangements whose existence is required for the policy to start rolling, and in which members/ participants are required to produce specific outputs such as oversight reports or policy proposals to improve implementation, to involve *high levels of participation*. Councils that engage in deliberation, oversight,

---

[9] For a discussion, see Cornwall (2008); Goldfrank (2007); Van Cott (2008).
[10] On the operation of participatory arrangements, see Avritzer (2009); Baiocchi (2005); Cornwall (2008); Goldfrank (2007).

or consultation but are not required to produce any actual institutional output, and/or whose existence is temporary or not a prerequisite for the launching of the program, entail *moderate levels of participation.* Arrangements in which organizations are engaged in any of these activities but meet infrequently and produce no institutional output and are therefore rather ceremonial, as well as less stable arrangements such as participation in information campaign activities in partnership with state agencies, indicate *low levels of participation* (see Appendix 1). Finally *no participation* involves the absence of participatory arrangements or their existence on paper alone.

A critical question concerns whether participatory arrangements may become ambits for clientelism. If council members have the power to "authorize access and/or withdraw benefits," then I assume that councils are vulnerable to clientelism or prone to engage in the manipulation of beneficiaries. As discussed in the empirical chapters, policies that constitute cases of "expansion" in the countries under investigation lack this type of associational intermediation, as policy makers and politicians generally rejected it due to fears that potential abuses or clientelism would discredit the policies.

The direct state implementation of nondiscretionary benefits empowers bureaucracies and often leaves little space for the circulation of information, demands, and concerns raised collectively by beneficiaries, or for the development of policy learning and skills on the part of beneficiaries or organizations representing them. Although nonparticipatory implementation may help develop bureaucratic capacity for policy implementation within environments in which such capacity is not widespread – Chile is an exception in this case (see Luna and Mardones 2014; Soifer 2015) –it may also limit the ability of beneficiaries to organize around and/or entrench specific policies.

These three institutional features – scope of coverage, benefit levels, and participatory versus state implementation – can combine to produce different social policy structures or models. In the cases of large-scale expansion under examination, they have combined to yield two distinct models that I term *inclusive* and *restrictive.* Inclusive social policies provide extensive benefits (universal or nearly universal) that are relatively generous and often uniform for all beneficiaries. At the same time, they allow for at least some participation by organizations in policy implementation. Restrictive policies generally provide more modest benefits to a smaller pool of outsiders, often leaving a significant number of people uncovered and/or underserved. At the same time, they approach implementation in a state-centric way without involving social organizations.

As we will see, inclusive policies are sometimes integrated with formal-sector programs and provide similar benefits to outsiders and insiders (often low-income formal-sector workers), while restrictive policies are generally constructed in parallel to formal-sector programs, resulting in two-tiered welfare structures. As found in the literature on institutional development, such separation of benefits may limit opportunities for joint action and common policy concerns across sectors.[11]

These two policy models are conceptual devices that help identify similarities and differences in the levels of welfare provision in policies for outsiders, and the involvement of beneficiaries in implementation, as well as in the policy choices of governments, social movements, and political parties involved in expansion across cases. While these two models introduce clear-cut distinctions between policy structures, policies may exhibit similarities across different models and may vary across policy areas within each model to some extent. Other models stemming from different combinations of levels on key dimensions of social policy are analytically possible. And countries may also be scored on a continuum of coverage scope, benefit levels, and participation. The choice of a discrete number of models in this book follows the empirical clustering of cases as well as the logic of typologies found in the welfare state literature (see Esping-Andersen 1990), which clearly emphasizes the coherence of policy choice in each model that results from expansion. This facilitates understanding of country-level political dynamics over policy-specific ones.

To determine whether policies within each country case cohere into one model or the other, I score each dimension within each policy area following the criteria in Appendix 1. When the policy's scope of coverage and benefit level are high or moderate with one being high, and when participation in implementation is present, I score the policy as inclusive. When a policy area has a moderate or low scope of coverage, a moderate or low benefit level, and no participation in implementation, I score it as restrictive. When the majority of policies are restrictive/inclusive, then the country-level model gets that label.

Table 2.1 scores policy areas in each of the four countries along the main dimensions of social policy around the year 2010. Among selected cases, Argentina and Brazil created inclusive social policies for outsiders, whereas Chile and Mexico built restrictive policies.

---

[11] See Jacob Hacker's (2002) work on the welfare state in the United States.

TABLE 2.1 *Inclusive and restrictive social policy models,*
selected countries, ca. 2010

	Inclusive		Restrictive	
	Argentina	Brazil	Mexico	Chile
Pensions				
Scope of Coverage	High (97%)	High (79%)	Low (48%)	Moderate (54%)
Benefit Level	High	High	Low	Moderate
Participation	Low	Moderate	None	None
Health Care				
Scope of Coverage	Free, universal	Free, universal	Free, poorest	Free, poorest
Benefit Level	High	High	Moderate	Moderate
Participation	Moderate	High	None	None
Income Support				
Scope of Coverage	High (74%)	High (72%)	Low (36%)	Moderate (58%)
Benefit Level	High	Moderate	Moderate	Low
Participation	Low	Low	None	None

Notes: In Scope of Coverage percentages refer to the share of the relevant outsider population that is covered (e.g., seniors, school-age children).
Sources and measures: Available in Appendix 1.

Despite some differences in coverage and benefit levels between Mexico and Chile, both countries' policies demonstrate a number of critical similarities, namely the absence of nearly universal or universal reach (more than 70 percent of the outsider population; see Appendix 1 for further reference); a clear preference for benefits that are significantly smaller than those afforded to low-income insiders; the segmentation of outsiders based on receipt of full or partially subsidized health benefits; and the absence of participation in implementation. At the same time, despite differences across Argentina and Brazil, both countries provide high (or universal) access, higher benefit levels – which are comparable to those low-income insiders receive – and both cases show participation in implementation playing some role.

2.3 EXPLAINING SOCIAL POLICY EXPANSION

What explains the expansion of social policy for outsiders in countries with marked insider–outsider divides? Why have some incumbents embarked on large-scale expansion of nondiscretionary social policy for outsiders while others have not? To account for expansion, the first component of this research, I present a theoretical framework that emphasizes the pressures on incumbents produced by high electoral competition for outsider voters and/or mobilization from below. These factors create incentives for incumbents to respond with social policy expansion at a time in which outsiders lack the basic social policy protections enjoyed by insiders.

Incumbents in the new democracies of Latin America were confronted with the long-standing question of how to address social needs and inequities. Like many of their predecessors, they often lacked both readily available economic resources and a social policy framework to easily include outsiders, as existing social programs were linked with formal-sector employment everywhere in the region.

In this context, incumbents concerned about their parties' or their own continuity in power extended nondiscretionary social programs to outsiders when they faced credible challengers who could defeat them in elections by mobilizing outsiders and who often promised social policy expansion to gain outsiders' votes, and/or when they faced powerful social mobilization from below demanding expansion. Absent these conditions, expansion did not occur.

Conceptual Building Blocks: Electoral Competition for Outsiders and Social Mobilization

Electoral Competition for Outsiders

Throughout this book, electoral competition entails the existence of a party that can plausibly defeat the incumbent by gaining significant electoral support among outsiders. Electoral competition may occur when outsider voters either (a) are not aligned with any particular party and thus are ready to be mobilized by different parties, or (b) constitute the electoral bastion of a given party but encounter a credible challenger who seeks to gain their support. The dynamics characterized here thus entail a situation in which outsiders are not (or no longer) the secure constituency of any party.

Presidential elections are the most relevant factor in incumbents' decisions to expand social policy, as these most directly affect incumbents and their parties in the highly presidentialist systems of Latin America, where the president has especially strong powers and the national executive is the most important prize politicians and parties can win.[12] As this book shows, incumbents are likely to embark on large-scale, nondiscretionary

---

[12] On presidential systems in Latin America, see Mainwaring and Shugart (1997).

expansion to offset credible challengers when they face *competition for outsider voters in presidential elections.*

The growth of challengers in local elections does not present a direct threat to the continuity of the incumbent in national office. Challenges in these elections may be addressed with other types of resources and involve decisions and strategies of subnational authorities, particularly, though not only, in federal systems. Legislative elections, while important, do not clearly implicate the ability of other parties to pose a challenge to the continuity of the incumbent president or national governing coalition, or of rising candidates to effectively challenge the incumbent in future presidential elections. As this study's cases show, challenges in legislative elections may respond to the dynamics of competition in different districts and affect those districts' political authorities. The prize at stake, however, is less consequential for parties than the loss of national office. In some cases, party systems have shown higher fragmentation in legislative than in presidential elections, with factions of the largest parties – or local parties allied to national party coalitions – sometimes running alternative ballots to those of their national allies. These factions often have power in some districts but lack the ability to run a plausible winner in national elections on their own.[13] Although results from legislative elections may affect the capacity of governments to effectively pass legislation, competition for outsider voters in these elections does not produce incentives for the incumbent to solidify the outsider electorate behind her party or coalition, as it does in presidential elections.

Although these expansions may be confounded with an incumbent's *individual* project, continuity should be understood as that of an incumbent president or that president's party – especially when parties are not simply electoral vehicles but organizations that routinely submit candidates in elections.[14] In short, social policy expansion in the face of electoral competition for outsiders is a project national incumbents undertake in nascent Latin American democracies in response to challenges to their own or to their parties' control of the presidency.

It should be noted that in some cases, outsiders are not a majority of the population, and the party that wins the elections may not have significant outsider support. According to my data, this is the case in Argentina in 1983, when the Radical Party won the presidency without

---

[13] On Brazil, see for example Borges (2011).
[14] On political parties in Latin America, see Levitsky, S., J. Loxton, B. Van Dyck and Domínguez (2016).

significantly challenging the Peronist or Justicialista Party's (PJ) historical electoral stronghold among outsiders, and the size of that population was close to 40 percent at the time. When the PJ returned to power in 1989, it continued to enjoy support from outsiders, an electorate that was not being disputed by another party.

To measure electoral competition for outsiders, I analyze existing pre- and postelection surveys,[15] as well as ecological data of national-level election results across districts (municipalities or *departamentos*) since re-democratization compiled for all cases.[16] Given the lack of data on national elections before 2000 for Mexico, I analyzed local elections since the 1980s as well as national elections since 2000. I also carried out interviews with candidates and politicians involved in campaigns, analyzed documents of political parties (e.g., campaign platforms), and searched for candidates' statements in the press to understand whether credible challengers were seeking to mobilize outsider voters and how they sought to do so.

I have built two systematic indicators of electoral competition for outsiders' votes. The first indicator is the *vote margin between the first and second party among outsider voters*; the second is *challenger victory among outsider voters*. I measure these indicators with two types of data: existing polls and ecological data. Using votes reported by respondents I classify as "outsiders" in existing survey data, I measure the vote margin of the most voted party, and whether the challenger garners the most votes among outsiders. I consider elections to have electoral competition for outsiders when this margin is less than ten percentage points or when a challenger disputing outsiders' support from the incumbent effectively wins.

With ecological data, I measure the margin of victory between the two most voted parties as well as challenger victories at the district level for every presidential election since re-democratization. Acknowledging the shortcomings of ecological data, namely the problem of ecological fallacy, I focus only on districts where outsiders are a majority – representing at least 55 percent of the population – and call these districts "outsider." This does not eliminate problems with ecological data, but mitigates them to some extent. I consider elections to have electoral competition for outsiders if at least 50 percent of the outsider districts

---

[15] Systematic national polls of Argentina's elections were not available.
[16] For some countries I also build on existing data sets, such as Zucco's (2009), and the historical electoral data from Universidad Diego Portales (accessed in 2013).

and/or if 50 percent of the outsider population in outsider districts experience competition (see Appendix 3).

The focus on outsider districts also stems from the fact that because several of these districts are low income and far from large cities, I assume competition tends to emerge later in these areas, and when it does take place, it probably means that competition for outsiders is also high in these other districts.[17] When I have both ecological and survey data for a given election, the measures coincide.

Overall, this way of measuring electoral competition best captures the notion that a particular level or *threshold* of electoral competition threatens incumbents' survival and compels them to reach out to outsiders through social policy. A continuous measure of electoral competition in which the impact of this factor on incumbents' decisions would be based on more or less competition regardless of its absolute level would not capture the analytical argument.

This data collection, classification, and analytical endeavor constitutes, to my knowledge, the first attempt to systematically conceptualize and measure the presence of competition for the votes of outsiders (informal, unemployed, self-employed rural workers and their dependents) since the third wave of democratization in Latin America. Other studies have referred to electoral competition while seeking to explain types of social policy reforms in Latin America (Haggard and Kaufman 2008; Huber and Stephens 2012; Pribble 2013), yet these studies do not theoretically explain what type of competition or what elections (presidential, local, legislative) matter to social policy reformers. Moreover, these studies do not conceptualize or measure electoral competition systematically.

As presented in the empirical chapters, the data show the presence of electoral competition for outsiders in the 1999 elections in Argentina and the 2002 elections in Brazil as well as in all presidential elections in Chile and Mexico from 1999 and 2000, respectively, through the end of the period under examination, 2010. In these latter cases, electoral dynamics are fundamental for social policy expansion across different policy areas.

Social Mobilization

The second path to expansion is triggered by social mobilization from below, here defined as a sustained process launched by a coalition of

---

[17] On Mexico, see Gibson (1997); Lujambio (2001); Magaloni (2006). On Brazil, see Fleisher (2002); Hunter (2007).

social movements and labor unions making demands on the state for broad, universal benefits for outsiders. The significance of these processes of social mobilization from below rests in (a) the presence of powerful organizations representing outsiders and (b) the movements' alliance with labor unions, which represent insiders and have been understood to have opposing interests to those of outsiders (see Weyland 1996a). Throughout this book, I will refer to these alliances as social movement coalitions (SMC). Next I discuss each component of these coalitions, and the conditions under which they formed.

SOCIAL MOVEMENTS REPRESENTING OUTSIDERS. Social movements that represent outsiders include national-level federated groups with large membership bases, as well as smaller grassroots organizations. Those analyzed here were initially formed by outsiders themselves or jointly with other groups advocating social policy for outsiders, such as doctors, health care workers, and NGOs.[18] As scholars of contention have noted, these social movements are loose networks of organizations and federations in which no single organization has a dominant position (see Diani 2003: 9), and claim to represent outsiders beyond their adherents and leaders, a feature that generally characterizes social movement organizations (Amenta 2006: 7).

Given the prevailing pessimistic view about the capacity of outsiders to engage in collective action and influence national policy, a relevant question becomes what conditions favor the emergence of outsider movements. Building on the classic social movement literature,[19] Yashar (2005) has found that social movements representing excluded ethnic groups (an outsider group) in Latin America formed when three factors combined: motives to organize, which were generated by state policy negatively affecting indigenous communities; organizational capacity provided by networks formed by activists, churches, or the state that afforded communities with resources, skills, and ties; as well as associational space, which allowed for organizations to freely flourish. Associational space and resources provided by other organizations and allies also augur in favor of the emergence of the movements studied in this book.

Other factors have also played relevant roles in the emergence of these movements. In the following chapters we see that state programs may also galvanize large-scale collective action and favor the formation of a

---

[18] For a discussion of federated organizations, see McCarthy (2005: 196).
[19] McAdam (1999); McAdam, McCarthy, and Zald (1996); Tarrow (1998).

common identity that provides the basis for social movement organizations to emerge and grow. As analyzed in Chapter 5, in Argentina, the
selective distribution of social benefits by the government in response to
isolated protests of unemployed workers led to the spread of collective
action by groups seeking similar responses and contributed to the emergence of a powerful movement of unemployed workers. Social benefits
provided resources and a target for demands, and helped develop a collective identity among the unemployed.[20]

State-structured associations formed by outsiders can also provide
the basis for more autonomous, national-level activism over time. Rural
unionization in Brazil was initially sponsored by the state to control contention and to mobilize rural unions as a support base by João Goulart's
administration (1962–4).[21] The military that overthrew Goulart purged
the National Confederation of Agricultural Workers (CONTAG), and
distributed resources through the unions to demobilize and co-opt them,
producing a dramatic increase in unionization.[22] With the democratic
transition in the 1980s, these state-sponsored unions built alliances with
other labor unions and popular organizations and pressed for social policy expansion and for agrarian reform.

Thus, according to existing scholarship, a number of enabling factors
appear fundamental for the formation of movements of outsiders. First,
critical allies may help outsider interest organizations to germinate and
grow.[23] These allies help develop leadership, skills, and connections across
different organizations. Second, a favorable democratic environment – or
a democratic transition – is also fundamental for movements to scale up
and press the state for resources or social change, as systematic repression
of organized movements is costly for incumbents in liberalizing or democratic polities. Although the emergence of mobilization is not impossible
under authoritarian regimes, state responses to demands of autonomous
groups are highly likely to involve repression, limiting the impact and
growth of a movement. The third wave of democracy has been, in this
respect, a crucial environment for social movement formation, especially
for the emergence of national movements. Finally, access to resources and
the formation of a common identity may be facilitated by existing state
policy, which may help organizations representing outsiders advance

[20] See among others Delamata (2004); Garay (2007); Svampa and Pereyra (2003).
[21] See Houtzager (1998); Maybury-Lewis (1994); Novaes (1991).
[22] On patronage under the military, see especially Jenks (1979) and Hagopian (1996).
[23] See Tarrow (1998).

common demands or oppose common state projects. Thus, mobilizing structures and powerful allies, an open democratizing polity, and sometimes small-scale state programs are important for outsiders' organizations and movements to form and scale up.

LABOR UNIONS. Labor unions that forged alliances with social movements are termed "social movement unions" because they press for workplace, social, and political issues that affect their members and broader communities (Sader 1988; Seidman 1994: 28). Social movement unions emerged under the broad macrosocial processes of market-oriented reforms and democratization. Changes produced under these shifts led more combatant unions in countries with powerful or rising labor movements, such as Argentina and Brazil, respectively, to form alternative labor-union confederations[24] the Central Única dos Trabalhadores (CUT) in Brazil and the Central de Trabajadores de Argentina (CTA).[25] Industrial labor unions formed the CUT during the democratic transition to press for democratization and social demands, which they brought under the broad umbrella of citizenship rights (see Keck 1992). Public-sector workers and teachers' unions created the CTA in opposition to the market reforms that the rest of the union movement endorsed in the 1990s and sought to represent the working class rather than to advance the more narrow interests of their members (CTA 1992; Godio 2000). Over time, both confederations became largely composed of public and social service unions (da Silva 2001), which have tended to be closer to the needs of low-income communities.

Social movement unions did not emerge as forcefully in Mexico and Chile, where labor unions have been exceedingly preoccupied with their own inability to organize the formal workforce as a consequence of detrimental labor laws that curtail unionization and/or the centralization of union organizations and thus their influence (see Bensusán and Cook 2003; interviews, UNT leader Hernández Juárez, Mexico; national board of CUT, Moraga, Chile). Until recently, broad social movements were not available for cross-sector alliances either. In the case of Chile, a lack of economic resources to engage in mobilization on the part of labor unions appears to have been a limiting factor for unions' ability to engage in wider coalition building as well (interview, CONFENATS, Chile).

---

[24] Higher level organizations that represent federations.
[25] See, among others, Bensusán (2000); Godio (2000); Sader (1988); Seidman (1994).

SOCIAL MOVEMENT COALITIONS (SMC). Coalitions between social movements representing outsiders and labor unions are the critical actors in the processes of social mobilization analyzed in this book. These coalitions possess two main features. First, alliances with social movements and organizations constitute a central concern of the confederations formed by labor unions. For example, since its creation, and against a tradition in which confederations only organized labor union federations of formal-sector workers, the CTA sought to establish "direct affiliation" of workers and organizations other than labor unions, such as informal-sector and unemployed workers and cooperatives. Second, these alliances share a common social policy agenda. The development of such an agenda is a fundamental way through which these confederations sought to create or sustain ties with social movements over time (interviews, Lozano, national board of CTA; Dau Motta, national board of CUT). Focusing on citizens' rights instead of workers' rights (Dau Motta) or on income instead of wages (Lozano) were ways in which unions redefined their subjects and goals to include outsiders).

Across cases, labor unions pursued these alliances to increase their strength and numbers in order to advance their own demands for democracy and/or against state adjustment, and to create a labor movement with greater solidarity. Social movements in turn often acquired a national scope when they were aided by the capillarity of the labor unions' structures, especially in the case of public service unions, and were thus able to target the state in a sustained way, which is fundamental for social movements to achieve their goals. At the same time, coalitions with labor unions generally helped social movements elaborate their social policy agendas. Moreover, these national confederations helped articulate different movements that pressed for benefits and services for outsiders in different policy areas. This was especially true in Brazil, where different social movements made policy demands within different policy areas (e.g., pensions, health care, and agrarian

I measure the existence and level of social mobilization. For the first question, I explore whether there are organizations representing outsiders and if they have established coalitions with labor unions. Second, to measure whether this social mobilization is sustained and large scale, I assess the size of the SMCs' membership bases, alliances between outsiders' organizations and other groups such as NGOs, and indicators of protests and other tactics such as the collection of signatures, petitions, participation in formal policy formulation, lobbying, and formal and informal meetings with public authorities. I also measure the presence of SMC–incumbent alliances and the participation of social movement members in government positions, which constitute ways in which they may influence policy.[26]

Dynamics of Social Policy Expansion

This section lays out the argument linking electoral competition for outsider voters and social mobilization with incumbents' decisions to expand social policy for outsiders. It presents the mechanisms by which these two factors affect decisions to expand large-scale social policy and explains why they incentivize adoption of nondiscretionary benefits instead of clientelistic provisions. One of the key issues in this discussion is to highlight the presence of democracy, which is necessary for these two factors to fully develop and generate incentives for the expansion of large-scale nondiscretionary policy.

As put forth by Dahl, real-world democracies are those with inclusive electoral institutions that extend the right to vote to the vast majority of the population and enable contestation, which allows for the opposition to grow, express itself, and compete in elections.[27] Social groups and political parties are allowed to organize in democratic regimes without members fearing intimidation, repression, or exclusion. Authoritarian regimes by contrast limit civil freedoms and may ban, manipulate, or restrict suffrage and the political and social groups that can contest power. Despite the fact that authoritarian regimes may vary, their defining features are that the scope of contestation and/or inclusion are seriously restricted. Elections may exist but are not free and/or not fair, and particular groups may be excluded from the vote and/or be the subject of systematic intimidation, repression, or persecution.[28]

As broadly discussed in the literature, incumbents in authoritarian regimes have other tools for dealing with the rise of electoral competition and social mobilization. These include limiting or repressing the opposition and social organizations, co-opting movement leaders, and

---

[26] The data come from a systematic analysis of newspaper articles and interviews with social movement leaders, activists, politicians, and policy makers, as well as an analysis of publications of social movements and labor unions. The secondary literature is also a source of information. See Appendix 2 for further information on measures and scores.

[27] More specifically, Dahl defines real-world democracies or polyarchies as characterized by free and fair elections in which citizens can elect and be elected, in which there are alternative sources of information, freedom of expression is afforded and citizens have the right to form and join organizations. On Polyarchy, see Dahl (1971).

[28] See for example, Levitsky and Way (2010); Magaloni (2006); Masoud (2014).

distributing benefits selectively – even if these benefits are broad – in order to dampen pressures and demobilize activists. These incumbents lack the incentives for expansion present under democratic regimes in which power is contested openly, freedoms are granted, and the systematic repression of opposition candidates can hardly go unpunished, especially in national politics.[29] I return to this question in Chapter 3 when I discuss systematically the origins of the social policy divide between insiders and outsiders.

Electoral Competition for Outsiders: Incumbents, Challengers, and Social Policy Expansion

The argument of this book is based on the premise that incumbents care deeply about their or their parties' continuity in power. Continuity is uncertain in democratic regimes in which parties compete in free and fair elections. In these environments, the rise of a challenger vigorously appealing to outsiders to win office may undermine incumbents' continuity, especially when outsiders constitute a significant portion of the electorate. When incumbents face electoral competition for outsiders, they have a strong incentive to appeal to this sector and secure its support. Social policy expansion is deemed a critical tool to that end.

These incentives, however, may be severely undercut by the particular features of the institutional environment that reduce incumbents' time horizons. More concretely, incumbents expect continuity under two conditions: when incumbent presidents can be reelected and when their parties are minimally stable organizations. The absence of both of these basic institutional arrangements (reelection provisions and stable party organization) restricts the possibility of continuity in power, and undermines the incentives for embarking on social policy expansion. Democracies without consecutive reelection provisions and/or without minimally stable parties are few in Latin America. Since the 2000s, Peru has possessed these two features (Levitsky 2013; Levitsky and Cameron 2003), which, as analyzed in greater detail in Chapter 8, significantly reduced incumbents' incentives for social policy expansion.

With these scope conditions in mind, incumbents who face competition for the votes of outsiders in presidential elections may choose to offset challengers' appeals to outsiders with social policy expansion for a number of reasons. In third-wave democracies, outsiders are numerous

[29] ibid.

and lack the social protections provided to insiders, which makes access to social policy an especially important common need across outsiders. Because of outsiders' heterogeneous and often precarious employment situations, work-related policies are a challenging method for reaching them broadly and decisively. While land distribution helped mobilize a substantial share of outsider support earlier in the twentieth century, urbanization since the 1960s reduced the size of the rural sector significantly, raising the question of how to reach urban outsiders. In this scenario, social policy became a particularly useful way to reach out to the diverse universe of the urban informal sector, the unemployed, and rural workers, and an easier strategy for incumbents to pursue. By extending social policy (or promising to do so if elected), incumbents and challengers can reach out with (promises of) divisible and tangible benefits to voters who lack access to the social protections received by insiders and who typically live in poverty.

In an environment of social policy exclusion, challengers in fact often appeal to outsider voters through promises of social policy expansion in an effort to mobilize their support. Once a challenger places the issue of expansion on the public agenda, the competitive environment and the threat of replacement in office are likely to compel incumbents to respond. Though not always practically possible before elections, the threat of defeat followed by the inauguration of social benefits by a new administration is a potent incentive for incumbents to initiate reforms promptly during their tenures or to promise to expand benefits if they or their parties are elected for another term. If they manage to initiate expansions before elections, incumbents may then present themselves as first movers, establishing institutions of social inclusion proposed by their opponents.

In the cases studied here, incumbents expanded social policy when (a) responding to threats to their continuity in office raised by a challenger courting outsiders in elections, and (b) when they came to power in elections that were marked by competition for the vote of outsiders, and launched social policy innovations in an effort to secure outsiders' electoral support. In both of these cases, the logic is similar: Incumbents seek to consolidate contested outsider support in an effort to ensure continuation in power.

Seeking to diffuse the momentum of competitors and to claim credit for expansion, incumbents are likely, then, to conceive of social policy expansion as a viable tool to help them continue in office. The promise of expansion may then become a double-edged sword for challengers: On one hand, it may help politicians to advance in opinion polls before elections; on the other hand, it prompts incumbents to try to initiate challenger-proposed reforms during their tenures or promise comparable initiatives before elections. Competition for the votes of outsiders therefore compels both credible challengers and incumbents to make appeals to outsiders with social policy, proposing expansion and supporting it decisively.[30] For example, when he ran for Mexico's presidency in 2006, Andrés Manuel López Obrador of the Party of the Democratic Revolution (PRD) promised to create a universal pension for seniors. A similar initiative during his tenure as mayor of Mexico City had won him and his party massive support (interview, PRD social policy expert), and the promise of launching this benefit nationally allowed him to place the issue at the center of the campaign debate (interview, campaign advisor of López Obrador). After criticizing the proposal as populist, however, the incumbent president from the center-right National Action Party (PAN) launched a pension program in the last months of his tenure, when López Obrador threatened to defeat his party's candidate for the presidency.

Challengers' and incumbents' promises of social policy lower barriers to obtaining funding for new programs. Once social policy expansion becomes a salient issue, politicians face higher costs in opposing or blocking funding for such innovations. After elections, the newly elected incumbent who comes to power has strong incentives to expand social policy to consolidate support among outsiders and the competitive environment in turn discourages challenger opposition to these initiatives.

Competition for outsider voters then motivates expansion through three different mechanisms. First, competition for outsider voters by a credible challenger poses a *threat of replacement*, which motivates incumbents' responses. Second, it raises the *salience of social policy* issues affecting outsiders and places expansion at the center of the public debate generating incentives for incumbents to respond. Finally, when social policy expansion is publicly discussed and promoted by challengers, incumbents fear *declining popularity* if they fail to expand policy themselves. Both to curry favor with outsider voters and to present the administration as competent, incumbents are motivated to favor expansion. The opposition faces similar pressure, as it can block expansion to undermine the incumbent, but the salience of the social policy debate makes it an unpopular measure and a losing strategy.

---

[30] On policy expansion and how it allows politicians to claim credit, see Pierson (1994: ch. 1 and 2).

Social Mobilization: Social Movement Coalitions,
Incumbents, and Social Policy Expansion

Incumbents who face broad mobilization from below demanding social policy have incentives to respond to this mobilization with social policy expansion in order to satisfy demands and dampen pressures that may destabilize the government, reduce its popularity, and even, in some cases, threaten its survival in office.

Social movement coalitions engage in three main types of social mobilization that can be schematically characterized as (a) protest, (b) pressure through institutional channels, and (c) pressure through an allied party in office. Although the three strategies may be adopted simultaneously, SMCs often rely on one strategy more than the others.

Social mobilization affects incumbents' behavior through different mechanisms. First, SMCs use pressure through institutional channels and protest activities to *increase the salience of an issue*, which creates compelling incentives for incumbents to address it in some way. Second, SMCs often attempt to marshal broader public support for their demands through communication campaigns, appearing in the media, organizing protests and demonstrations that give visibility to their demands, and collecting signatures for a policy proposal. If public opinion supports proposed changes, this threatens incumbents with *declining popularity* if they do not address social movement claims. In the case of protest, moreover, governments may seem incompetent if they do not effectively resolve an issue that brings thousands to the streets, often causing general disorder. Support for movement demands and/or frustration with disorder produced by protests may negatively affect the popularity of incumbent presidents (and their parties), which helps place movements' demands within the government's agenda. Incumbents respond in these cases mainly to regain or prevent a decline in popularity emerging from neglecting an issue that figures prominently in the public debate. Third, protest and the exit of a social movement ally from the government coalition may influence not only popularity rates but governability as well, and give rise to the *threat of destabilization*. Recurrent protests generate the impression that the government has a weak grip on power and cannot solve major issues. Several informants, for example, highlighted the overriding concern of Argentina's President Néstor Kirchner (2003–7) with protests, referring to his gesture of pointing to the recurrent mass of protestors outside the house of government as his "greatest problem." The fear of large-scale protests felt by the Kirchner administrations – what government informants called "losing the streets" – was a factor that influenced incumbents' decisions in different issue areas (export taxes, wage negotiations, and social policy). The threat of instability may be more pronounced. Large-scale antigovernment mobilizations propelled Fernando Collor de Mello's resignation in Brazil in 1992, as well as that of Fernando de la Rúa and other interim presidents in Argentina between 2001 and 2002 amid a dramatic financial meltdown. Fearful of the destabilizing effects of mobilization, successor presidents tried to dampen existing protests – including mobilization for social benefits that took place within these large-scale antigovernment protests – through negotiations or through strategic responses to demands.[31]

Next, I analyze different strategies of social mobilization and the corresponding incentives of incumbents to respond to demands in democracies. Governments generally also seek to claim credit for expansion, but the main motivation in these cases is to mitigate the pressure of social mobilization. In general, *protest* is employed by organizations that have little access to policy making, while *pressure through institutional channels* is employed by movements who have access but may not easily achieve results through the party system and thus need to coordinate broadly with other actors and often appeal to public opinion to bring attention to their demands and achieve policy change. Finally, *pressure through a party ally* takes place when a party ally is in power. This may be a party SMCs created to act as a vehicle for advancing their interests, or a party that integrated or created an alliance with SMCs once the party was in power.

PRESSURE THROUGH PROTEST. To press for social policy expansion, SMCs sometimes engage in marches, demonstrations, roadblocks, encampments in public spaces, and occupations of buildings. Once these protests[32] become large-scale and sustained, frequently driving thousands to the streets, incumbents are likely to respond to their demands. Three mechanisms may motivate incumbents' responses: the relevance of demands in the public debate; the fear of a decline in popularity produced by disorder and/or public support for the protestors – which is often what social movements keenly pursue – and the destabilizing effects of incessant large-scale protest.

---

[31] Based on the data set of protests, Argentina (1996–2010) and the Database of Policy Making, Brazil. For the case of Collor, I surveyed *Folha de São Paulo* during 1992 to further explore the evolution of the impeachment movement. On presidential falls, see Hochstetler (2006) and Pérez-Liñán (2007).

[32] I use the terms *contention* and *protest* interchangeably.

Governments can respond to protest in different ways. They can use repression, extend smaller concessions, or acquiesce to the more generous social policy demands SMCs pursue. In the cases of the third-wave democracies analyzed here, repression has not been a successful strategy, especially in the face of large-scale mobilization.[33] It has often backfired, driving more people into the streets and expanding the scope of contestation to new protestors and topics (such as civil liberties and state abuse). Across cases, smaller concessions that benefit movement leaders and members – what the literature often calls "club goods" – are sufficient enough to dampen pressure when movements are small or rising. Yet, when they face large-scale social mobilization by SMCs, incumbents are pressured to respond (also) with more meaningful measures to diffuse contention out of fear of *declining popularity* and/or *destabilizing protests*. Club goods targeting social movement leaders and adherents may grease the wheels of negotiations but are not enough to dampen large-scale contention.

Intense protest may produce destabilizing effects on the government. The presence of large-scale contention and public support for protestors' demands may create fissures within the incumbent coalition about how to respond, debilitating the government. It may also lead to a dramatic withdrawal of support and generate an image of a power vacuum that severely undermines the government. This has often occurred in cases in which a broader cycle of protest driven by several demands and involving large sectors of the population also emerged in addition to those placed by SMCs pressing for social benefits. These cycles of widespread contention are especially threatening for incumbents, making them both vulnerable to pressure and more likely to respond quickly to social policy demands. In these cases, incumbent responses reflect not only the power of individual groups demanding social policy expansion, but, as Tarrow points out when analyzing cycles of contention, "the degree of turbulence" in society as well (Tarrow 1998: 25).[34]

PRESSURE THROUGH INSTITUTIONAL CHANNELS. The strategies of influence SMCs employ to advocate expansion through institutional channels often involve lobbying legislators and officials at different

---

[33] A broad literature addresses repression of collective action. See, for example, Beissinger (2002); McAdam (1999); Tarrow (1998); Yashar (2005). For the cases under investigation, see Garay (2007) and Ondetti (2008).

[34] See Tarrow (1998, ch. 8).

levels of government in order to achieve policy change. When social mobilization is high, this pressure is often accompanied by efforts to mobilize the public in favor of reform through public opinion campaigns and different forms of participation in the public debate. After placing the issue of policy change on the agenda, social movement organizations may also become government advisors on policy reforms, and may even accept positions in the state to influence policy adoption and implementation. The choice to pursue institutional channels depends on the existence of venues where organizations can access policy making and advance demands not decisively addressed by political parties. These channels are usually opened or initially established as a response to pressure from organizations that demand participation in decision making.

Institutional channels may be formal (established by legislation) or informal (created ad hoc to integrate SMOs and state officials in regular conversation). Organizations may hold regular meetings with policy makers to explain their positions, or may brief them on particular issues affecting the policy debate and meet to clarify specific points. Movements may also run meetings, conferences, and workshops with public officials, and organize forums while a reform process is under way. For example, constant formal and informal interactions between social movement activists and public officials characterized the setting of the public agenda around health care reform and subsequent policy formulation and design in Brazil during the democratic transition.

SMCs that act through institutional channels may also use demonstrations to attract attention to and provide visibility for their claims. For example, when seeking to promote citizen participation in debates over the constitutional reform in Brazil, social movements organized activities such as the "caravan of the constitution," which went around towns disseminating information on ways citizens could influence the constitution's text and organizing cultural activities related to citizens' rights.

In order to affect incumbent's decisions, social movements need to persuade them that change is preferable to the status quo. Social movements seek to highlight "the repercussions" of not supporting their cause and often do so through "demonstrations of support" (Amenta 2006: 17). Unlike contention, SMCs employing institutional channels demonstrate the level of support in favor of a particular policy proposal through measures such as the collection of signatures, surveys, referendums, and petitions. For example, the lobby to get disability pensions adopted and implemented in Brazil was led by a group of activists who gathered more than 600,000 signatures nationwide in favor of the social assistance law that regulated these benefits in 1993.[35] Signatures provided demonstrated support for the cause and a measure of the size of the population expecting a response from the government.

Another way in which social movements seek to pressure policy makers is by holding individuals responsible for the approval or lack of approval of policy change. By exposing politicians' decisions to their electoral constituencies, social movements threaten them with *declining support*. For example, activists in Brazil during the Constituent Assembly publicized legislators' votes in their local towns, filmed congressional sessions to inform constituencies of their legislators' choices regarding social issues, and posted information on local media outlets, public buildings, and the streets. By threatening to hold them responsible for blocking policy responses, activists raise the costs for legislators opposing their demands.[36]

Social movement coalitions may also build alliances with other actors involved in proximate causes in order to achieve policy change. A broader coalition of organizations may give a stronger air of legitimacy to the issues proposed and mobilize broader levels of support across different sectors of society. At the same time, organizations may also mobilize local-level public officials in an effort to advance their demands and prompt the national government to respond, as was the case during health care reform in Brazil.

Finally, social movement organizations pressing for reforms through institutional channels may also gain leverage for their demands when governments face more radical demands from other groups addressing or representing similar constituencies. Amenta has argued that officials in the Franklin D. Roosevelt administration invoked the Townsend Plan (a pension proposal supported by a large social movement) "to try to scare conservatives into supporting the administration's more moderate old-age legislation" (2006: 7).

Incumbents are likely to respond to pressures through institutional channels when support for reforms is high – demonstrated through surveys, petitions, signatures, or the mobilization capacity of the SMCs involved, among others. Incumbents may nonetheless try to delay

---

[35] See Chapter 4.
[36] Ibid.

implementation and sometimes curb the scope of changes if they perceive that SMCs might have a hard time putting new pressures on the state to guarantee implementation. The cases of expansion in Brazil in which incumbents responded to pressure through institutional channels were drawn-out reform processes involving continuous pressures and coalition-building efforts by SMCs to achieve policy adoption and implementation.

Pressure through a Party Ally

SMCs also exert pressure for policy expansion through a party ally from within the state when this party is in power. When allied parties are in power, social movement leaders and/or allied experts gain positions in ministries and state agencies and may often even reach elected office. From these positions, SMCs pursue their agendas and negotiate their priorities with other members in the governing coalitions. Programmatic commitments and promises political parties make to SMCs become sources of active pressure when the allied party is in office.[37]

Alliances between parties and social movement coalitions may be recent or long-standing. If these alliances are formed when parties arrive in power – or to support them in their quest for power – ties between movements and parties are more fluid and potentially unstable. These alliances are often struck when governments seek to contain sustained mobilization and garner the support of SMCs. This is the case of the Peronist Party's alliance with some of the unemployed and labor union movements in Argentina beginning in 2004, and of the Confederation of Indigenous Nationalities of Ecuador (CONAIE), who supported the candidacy of Lucio Gutiérrez for the presidency in 2003. When parties ally with social movements, often to curb contentious activity, they generally respond to the movements' demands in order to preserve such alliances and avoid destabilizing their governments with the movements' exit. However, movements' demands may take a back seat when they integrate with a governing coalition, as SMCs may need to articulate their priorities with other sectors in that coalition. Moreover, when SMCs are allied with the governing coalition they are less able to mobilize in the streets for policy change.

---

[37] Note that alliances of social movements and parties in Latin America have been much less institutionalized than those existing among leftist parties and labor unions in the welfare state literature on Western Europe.

Social movements and unions may also form their own political parties that end up reaching office. The alliances between these parties and social movements are stronger and based on long-term relationships of trust and shared experiences (see Madrid 2012; Van Cott 2005). This is the case of the Movement for Socialism (MAS) in Bolivia, which was formed by labor and indigenous movements and reached the presidency in 2006; and of the Workers' Party (PT), in Brazil, originally founded by labor unions, social movements, and left and church activists, which, after more than two decades of electoral participation, won the presidency in 2002.[38] Parties and movements share common programmatic commitments that incumbents may promote while in power.

However, attaining their goals when allied presidents are in power is not always easy for SMCs. The incumbent governments are often based on party alliances, and presidents have to cater to different constituencies and demands. At the extreme, some governing coalitions marginalize social movements if presidents consolidate strong power, and (parts of) SMCs then depart from such coalitions or challenge government policies to the point that the coalition is terminated. The latter case occurred in the break up between Ecuador's indigenous movement and president Lucio Gutiérrez (2003–5) after the movement had supported his ascent to power and joined his government (see Madrid 2012: 101–2).

Incumbents have to accommodate social movement pressures as well as demands from other sectors within their coalitions. Social movement demands may at times contradict the priorities of other coalition members, and incumbents may then delay their responses by administering the timing of social policy decisions and slowing down the pace of implementation, or they may try to respond to movement demands with benefits targeted at movements and their adherents alone. These benefits include selective incentives – such as literacy promotion, education, or job training programs – to attract more movement members. They also provide resources to develop infrastructure investments in areas where movements are strong, channeling these investments through cooperatives and microenterprises. Movements allied with incumbents such as the MST (which is involved in agrarian reform, not social policy) and the CONTAG in Brazil, and the unemployed workers' movements in Argentina, administered selective benefits that helped them empower their organizations, recruit and retain members, and obtain resources to

---

[38] See Hunter (2007); Keck (1992); Samuels (2004); Seidman (1994).

coordinate movement activities nationally, as well as establish linkages with other grassroots organizations.

However, in the cases analyzed here, large-scale coalitions of outsiders and insiders also demanded social benefits for a broader universe of beneficiaries. In particular, activists who remained excluded from party alliances, or sections of SMCs willing to break such alliances to protect their founding policy agendas in the absence of concrete responses, placed intense demands for broad-based benefits. Because the social policy agenda is a building block of these SMCs, the agenda's abandonment in an alliance with parties in office may strongly debilitate the movements. In Argentina, for example, some of the unemployed and their union allies joined the Néstor Kirchner administration and obtained state positions. Other movements instead interacted intensely with the state through informal channels. When the government consolidated massive power and these informal meetings with organizations outside the governing coalition became more infrequent, social movements initiated renewed protest campaigns to capture state attention and press for universal benefits more vocally.

Movements allied to a party in office advance their demands through persuasion and negotiation within the government, or use contention and threats of exit if demands are left unattended. Movements often act on these threats, thereby pushing governments to respond with concessions, either out of fear of being weakened if social movement alliances are not maintained, or in anticipation of protests.

The Choice of Nondiscretionary Benefits
Why did incumbents in Argentina, Brazil, Chile, and Mexico launch nondiscretionary benefits to include outsiders? Why did they not adopt discretionary provisions that could be manipulated in exchange for targeted electoral support? Against the background of clientelism and the continuing presence of discretion in the allocation of some social investment projects and food programs, the creation of large, nondiscretionary health care services, pensions, and income-support programs for outsiders is surprising, and its causes are one of the least explored aspects of these processes of expansion.

This study argues that the design of nondiscretionary policies is the result of the strategic interests of politicians and social movements involved in decisions over social policy expansion. In democracies with intense electoral competition for outsiders – one of the drivers of expansion – incumbents launching broad policies for outsiders are accountable to opposition politicians who vigorously press for new programs to be nondiscretionary in order to prevent incumbents from manipulating large-scale benefits to their advantage. Challengers fear that incumbents manipulate benefits to hinder their chances of winning. Incumbents in turn fear that if large-scale policies are discretionary, allegations of clientelism by challengers will discredit them, increasing their electoral vulnerability.

Particularly when machine parties lock in outsiders and rising parties are competing for their vote, allegations of clientelism in national programs made by opposition politicians are likely to appear credible in the eyes of the public and to discredit incumbents' motivations and their social programs. When launching large expansion in the context of intense competition, incumbents – whether of machine parties or not – strive to minimize (unintended) biases in implementation that can feed accusations of clientelism. Opposition parties who seek to mobilize the outsider vote and defeat the incumbent are compelled to monitor implementation of the benefit and thereby raise the cost of discretionary allocations in large-scale programs, lowering the potential benefits of clientelist targeting.[39]

In a highly competitive environment for outsider voters, in which large-scale, visible benefits are launched, both incumbents and opposition politicians thus prefer nondiscretionary policies that can allow incumbents to effectively claim credit for expansion while simultaneously preventing them from gaining support by manipulating benefits or threatening beneficiaries with losing their benefits if they deprive them of their vote. In this environment, as noted, it is not advantageous for the opposition to block expansion. While clientelistic distributions in large-scale initiatives reaching millions of households may undermine challengers, they may also provide ammunition for opposition politicians to discredit incumbents by claiming that these programs are only implemented to get votes.

A similar dynamic emerges when social movements press for large-scale social policy expansion, and incumbents decide to expand in response to such demands. Social movement leaders demand transparent access to social benefits with clear eligibility rules out of fears that they will be excluded and/or that policies will empower clientelistic networks

---

[39] See Grzymala-Busse's seminal work on robust competition and state exploitation in postcommunist democracies. In particular, see her argument on the cost of discretion for politicians facing competition (2007: 12–13).

or patronage-based organizations to carry out the selective allocation of social programs.

Incumbents fear accusations of discretion in the administration of large-scale benefits that may spark further social conflict and project an image of incompetence or manipulation among potential beneficiaries and public opinion, diminishing the government's popularity. This would shatter incumbents' goals in creating large-scale policy provisions.[40] As in the context of electoral competition, accusations of discretion in large programs can also harm incumbents among electoral constituencies other than outsiders and decrease their popularity. For that reason, social mobilization increases the costs of and diminishes the advantages incumbents may obtain with discretionary distribution of large-scale social programs.

In short, intense electoral competition for outsiders and mobilization from below incentivize not only large-scale policy expansion, but also avoidance of discretionary policy designs in these benefits. Invariably, incumbents in these circumstances prefer to provide pensions, income transfers, and health care services through nondiscretionary, institutionalized policies. Concerns about the potential manipulation of benefits figure prominently in interviews with key informants, in the transcripts of congressional debates, in public statements made by politicians, and in institutional efforts to diminish the likelihood of biased allocation, as discussed in the next chapters.

Of course, this does not mean clientelism is no longer a feature of political dynamics in Latin America or within the cases under study (see Luna and Mardones 2014; Magaloni et al. 2006; Stokes 2005). Rather, this argument contributes to existing scholarship on clientelism by identifying when large-scale social programs that explicitly seek to avoid discretion are designed. Within this literature, Weitz-Shapiro (2014) looks at a food program in Argentina and argues that the presence of electoral competition and a larger middle class limit discretion across municipalities because mayors face electoral punishment from middle-class voters if they engage in the exchange of food provisions for poor peoples' support. Unlike the benefits studied in this book, this food program is a decentralized provision in which critical design issues and access are determined

---

[40] The exclusion of activists from program benefits is a typical tool political machines employ.

at the subnational level. Having such differences in mind, this book's argument can be considered complementary to the one Weitz-Shapiro advanced as it highlights the incentives to reduce clientelism created by electoral competition. The arguments differ on some matters, however. In Weitz-Shapiro's analysis, local governments are competing for middle-class voters – who are a relatively large electorate in the municipalities in which mayors opt for programmatic benefits – and care about their views particularly. In the cases analyzed in this book, the electoral competition that matters concerns outsiders as well, regardless of the size of the middle classes. In other words, although the reaction of middle-class voters may be a concern of incumbents facing competition for outsiders, the reaction of outsider voters – regardless of the size of the middle-class constituency – also matters to incumbents in presidential elections. This is evident in countries with both relatively larger and smaller middle classes (e.g., Argentina and Mexico, respectively). As Zarazaga's research on clientelism shows, low-income populations also condemn clientelistic distributions (2014: 29). Second, this book further finds the presence of mobilization from below demanding programmatic benefits a fundamental factor explaining the choice of non-clientelistic benefits in some cases. This is especially important because electoral competition may not be a feature of national elections, but SMCs demanding transparent benefits can nonetheless propel adoption of nondiscretionary programs.

Other studies argue that nondiscretionary social programs in developing countries are a function of the absence of a machine party in the political system and the presence of a strong bureaucratically capable state, with Chile fitting this characterization (Luna and Mardones 2014: 39). The argument advanced in this book differs from Luna and Mardones, as I find that governments under the particular circumstances of electoral competition for outsiders and mobilization from below have strong incentives to create benefits that are nondiscretionary and actually accomplish it even in the absence of strong states and programmatic parties, including situations in which a machine party is in power.

The development of bureaucratic capacity to attain expansion is not a minor question. It has oftentimes shaped the process of implementation in different ways. To avoid potential biases, incumbents sometimes delayed implementation, created agencies with bureaucratic capacity, or concentrated the administration of benefits in the most capable agency in the central government, signaling concern for potential manipulation.[41]

It bears mention that in the cases under investigation, the early distribution of benefits – especially of cash transfers – often suffered from allegations of clientelism and political abuses. Typical accounts refer to local brokers threatening beneficiaries with withdrawal of benefits if support was not given to a particular candidate or party, even if these brokers were neither authorized nor capable to determine access to or exit from benefits. These accounts also highlight the presence of specific categories of beneficiaries who illegally accessed benefits due to loopholes in the supervision of eligibility. Early problems in implementation were corrected with measures such as the introduction of magnetic cards, improved checks of eligibility conditions, and the exclusion of fraudulent claimants of benefits, as detailed in the empirical chapters. These and other blunt problems in access subsided as institutional features unintentionally favoring abuses were eliminated or corrected by national authorities to maintain credibility for the programs. In some cases, changes in program features were small, while, in others, they constituted in part the rationale for a shift in a program's structure with its replacement with a new scheme.

2.4 EXPLAINING POLICY CONTENT: RESTRICTIVE VERSUS INCLUSIVE POLICIES

The choice of policy model is the second component of this book's theoretical argument. In the face of electoral competition for outsiders and/ or mobilization from below, why did some incumbents in democracies launch large-scale massive benefits while others created programs with a more limited reach? Why did some programs but not others include social participation in implementation?

Once the decision to adopt new benefits is made, a distinct analytical stage is that of designing the content of the new policies. Within the "design phase," the actors involved in adoption as well as new actors – such as social movements who were not active in expansion but may be affiliated to the incumbent party – may also want to influence the content of the new policies (in terms of scope, benefits, and implementation characteristics).[42]

---

[41] On state capacity, see Evans (1995); Rothstein (2011).
[42] On the need to differentiate adoption and content, see Murillo (2009).

As students of institutional development point out, public policy designs are the object of political contestation (Thelen 2004: 31). Actors participating in policy design or with the capacity to influence policy making try to imprint particular features on the policies that affect them. Political actors rely on assessments of their interests (or those of the constituencies they represent) and on existing policy blueprints and institutions, which often inspire ideas about how to better design new policies.[43] Existing policies may inform the preferences of technocrats designing new benefits for outsiders, as well as those of SMCs pushing for expansion and politicians competing for outsiders' votes. When designing and negotiating new policies, politicians try to make them compatible with the preferences of the constituencies they represent and their own goals to remain in power. SMCs demanding expansion in turn generally try to link their proposed benefits to those of insiders, creating broad-based inclusive benefits.

The choice of *restrictive* or *inclusive* programs – defined in terms of the scope of coverage, the benefit levels, and whether programs involve participatory or state-centric implementation – depends on (a) the coalitions participating in the process of policy design, (b) these coalitions' preferences, and (c) their power to influence decision making.

Among the cases under investigation, SMCs and/or politicians from different parties participated in policy design with incumbents who often negotiated or strategically responded to their demands. Schematically, two primary types of policy design processes are identified: one involving the incumbent and congressional parties, and the other involving these parties as well as SMCs. As outlined later, the first type of policy design process yielded restrictive policies, while the second yielded inclusive policies. Variations within each model are further accounted for by the differential power of these actors within the policy-making process.

This understanding of the drivers of policy variation differs from the literature on the welfare state in which the power resources of labor (Esping Andersen and Korpi 1984) and cross-class coalitions (Esping Andersen 1990) shape different welfare regimes in industrialized democracies. Although the social mobilization dimension of policy change may resonate with this literature, SMCs involve a more heterogeneous group of actors, and they play a role in policy design that is not always, as in the power-resources argument, channeled through left parties, or through

---

[43] See, among others, Hacker (2002); Hall and Taylor (1996); Mahoney and Thelen (2010); and Thelen (2004).

any party. What is indeed similar to the literature on the welfare state are the policy preferences of conservative and popular-based or left parties, as described next.

These dynamics of policy design also differ from the processes that originally shaped programs for insiders in Latin America, in which political parties played a limited role (Mesa-Lago 1978: 9). According to Carmelo Mesa-Lago, and as described in Chapter 3, different occupational groups were granted social benefits according to their capacity to pressure the state, which resulted in social programs that were highly segmented and provided different occupations with different provisions. SMCs representing outsiders, by contrast, press for uniform benefits for all, and their involvement in or absence from the policy design process is a key factor explaining variation in policy content. Political parties, in turn, also play more fundamental roles in some cases.

Next I analyze the politics of design. In the final sections of this chapter I analyze the strategies incumbents develop to deal with program stakeholders and vested interests that might oppose expansion or want to influence policy content and implementation. Lastly I address the critical question of how new policies get funded.

Restrictive Policies: Negotiations Involving Incumbents and Congressional Parties

One type of negotiation over social policy design involves incumbents, their parties, and the opposition in Congress. This type of negotiation is likely to emerge when decisions to protect outsiders are triggered by high electoral competition for their votes.

As discussed earlier, when competition for outsider voters takes place, blocking expansion is a costly option for opposition parties, as the incumbent (or factions within the incumbent party) can easily blame the opposition for impeding expansion, which can be electorally costly. Therefore, the opposition has few incentives to block proposals to expand these benefits when competition is high and especially when these initiatives have been placed in the public debate. Opposition politicians may delay the approval of new benefits, but at least in the period under investigation, parties in Congress did not block any incumbents' proposals to expand social benefits for outsiders when electoral competition for these voters was high and when outsiders were unprotected within these policy areas.

Opposition parties in Congress are likely to try to affect policy design and negotiate programmatic features with the incumbent and the incumbent's party. Aside from making sure that they are nondiscretionary, opposition parties expect new benefits to reflect their own preferences regarding social policy. In contexts of electoral competition for outsider voters, it is likely that opposition parties have some meaningful share of seats in Congress to influence policy design, as political competition as here defined often takes place in contexts of relatively stable party systems, in which decisions are made with some negotiation with opposition parties. The process of policy design may therefore involve negotiations, and the final shape of the policies depends on the preferences of different partisan coalitions and their institutional power in the executive and in Congress (which is here measured by share of seats).

Social policy preferences relate to the parties' core constituencies, which are the critical sectors shaping their agenda and policy goals (Murillo 2009). According to Gibson, the importance of the core constituencies "lies not necessarily in the number of votes they represent, but in their influence on the party's agenda and capacities for political action" (1996: 7). Aside from representing their core constituencies, parties also seek to retain and to win power, and thus must make their policy proposals compatible with the twin goals of winning elections and responding to core constituencies' preferences (see Gingrich 2011).

In line with the welfare state literature, two broad types of political parties or coalitions can be distinguished when it comes to social policy preferences: conservative coalitions and left or popular-based coalitions. The distinctive feature of conservative coalitions is that economic elites and/or higher-income middle classes represent their core constituency and their preferences are articulated in the coalition's social policy priorities, whereas the core constituency for popular-based or leftist coalitions is located within the organized lower and middle classes, whose preferences regarding social policy are reflected in these coalitions' proposals. To be sure, these are schematic characterizations. Populist parties that have been critical actors historically in some of the cases under investigation (Collier and Collier 1991; Levitsky 2003; Murillo 2001) have never been ideologically "left parties," with their leadership converting from statist to more conservative ideologies in the 1980s and 1990s, implementing market-oriented reforms and forging alliances with business and conservative politicians, including technocrats from think tanks linked to business and financial-sector interests.[44] In the 2000s, the leadership of some of these parties shifted to more left-wing positions, eschewing

---

[44] Gibson (1997); Kessler (1998); Levitsky (2003); Murillo (2001, 2009).

alliances with large business and condemning the market-oriented policies of the 1980s and 1990s.[45] Due to the fact that populist parties have
manifested unstable policy preferences during the period under investigation, their characterization as conservative or popular-based depends
on the coalitions built within each administration examined and on the
party leadership's social policy agenda.[46]

In the episodes of expansion analyzed here, the social policy preferences of conservative and popular-based coalitions are comparable to
those identified in the literature on the welfare state in advanced industrialized countries (see Gingrich 2011; Huber and Stephens 2012; Pierson
1994). Conservative coalitions frequently prefer inexpensive programs
that do not entail significant direct state intervention. They also favor
market incentives and private provision of services over large-scale state
intervention. In the case of transfers, they generally advocate expansion
that reaches a relatively smaller pool of beneficiaries with less generous
provisions than those of low-income insiders. Regarding health care
services for outsiders, conservative coalitions generally prefer to provide extensive free coverage to the extremely poor, and offer voluntary,
partly subsidized services to the rest, who are required to pay for services
according to their income. Thus, health insurance systems advocated
by conservative coalitions tap payment capacity from non-indigent (or
extremely poor) outsiders. These health care schemes provide modest services, often encourage private provision of services for the lower income
– even if private providers often fail to expand in accordance with policy
makers' expectations – and are compatible with the preferences of core
conservative constituencies for limited state involvement. In fact, the evolution of health care services might eventually alter the preferences of
conservatives, leading them to include more subsidies for outsiders, and
to rely more on public infrastructure in the absence of new private providers that serve low-income populations.

When they are competing for the votes of outsiders, popular-based
coalitions in turn prefer programs that protect a broader share of outsiders than conservative coalitions, and they favor direct state intervention
over the market-based provision of services. In the case of pensions and
income-support schemes, they generally favor broad coverage, hoping

---

[45] For Latin America, see Levitsky and Roberts (2011); for Argentina, see Etchemendy and
Garay (2011).
[46] A broad literature exists on populist parties and their choices in the 1990s and 2000s,
including Burgess and Levitsky (2003); Gibson (1997); Levitsky and Roberts (2011);
Murillo (2001, 2009); Weyland, Madrid and Hunter, (2010).

to reach both low-income and especially lower-middle-class outsiders with social policies. With regards to health care, they generally prefer more even benefits rather than segmentation, which conservatives favor. Popular-based coalitions sometimes even advocate solidarity or cross-subsidization across insiders and outsiders. This mechanism allows more affluent beneficiaries (formal workers) to partially subsidize benefits for outsiders through their contributions or through special solidarity funds created for such purposes.

Despite these differences in the content of social policies, both conservative and popular-based politicians – which, as noted, include both left and left-populist – have generally preferred nonparticipatory, bureaucratic implementation of new policies. This preference is motivated by concerns about social demands that might emerge within participatory arrangements, potential opportunities for discretion stemming from social participation, as well as concerns over partisan opponents taking over local participatory arrangements. When expansion emerges as a top-down project, incumbents simply seek to create social policies that contribute to their electoral survival and, unless pressured by social movements, prefer not to include organized participation in policy implementation. A more direct implementation of benefits is easier; it reduces the emergence of demands and the need to respond to concerns from beneficiaries and their organizations on the ground.

The balance of power of incumbent and opposition parties shapes policy content. Theoretically, a conservative-dominated policy process, or one in which both conservative and popular-based coalitions share power, should yield restrictive models, with some variation within the restrictive model in the scope of coverage and benefit levels depending on the power of each coalition. When a popular-based coalition dominates policy design, then policies should be broad-reaching but not participatory.

Empirically, it is generally the case that conservative (right, center-right, and populist-conservative) parties hold institutional power in Congress in Latin America. The process of designing large-scale benefits for outsiders under these circumstances then yields a *restrictive model*, in which the preferences of conservatives for more modest (non-universal) benefits are reflected at least to some extent due to the plurality of interests involved or simply their relative presence in Congress. Some episodes of expansion witnessed conservative coalitions large enough to include little input from popular-based coalitions in social policy design. This occurred, for example, when a populist party, which typically has both conservative and left-wing politicians within its ranks, had a large conservative faction. The case of Mexico in Chapter 6 is illustrative in this regard; the Institutional Revolutionary Party (PRI) had a large bloc in Congress during the Fox administration (2000–6) of the conservative PAN, and it shared fundamental aspects of the PAN's social policy agenda. The PRI largely supported the content of Fox's social policy proposals without engaging in too much negotiation over the levels and scope of coverage of new benefits. The PRD, a left-wing offshoot of the PRI, had a small share of seats in Congress and could not influence policy design.

At the same time, and across cases, not one episode of policy design involved popular-based coalitions with sufficient power to make decisions about policy content without negotiating with conservatives or, in anticipation of conservative preferences, without putting together policy design proposals that conservatives would approve with little change. Cases in which popular-based coalitions dominated the executive and Congress were characterized either by (a) an absence of competition for outsider votes – therefore meaning that no process of social policy expansion (as defined here) was under way (Venezuela) or (b) by social movements representing outsiders participating in policy design – either from outside or within the governing coalition – and thus following another type of negotiation, which is discussed ahead and in which movements influence policy design through institutional channels or as members of governing coalitions.

As summarized in Figure 2.1, the important point to highlight is that the *restrictive model* emerges out of negotiations in which conservatives have sufficient institutional power to at least influence the content of resulting policy designs. Those negotiations have taken shape in the context of electoral competition for outsiders and in the absence of SMCs involved in the policy design process.

A number of issues characterized negotiations over social policy design among incumbents and congressional parties in which conservatives have institutional power. As noted, conservatives strive for smaller policies that allow them to court outsiders in a manner compatible with the preference of their core constituency, thus limiting the scope and benefit level of the resulting policies. In negotiations over policy design, conservative politicians emphasize the creation of tight eligibility criteria, and often establish annual quotas for the number of benefits granted, notwithstanding the number of eligible individuals or households. Both features have been the target of criticism by popular-based politicians in Chile and Mexico, the two cases analyzed here in which restrictive models were created.

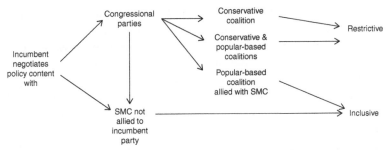

FIGURE 2.1 Negotiations over policy content: who is involved and resulting models.

Despite those criticisms, quotas and waiting lists remained a feature of several policy interventions in the restrictive model throughout the period. In Chile, when center-left politicians had more power in Congress under the Michelle Bachelet administration (2006–10), they were able to exert leverage to eliminate quotas in some programs for outsiders.

When both coalitions have comparable representation in Congress, and when elections are not imminent, negotiations can take a long time. Policy makers may submit policy proposals that strategically anticipate the feasibility of opposition support, or may split legislative proposals into different draft bills to achieve at least piecemeal change (as in the case of health care reform in Chile) by discussing the more controversial aspects of reforms without jeopardizing less polemic aspects of the entire project when legislators hold divergent views (see Chapter 7). They may also initiate a pilot project first to demonstrate the viability of a policy, obtain ammunition to defend it – including defending it against claims that it is discretionary – and then launch expansion.

In sum, facing electoral competition for outsiders, incumbents negotiated the policy content and funding of programs with opposition parties. If social movements were not involved in policy design, then the presence of conservatives in Congress and/or the executive yielded policies that are restrictive across cases, with some variation in the scope of new benefits depending on the balance of partisan power.

Inclusive Policies: Negotiations Involving Social Movement Coalitions

Incumbents who face broad demands for expansion by SMCs, either from outside or within the governing coalition, are compelled to engage in formal and informal negotiations with movement leaders around policy change and/or respond strategically to movements' demands. Incumbents who seek to mitigate protest, respond to institutional pressure, or cater to the demands of an allied movement are likely to respond with policy designs that coincide or are compatible with movements' preferences. In the cases under investigation, SMCs often participated actively in policy making and sometimes even negotiated policy choices with presidents and ministers.

The channels through which movements participate in policy design in each episode of expansion are open due to movement pressure surrounding that particular episode or to previous episodes of mobilization that resulted in broader access to the state. Participation in policy design therefore may occur through three different paths:

- Governments open formal or informal channels of negotiation to protestors in order to dampen contention. These include meetings with the president and ministers, ad hoc councils, and channels of permanent communication with the executive and sometimes also with Congress.
- Channels for participation are already in place and movements pursue social policy demands and participate in policy design through such channels (lobbying, meetings with policy makers, and seats in councils), which allow them to influence the shape of policy decisions.
- Movements allied to the government participate in policy design via their positions within the state, as movement leaders sometimes hold important roles in allied administrations or as members of the governing party.

The process of policy negotiation raises the visibility and status of social movements within the political system. As mentioned previously, movements sometimes negotiated policies with presidents and ministers that Congress later passed. At other times, presidents themselves modified legislation, issued decrees, or passed ministerial resolutions that could speed up the response to social mobilization and demonstrate their commitment to movement demands. This was especially the case in Argentina, where incumbents responded to movements and typically avoided negotiations with Congress around these reforms, or waited to carry them out after the policy was already in place in order to facilitate adoption of their proposals. Incumbent and opposition parties also negotiated with social movements over the shape of the resulting programs, as was the case in Brazil during the Constituent Assembly, which is analyzed in Chapter 4.

In the cases of Brazil and Argentina, where they participated in policy design, powerful SMCs demanded broad-reaching benefits, in addition to participation in policy implementation. Social movements advocated benefits similar to those low-income insiders enjoyed, pressed for inclusions within existing programs for insiders, called for the creation of new programs from scratch, or requested that smaller benefits for outsiders be transformed into broad-reaching programs. In Brazil, for example, the health care reform movement advocated the creation of an entirely new universal system that would replace the contributory-based health care system and cater to both insiders and outsiders.

Social movements also demand participation in relatively permanent structures of oversight and policy deliberation. Participation offers different advantages. First, social movements view participation as a mechanism to help prevent the manipulation of benefits. In that sense, the idea of participation springs from movements' mistrust of the state and the history of clientelism embedded in state structures in Latin America. Second, movements see participation in implementation as a mechanism to perpetuate their influence in policy making.[47] Participation makes leaders of SMCs more permanent "advisors" to the state and provides them with information about and experience in policy implementation. Finally, movements sometimes want to administer benefits themselves by distributing resources and identifying beneficiaries. This level of participation – or the "delegation" of critical state functions to social movement organizations – was not a constant demand of social organizations in the episodes of expansion analyzed, but it did arise within social movements that had been previously involved in the administration of small programs.[48]

In a context of large-scale social mobilization, incumbents often respond with policies in line with those advocated by social movements, in terms of the scope of coverage, benefit levels, and participatory structures. Other interventions, such as small benefits or highly technocratic programs that do not include social movement input, may not satisfy social movements engaged in large-scale activism. If they are dissatisfied with government responses, social movements may then press for

---

[47] There is an abundant literature on participatory institutions in Latin America. See essays in Coelho and Nobre (2004) and Fung (2006). On the participation of organizations in policy administration, see Houtzager (1998); Maybury-Lewis (1994); Novaes (1991). On the welfare state, see Anderson (2001); Mares (2003); and Rothstein (1992).

[48] On the concept of "delegation," see Giugni and Passy (1998: 84–5).

further changes, reject the policy, or refuse to support it. If incumbents seek to respond to social movements with expansion, then adopting policy designs that are different from those social movements advocate is not the best strategy for demobilizing leaders and activists or preventing an allied movement from breaking its alliance with the incumbent.

Participatory implementation has some advantages for incumbents facing social mobilization. First, if incumbents are facing protests, it serves the purpose of channeling protest activism into policy implementation and away from the streets – something of paramount importance for incumbents. Furthermore, it can help check or control the implementation of the policy and keep movements engaged in policy-making collaboration with the state. Of the demands SMCs pose, policy makers did not agree to involve them in the distribution of benefits. As discussed previously, in the context of large-scale mobilization, incumbents worry that costly, visible, large-scale benefits might be manipulated and thus they strive to create mechanisms of transparency. Incumbents fear that if programs become clientelistic, they may become unpopular and even generate more social movement pressure, as discussed in Chapters 4 and 5. For these reasons, in the cases analyzed here, incumbents avoided delegation of program administration to social organizations of any kind (allied or not), including them only in structures of oversight, control, consultation, or in outreach information campaigns. The administration of program benefits could give movements the power to allocate resources themselves, a prospect incumbents strongly rejected in these large-scale benefits.

There is some variation across inclusive policies depending on whether social movements promoting expansion are allied to the incumbent coalition. Incumbents are often more pressed to open up channels of participation in implementation when movements demand inclusion through contention or lack strong linkages with the incumbent party than when some or all of the components of SMCs are allied with the governing coalition. In the latter cases, incumbents and/ or allied movements often find participatory mechanisms less relevant or their creation much less pressing, as communication between the state and the movements is already fluid. In these cases, the resulting implementation is either less participatory or the adoption of participatory mechanisms is less decisive, relative to cases in which movements engage in policy design from outside the party system. Informal channels of participation in oversight and consultation are often also created in these cases, but policies are generally not as participatory as innovations launched when movements push their demands in the streets or combine protest and pressure through institutional channels.

As we see in Chapters 4 and 5, social movements in Brazil and Argentina participated through different ways in the design of social policies introduced in each policy area. During episodes of expansion in Argentina, social movements mainly pressured governments into negotiation through protest, although social movements and allied unions also proposed specific policies adopted by incumbents through institutional channels of negotiation that opened up after protest peaked in 2001 and 2002, and through an allied party when some movements joined the incumbent coalition in 2004. The resulting model in Argentina was inclusive, with some benefits even being incorporated into the structure of formal-sector programs, and with varying degrees of participation across policies depending on whether at least part of the SMCs were allied with the incumbent government.

In Brazil, a number of SMCs pressing for social policy through institutional channels primarily led to incumbents expanding health care and pension programs in the new democracy. Protest did take place, but social movements enjoyed access to policy-making venues, especially when they managed to attain access to the Constituent Assembly, where policy adoption was critical. The resulting policies were inclusive and featured participatory structures of policy implementation. Incumbents then launched income transfers in the context of the high electoral competition for outsider voters that emerged in the new century. When the left-wing Workers' Party came to power, broader social transfers were designed with the influence of social movements linked to the party. These movements were not strong enough to achieve social policy expansion on their own, yet once the allied party was in office, they could influence critical features of the model of income transfer programs from within the coalition.

2.5 OVERCOMING CHALLENGES TO SOCIAL POLICY EXPANSION: OPPONENTS AND FUNDING FOR NEW BENEFITS

Two critical issues further affect the process of social policy expansion: (a) the surge of opposition from program stakeholders and subnational actors who might lose power as a result of the expansion of social benefits for outsiders, and (b) the need to raise revenue to launch new benefits. These issues deserve attention because they have been said to be important obstacles to social policy reforms (see Haggard and Kaufman 2008; Nelson 1992). However, in the cases under investigation, incumbents employed a set of observable strategies that allowed them to deal effectively with each obstacle to expansion, as discussed later.

Opponents to Expansion

As students of social policy have argued, expansion is an exercise in credit-claiming that can generate easy majorities in favor of new social policy provisions (Pierson 1994). Opposition to expansion can nonetheless emerge within sectors that feel threatened by the political effects of new policies, or that refuse to allocate substantial resources to new programs. Opposition to expansion was particularly consequential during the decades in which outsiders were not politically relevant sectors of society due to authoritarianism, the absence of competition for their votes, or lack of large-scale mobilization. As analyzed in Chapter 3, proposals for social policy expansion advanced by progressive politicians concerned about the welfare of the poor were unlikely to succeed in that context. In the context of high competition or large-scale mobilization, by contrast, such opposition faced steeper obstacles in challenging expansion and articulating claims against new provisions. Nevertheless, incumbents still had to find ways to bring opponents on board or neutralize their pressure in order to ease the process of policy adoption. Two primary types of opponents emerged in the context of expansion: program stakeholders and subnational authorities.

Program Stakeholders

Program stakeholders include a broad set of actors, such as doctors, providers, or social security agencies that may see their powers curtailed by the reforms involved in expanding benefits to outsiders. The specific behavior of these stakeholders is analyzed in the empirical chapters. None of these actors successfully blocked expansion in the policy areas under study in the face of electoral competition for outsiders and mobilization from below. Program stakeholders were not powerful enough to counterbalance the incentives for expansion that incumbents faced, or to form critical alliances against expansion. Because expansion was usually a popular measure and opposition to expansion was costly, politicians hardly sought to defend the status quo. Moreover, expansion may generate mixed blessings for program stakeholders. For example, in the case of health care, it may increase service provision but also generate higher levels of control and monitoring of policy delivery, and may reduce the relative power of agencies and providers that cater to insiders. In these cases, program stakeholders were unable to marshal opposition to expansion.

In some cases, stakeholders aggrieved by the process of expansion did try to steer the new programs to their advantage by seeking to affect policy design and/or implementation of the programs. In Brazil, for-profit hospitals organized in the Brazilian Federation of Hospitals (FBH) were major opponents to the expansion of health care, especially because it entailed an overhaul of the existing system for insiders. The FBH fought to limit the expansion of the state's regulatory role in the private system (in particular, the modification of contracts governing health provisions), as well as the decentralized structure of public-private contracting that the new system introduced. While the FBH could not block the adoption of the new system, as discussed in Chapter 4, it opposed it consistently by attempting to introduce different institutional mechanisms to alter the pattern of universality of health care services in pursuit of higher profits or rents that hospitals enjoyed in the old system.

While opposition from existing stakeholders can be dramatic, and may even threaten – and sometimes manage – to delay policy adoption, the longitudinal analysis of the four country cases has not found a single episode in which expansion in the context of dramatic mobilization or high electoral competition for outsiders failed to be adopted or implemented. Although changes to policies and delays in policy adoption sometimes did occur as a result of pressures from program stakeholders, this did not alter the policies significantly.

Subnational Authorities
Within the federal systems of Argentina, Brazil, and Mexico, state governors often initially contested the expansion of large-scale national social policy programs or sought to influence their design in order to increase their involvement and control over new resources, ideally administering benefits themselves. In the absence of high electoral competition or large-scale mobilized pressures to expand social policy for outsiders, governors' refusal to support a new policy could be decisive in reshaping or blocking implementation, as was the case of the Solidary Bonus (BS) in Argentina in 1989 (see Chapter 3). Yet governors were unable to block expansion in the presence of strong competition for outsiders or mobilization from below.

Governors initially opposed new policies for outsiders because of their limited role in these projects. Governors do not play a central role in the implementation of pensions and transfers, though they do play some role in health care programs (which varies across countries). Given the relevance of these policies, and their inability to claim credit from their implementation, subnational authorities often feared that those benefits would undermine their political standing and their hold on power if the national government backed alternative candidates in their districts, or even just overshadowed them.

Subnational incumbents often demanded inclusion in the administration of new benefits, which nonetheless remained largely under the purview of the national government. In the face of limited participation in policy implementation, governors sometimes initially refused to cooperate with the national government. For example, governors sometimes resorted to "passive resistance" by delaying implementation in their states (e.g., by not signing agreements with the national government to initiate implementation), or to more "aggressive resistance" (e.g., by launching programs similar to those initiated by the national government). This was especially the case in wealthier subnational units and states in which leaders sought to compete for national office. If provinces were already running a provincial-level social program for outsiders, governors often refused to share existing records of program beneficiaries, a tactic found in all three federal systems analyzed here (Argentina, Brazil, and Mexico).

Incumbents often negotiated with subnational authorities in order to gain their support, employing two strategies. First, national governments developed ways to *share credit* with subnational authorities, even if they did not share policy administration. This idea was explicitly articulated by President Luiz Inácio "Lula" da Silva (2003–10) as he negotiated Bolsa Família with governors in Brazil in 2003. Virtually everywhere, national-level technocrats and presidents organized public events with governors and mayors to promote the policies and share the credit for expansion on the ground.[49] Subnational administrations also sought to produce program materials and print magnetic cards for program beneficiaries that carried the provincial government's insignia, as a way to figure into the process of expansion.

National incumbents also often *compensated* subnational authorities with other benefits or resources that they could administer at their discretion. Nondiscretionary transfers and services continued to exist alongside more discretionary policies implemented by subnational authorities. For example, public works were often used to placate governors' demands

---

[49] See Chapters 4–6.

in Argentina in the 2000s. In Mexico, decentralization of social invest-ments in the late 1990s granted massive discretion without accountabil-ity mechanisms to subnational authorities in the allocation of resources for education and social infrastructure, which subsequent governments found hard to modify.

These dynamics may be part of the initial process of policy expansion and design, or may take place during the process of policy implementa-tion. In fact, once the program is rolling, subnational authorities may be able to influence implementation in different ways. Understanding the evolution of implementation of these policies over time is beyond the scope of this project.

Funding for New Benefits

Funding is a major issue for governments pursuing expansion, either as a project from above or in response to pressure from below. Presidents and congresses in countries burdened by large debts and competing funding priorities have a long list of issues on which they should spend resources; obtaining funding for expansion is thus not an easy task in any economic environment.

Without engaging in the complex question of taxation, which has its own political dynamics and actors and is beyond the scope of this book to explain, five specific mechanisms for allocating resources to previously neglected populations can be identified in the episodes of expansion:[50] (a) the creation of temporary taxes, (b) the reallocation of funding from existing benefits, (c) the inclusion of new benefits into programs for insid-ers, (d) the phased implementation of expansion over a number of years to raise sufficient funding for full-scale program implementation, and (e) the creation of taxes earmarked to new benefits.

Creation of Temporary Taxes

Temporary taxes may be an easier option than permanent taxes for incumbents hoping to fund a new policy and to speed up policy adop-tion. For opponents of new taxes, these are more palatable initiatives, as they can be removed if support for them wanes. Thus, their adop-tion may be politically more feasible. Temporary taxes proved effective strategies to initiate programs in the context of scarce resources. Once

---

[50] On the politics of taxation in Latin America, see Fairfield (2015); Lieberman (2003); Weyland (1996a).

a large-scale policy is implemented, the ability of opponents to abolish it decreases and thus elimination of temporary taxes leads to the search for alternative funding mechanisms. Brazil provides a critical example of how temporary taxes helped incumbents move forward with policy implementation. With no resources to fund the implementation of health care expansion, the Brazilian minister of health proposed a temporary tax on financial transactions in 1993. Debate over the temporary tax was initiated in Congress under the Franco administration (1992–5), and a first initiative was approved in 1993; a more lasting version, Temporary Contribution on Financial Transactions (CPMF), was approved in 1996. Over the years, this tax grew to include new revenue and outlays until it was eliminated in 2007 and its funding for social programs was replaced by direct state revenue.

Reallocation of Funding from Existing Programs

Resources from smaller social programs may be reallocated into a larger program to facilitate its implementation. The initial funding for Remediar, the free prescription drugs program in Argentina, came from the reallocation of funding for primary care, which had been underspent by the prior government. Reallocation often turned "vice into virtue" (Levy 1999) or redeployed unfair or inefficient resources toward new schemes; in several cases, it contributed to the initial funding for these programs.

Inclusion of New Benefits in Existing Programs

To be able to fund the newly created programs, governments sometimes used the existing social security funds of formal-sector workers, which are funded with payroll contributions and other earmarked taxes. By cross-subsidizing benefits for outsiders with payroll contributions from insiders, governments have been able to extend benefits without creating new taxes and generating uproar from taxpayers. In Brazil, pensions for rural workers were initially funded with resources from the existing pension system. The remarkable absence of labor union opposition to the use of insiders' funds for outsiders' benefits challenges widely held assumptions that insiders are inherently defensive or prioritize their own interests at the expense of outsiders. It further challenges the idea that new benefits are specifically funded with general revenue (Carnes and Mares 2014). Incumbents facing social mobilization from below are more likely to adopt this funding strategy initially, as at least part of the union movement is supportive of the demands of outsiders.

Gradual Implementation

Another way of dealing with an initial shortage of funding has been to embark on a phased expansion by which benefits are rolled out gradually over a scheduled period of time, allowing governments to collect necessary resources along the way. Phased expansion allowed presidents to announce massive program adoption early on and gradually pay for these innovations over the course of their tenures. Several initiatives in Mexico and in Chile were launched in phases, requiring increased funding over the years as the programs became more entrenched and well received. To avoid discretion, phased expansion is generally structured along specific measurable criteria, such as income, demographic factors, and/or geographic targeting, with each phase incorporating a new age group, municipalities with larger populations, or higher income or human development indicators.

New Taxes

Of course, a final way of funding benefits is to tie them to tax reform. As shown by Fairfield (2015), the VAT increase in Chile under the Ricardo Lagos administration (2000–6) was linked to social benefits negotiated at the time by the incumbent and opposition parties in Congress (i.e., health and social programs). But the creation of permanent taxes for new benefits has not been a much-preferred strategy probably due to the strong resistance new taxes might generate and the risk of compromising expansion. In most cases in which new taxes were raised for social benefits, they were created at a later stage or temporary taxes were launched after other sources of funding proved inadequate.

In sum, incumbents that embarked on the process of expansion faced challenges posed by program stakeholders and subnational actors concerned with the potentially pernicious effects on their interests stemming from the establishment of these new policies. Program stakeholders, especially those involved in service provision, feared increased demands for services and dwindling profits or benefits for themselves. The expansion of health care services, for example, often faced this type of resistance. Although claims of program stakeholders could not counterbalance the incentives politicians faced to provide benefits to outsiders, they could occasionally affect aspects of policy design with the support of receptive politicians. Subnational authorities sometimes felt aggrieved by their limited involvement in the new programs. In these cases, governments compensated them with the continuity or expansion of other, more discretionary resources, and often engaged in strategies to share credit on the ground, as described in the chapters that follow.

Funding also required political negotiations and creative solutions. The mechanisms described in subsequent chapters allowed incumbents to initiate implementation, though they often initially left programs with unstable or short-term funding sources, requiring further negotiation to ensure stable sources of revenue. Incumbents, activists, and beneficiaries had one advantage in this quest, however. Once programs were in place, they were hard to scale back, and new, more permanent, funding sources were generally provided. Brazil, the early reformer, clearly demonstrates this dynamic; other cases have also experienced changes in and negotiations over sources of funding for these benefits. As students of the welfare state have convincingly shown, once policies are implemented, they take on a life of their own, acquiring their own supporters among program beneficiaries (Pierson 1994; Skocpol 1992). This is especially the case when policies reach millions of people and achieve popular support, as the social policy innovations described in this book have done to date.

3

The Social Policy Divide in Latin America

3.1 INTRODUCTION

In Latin America, the divide separating a well-protected segment of the population and a vast share of unprotected or underserved outsiders has its origins in the first half of the twentieth century, when social insurance benefits were established for workers with formal-sector jobs such as civil servants, railroad workers, and blue-collar industrial workers. Initially a minority of the working class, these workers came to enjoy pensions, health insurance, and family allowances comparable to those provided in Western Europe. By contrast, workers who were hired off the books, employed in informal-sector firms, self-employed, street vendors, peasants, or unemployed remained – along with their dependents – at the margins of such protections for most of the twentieth century.[1]

In explaining this social policy divide, experts and conventional wisdom have often emphasized Latin America's limited economic development – especially industrial development – as constraining the scope of the formal-sector workforce, and thus, the reach of social programs. Given that social benefits were extended through social insurance systems paid with payroll contributions, the presence of a limited formal workforce that could pay for those benefits, and that could press the state to launch social programs, impeded universal coverage.[2]

---

[1] On the origins of social protections for insiders, see Borzutzky (2002); Feldman, Golbert, and Isuani (1988); Malloy (1979); Mesa-Lago (1978).

[2] See discussion of social security adoption in Collier and Messick (1975); ILO (1960); Malloy (1979); Mesa-Lago (1978).

79

While socioeconomic conditions likely affected the reach of social security, these conditions alone do not explain why this social policy divide persisted and even deepened as benefits for insiders consolidated over time. Why did policy makers not seek to extend coverage to outsiders, or look for alternative ways to provide or finance universally needed protections such as health care services? Although governments primarily relied on payroll contributions to fund social insurance programs, over time they also resorted to state revenue to fund benefits for insiders.[3] Despite funding constraints, they also used general revenues to pay for the few costly social policy innovations reaching outsiders initiated in Argentina in the 1940s and 1950s and in Chile in the 1960s and 1970s, as well as some discretionary benefits such as pensions for rural workers in Brazil in the 1970s. These cases indicate that when governments prioritized broad-based expansion, funding restrictions were not an insurmountable hurdle.

The lack of social policy models to protect outsiders is not a good reason explaining this divide, either. The 1942 Beveridge Report, which inspired universal programs in advanced industrial democracies, was disseminated in the region, and international agencies such as the International Labor Office (ILO) also offered recommendations to expand social programs to the unprotected (see ILO 1960; Malloy 1979; Ross 2007). Since the early twentieth century, moreover, health care conferences promoted sanitation measures, maternal health care clinics, and preventive care. Politicians and policy makers who participated in knowledge-based epistemic communities were exposed to these ideas and several unsuccessfully promoted or attempted to implement similar initiatives (see Malloy 1979).

In this chapter, I argue that political dynamics played a fundamental role in shaping whether governments expanded broad nondiscretionary social protections for outsiders. Relying on the argument presented in Chapter 2, I will show that if the political regime was a democracy with electoral competition for outsiders and/or social mobilization for benefits, then incumbents were likely to expand social policy for outsiders. These political conditions were not present, however, in most Latin American countries until the third wave of democracy. As we see in the following section, for a significant part of the twentieth century, the cases under investigation – and most Latin America countries – saw long

---

[3] States subsidized payroll contributions, construction of private hospitals serving insiders, and pensions when systems matured.

TABLE 3.1 *Regime type, political conditions, and social policy for outsiders*

		Regime Type	
		Democratic	Authoritarian[a]
Electoral Competition for Outsiders/Social Mobilization?	Yes[a]	*Large, nondiscretionary*	*Discretionary, often relatively large*
	No	*Small, often discretionary*	*No significant initiatives*

[a] In authoritarian regimes, social mobilization and electoral competition for outsiders are generally not high (unless there is a transition to democratic elections) due to constraints on organization and elections.

periods of authoritarianism, including military dictatorships and competitive authoritarian regimes.

As summarized in Table 3.1, in authoritarian regimes incumbents lack the main incentives to initiate social policy expansion for outsiders. In these settings, outsiders cannot vote incumbents out of office – because in these regimes elections do not determine access to power – and they are also unlikely to mobilize and press for benefits, due to the absence of democratic freedoms (Table 3.1, bottom right). However, if social mobilization takes place or if elections are held and some electoral competition occurs within an authoritarian regime, incumbents are likely to combine repression and intimidation of opposition or social movements with the extension of some social provisions that do not qualify as expansions as here analyzed. As shown in the next section, authoritarian incumbents in these particular settings likely launched social policy initiatives that were sometimes quite large but also discretionary and/ or temporary, and they would use social provisions as a form of patronage to undermine the opposition or to co-opt and demobilize social movements (Table 3.1, top right). Finally, when democracies lack social mobilization or electoral competition for outsiders, incumbents are not pressed to change the status quo and initiate large-scale protections for outsiders, and thus expansion is less likely to occur. Incumbents may create small – and sometimes discretionary – benefits to show some concern for the poor but are unlikely to embark on large-scale expansion (Table 3.1, bottom left).

In the next sections, I analyze the historical evolution of the social policy divide in each of the cases under study to understand why social policy expansion for outsiders occurred in only a few cases and why governments sometimes chose to adopt other kinds of social policies (e.g., benefits that were large but discretionary, or small-scale benefits), before initiating the large-scale expansions that are the focus of this book. The analysis is structured along the main historical stages that character-ize the development of social security for insiders: (a) origins, involving the creation of the main social programs for insiders; (b) consolidation, meaning the deepening of these programs; and (c) reform, consisting of changes involving a substantial transformation of the role of the state in administering social security programs and in setting the conditions that determine access to benefits. As discussed later, throughout the first two stages, proposals to protect outsiders emerged and different responses were launched, which – with the exception of health policy expansion in Argentina in the 1940s and Chile in the 1960s and 1970s – did not result in the extension of large-scale nondiscretionary benefits. During the third stage, by contrast, some governments began the process of expansion of large-scale nondiscretionary benefits, which will be discussed in subse-quent chapters.

3.2 THE SOCIAL POLICY DIVIDE: ARGENTINA, BRAZIL, CHILE, AND MEXICO, 1920S–1990S

The Origins of Social Programs for Insiders

Social security benefits were extended to several categories of formal-sector workers between the 1910s and 1940s. This expansion usually coincided with the process that Collier and Collier (1991) understand as the incorporation of the labor movement – the process by which the state legitimates and shapes an institutionalized labor movement through legislation, regulating aspects such as collective organization and bar-gaining, as well as the right to strike and engage in political activity.[4] This process occurred at a time of rising labor conflict and, as Mesa-Lago noted, the scope of welfare programs established for formal workers largely depended on the power of labor organizations to press the state and obtain concessions (1978: 8–9), as well as on the goals of incum-bents who sought to mobilize and/or control labor unions as part of their political projects.[5]

Several proposals to create benefits for outsiders did not succeed dur-ing this period. Contributory benefits for the self-employed and rural

---

[4] For this process see Collier and Collier (1991), chapter 2, chapter 5, and glossary.
[5] On the goals of incumbents during incorporation, see Collier and Collier (1991).

workers – some of which were voluntary – were enacted in a few cases. However, as a 1960 report on social security in agriculture in Latin America highlighted, "a great discrepancy" existed between social security's "theoretical" coverage and its "actual" reach (ILO 1960: 136), which was almost nonexistent.

The exception among the countries under investigation was the establishment of comprehensive health care services in Argentina in the late 1940s. After winning the 1946 elections in the context of universal male franchise and electoral competition for popular-sector votes, Juan Perón (1946–55) launched this innovation as part of his effort to consolidate popular support. The other cases in this study lacked the political conditions for expansion. In Brazil and Chile, the electorate was small due to limitations on suffrage, and outsiders did not organize to demand social policy benefits. Unionization was strongly resisted in rural areas, where a large share of the outsider population resided. In Mexico, the absence of electoral competition within a political regime that became increasingly authoritarian coupled with the lack of mobilization for social policy by outsiders created no strong incentives for expansion.

Argentina

Social security benefits were expanded gradually in Argentina in response to demands for wages and better working conditions (Feldman et al. 1988: 28–9). Despite the fact that the country's labor movement was probably the most powerful in the region (see Collier and Collier 1991; Torre 1990), by 1940, only 7 percent of the economically active population accessed social security benefits (Feldman et al. 1988: 31). Health care services were provided by a limited number of public hospitals and clinics, and some labor unions and immigrant communities had their own mutual-aid associations and hospitals in large urban areas.[6] Unlike Brazil and Mexico, where the rural population is vast, in 1947, 62.5 percent of the Argentine population was urban (census data in Veronelli 1975: 132)

The country's politics were highly unstable. The Radical Party (UCR), which advocated clean and fair elections at a time of conservative dominance by the agro-export economic elite, won the first, and subsequent, democratic elections beginning in 1916 until a military coup ended democracy in 1930. Conservative politicians then perpetuated themselves in power through fraud and the proscription of opponents until another military coup in 1943 (see Rock 1993).

---

[6] See Belmartino (2005) and Thompson (1985) on nonprofit hospitals; see Garay (2000).

Extension of social security benefits occurred in these decades by occupational groups as a result of labor union pressure. Proposals by socialist and UCR legislators to create broad-reaching social insurance in the 1910s and 1920s were defeated by opposition from employers and conservative politicians.[7] Between the 1930s and early 1940s, health professionals in state agencies and socialist politicians – several of whom were doctors – attained some modest accomplishments, such as the adoption of a milk distribution program, inauguration of family allowances for poor families in a few districts, and establishment of twenty-four maternal health care clinics.[8] Though they reached small segments of the population only, these initiatives reveal politicians' concerns with the social needs of the excluded and knowledge of effective policy tools to address them.

Broader social policy changes occurred in the 1940s. Concerned about the deteriorating legitimacy of governments sustained on fraud, and fearing an escalation of labor unrest due to unmet social demands, the military launched a coup in 1943. Secretary of labor, Juan Perón, one of the promoters of the coup, extended strong linkages with labor unions to contain conflict and to win their support. Perón supported wage demands as well as extension and enforcement of labor and social security legislation reaching various occupational groups (Belmartino and Bloch 1989; Thompson 1985).

Perón's policies met with growing opposition within the government and from employers and resulted in his removal and imprisonment (see Torre 1990, 1995). Facing popular mobilization after Perón's removal, the military reinstated him and called for elections. Supported by a coalition formed by the new Labor Party – which was molded on and had adopted a similar policy agenda as the British Labour Party – as well as UCR and conservative dissidents, Perón won the presidency in 1946 with 52 percent of the vote, against 43 percent for a his opponent, a coalition including UCR, socialist, communist and conservative politicians concerned about the rising leader who was competing intensely for workers' and low-income voters' support (see McGuire 1995: 209–10).

Both the UCR and the Socialist Party had courted workers' and lower-class votes before the ascendancy of Perón (Torre 1995: 39). Perón disputed that support to win office and sought to consolidate it once in power. A critical way to do so was through inauguration of social programs. The

---

[7] On the history of social security see Isuani (1985); Lvovich (2006); Mesa Lago (1978).

[8] Ross (2007: 32); see also McGuire (2010: 121–2); Mercer (1990: 117); Nari (2004: 225–6).

most important innovation – unique in the region at the time – was the expansion of broad-reaching health care services based on a plan that was "remarkably similar to the organization of the British National Health Service" (Ross 2007: 148). In fact, "socialization of medical services" had been included originally in the platform of the union-based Laborist Party. Beginning in 1946, hospital infrastructure grew nationwide, and hospital beds doubled by 1955 (see Belmartino and Bloch 1989: 500). Through large-scale immunization campaigns, measures to prevent infectious diseases, and nutrition programs, infant mortality rates declined sharply (see Neri 1982; Ross 2007: 113). Despite these achievements, the Ministry of Health lacked sufficient funding and political support to accomplish its titanic goals of building adequate infrastructure and coordinating health care services throughout the country (Ross 2007). A testament to this was the Ministry's inability to accomplish the plan to build 800 primary care health centers to cover the entire population by the late 1950s (Veronelli 1975: 69–71).

Scholars have argued that Perón's implementation of coordinated universal health care services was undermined by the expansion of the union-run health funds he also sponsored, as well as by the Eva Perón Foundation (FEP), which controlled some public hospitals.[9] However, as Thompson described, union-run health funds were "complementary" at the time; health insurance of formal workers was voluntary, and public hospitals served insiders and outsiders (1985: 36). Ross further suggests that the FEP collaborated with the Ministry of Health (2007: 157), and its hospitals were eventually transferred to that agency (Veronelli 1975: 67). It is likely that because Perón gained massive electoral support from outsiders, further efforts to secure funding, expand infrastructure, and achieve institutional coordination of health services in his second term were deemed too costly and politically less urgent, and were therefore neglected. Further health care expansion was not on the agenda in subsequent years. Perón's overthrow by a military coup in 1955 – in a context of economic troubles, accusations of intimidation and denial of media access to opponents in the 1951 elections, as well as conflict with the Catholic church – inaugurated almost twenty years of nondemocratic rule (McGuire 1995: 212–13).

---

[9] The FEP was created out of the transformation of a long-standing public beneficence organization, the Beneficence Society, which was funded by the state, run by presidents' wives, and previously administered most social assistance programs. On the FEP, see Ferioli (1990).

In sum, social security benefits initially grew gradually in response to pressure by labor unions and were then expanded into a broader universe of services and benefits that reached the formal workforce. Seeking to consolidate the support of low-income voters who had been previously mobilized by other parties, Perón expanded comprehensive health care services to reach those sectors. Although contributory social security legislation was extended to self-employed and rural workers, noncompliance and evasion were high and these initiatives were not ultimately implemented in full due likely to the limited power of rural unions, and the informal sector's lack of organization. In 1954, an estimated 40 percent to 50 percent of the economically active population (EAP) were still outsiders, despite the existence of broad-reaching social security legislation (Feldman et al. 1988: 36).

Brazil

As in the other cases analyzed here, the first social benefits in Brazil were granted to workers in critical economic activities (i.e., railroads and docks). These concessions were designed "to dampen social protest and weaken radical labor organizers" (Malloy 1979: 45). The expansion of similar benefits to other categories of workers, and the later creation of a broader system of social security, took place with the incorporation of the labor movement under Getúlio Vargas in the 1930s and 1940s.

After assuming office through armed insurrection Vargas (1930–45) passed social legislation providing pensions, disability benefits, and health insurance to a number of sectors on a group-by-group basis (Malloy 1979: 69). These benefits were later collapsed into a few social security funds in the 1940s. Labor and social security legislation passed by Vargas aimed at controlling and co-opting segments of the labor movement (Collier and Collier 1991; Malloy 1979: 56–7). Unlike Perón in Argentina, who sought to control and mobilize labor support, labor legislation under Vargas sought to severely constrain and depoliticize labor unions – even to the extent of repressing labor leaders – with the goal of avoiding social conflict (Collier and Collier 1991: 169; Malloy 1979: 57).

Rural workers, urban informal workers, and the self-employed, all of whom were largely unorganized, were excluded from social security (see Malloy 1979: 56–7, 62). Given the scope of the rural population, which represented 64 percent of the total population in 1950 (Love 1970: 17), social security benefits reached a small minority of the workforce, protecting only 20.8 percent of the economically active and 6.8 percent of the total population (Malloy 1979: 95).

Over the years, the administration of pensions – the most developed social security program – became a source of patronage for labor leaders and politicians in the Brazilian Workers' Party (PTB), the party Vargas created in 1945 (Malloy 1979). Health care, by contrast, was less developed during this period, with some occupations receiving no medical benefits at all. Health care services were not a priority of social security funds and were provided "only after other obligations had been met" (Malloy 1979: 110). Attempts to standardize and universalize pensions were thwarted under Vargas in the 1950s – when he came back to power through elections within a still nondemocratic regime – and under Kubitschek (1956–61) of the Social Democratic Party (PDS), the other party created by Vargas but that was rooted in the rural elites (Malloy 1979: 95–7; 103). In both cases, strong opposition from rural-based parties and employers thwarted the initiative.

Until the early 1960s, when the consolidation of social security programs begins, the political regime was either authoritarian – prior to 1945 – or, after 1945, a limited democracy, given the small scope of suffrage. The percentage of the adult population registered to vote ranged from 13.4 in 1945 to 18.1 in 1960 (Chilcote 1974: 137; Love 1970: 9). Despite women's suffrage and compulsory voting, which were established in the 1934 constitution, literacy requirements excluded the illiterate. In the 1960s, for example, half of the population was disenfranchised due to literacy stipulations (Love 1970: 24). This was particularly acute in rural areas, where about 55 percent of the population resided in 1960 and where electoral manipulation was pervasive (Love 1970: 17 and 12).

Overall, until the 1960s, social benefits were granted only to workers and their dependents in the formal sector. This was a small minority, which, according to Malloy's estimates, reached only 7.4 percent of the total Brazilian population in 1960 (1979: 95). Because outsiders lacked political relevance, that is, they were largely disenfranchised, and were not organized, incumbents lacked strong incentives to mobilize their support through broad-reaching nondiscretionary social policy.

Chile
Benefits were initially extended in Chile on a group-by-group basis beginning in 1910 and were institutionalized in a more comprehensive social security system in 1924. These social innovations were part of a broader process of labor incorporation, which was carried out in Chile under military intervention and unstable political dynamics (Collier and Collier 1991; Scully 1995).

In a context marked by labor mobilization, Arturo Alessandri of the Liberal Alliance was elected to the presidency on a platform that promoted social and labor legislation (Mesa-Lago 1978: 24). Yet conservatives in the Chilean Congress – from both the Liberal Alliance and the Conservative Party – blocked Alessandri's social reform as well as the Conservative Party's alternative project and virtually all legislation of any kind (Borzutzky 2002: 14; Scully 1995: 107). In the face of a stalemate, army officers showed up in Congress putting pressure on lawmakers to pass legislation, and labor and social security bills were quickly approved (see Scully 1995: 107; Borzutzky 2002: 47-8). Congress approved a labor law that included key aspects of both the liberal and conservative projects and created a fragmented union structure with serious limitations on collective action (see Scully 1995:107; Collier and Collier 1991: 533–41). At the same time, and reflecting conservative preferences, Congress established social security programs that included highly segmented benefits along occupational lines (Borzutzky 2002: 47–8). After these reforms were passed, Alessandri resigned; the military took control of the government for a few months, and between 1924 and 1932, "five military coups interrupted a vitiated political process" in which no president finished his term (Scully 1995: 108).

The segmentation of benefits remained a feature of the social security system. As a testament to this, between 1924 and 1964, there were 160 different social security funds and dozens of old-age pensions and disability, maternity, and family allowance programs (see Borzutzky 2002: 49). At the same time, health care services attained only uneven reach during this period. The National Health Service, established in 1952 for blue-collar workers and the indigent, provided preventive care to all and medical services to blue-collar urban workers only. Through their respective insurance systems, some white-collar workers (e.g., bank workers) and the military could fund their own health care facilities and offer comprehensive medical services to their affiliates (see Borzutzky 2002).

Outsiders in urban and rural areas lacked protections; even if some benefits for blue-collar workers were applicable to rural workers, these were undermined by lack of compliance and evasion (see Borzutzky 2002: 53–5; Loveman 1976).[10] The absence of protections for outsiders resulted from these sectors' lack of political power. Despite the fact that Chile's democracy has been frequently presented as one of the most

---

[10] Loveman documents the absence of social security payments, deplorable working conditions, and physical punishments of workers in several rural estates (1976: 93–5).

stable in Latin America, and that its parties are considered fundamental actors of representation and policy making (Valenzuela and Valenzuela 1986: 185–6), democratic rule was based on a limited franchise until the 1960s.[11] Restrictions on suffrage operated through literacy requirements and the absence of secret ballot, which particularly affected rural voters and helped conservatives to win majorities in rural districts (see Scully 1995: 117). In 1950, 40 percent of the population resided in rural areas (INE n/d). At the same time, overrepresentation of rural districts in Congress allowed conservatives to gain institutional power and curtail or block more encompassing social legislation (see Borzutzky 2002: 23).

Social organization in rural areas was also restricted, constraining collective action among outsiders. Although unionization was approved in 1931, landowners managed to block union formation by forcing the government in 1938 to issue a temporary suspension, which remained in effect until 1947 (Loveman 1976: 95–116).[12] From then until the mid-1960s, although peasant unions were legally permissible, they were blocked by administrative action (Kurtz 2004b: 101).

In Chile, in sum, a relatively stable polity that largely excluded outsiders from the vote – as in Brazil – together with the lack of mobilization from below, which was stringently restricted by conservatives in rural areas, created an environment in which incumbents had little incentive to expand social benefits to outsiders. At the same time, and in spite of their early development, benefits for insiders featured marked differences across occupational groups, a fact typically attributed to the fragmentation of both the labor movement and the party system.

Mexico

Together with Brazil, Mexico stands out for the limited reach of social security during this early period. Estimates indicate that in 1963, only 17 percent of the total Mexican population was covered by one of the two large social security institutes, the Mexican Institute of Social Security (IMSS) and the Institute of Social Services for State Employees (ISSSTE).[13]

---

[11] The main parties in Chile were the Liberal and Conservative Parties (both elite), the Radical Party (also elite and middle class), the Communist Party, and more recently the Socialist Party (founded in 1933) and the Christian Democratic Party (established in 1957 when the Radical Party began to decline).

[12] See Kurtz (2004b) and Loveman (1976).

[13] According to Mesa-Lago, coverage reached 17 percent of the population and 18 percent of the EAP (1978: 219).

Beginning in the 1930s, social security benefits were extended in a piece-meal way to different occupational groups such as railroad and petro-leum workers in response to their pressures (Mesa-Lago 1989: 144–5). These innovations were rather limited and they pale in comparison to the comprehensive social security proposal drafted by the Álvaro Obregón presidency (1920–4), as well as to other broad-based initiatives such as those advocated by labor unions and those proposed by the Lázaro Cárdenas administration (1934–40), which seriously considered extend-ing pensions to peasants in the 1930s (Pozas 1992: 32–3). These alter-native proposals met strong employer resistance and were either not submitted to Congress or were never approved (Dion 2010: 57; Mesa-Lago 1978: 212; Pozas 1992: 33). The absence of social mobilization from below or electoral competition for outsiders discouraged the deci-sive creation of programs that would benefit them.

The Cárdenas administration made important efforts to organize popular support for his government and for the Party of the Mexican Revolution (PRM), which was the predecessor of the Institutional Party of the Revolution (PRI), the party that would govern Mexico until 2000. Cárdenas fostered the formation of a unified labor confederation of industrial workers, the Confederation of Mexican Workers (CTM), and a peasant organization, the National Peasant Confederation (CNC). Although Cárdenas encouraged the unity of the labor movement, he also opposed the CTM's intention to organize blue-collar workers, rural workers, and peasants within the same confederation, pursuing a divide-and-conquer strategy that would curtail the CTM's power to the advan-tage of the PRM (Middlebrook 1995: 91).

Cárdenas launched a vast land reform program to solidify support of the rural sector, which comprised between 74 percent and 66 percent of the population.[14] In reaction to labor mobilization under Cárdenas, a conser-vative party, the National Action Party (PAN), was formed to express the interests of the industrial elite. Fearing a decline in elite support, the PRI relegated its pro-labor agenda and shifted to the center, electing conser-vative politician Manuel Ávila Camacho (1940–6) to succeed Cárdenas (Collier and Collier 1991: 407–20). The extension of pensions and health care for industrial workers occurred under Ávila Camacho. After prom-ising the adoption of such benefits during his campaign and inaugural speech, Ávila Camacho formed a commission with representatives from

---

[14] Depending on whether rural populations are defined as those living in localities with fewer than 2,500 or 5,000 inhabitants. See INEGI (www.inegi.gob.mx).

labor, employers, and the state to draft a social security bill. The law was passed by Congress in 1942 at a time of high labor agitation, and began implementation in 1943 with the creation of the IMSS (Mesa-Lago 1978: 215). Social security legislation reflected the CTM's long-standing demands and has been understood as resulting from labor's pressure on the government in exchange for its political support (Dion 2010: 84). The implementation of social security in subsequent years was slow, however, and coverage grew at times of labor conflict, which the PRI handled through concessions and sometimes repression (see Mesa-Lago 1978: 215–19).

Although social security reforms were important achievements of the labor movement, the influence of organized labor on the government declined and its role in the governing coalition became more subordinate beginning in the 1940s, probably limiting the pace of implementation. In subsequent years, the PRM and its successor, the PRI, managed to co-opt most of the opposition from business and the right into a more conservative PRI coalition (Collier and Collier 1991: 408–12). The PRI-led peasant confederation was also state-penetrated to control and dampen demands while selectively delivering goods (see Collier and Collier 1991). A nondemocratic regime with a dominant-party system was strengthened by limiting dissent, consolidating the power of the party apparatus – which was increasingly merged with the state – and weakening popular organizations (see Collier 1992; Magaloni 2006). The PAN in turn lacked meaningful ties to low-income populations. The urban and rural popular sectors, which were enfranchised, were locked in by the PRI for decades, with the rural sector becoming the party's electoral bastion.

In sum, the consolidation of a nondemocratic regime dominated by the PRI, as well as the penetration of popular organizations by the party, limited both collective action by peasants and the expansion of opposition parties, raising no significant challenges to incumbents' continuity in power. In this environment, expanding social policy for outsiders was not on the agenda.

Consolidation of Social Security Systems

From the 1960s through the 1970s, the formal sector grew in the context of industrialization. Social security systems consolidated by incorporating new protections to those who were already insured, covering new occupational groups, rationalizing administration of social security programs, and effectively providing medical services – often the least developed

social insurance program during the previous period (see Malloy 1979;
Mesa-Lago 1978). Incumbents facing labor mobilization often extended
these innovations to contain activism and sometimes to mobilize labor
unions as allies.

Important transformations also affected outsiders' political participation and social policy. The growth of inward-oriented industrialization encouraged migration from rural to urban areas and the creation of
broader urban electorates, which sometimes upset the bases of conservative parties that had been sustained by the manipulation and/or exclusion
of rural voters. At the same time, and to different extents, mobilization
broke out in rural areas propelled by movements of rural laborers as well
as workers employed in agricultural industries (e.g., sugarcane). These
movements were often sponsored by church-based groups and/or left-
wing militants, and some rising rural organizations were also mediated
by newly created parties, as in Chile. This mobilization was particularly
strong in the 1960s and early 1970s, inspired by the Cuban Revolution
(1959) and by Catholic groups advocating liberation theology's commitment to the poor, as well as by often declining agricultural conditions.
In Chile, transformations were particularly intense as urban migration
coincided with changes in electoral rules and the broadening of suffrage,
which generated high electoral competition for the newly enfranchised
voters, most of whom were outsiders.

Several attempts to extend protections to outsiders were undertaken.
In Argentina, during a brief democratic interregnum, proposals were discussed and legislation was enacted to deepen and enforce benefits for
outsiders that had been created in the 1940s. High levels of regime instability, followed by open political violence, thwarted the implementation
of these initiatives. Large-scale expansion occurred only in Chile, which
experienced high electoral competition for outsiders and a more inclusive democracy beginning in the 1960s. By contrast, discretionary and
unstable benefits were extended by authoritarian regimes facing pressure
from below in rural areas in Mexico and more prominently in Brazil in
the late 1960s and early 1970s.

Given the "vertical" expansion of benefits – accumulation of protections by those who were already insured (see Mesa-Lago 1978: 217) –
and the failed attempts at protecting outsiders, the social policy divide
deepened, particularly in Brazil and Mexico, where health care expansion
for rural and urban outsiders did not materialize and where benefits –
if granted in rural areas by authoritarian regimes – were small and/or
selective.

Argentina

Between the overthrow of Perón in 1955 and re-democratization in 1983, few social policy innovations were implemented in Argentina. Health insurance was made compulsory for insiders and family allowances were extended to most categories of formal workers. Social security pensions, health care, and family allowance programs were merged into a few national systems, reducing the high dispersion of benefits that characterized their early development. In the context of some rural mobilization, policy proposals to strengthen benefits reaching outsiders were also enacted, yet no meaningful and lasting social policy expansion took place due to the profound instability of the political regime and, for the most part, the absence of democratic rule.

From 1955 to 1973, the military banned the Peronist Party and kept Perón in exile. In 1958, Arturo Frondizi, of the Intransigent faction of the UCR (UCRI), managed to win the presidency by forging ties with Perón in exile and courting labor support.[15] In office, Frondizi sought to integrate the Peronist labor unions with promises and concessions (James 1976: 274). As part of his appeal to workers, Frondizi standardized and increased pension benefits substantially (Feldman et al. 1988: 45). Yet despite the alliance he had built with unions, labor protest was repressed (see Di Tella 1986: 51–3). Labor discontent and pressures from the military to curtail working-class demands weakened the Frondizi administration and facilitated its overthrow in 1962 (see James 1976).

Elections were held again in 1963, with the proscription of the Peronist Party and Frondizi's UCRI. Arturo Illia (1963–6) of the UCR of the People (UCRP) came to power with little popular legitimacy. With respect to social policy, Illia sought to strengthen the health care system by increasing access to pharmaceuticals through a bill passed by Congress. In a context of strong military and conservative pressure in which he faced massive labor union unrest,[16] Illia was ousted by a coup in 1966.

The new military government led by Juan Carlos Onganía initiated a process of industrial deepening, setting up what O'Donnell has called a bureaucratic-authoritarian state (1979). With respect to social policy, it repealed Illia's pharmaceutical law, reduced health care expenditure,[17] and sought to limit the role of unions in health insurance. The leadership

---

[15] The Radical Party split in 1956. The UCRI promised to preserve Perón's social and labor legislation. The UCR of the People Party (UCRP) wanted to repeal many Peronist laws and supported the military's efforts to de-Peronize society (McGuire 1995: 213).

[16] For example, 11,000 factory occupations. See Di Tella (1986: 64).

[17] Congreso Nacional, Cámara de Senadores, Volume 5, April 24 and 25, 1973: 4065, 4079.

of the CGT in turn demanded a law establishing compulsory registration of all employees into the union-run health insurances, and a union-
friendly law governing their administration.

High levels of political contestation and instability emerged in the late
1960s. In response to massive protests by combative labor unions,[18] the
military agreed to demands from the more moderate CGT to mandate
enrollment in union-administered health funds. As a result, coverage
grew significantly in the following years to reach at least 60 percent of
the population in 1980 (see Neri 1982: 92).

As in the other cases under study, rural mobilization grew in the late
1960s and early 1970s. Originally sponsored by the Catholic Church,
agrarian leagues were formed in several low-income provinces to demand
better conditions for rural producers, including medical facilities and
noncontributory pensions for agricultural laborers (see Ferrara 1973:
233; Roze 1992). Sugarcane workers affected by the military's policy
of closing down sugar mills formed alliances with combatant industrial
unions and activists, and in part provided the basis of a guerrilla movement inspired by the Cuban Revolution (Mattini 1990; Pozzi 2004). In
this context of mobilization, and seeking legitimacy for the regime, the
military dictatorship launched a health care program for formal-sector
pensioners (Belmartino and Bloch 1989: 506) and for rural workers that,
though limited, improved access to health care services in rural areas.

Confronted with high instability and popular demands for regime
change, the military allowed democratic elections. In 1973, Hector
Cámpora of the PJ came to power. New elections were soon held for
Perón to return from exile and run for the presidency, which he won
comfortably with the traditional loyalty of outsider voters. Under these
administrations, social security for rural workers saw a mild increase
in access (Feldman et al. 1988: 54), and benefits for insiders were also
improved.

The most important initiative for outsiders launched in this period
concerned health care. The government sought to consolidate and
strengthen public health care services, which had deteriorated as a consequence of neglect and cutbacks on critical programs. In 1974, shortly
after Perón's death, Congress passed a new health care law that established the Integrated Health System (SNIS). The SNIS would standardize, coordinate, and provide funding for health care services. It offered
voluntary incorporation to provinces and labor unions, which ran health

---

[18] Classist non-Peronist unions were strong in the auto industry. See James (1976; 1978).

insurance services for their workers. Congress further approved legislation regulating training, certification, and promotion for health care professionals. Low-income provinces were enthusiastic supporters of the SNIS, as it would provide them with fresh funding to develop greater institutional capacity and improve service delivery.[19]

Political violence escalated under the administration of Perón's wife and successor, Estela Martínez (1974-6), and extreme divisions among Peronist factions widened further (see James 1976: 287). In this context, the SNIS was not implemented. The universalization of family allowances to reach outsiders, which the Ministry of Social Welfare sponsored,[20] was not pursued, either. In 1976, a coup inaugurated a new military dictatorship (1976–83) that produced massive, unprecedented state repression and human rights violations, with thousands of people murdered and disappeared.

The military retrenched social programs; it eliminated employers' contributions to social security – which were subsequently restored in the new democracy in the 1980s – excluded unions from the administration of benefits, and reduced social expenditures (see Neri 1982).[21] At the same time, the law creating the SNIS was repealed. Facing growing discontent with the regime, the dictatorship ended with the defeat of the military in the Malvinas War in 1982, which ushered in a transition by "collapse" that paved the way for the return of democracy in 1983 (See Collier 1999).

Overall, mobilization in the late 1960s and early 1970s did lead to minimal improvement in access to rural pensions – which did not amount to an expansion as the majority of rural workers remained unprotected – and an attempt to improve the universal public health care system, which was never implemented due to profound political instability and violence followed by regime breakdown. The absence of democracy during virtually the entire period, and the lack of sustained mobilization from below by organizations representing outsiders – save briefly in the early 1970s – generated no potent incentives for incumbents to adopt or implement broad, nondiscretionary social benefits to secure their support.

Brazil

An important phase of social security consolidation for formal workers in Brazil began during the authoritarian regime inaugurated in 1964. In the 1970s, noncontributory pensions and some minimal health care

---

[19] See Congreso Nacional, Cámara de Senadores, Volume 5, April 24 and 25, 1973.
[20] See *La Nación*, August 30, 1974.
[21] See also Belmartino and Bloch (1989) and Belmartino (2005), among others.

services were extended to outsiders in rural areas. Incumbents further introduced a short-lived primary care program as well as more flexible rules for accessing pensions for low-income insiders in urban areas. Of these innovations, the provision of rural pensions was the most meaningful, albeit discretionary.[22] Often in combination with the repression and intimidation of activists and the banning and exclusion of politicians, authoritarian incumbents initially inaugurated these benefits to dampen pressures from below in rural areas, and later on to increase the appeal of allied parties during the democratic transition when some restricted form of electoral competition was allowed.

The 1964 coup was a reaction to the administration of João Goulart (1962–4), which sought to organize and mobilize popular support behind his administration at a time of increased activism.[23] Mobilization was growing in rural areas among sharecroppers, landless families, and especially sugarcane laborers (Houtzager 1998: 106).[24] In the low-income northeast, some of these workers were organizing a movement of peasant leagues[25] that challenged the status quo in the countryside (Chilcote 1974: 156; Pereira 1997). According to the leader of the peasant leagues at the time, Francisco Julião, their demands centered on "land reform and the vote of the illiterate."[26] Although rural mobilization was neither large scale nor coordinated among different groups, some politicians and the military even feared a Cuban-inspired revolution in the countryside.[27]

Confronted with rural activism, Goulart sponsored the Statute of the Rural Worker (ETR) and social security legislation, both of which Congress passed in 1963, as well as an agrarian reform proposal, which did not prosper (Houtzager 1998: 106–10).[28] The ETR extended labor

---

[22] Note, however, that noncontributory pensions reached less than 35 percent of all outsiders aged sixty and over and did not constitute what is here defined as an expansion. Estimated with data from *Anuário da Previdência Social*.

[23] When leaders of mass groups, such as the peasant leagues or the unions' strike committee, ran for office, they would do so through the PTB, but their ties to parties were tenuous at best (Jenks 1979: 74).

[24] See Chilcote (1974: 155–60); Houtzager (1998); Maybury-Lewis (1994); Novaes (1991); Pereira (1997).

[25] The peasant leagues formed in the northeast between 1955 and 1964. They demanded redistribution of land to cultivators and launched unprecedented waves of protest (see Pereira 1997: xv). They were banned in 1964 and several members formed part of the rural unions established by the ETR.

[26] *Folha de São Paulo*, August 8, 1960.

[27] See Houtzager (1968).

[28] Goulart had previously attempted social and labor legislation for the countryside in the 1950s, when he was Vargas's minister of labor.

legislation to the countryside and established a corporatist structure of representation similar to that used for the urban labor force. According to Houtzager, congressional approval of these reforms was facilitated by the fact that conservatives believed this legislation would never be enforced. Goulart in turn hoped that the new union structure the ETR established would allow him to mobilize a rural support base (1998: 108, 110). By 1964, 2,000 rural unions,[29] as well as a national confederation, CONTAG, which was controlled by Communist Party affiliates, were formed (Chilcote 1974: 159).

Goulart's societal mobilization alienated the largest parties in his coalition, the populist PTB and the PDS, and was opposed by the right-wing National Democratic Union (UDN) – which drew support from elites in rural areas – as well as by the military. After overthrowing Goulart, the military disregarded the new social and labor legislation, purged urban and rural unions, and allowed for only moderate union leadership (see Chilcote 1974: 159; CONTAG 2003; Maybury-Lewis 1994). However, the persistence of rural mobilization and the fear of "an agrarian insurgency" prompted the military to implement both the ETR and the social security benefits (see Houtzager 1998). In 1968, a strike of sugarcane workers broke out in Pernambuco, raising fears of widespread unrest in the northeast. In response, the military recognized the unions' demands, granted social security benefits, and threatened repression if the strike continued (Houtzager 1998: 117). Social benefits were then extended to the whole countryside in 1971 to prevent the spread of militancy and to co-opt rural unions by including them in the administration of health care services for their affiliates. Pensions grew significantly in the following years while the provision of medical services, which represented selective incentives for unions to recruit members and dispense patronage, remained very limited (see Malloy 1979: 138).

Repression and the distribution of social benefits helped the military deactivate union militancy and prevent the emergence of coordinated mobilization in the countryside. In an authoritarian environment, rural unions could not denounce the selective repression of union leaders and the manipulation of benefits. As analyzed by Maybury-Lewis (1994), some unions succumbed to clientelism, while others used resources to strengthen their organizations and survive the dictatorship. Given the unions' intermediary role in access to benefits, membership grew

---

[29] Even before the ETR was approved, these activists set out to create rural unions to compete with the peasant leagues (see *Folha de São Paulo*, November 11, 1962).

significantly under the military (see Maybury-Lewis 1994). Aside from the administration of health care services, the power of rural unions emanated from their authority to certify the status of rural workers, which was a requirement for accessing rural pensions.

The military also introduced managed partisan competition by establishing a two-party system formed by the military National Renewal Alliance (ARENA) party and the opposition Brazilian Democratic Movement (MDB). In contrast to other military dictatorships in the region, the Brazilian military leadership did not see parties as a source of chaos, but rather as a tool for governing: parties were a way to determine access to state positions, to achieve legitimacy, and to deal with subnational political strongmen, some of which were eventually accommodated into the military coalition.[30] The opposition in turn was severely curtailed by the exclusion of candidates and the absence of elections in areas where it could pose an electoral threat to the incumbent.

Rural pensions helped create a patronage structure of local offices staffed by ARENA politicians who initially administered these benefits (Weyland 1996a: 100). The military had an ambivalent relationship with patronage politicians. While they sought to undercut pervasive patronage in the state (Jenks 1979: 77–8), the military nonetheless needed support from these politicians in order to govern. On several occasions, the military tried to undermine the archaic institutions on which the power of politicians and ARENA-affiliated rural oligarchs was based. Aside from attempting what would be a failed agrarian reform, it tried to extend the vote to illiterates, an initiative that ARENA in Congress rejected (Jenks 1979: 92), and to centralize the administration of rural pensions in 1977, which ARENA vigorously though unsuccessfully opposed.[31]

In the early 1960s, formal-sector employment was still small but began to grow rapidly with industrialization and urbanization. The military then strengthened health care services for insiders, which were inadequate at the time, by increasing private-sector involvement in both insurance and service delivery. In 1974, it began to subsidize the construction of private hospital facilities that would provide services through social security institutions (Medici 1997: 27).

Facing divisions over the continuity of the regime, the military created a limited political opening in the early 1970s, which was immediately

---

[30] For parties and oligarchic power under the military, see Hagopian (1996), Jenks (1979), and Moreira Alves (1985).

[31] *Jornal do Brasil*, February 6, 1977.

followed by the unexpected showing of the MDB in the legislative elections of 1974. Critiques of deplorable social conditions – despite the "miracle" levels of growth that Brazil experienced in the 1960s and early 1970s – were intensified by outbreaks of meningitis in São Paulo in 1972 and especially in 1974 (see Iversson 1976: 12–13), raising concerns about potentially declining electoral support. Although censorship initially hid the spread of the disease, the military administration of Ernesto Geisel (1974–8) eventually launched an unprecedented vaccination campaign that reached between 75 percent and 80 percent of the population to combat the epidemics (Knight and Moran 1981: 24).[32] The campaign demonstrated the effectiveness with which the state could reach the population "when political priority was high" (Knight and Moran 1981: 24). It also revealed the sheer absence of adequate health care infrastructure and motivated some responses.

In 1976, the military launched an incipient – and short-lived – expansion of primary health care services for outsiders through the Interiorization of Health and Sanitation Actions Program (PIASS). PIASS aimed at establishing health posts and training health agents in local communities in the northeast. The Secretariat of Health in the city of São Paulo launched a similar initiative in 1978. While the São Paulo initiative continued, PIASS was defunded by the end of the decade.[33]

The importance of these two programs, however, resides in the network of doctors and local community ties they helped form. As documented in the literature, the inclusion of left-wing public health professionals in the national and state-level health care bureaucracy to implement these and related training programs, as well as the linkages these doctors developed with research institutions, public health schools, labor unions, local communities, and popular health movements – especially in São Paulo – facilitated the eventual formation of an influential movement for health care reform (see Escorel 1999; Lima et al. 2005). This movement promoted a universal, participatory health care system, which became a critical popular demand during the transition to democracy in the 1980s (see Lima et al. 2005).

In the context of an increasingly competitive political system, the military further launched more accessible contributory pensions for low-income seniors and disability benefits. These provisions were extended to increase the appeal of conservatives and to dispense patronage.

---

[32] Built with a systematic search of newspaper articles in FdSP from 1972 to 1975.

[33] There is scarce information on the evolution of PIASS; see, for example, Medici (1997).

Beneath the veneer of concern for the poor, the electoral competitiveness of ARENA politicians was the main driving force of social policy creation. This can be observed in the importance granted to social benefits in electoral campaigns. Though literacy requirements restricted outsiders' electoral participation, in 1976, for example, the party leaders instructed the national board of ARENA to emphasize "Social security, rural pensions ... vaccination against meningitis" (quoted in Grinberg 2009:200).

In sum, the military dictatorship extended pensions to rural workers and provided minimal access to health care services. By the 1980s, rural pensions, despite being meaningful, were discretionary and had not reached the minimum threshold of expansion, here considered 35 percent of outsiders. Both programs were selectively used to defuse contention and co-opt rural unions. During the political opening, the military further expanded some basic though rather unstable primary care initiatives that were later defunded. Rural unions and a movement for health reform – both of which gained momentum during the transition and formed around these initiatives – put pressure on the state to enact social policy change and achieved significant expansion in the new democracy, as discussed in Chapter 4.

Chile

In the 1960s, social security systems consolidated, featuring improved access to health care services and a lower segmentation of benefits across occupational groups. In this period, the expansion of health care services for outsiders constituted a fundamental innovation and the only large-scale nondiscretionary initiative implemented among our cases. Intense electoral competition propelled by electoral reforms, expansion of the suffrage, and the emergence of new parties seeking to mobilize outsiders increased the relevance of these voters. Promises of social policy expansion became a critical tool for politicians competing for outsiders to mobilize their support, and expansion became a strategy to consolidate it once in power.

Starting in the 1950s, Chile underwent further democratization with a significant expansion of the electorate. The number of registered voters grew due to the extension of female suffrage in 1949 and electoral reforms in 1958 and 1962 that effectively introduced the secret ballot in the countryside (Scully 1995: 117) and simplified registration and created penalties for not registering or voting (Oxhorn 1995: 50). Furthermore, in the early 1970s, literacy requirements were eliminated (Oxhorn 1995: 50). Estimates show that between 1958 and 1970, the percentage

of registered voters more than doubled (Scully 1995: 117). These transformations incentivized party competition for the urban poor (Schneider
1995: 48) and for previously disenfranchised sectors of the rural population (see Scully 1995: 119).

The party system experienced changes. Within a fragmented party system, the expansion of the left – with the near victory of Salvador Allende
in the 1958 presidential elections – combined with the creation of the
Christian Democratic Party (DC) in 1957, increased competition for outsiders. The DC sought to mobilize the new electorate at the expense of
the Conservative and the Radical Parties[34] by offering a socially oriented
conservative alternative that would be more appealing to outsiders and
the middle classes than the more exclusionary right parties and more
moderate than the Socialist and Communist Parties.

In the 1964 presidential elections, DC candidate Eduardo Frei-
Montalva managed to win a significant share of outsider and women
votes (see Fleet 1985: 43; Scully 1995: 119).[35] Once in power, the Frei
administration (1964–70) sought to consolidate this support. As stated in
his first speech as president, the sectors his "Revolution in Liberty" would
try to protect were precisely the peasants and those at the urban margins, roughly "55 percent of the population" (Frei quoted in Borzutzky
2002: 81). Social policy was a fundamental tool to achieve this goal.
With a focus on mother and child programs, the government improved
preventive health care services, constructed health posts, and extended
free universal meals for children in public schools (Borzutzky 2002: 111;
Graham 1991: 10). It further increased investments to effectively extend
medical services for marginal urban and rural populations foreseen in
existing legislation. To entice the low-income rural vote, Frei made important efforts to enforce existing social security legislation and managed to
get congressional approval for an agrarian reform and a new unionization law for rural workers and peasants – which permitted the formation
of 500 rural unions by 1971 (Borzutzky 2002: 86–93). These measures
alienated potential conservative allies, and threatened to deprive parties
of the left of their electoral base (Scully 1995: 121).

The Frei administration further launched a vast program of popular
promotion that organized residents in shantytowns on the basis of their
consumption needs, particularly housing (Oxhorn 1995: 51–2). These

---

[34] In 1966, these parties formed the National Party (Pollack 1999: 27). For the DC, see
Pollack (1999: 25–7).
[35] See Fleet (1985: 70) and Schneider (1995: 48).

organizations were expected to provide support for the government among the marginal urban populations (Fleet 1985: 87). As expected in this book's argument, however, in a context of electoral competition for outsiders, opposition parties feared manipulation of social organizations by the DC and rejected the program, limiting its funding, until it was discontinued in 1967 (Borzutzky 2002: 83; Fleet 1985: 87).

In the late 1960s, three blocs competed vigorously for the vote of outsiders, including a coalition of center and right parties, the Popular Unity (UP) formed by the Socialist and Communist Parties, and the incumbent DC, which faced growing inflation and heightened popular demands in office (see Oxhorn 1995: 54; Valenzuela and Valenzuela 1986: 197). Promises of social policy expansion figured prominently in the campaigns of politicians seeking to court outsiders. Salvador Allende of the UP, who won the 1970 presidential election by a slim margin, promised universal social security funded with direct taxes and free medical services delivered by a participatory unified health care system (Stallings 1978: 126–7).

During his brief tenure, Allende (1970–3) accomplished an extension of contributory social security for self-employed workers, which was nonetheless undermined by compliance problems, and a significant expansion of medical services, achieved through the inauguration of new clinics and health centers in low-income areas (Borzutzky 2002: 140–4). Like the Frei administration, particular emphasis was placed on reaching mothers and children through primary care, milk distribution, and vaccinations (Borzutzky 2002: 144). In combination with other social improvements, the health initiatives of the Frei and Allende governments contributed to a dramatic decline in infant mortality rates, from 102.9 per thousand in 1964 to 26.9 in 1973 (Borzutzky 2002: 103, 145).

Political mobilization of the popular sectors under Frei and Allende was at times hard for governments to control. Growing activism, together with Allende's nationalization and redistributive measures (e.g., increased taxes, agrarian reform) generated a tremendous backlash (Scully 1995: 121) with street marches, demonstrations, and employers' lockouts in 1972 (Stallings 1978: 141–4). After failed attempts at forming a coalition government, mobilization culminated in a military coup that, as in Argentina, inaugurated a dictatorship that engaged in harsh repression of popular organizations and activists.

In sum, the expansion of the suffrage increased the relevance of outsiders and incentivized high electoral competition for their votes. The DC, which sought to achieve power and opposed both traditional conservative parties in their manipulation and neglect of low-income constituencies as well as the more statist and egalitarian proposals advocated by the left, initiated a vigorous attempt to mobilize the rural sector and urban informal workers. This resulted in high competition for these voters between the DC and the left. To court outsiders and consolidate their support in office, Frei and Allende expanded large-scale health care services and attempted to extend social security for rural workers and for the self-employed, which proved hard to implement and thus saw only modest changes in coverage in this period.

Mexico

Social security coverage in Mexico experienced an important leap in the 1970s, from 20 percent of the total population in 1970 to about 40 percent in 1980.[36] Expansion was propelled by the growth of formal jobs in industry and the state, as well as by the regional extension of the IMSS and the creation of the social security institute for state workers (ISSTEE) in 1959 (see Mesa-Lago 1978: 215–19). The 1970s also witnessed the inauguration of limited health care services for outsiders in rural areas – which did not amount to an expansion as defined here – as well as land distribution. These measures were responses to rural unrest by incumbents in an authoritarian regime that primarily resorted to the selective distribution of benefits, co-optation, and eventually repression to quell discontent.

The 1960s and 1970s saw the emergence of peasant protest amid declining living conditions. As elsewhere in the region, this coincided with a surge in social activism in urban areas as well. Rural mobilization gained state attention and policy responses in the 1970s. Underlying demands in the countryside were a profound economic crisis in agriculture (interview, Araujo, head of CNC), and the sharp decline of the ability of the PRI-affiliated peasant confederation to mediate rural conflict given the slower pace of land distribution that began in the 1940s (Kurtz 2004b: 170). Activism in the countryside resulted in the formation of more autonomous peasant groups (see Grammont and Mackinlay 2006: 699). These rural organizations understood that their needs would be solved with public policies and development investments, and thus demanded not only land distribution, as peasant groups had traditionally done, but also production-oriented programs (interview Araujo).

Legislation to expand social security to the rural sector and the uninsured failed to gain support within the PRI during this period (Mesa-Lago

---

[36] 1970 figure built with data from Zorrilla Arena (1988: 207), and INEGI. Similar estimates in Mesa-Lago (1989: 150).

1978: 219). In response to demands, incumbents extended discretionary policy provisions, and distributed them strategically to manufacture support and quell contention. Luis Echeverría (1970–6) initiated a new wave of land distribution that was mediated by the CNC, and extended other initiatives to rural populations to appease unrest (see Grammont and Mackinlay 2006). Rural credit institutions such as BANRURAL were established, and existing agencies such as CONASUPO were revamped to better help peasants market their produce and provide higher price supports for their crops. The Public Investment for Rural Development Program (PIDER) was launched to provide technical assistance, improve local infrastructure, and extend funding for microenterprises (interview, Rolando Cordera Campos; Fox 1994: 159–60).

These initiatives provided the state and the CNC with resources to exchange with the peasantry and mobilize their support (see Kurtz 2004b). The PRI also channeled resources through some of the dissident organizations as a way to dampen protest, undermine local bosses who discredited the party, and gain some legitimacy for the regime partly by integrating these groups (see Collier and Collier 1991: 605; Fox 1994). This latter strategy was pursued as long as these groups' involvement could be controlled through some measure of co-optation and the threat of coercion (see Fox 1994). Eventually, several of these dissident organizations and leaders threw their support for the PRI (see Collier and Collier 1991: 605, interview Araujo). Though these groups were capable of extracting some concessions, they were not strong enough to achieve broad-based mobilization in the context of an authoritarian regime.

The strategy to increase the regime's legitimacy by reshaping discredited local structures of brokerage that undermined support for the PRI through the integration of new leaders – this time not organized in protest groups, however – resurfaced with the first electoral challenge to the PRI in the 1980s, which led to the creation of a more ambitious development strategy, the National Solidarity Program (PRONASOL) that also reached urban areas, as discussed in the next section.[37]

Echeverría's successor, José López Portillo (1976–82), launched the Commission for Depressed and Marginal Areas (COPLAMAR) to develop infrastructure and credit, extend training, and provide health care for rural populations. The provision of primary health care services in remote rural areas was the only one of the COPLAMAR initiatives

---

[37] Some of the technocrats who participated in PIDER and COPLAMAR played important roles in PRONASOL (interview, Cordera-Campos).

that was eventually implemented; the remaining strategies were abandoned during the economic collapse of 1982. IMSS took charge of setting up and providing these health care services through a special program, IMSS-COPLAMAR (interview, head of IMSS-COPLAMAR and IMSS-Solidaridad). Despite its importance, the extension of health care services was uneven and limited, not amounting to an expansion as it is defined here.

Overall, within a nondemocratic regime, rural protest led incumbents to extend discretionary benefits to the countryside to reinforce the PRI's dominance in rural areas. Selective distribution of land and of production-oriented goods was employed to deactivate protest. IMSS-COPLAMAR was an important health care initiative for rural areas, but due to the political constraints mentioned here, it did not reach a meaningful proportion of outsiders.

Reform of Social Security Systems

The debt crisis in the early 1980s and the economic recession that followed put pressures on middle-income countries in Latin America to initiate market-oriented reforms. Economic liberalization and the privatization of state companies and social security programs were increasingly viewed as the most appropriate solutions to the difficulties experienced by economies based on inward-oriented industrialization and debt-led growth (see Bulmer-Thomas 2010). With respect to insiders' benefits, privatization varied across countries despite a growing consensus in policy circles about the need to retrench social security systems – which came to be increasingly portrayed as unfair – and to create limited safety nets for the very poor.

In this context of market expansion and state retrenchment, there is broad cross-national and cross-temporal variation in social policy initiatives for outsiders. The framework proposed in this study contributes to our understanding of the reasons behind these differences. Chile initiated market adjustment early and under a military dictatorship. Market reforms served the goal of addressing economic troubles, but more importantly, they formed part of a broader strategy to radically transform the political dynamics that predated the military coup. In this case, social benefits for outsiders were launched when the authoritarian incumbent faced social protest and the prospect of electoral competition surrounding a plebiscite to determine the continuity of the authoritarian incumbent or the transition to democracy in the late 1980s. Some of these benefits were broad-reaching but discretionary and often temporary. A comparable strategy was followed by the incumbent PRI in Mexico, which did not launch any meaningful expansion during the 1982 debt crisis, but did inaugurate social policy innovations in response to unprecedented levels of electoral competition in some urban areas, especially in Mexico City in the 1988 presidential election. As in Chile, policies launched by the Mexican government were temporary and coexisted with intimidation and repression – though this was much milder and decentralized in the case of Mexico. In the absence of a strong opposition or a sustained national social movement that could limit discretion and demand benefits within a free regime, incumbents selectively used social benefits, co-optation (in Mexico), and repression to achieve their political goals.

In Argentina, and in Chile after the return of democracy, the initial lack of electoral competition and of pressures from below generated no compelling incentives for expansion. Small social programs for outsiders were launched in these cases. In Argentina, the absence of meaningful protections, that is, nondiscretionary policies covering a significant portion of the outsider population with stable benefits, continued even after a crisis of hyperinflation that produced dramatic hardship. In Chile, the new democratic governments did not expand benefits despite very high poverty levels in the early 1990s and despite the country's economic growth, which is analyzed in Chapter 7. In Brazil, by contrast, high levels of mobilization from below during the democratic transition led to the expansion of social policy for outsiders in the new democracy. This is analyzed in Chapter 4.

Argentina

With the return of democracy in 1983, social programs for outsiders were given serious consideration, yet no major initiative was effectively implemented until the emergence of large-scale mobilization, which began in the late 1990s and is the subject of Chapter 5. During this period, the PJ managed to keep the bulk of outsider electoral support intact, which, together with the absence of social mobilization, generated no incentives for expanding benefits. Initiatives to placate economic hardship during this period were small, temporary, or failed to be implemented. This was the case with the Solidary Bonus (BS), a broad food stamp program launched under the first administration of Carlos Menem (1989–95) of the PJ.

Raúl Alfonsín (1983–9) was the first UCR candidate ever to defeat the PJ in fair competitive elections, and in 1983 he inaugurated what would be the longest period of democratic politics in Argentina. Although competition was important in these elections, outsiders remained the PJ's electoral support base (see Catterberg 1991; Ostiguy 1998; author's calculations). Upon taking office, Alfonsín got congressional approval for the National Food Plan (PAN), which sought to improve declining living conditions produced by the debt crisis. The scheme was designed in a technocratic top-down way and initially reached 5 million people, about 40 percent of all outsiders.[38] PAN was intended to be a nondiscretionary scheme. It ran through a parallel government structure "to bypass the heavy state bureaucracy and make it more transparent" (interview, Aldo Neri, Alfonsín's minister of health and social welfare). Households were selected according to need, which was assessed using a map of poverty built with 1980 census data and with information from municipal governments.

Despite the government's concern for transparency, the implementation of PAN was marred by clientelism, which backfired against the government and reduced support for PAN's continuity. Discretion operated in two ways. First, when PAN was announced, provincial governments demanded involvement in the program, fearing that a large-scale program operated directly by the national government would affect provincial politics. Under this pressure, the Alfonsín administration involved governors in appointing PAN's agents, who were in charge of controlling the distribution of food boxes and providing nutrition education to beneficiaries, and whose role was crucial to the program's transparency. This decision undoubtedly introduced biases in implementation. As a key official of PAN pointed out:

In direct assistance programs ... you have a struggle that has no political color: Who controls? Is it the federal or the provincial government? This is raised by members from your own party, and is more intense when governors belong to the opposition. We managed this well with PAN.... We negotiated with each governor that half of PAN's agents, who were those in contact with the community and with the ones who distributed the food, and who needed some training to perform their task, were appointed by the governor. We appointed the other half from the central office of PAN in the national government. By doing this, we could achieve some political equilibrium. (interview)

Second, because they lacked systematic data to use as a basis for selecting beneficiaries, municipal governments eventually became "a principal

[38] Interview, Neri. See also Grassi, Hintze, and Neufeld (1994: 194–6).

source of information" (interview, Neri) to determine eligibility, which allowed for discretion given the absence of standardized municipal information systems. Furthermore, PAN agents often selected beneficiaries themselves (Grassi et al. 1994: 195), which undoubtedly biased access, as agents were appointed through political negotiations between the provincial and national government.

Although it is not within the policy areas under study, the importance of PAN lies in that it illustrates the political consequences of the discretionary implementation of a broad-reaching, visible national program, even in a case in which discretion contradicted the incumbent's aspirations. The inability of the state to enforce the rules and to control distribution of food boxes on the ground undermined the program and made it an exemplar of clientelism in public opinion. Despite Alfonsín's intention to build a nondiscretionary benefit, the PJ leadership – whose party structure was embedded within outsider neighborhoods – used accusations of clientelism to discredit the program and the national government.

After a failed stabilization plan, the Alfonsín administration faced high inflation, hyperinflation, and a dramatic power vacuum. In the context of a profound recession, PAN was gradually defunded, providing increasingly fewer benefits to fewer households just when these households were most in need of assistance (interview, Neri). Alfonsín stepped down six months before the end of his tenure amid lootings, high inflation, and a deteriorated economy.

The PJ won the presidential elections in 1989 with a smashing victory that included massive support in outsider districts (author's dataset). Concerns about lootings and the potential emergence of social conflict led newly appointed President Menem to issue a decree establishing the BS.[39] The scheme was inaugurated in a few metropolitan areas as soon as Menem took office, while a bill proposing BS worked its way rapidly through Congress. The benefit would provide a voucher for medicine and food stamps equivalent to half a minimum wage to all families earning below the minimum wage – about 20 percent of total households – and would be funded with a new corporate tax.[40]

The program was launched in a few provinces but was not fully implemented, however.[41] First, lootings – and thus fears of social conflict – dissipated soon after Menem took office. Second, after being approved in the Lower Chamber, PJ senators rejected the policy, denouncing BS as

[39] See "Menem firma el decreto del Bono para carenciados," *Clarín*, July 31, 1989.
[40] "Todos los detalles sobre el Bono Solidario de Emergencia," *Clarín*, August 12, 1989.
[41] "Lanzan hoy el Bono Solidario," *Clarín*, August 24, 1989.

an incursion of the national government in their provinces and accusing the program of discretion in the distribution of benefits.[42] PJ senators demanded the decentralization of BS and the distribution of funding following the revenue-sharing criteria, which rewarded the less populated provinces and would deprive hard-hit metropolitan areas of critical resources to mitigate declining living conditions and potential social conflict.[43]

In the absence of social conflict, whose threat had motivated the initial adoption of BS, governors' resistance made Menem reconsider the program's implementation. Despite Congress' approval of a watered-down, temporary version of the BS, Menem announced that a workfare program run by municipalities and social organizations called Plan Trabajar (Work Plan) would replace BS in the following months.[44] BS soon petered out; yet the Work Plan was not implemented until years later, as discussed in Chapter 5. Absent the conditions propelling expansion, electoral competition for outsiders or mobilization from below, and given governors' resistance to a large-scale national benefit, Menem shifted course and a deep hyperinflation crisis was navigated without any significant nationwide social provision palliating its effects on the poor.

State shrinkage was vast in Argentina. Immediately upon taking office, Menem launched one of the most sweeping programs of economic liberalization in Latin America (Etchemendy 2011). As a result of such transformations, Argentina gained access to financial markets, inflation was tamed, and economic growth resumed. Reforms affected benefits for formal-sector workers. Menem negotiated pension privatization in Congress with labor unions, yielding a partly privatized pension system (Alonso 2000; Brooks 2009; Isuani and San Martino 1994). He further established tighter eligibility requirements – thirty instead of twenty years of contributions to qualify for a pension – and deregulated the union-run medical insurance system, allowing the union-run funds to compete for formal-sector affiliates.

Despite growing unemployment as economic growth resumed, Menem launched no significant social policy for outsiders. Because outsiders were not organized into a social movement and no credible challenger was competing for this loyal PJ electorate, Menem had no incentives to

---

[42] "Media Sancion en Diputados al Bono Solidario," *Clarín*, September 15, 1989; "Duro debate por el Bono," *Clarín*, September 23, 1989.
[43] ibid.
[44] See "Aprobaron la Ley del Bono Solidario," *Clarín*, September 29, 1989 and Garay (2007).

launch large-scale policies. Instead, the Menem administration pursued a two-pronged social policy strategy whose main goal was to maintain the status quo and prevent the emergence of protest and voter disaffection, especially in metropolitan areas hard hit by economic reforms. On one hand, the national government launched small, temporary social programs to show concern about poverty.[45] These programs were often implemented in selective ways, as the more or less technocratic agencies that run these programs did not fully control the selection of beneficiaries or the allocation of social investments on the ground (interview, Minister of Labor Caro-Figueroa). At the same time, governors implemented discretionary programs in strategic electoral bastions of the PJ to prevent voter disaffection.[46] The *conurbano* (greater metropolitan area) of Buenos Aires, a critical stronghold of the PJ, was rewarded with a special fund – the Conurbano Reparation Fund (FRHC) – that helped Governor Eduardo Duhalde (1991–9) feed a powerful machine through the discretionary allocation of public works and social programs (see Danani, Chiara, and Filc 1997; Levitsky 2003).

The national ministries of labor and social development did not distribute social benefits in the *conurbano*, despite being the largest metropolitan area and one especially hard-hit by unemployment, until the emergence of mobilization from below in the late 1990s (interviews, Amadeo; high official, Ministry of Labor). The area was viewed as "another territory" and the intervention of the national government there was perceived as a drop in the bucket (interview, Amadeo). Duhalde's FRHC funded a food program, the Life Plan, under the supervision of his wife. Reaching about 20 percent of the *conurbano*'s population, the Life Plan was distributed on the ground by 30,000 volunteer women (*manzaneras*) from low-income neighborhoods who formed a complex network of information and support for the Duhalde administration.

The principal role of the *manzaneras'* network, as well as PJ local party offices, was to identify discontent and respond accordingly to preserve the status quo (see Zaramberg 2004). The absence of electoral competition for outsiders – and the absence of other parties on the ground, which could denounce manipulation – facilitated the expansion of clientelism before the emergence of unemployed workers' movements, which

---

[45] Based on several interviews, program documents, and materials from the Secretariat of Social Development (1996; 1994; 1999).
[46] Sometimes funded with highly discretionary "emergency" transfers of the national treasury (ATNs) created by Menem.

confronted such abuses and amplified communities' frustrations with these practices. As suggested by the leader of an unemployed workers' organization that formed in the *conurbano* in the late 1990s:

The peronists are always present on the ground, with their local brokers, the social plans. They have thermometers and they control everything... In poor neighborhoods here, you can find 6 or 7 *basic units* [PJ party offices] and there is no single UCR *comite* [party office]. [Other parties] don't have thermometers... The peronists pick up the phone and say: "There's trouble here, things are getting nasty" ... and they intervene. (interview, unemployed leader # 3)

Overall, in the first decades of the new democracy, despite some failed attempts to expand broader nondiscretionary benefits, small-scale social assistance was provided to outsiders to maintain the status quo. The main reason for this was the absence of electoral competition and/or social mobilization. This scenario began to change in the late 1990s, as analyzed in Chapter 5.

Chile

The Augusto Pinochet dictatorship (1973–89) implemented sweeping market-oriented reforms (Etchemendy 2011; Schamis 1999; Silva 1996) and significant changes in social policy.[47] The dictatorship reorganized health care services, which had undergone significant expansion in the previous years, and privatized the pension system, becoming a worldwide pioneer in this area. The health care reform established free health care for the poorest populations, while all other outsiders paid according to their income. It also introduced private health care funds within social security health insurance, which were targeted to higher income workers. The military further eliminated employers' contributions to social security and reduced social expenditures.

The dictatorship implemented important changes in programs for outsiders. Aside from segmenting access to the health care system, Pinochet reduced the school meals program created by Frei, and expanded small-scale transfers to low-income households facing declining living conditions in the mid 1970s. Those transfers included workfare benefits, which were expanded dramatically in 1982 and 1983, during a deep economic crisis that prompted social protest. In the early 1980s, Pinochet gradually established a small program of family allowances that reached close to 29 percent of outsider children at the end of the dictatorship.

---

[47] There is a broad literature on Pinochet's social policy reforms. See Castiglioni (2002); Madrid (2003); Medlin (1999); Mesa-Lago (1994); Razcynski (2000).

The military, led by Pinochet, seized power in a context of popular mobilization with the goal of depoliticizing civil society and putting an end to transformations introduced by the left. Parties were banned, and leaders and activists were repressed, exiled, and murdered. The Pinochet dictatorship not only sought to prevent what the military understood as the political mobilization of the lower classes by "opportunistic politicians" (Scully 1995: 122), but its "cardinal objective" was to impose a long-term transformation by force that would "do away with the traditional party system" (Valenzuela and Valenzuela 1986: 192).

The market-oriented reforms Pinochet adopted initially produced high unemployment and poverty. When state downsizing began, and unemployment grew to two digits, the military extended small-scale workfare programs and noncontributory pensions. Further expansion of temporary employment programs took place after a dramatic collapse of the economy in 1983, which spawned widespread popular protest against Pinochet. Protests involved labor unions, groups of shantytown dwellers, and political parties, which further called for a return to democracy (Oxhorn 1995; Schneider 1995: 160; Scully 1995: 123).

As advanced in this study's framework, facing protests by previously activated popular sectors, the authoritarian incumbent – in this case a harsh military dictatorship – used both repression and discretionary provisions to quell unrest. Between 1983 and 1985, at least 200 people were killed by the military in demonstrations and hundreds were wounded, arrested, and tortured (see Schneider 1995: 182). Temporary workfare benefits were extended broadly and, as Huneeus argued, were implemented selectively. The military would cut benefits to punish unemployed workers who mobilized against the dictatorship; the most dramatic cuts occurred in areas where protest activity was most intense (2007a: 365). Social benefits were therefore used both to alleviate the harsh living conditions produced by the crisis and, by selectively excluding activists, to "repress opposition at the grassroots level" (Oxhorn 1995: 194–5). Both repression and the extension of social provisions – which could be selectively withdrawn to punish protestors – have been seen as major factors in reducing unrest (see Graham 1991: 17; Huneeus 2007).

Other benefits were also extended in the early 1980s, though their reach was more limited. In 1980, the military had sought to defuse international pressures by agreeing to conduct a plebiscite in 1988 to determine whether the autocratic regime would continue or whether elections would be held. Confronted with the imminent plebiscite, and facing dramatically high poverty rates, the dictatorship extended family allowances to extremely poor families. The program was further expanded after the economic crisis and after protest erupted in 1983. Family allowances were meaningful but relatively smaller in scale than what is here considered an expansion. By the time the new democratic elections were held, the program reached 29 percent of outsider children.[48]

Social policy initiatives launched by the dictatorship were designed by a conservative political current within the government, the *gremialistas*, originally formed by students at the Catholic University in 1965, after the DC youth movement had begun to actively organize the poor (see Etchemendy 2011; Huneeus 2007a: 231–2). *Gremialistas* sought to extend top-down ties to the poor with the goal to build support for the right. In their view, the right's inability to reach outsiders, especially since the extension of suffrage in the 1950s and 1960s, had facilitated the rise of the Christian Democrats and the expansion of the left, both of which had fostered runaway social mobilization. Benefits administered by local governments have been found to serve the development of support for future politicians of the Independent Democratic Union (UDI), the "political branch" of the *gremialista* current, which formed at the end of the dictatorship.

In sum, the dictatorship implemented harsh state-shrinking measures affecting both insiders and outsiders. It also created meaningful but discretionary social benefits for outsiders to deactivate mobilizations during the 1982–3 crisis and to face subsequent electoral challenges as the plebiscite approached. However, in contrast with cases involving a democratic incumbent, discretionary benefits and repression were fundamental tools the Pinochet dictatorship used to control mobilization and build support.

Mexico

The dramatic economic collapse produced by the debt crisis of 1982 affected Mexican politics and policy in fundamental ways. In an international climate that was favorable to the expansion of markets, President Miguel de la Madrid (1982–8) embarked on state adjustment to cope with the crisis, producing no meaningful compensatory social policy despite hardship. Following harsh austerity measures, Carlos Salinas (1988–94) launched a large social-investment fund, PRONASOL, soon

---

[48] Given the method of distributing benefits, by which municipalities received a quota of provisions they had to distribute to eligible households, which often exceeded this quota, it is likely that discretion affected the program's implementation.

after he assumed the presidency in 1988.[49] Estimates calculated for this project indicate an absence of high electoral competition for outsiders nationally in 1988 (Dataset of Elections). However, the unexpected rise of a challenger and the uncertainty about its subsequent growth motivated responses to secure and rebuild support for the PRI. In an authoritarian regime in which incumbents also resorted to fraud, repression, and intimidation to maintain the PRI's grip on power, PRONASOL constituted a visible initiative to appeal to outsiders – and other sectors – through highly discretionary and temporary provisions. As discussed later, aside from demonstrating the incumbent's concern for ameliorating poverty, PRONASOL sought to reconstitute the social bases of the PRI by integrating new community leaders emerging from PRONASOL's participatory implementation into the party structure.

After experiencing decades of uncontested power, with landslide victories in presidential and subnational elections, and enjoying supermajorities in Congress, the PRI faced serious electoral challenges in the late 1980s. Three factors have been linked to the erosion of the PRI's electoral power (see Collier 1992; Magaloni 2006). The first is the reaction of different segments of the electorate to the measures the PRI adopted to cope with the debt crisis. Some middle-class voters and businesspeople began to support the PAN more actively in the face of the anti-business rhetoric of President López Portillo (1976–82) and his statist measures, such as the nationalization of banks (Lujambio 2001: 76; Mizrahi 1994: 83). Voter dissatisfaction further grew with the social cost of the state adjustment measures the de la Madrid administration launched beginning in 1983, which contradicted the responses of his predecessor.

The second factor identified is the PRI's open use of fraud to ensure legislative supermajorities in 1985, further igniting voter disaffection (see Collier 1992 (Lujambio 2001: 77; Rodriguez and Ward 1995: 7). Finally, the PRI's delayed response to an earthquake that ravaged Mexico City and caused extensive material losses in 1985 raised popular discontent with the incumbent. Lack of prompt state responses propelled the surge of autonomous social organizations in Mexico City, which later coalesced in a popular movement, Assembly of Neighborhoods. This movement made demands for housing policy and mobilized against the PRI (see Bruhn 1997; Ramírez Sainz 1994).

[49] On PRONASOL, see Cornelius, Craig and Fox (1994), Dresser (1994) and Magaloni (2006).

Disaffection with the PRI fueled unprecedented electoral competition in the dominant party system. The availability of discontented voters undermined elite cohesion in the PRI (Bruhn 1997; Magaloni 2006). The Democratic Current, a PRI faction with strong ideological differences with De la Madrid's economic policies, found incentives to split as existing discontent raised chances of gaining electoral support outside the party (Bruhn 1997: 114; Magaloni 2006). In 1987, a few months before the elections, PRI politician Cuauhtémoc Cárdenas formed the National Democratic Front (FDN) – which later on became the Party of the Democratic Revolution (PRD) – in alliance with small parties that had tended to support the PRI. The FDN initially showed few chances of seriously challenging the PRI in the 1988 presidential election. In fact, the PRI leadership did not foresee electoral challenges until shortly before the elections, when public opinion polls – which were infrequent in Mexico – showed the unexpected growth of the FDN (Salinas quoted in Castañeda 1999: 265; interview, Cárdenas).

Facing electoral results that showed a dramatic decline in support, the PRI allegedly manipulated the returns to assign itself a 50-percent vote share, which generated strong reactions and postelection conflict. In this new context, the PRI lacked the legislative supermajorities of the past. Despite initial postelection conflict, the PAN negotiated legislative support for reform proposals that coincided with its pro-market agenda in exchange for enacting institutional changes to make elections more transparent, which helped push democratization forward.[50]

In the more competitive environment, and seeking to enhance support for his government, Salinas managed to manufacture a new coalition through the distribution of rents from privatizations and by incorporating new groups who would benefit from market reforms into his government (see Gibson 1997; Kessler 1998). At the same time, Salinas sought to revamp the PRI to make it electorally effective in a more competitive environment. PRONASOL, which was announced in Salinas' inaugural speech and implemented immediately after he assumed office, was critical to this goal.[51]

Aside from mobilizing the vote through distribution of targeted benefits, Salinas sought to recast the PRI's connection to society. Existing organizations mediating such linkages (such as PRI-affiliated peasant and labor unions) as well as some local politicians were perceived as an

[50] On these reforms, see Magaloni (2006).
[51] Reproduced in *La Jornada*, December 2, 1988. PRONASOL initially concentrated some existing social investment, and later received further funding from privatizations.

obstacle to the future electoral success of the PRI. The view in the Salinas administration was that low-income communities wanted "a different type of relationship than the one traditionally established between the PRI and the poor" (interview, Cordera Campos, PRONASOL's Council).

To forge a new relationship with lower-income communities, PRONASOL was initially coordinated from the office of the president, bypassing local administrations and other traditional channels of distribution on the ground. Furthermore, the implementation of the program's various schemes was done through PRONASOL, solidarity committees formed by local communities. These solidarity committees were in charge of performing different tasks: proposing and implementing projects, and selecting beneficiaries. It is estimated that 100,000 solidarity committees formed between 1989 and 1994.[52]

Solidarity committees interacted directly with PRONASOL officials. Despite differences in the operation of the various schemes, the standard procedure was that solidarity committees submitted project proposals that were voted on in popular assemblies and approved by PRONASOL officials. PRONASOL provided "fast-flowing" resources for these community projects in order to demonstrate its power and effectiveness vis-à-vis the local vested interests and party politicians (interview, director of PRONASOL scheme). This direct connection between authorities and communities can be seen further in the way presidential involvement worked. As noted by the director of one of PRONASOL's schemes, "[When he visited communities,] who did the president meet with? With PRONASOL committees, not with local politicians" (interview).

PRONASOL officials were further expected to facilitate the incorporation of community leaders into the PRI to boost the party's electoral strength. Solidarity committees helped PRONASOL staff identify and link up with such community leaders to "absorb them into the PRI" (interview, regional director of social organization, PRONASOL) and increase the party's electoral power by embedding it within the community. Although the then-director of PRONASOL maintained that identifying new leadership was "not an intention of the program," he noted that it was rather "a natural outcome" as "leadership rapidly emerged with the formation of committees" and communities "appointed to the committees the people they found most representative" (interview, Carlos Rojas). Given the relevance of solidarity committees, special PRONASOL schemes were developed with the goal to foment social participation in

---

[52] See Consejo Consultivo del Programa Nacional de Solidaridad (1994: 10-11).

communities in which committee formation was challenging (interview, regional director of social organization).

PRONASOL's projects were implemented selectively. Discretion operated at two levels: first, in the selection of the communities and projects that would be funded, and second, in the selection of groups of beneficiaries within the communities. Interviews with directors of PRONASOL schemes indicate that resources were distributed according to "the political map" in the communities rather than according to programmatic eligibility rules.[53]

The selection of beneficiaries was often left in the hands of solidarity committees, and followed no clear rules. There is no systematic data on whose projects were approved, how PRONASOL mobilized communities to form solidarity committees, or which individuals benefited. With respect to beneficiary selection, the former director of PRONASOL suggests, "People are wise. We told them, 'there are fifty scholarships for this school' and it is impressive the way, the neatness, with which they would choose the beneficiaries" (interview, Rojas).

PRONASOL was launched by the incumbent of a nondemocratic regime facing unprecedented electoral competition, especially from disaffected middle- and upper-income voters, and some – though not high – competition for outsiders, especially in urban areas.[54] According to Rolando Cordera-Campos, PRONASOL was designed "in the heat of the [1988] campaign and the emergence of Cárdenas as a real alternative candidate" (interview, Cordera Campos). The fact that the political regime was nondemocratic and that the opposition – though growing – was still weak, facilitated the implementation of centralized, discretionary social programs through PRONASOL. These schemes were deployed according to the priorities of the Salinista leadership in the party, and did not develop long-term commitments between the state and beneficiaries. In fact, it was not even among Salinas's priorities to have solidarity committees active after public works and investments had finished (interview, Rojas), and most of them died out. The goals were to reconnect the state

---

[53] See Díaz-Cayeros, Estévez, and Magaloni (2007). I interviewed the director of PRONASOL; members of the advisory board; advisors and staff; as well as the heads of the following schemes: Social Concertation; Enterprises in Solidarity; Women in Solidarity; Jornaleros; Social Organization.

[54] No ecological data are available on the distribution of votes for the 1988 election. Municipal elections show dominance of the PRI in districts where outsiders are the majority of the population. Salinas recognized that the PRI lost in all 40 districts of Mexico City, and lost support in Michoacán and Baja California (see Salinas in Castañeda 1999: 267–8).

with communities through the program, to integrate new leaders into the PRI, and to recreate the party's ties with society in new ways. The relevance of PRONASOL as a key component of the president's political agenda was clear when Luis Donaldo Colosio, president of the PRI (1988–92) and secretary of social development (1992–3), was selected to succeed Salinas, who recognized Colosio "for his work with the social bases through PRONASOL," among other accomplishments (Salinas in Castañeda 1999: 290).

3.3 CONCLUSIONS

This chapter has shown that during most of the twentieth century, outsiders remained largely unprotected while social security benefits were first extended to workers in the formal labor market and later on deepened, with new benefits being added to those that already existed. It also showed that expansion of large, nondiscretionary benefits for outsiders occurred only under democratic regimes with electoral competition for outsiders. Finally, it demonstrated that authoritarian incumbents had no strong incentives for expansion of large-scale nondiscretionary benefits to prevent these dynamics from undermining support for the regime. Yet incumbents in authoritarian regimes with some electoral competition for outsiders or social mobilization were likely to launch discretionary, sometimes large, and often temporary benefits. Incumbents in these regimes generally sought to address mobilization from below or some electoral competition also with other strategies, such as intimidation of challengers, purging of social movements and parties, and repression. These tools are not available to democratic regimes, in which national incumbents cannot manipulate institutions to their advantage, utilize repression as a critical power-maintaining strategy, and go unpunished.

Table 3.2 combines the type of regime with the presence of competition and mobilization, and defines the likely response of incumbents in the face of each combination of political conditions. Each of these scenarios is illustrated with examples discussed in the preceding narratives.

The framework advanced here thus helps us to understand the evolution of social policy for outsiders. It was not the populist-left or left parties that expanded benefits, but rather those that faced competition or mobilization within democratic regimes. Expansion did not occur at particular moments, that is, during market reforms, or at the time of consolidation of benefits for insiders; it took place when the conditions motivating incumbents to focus on outsiders were present. For example,

TABLE 3.2 *Variety of Social Policy for Outsiders, Selected Countries,*
ca. 1930s–1990s

		Regime Type	
		Democratic	Authoritarian[a]
Electoral Competition for Outsiders/ Social Mobilization	Yes[a]	*Large, nondiscretionary* Argentina 1940s (health care); Chile 1960s–70s (health care)	*Discretionary, often relatively large* Brazil 1970s (pensions, primary care); Chile 1970s–80s (transfers)
	No	*Small, often discretionary* Argentina in the 1990s	*No significant initiatives* Argentina 1955–73; 1974–83* Mexico until 1960s** Chile until 1960s Brazil until 1960s

[a] Within authoritarian regimes, social mobilization and electoral competition for outsiders are not high (unless there is a transition to democratic elections) due to constraints on organization and elections.
* Initiatives were enacted in 1973–4, but implementation did not happen.
** I am not considering land reform.

in the 1980s and 1990s, the presence or absence of mobilization from below, electoral competition for outsiders, and the nature of the political regime had a significant influence on whether governments created protections for outsiders while implementing market reforms, and on what kind of benefits were extended. In Chile and Mexico, these benefits were discretionary and/or temporary; in Brazil they were broad-reaching (analyzed in Chapter 4), and Argentina did not produce any meaningful innovation during market reforms.

Social programs for outsiders did not coincide either with times of growth or crises, which happened at different moments throughout the twentieth century but did not give impetus to expansion. Though schematic and simplified, we can see that despite the constraints imposed on social policy by limited industrialization, the lack of expansion of protections was to a great extent a political matter in which governments invested in social programs for outsiders in different ways, choosing to create policies that were either discretionary or nondiscretionary, permanent or temporary, large or small-scale, depending on political factors rather than on the stage of development of social security benefits, their economic resources, or the availability of models of social protections to imitate and adopt.

4

Social Mobilization, Electoral Competition for Outsiders, and Inclusive Social Policy in Brazil

4.1 INTRODUCTION

In the twentieth century, Brazil exhibited one of the highest levels of income inequality in Latin America and in the world.[1] The social insurance system mirrored this inequality as it catered only to insiders, with some occupations receiving extremely generous benefits.[2] Against this backdrop, social policy innovations for outsiders were adopted and implemented gradually beginning in the late 1980s. Through these initiatives, governments established a universal health care system; broad-reaching pensions for rural workers, low-income seniors and the disabled; and a number of income-support programs for children conditional on school attendance, such as the prominent Bolsa Família established in 2003 (see Table 4.1).

This remarkable expansion of services and transfers has helped reduce inequality and child labor, increase school enrollment, and boost consumption benefiting low-income rural localities in particular.[3] Furthermore, these policies have established national and local policy councils for social movement organizations, NGOs, state officials, service providers, and labor unions to engage in policy consultation, deliberation, and/or oversight, contributing to policy learning and transparency.[4]

Aside from reaching deeply excluded populations, these policy innovations are puzzling in light of the predominant view in the literature

[1] On the characterization of inequality in Brazil, see Lieberman (2003).
[2] See Chapter 3 and Oliveira and Texeira (1985).
[3] See Delgado and Cardoso Jr (2000); IPEA (2006); Jaccoud et al. (2005); Schwarzer and Querino (2002); Zucco (2008).
[4] See Avritzer (2009); Coelho and Nobre (2004).

TABLE 4.1 *Social Policy Expansion and the Inclusive Model in Brazil, ca. 2010*

Policy Area	Scope of Coverage	Benefit Level	Participation in Implementation	Dates of Expansion
Pensions	High	High	Moderate	Rural pensions: 1988 (adoption); 1991–2 (implementation)
	79% of outsiders aged 65+	Equal to minimum pension of insiders	National deliberative councils; subnational deliberative and oversight councils	Social assistance pensions: 1988 (adoption); 1996 (implementation)
Health Care	High	High	High	Single Health System (SUS): 1988 (adoption); 1993 (gradual implementation)
	100% of outsiders	Free access to broad range of services and treatments	Deliberative national council; municipal deliberative and oversight councils	
Income Support	High	Moderate	Low	Bolsa Escola: 2001 (adoption); 2001–2 (implementation)
	72% of school-age outsider children	Less than 20% of the poverty line for a family with two children	Municipal oversight councils, most of which are not specific to transfer programs	Bolsa Família: 2003–4 (adoption); 2003–6 (implementation)

Notes: Dates of Expansion refers to the adoption of a policy and the launching of implementation. Characterization of Income Support refers to Bolsa Família, which replaced Bolsa Escola in 2003.
Sources and Measures: See Appendix 1.

that portrays Brazil's nascent democracy in the 1990s as one dominated by patronage and discretion. Scholars argue that fragmented interests (Weyland 1996a), an inchoate party system (Mainwaring 1995), and existing political institutions, especially open-list proportional representation and federalism (Ames 2002), discouraged the adoption of all-encompassing equity-oriented reforms and reproduced the status quo within a highly unequal system.

Given these adverse circumstances, why did incumbents establish large-scale nondiscretionary benefits for outsiders? And why did incumbents create an inclusive model of health care, pensions, and income support, with broad coverage and some level of participatory implementation?

To explain these outcomes, I argue that mobilization from below and electoral competition for outsiders – both of which occurred at different points in time – propelled incumbents to launch social programs for outsiders that tempered the existing social policy divide. There were two major moments of expansion. In the late 1980s, conservative incumbents adopted health care and pension innovations in response to pressure from coalitions of social movements and labor unions (SMCs) demanding these reforms. Incumbents sought to dampen pressures, avoid a decline in their popularity that might occur if these social policy initiatives were not adopted, and ultimately claim credit for them. Negotiations between movement leaders, state officials, legislators, and sometimes the president resulted in the design of social programs with inclusive benefits. Yet implementation faced initial delays owing to resistance from strong entrenched interests and the absence of adequate funding. Social mobilization persuaded President Fernando Collor de Mello (1990–2) and his successor, Itamar Franco (1992–5), to effectively start rolling the new benefits and services.

Social mobilization around income-support programs, on the other hand, was weak at this time; the largest social movements focused on poverty centered their efforts on the agrarian reform – which they believed would reduce rural and urban poverty – as well as on food distribution. These movements did not press for the creation of income transfers, a proposal advanced, at the time, only by some politicians of the left-wing Workers' Party (PT).

A second moment of social policy expansion occurred in the context of intense electoral competition for outsiders that emerged around the 2002 presidential elections. For the first time, the Workers' Party (PT) appeared as a credible challenger capable of effectively reaching low-income voters previously locked in by machine parties, challenging these parties' continuity in power, as discussed later. In response to the growth of the PT prior to the 2002 elections, local machines pressured their allies in the national government and mobilized in Congress to create taxes and social programs that would allow them to offset the appeals of PT candidates – who promised to expand social policy if elected – and maintain their bases of support. Income transfers were initially launched within this context of intense electoral competition. After winning the 2002 presidential election, the PT sought to consolidate support among outsiders by extending income transfers more massively. In response to demands from the social movements allied to the party, it created inclusive benefits, as predicted in this book's analytic framework.

In the next section of this chapter, I describe the evolution of the main factors accounting for social policy expansion since democratization through 2010: electoral competition for outsiders and mobilization from below. I then show how these factors created incentives for both conservative and left-wing incumbent coalitions to launch social policies for outsiders, and I characterize and explain the policies that were established. To facilitate the presentation and to assess cases where incumbents did not expand social policy despite the existence of a deep social policy divide, I examine each administration since the democratic transition, the incentives incumbents faced regarding expansion, and the responses they launched – or the proposals for expansion they ignored – across each policy area and why. The final section of this chapter explores alternative explanations for policy expansion and the social policy models. Two key points emerge from this discussion: (a) social policy expansion in Brazil occurred before the commodity boom, and was thus not driven by it, and (b) the left parties, though growing electorally, were not the main players driving social policy expansion before the 2000s. As presented in this chapter, incumbents supported by conservative coalitions and later on by left-wing coalitions adopted social policy innovations.

4.2 ELECTORAL COMPETITION FOR OUTSIDERS AND SOCIAL MOBILIZATION, 1989–2010

Electoral Competition for Outsiders

Electoral competition for outsiders was not a feature of presidential elections in Brazil until 2002. Between 1989, when Fernando Collor de Mello won the first direct presidential election in the new democracy, and 1998, outsiders tended to vote for candidates supported by conservative machine parties.[5] These included the Liberal Front Party (PFL), which was founded by former politicians of the National Renewal Alliance (ARENA),[6] as well as the Brazilian Democratic Movement Party (PMDB). Even if Collor de Mello created his own electoral vehicle to compete in the 1989 elections, machine parties mobilized the smashing support he received from outsiders in the runoff.[7]

The Brazilian Social Democracy Party (PSDB), which split from the PMDB in the late 1980s forming a centrist party that brought Fernando Henrique Cardoso to the presidency in 1994 and 1998, lacked a broad popular support base (see Samuels and Zucco 2012). To win office, Cardoso allied with the PFL and the PMDB (in 1998), as well as with other smaller machine parties, which allowed him to reach outsiders broadly.

Between 1989 and 2002, when it finally won the presidency, the left-wing Workers' Party (PT) came second in every presidential election. Until 2002, the PT did not form coalitions with non-left parties and had less than 11 percent of the seats in Congress. In the 1980s and 1990s, the PT drew most of its support from middle-class voters and those organized in labor and social movements, primarily in relatively wealthier metropolitan areas in the south and southeast of the country (Hunter 2010; Keck 1992). Before the party's territorial expansion in the late 1990s and more prominently in the 2000s, its inability to mobilize outsider voters throughout the country related to the lack of campaign resources and presence on the ground.[8] As PT politicians noted, during campaigns the party would organize caravans to connect with voters. Yet those contacts could not credibly compete with the steady presence of machine party politicians on the ground.[9]

Figure 4.1 depicts the absence of electoral competition for outsider voters until 2002. Using pre-election survey data from Datafolha, I identify those respondents with household incomes below five times the minimum wage as outsiders.[10] Until 2002, the vote margin between the two

[5] The 1989 elections were the first in which illiterates were enfranchised.

[6] ARENA was the pro-military party created by the dictatorship (1964–85). It was based on elite parties rooted in rural areas, such as the PDS and the UDN. See Grinberg (2009); Jenks (1979); and Kinzo (1988).

[7] Eighteen parties competed in the first round.

[8] See Boas (2010) and Hunter (2010) on the PT's campaigns and their transformations.

[9] See *O Globo*, March 31, 1998.

[10] I work with the survey data sets for the 1994 and 1998 elections. Vote intention of respondents in households with incomes below two times and between two and five times the minimum wage are comparable to the ones presented in Figure 4.1. More disaggregated income data was not available for the other two elections.

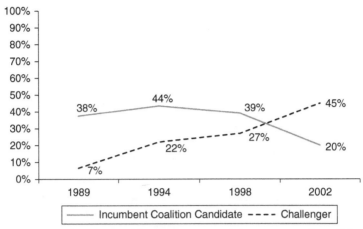

FIGURE 4.1 Vote intention of low-income voters for most-voted candidates in presidential elections, Brazil, 1989–2002.

Note: First-round elections. Incumbent coalition candidate: Collor (1989); Cardoso (1994 and 1998); Serra (2002).

Challenger: Lula (PT) 1989–2002.

Source: Datafolha 1989–2002 (1989 and 1994 data sets from Roper archive; 1998 and 2002 results from Datafolha's website accessed 2010).

most voted parties among these respondents was at least ten points and the incumbent coalition candidate won the most support, both of which indicate the absence of electoral competition for outsider voters. Note that in 1989, eighteen parties competed in the first round and machine parties supported several candidates. Yet these conservative machines supported Collor in the runoff election, and for that reason I label him as the incumbent coalition candidate.

Similar measures with ecological electoral data further describe this pattern (Figure 4.2). According to these data, electoral competition for outsiders was not present until 2002, when Lula won broad support from outsiders, defeating the incumbent candidate from the PSDB-led coalition. As in other cases analyzed in this book, electoral competition is measured as the proportion of outsider districts (municipalities) in which: (a) the margin of difference between the first and second party is less than ten points (close difference), and/or (b) the challenger who was seeking to gain outsider support comes first (challenger victory). As indicated in Chapter 2, there is electoral competition for outsiders if the proportion of districts with (a) and/or (b) is at least 50 percent of the total universe of outsider districts or if 50 percent of the outsider population in these districts experiences competition. As shown in Figure 4.2, electoral

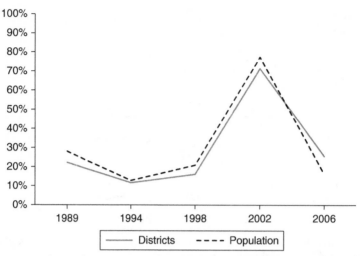

FIGURE 4.2 Electoral competition for outsiders in presidential elections, Brazil, 1989–2006 (% outsider districts and population in outsider districts with electoral competition).
Sources: Electoral data obtained from Zucco (2009) socioeconomic data from UNDP (2000). See Appendix 3 for the classification of outsider districts. For 1989 and 2002, I measure the runoff.

competition took place in 2002 in 71 percent of outsider districts and Lula, the credible challenger, won in 57 percent of these districts in the runoff.

Social Mobilization

Social mobilization from below flourished in Brazil's new democracy and was critical for social policy adoption and implementation through the 1980s and 1990s. As discussed in Chapter 3, new and long-standing social movements, labor unions, and civil society groups[11] began to mobilize actively for political and social changes during the democratic transition in the 1970s and 1980s.[12]

Left-wing and church militants were critical to the initial emergence of several of these movements beginning in the 1960s. Left-wing activists were often linked to the Brazilian Communist Party (PCB), which was

---

[11] On the new unionism, see Keck (1989, 1992); Seidman (1994). On the rural workers' unions and movements, see Houtzager (1998, 1997); Maybury-Lewis (1994); Novaes (1991); on urban movements, see Escorel (1999); Gohn (2003); Kowarick (1994); Mainwaring (1989); Sader (1988).
[12] See Collier (1999: 134–8); Skidmore (1989).

banned until the end of the dictatorship in the 1980s and had been perse-cuted in the past (Chilcote 1974: 94). Unable to compete in the electoral arena and constrained by electoral institutions that limited the franchise of the poor, permitting voter manipulation, the party's strategy centered on the formation of social movements and the penetration of existing ones to pursue social and political change. In the late 1960s, this strategy was intensified, and party militants focused on strengthening existing or forming new students', peasants', and women's movements, as well as on mobilizing professional groups around specific issues, such as doctors for health care reform.[13] The PCB sought to expand social organization as a necessary step toward political change, especially to attain the full exten-sion of the franchise (Chilcote 1974: 76).

The Catholic Church also set out to organize low-income communi-ties beginning in the 1960s. This deep involvement in community orga-nizing was partly led by priests and lay Catholic movements sympathetic to liberation theology's commitment to the poor. Ecclesiastical base com-munities (CEBs) were formed in the 1970s to improve the living condi-tions of the urban poor. Catholic activism also aimed at counterbalancing the left's expansion in rural areas, where it actively participated in the formation of rural unions.[14]

Ties among these groups and labor unions grew during the demo-cratic transition, contributing to the unprecedented upsurge of social mobilization. Left-wing and Catholic militants came to have similar agendas centered on mobilizing society for democracy and social rights, and often coalesced around specific movements, such as those linked to popular education, health care, and rural issues (Abrantes and Almeida 2002: 24–5; Chilcote 1974: 161; Houtzager 1998; Sader 1988). Activism was particularly strong in the metropolitan area of São Paulo, where social movements and CEBs became important allies of militant indus-trial unions in the 1970s (see Keck 1989; 1992). In 1980, when the dic-tatorship allowed for less restricted party competition, these unions and several social movements founded the PT to advance their interests in the partisan arena (Keck 1992; Meneguello 1989), and in 1983, they founded the "social movement" union confederation, CUT, which played a critical role in advancing social policy claims (see Seidman 1994).

The three social movement coalitions discussed next have been critical for the expansion of health care services and pensions.

---

[13] On the role PCB activists played, see Chilcote (1974); Coletti (1998); Escorel (1999); Houtzager (1998); Maybury-Lewis (1994).
[14] See Della Cava (1989); Mainwaring (1989).

Health Reform Movement (HRM)

The health reform movement (HRM) advocated the creation of a universal, participatory, and decentralized health care system, the Single Health System (SUS).[15] This broad movement was composed of public health doctors, health care–related organizations, labor unions representing health care workers, social organizations, CEBs, and the CUT (Abrantes and Almeida 2002: 24–5; Escorel, Nascimento, and Elder 2005; Vargas Côrtes 2009: 134).

The core of the HRM was formed in the early 1970s out of a group of public health doctors concerned about deleterious health conditions and the weaknesses of the existing health care system, which they perceived as highly centralized, exclusionary, and dominated by the interests of private providers and social security agencies (Escorel 1999). These doctors sought to universalize health care, with a special focus on preventive and primary-care services. In the 1970s, they founded two organizations that were critical for the articulation of the HRM and constituted important venues for the discussion and dissemination of health care reform proposals: the Brazilian Center for Health Studies (CEBES), and the Association of Graduate Students in Public Health (ABRASCO) (Escorel et al. 2005: 67–8; Fleury 1997).

Through these organizations, doctors extended ties to local health care movements, CEBs, and labor unions. The HRM emerged through these linkages and developed two major components: one formed mainly by public health doctors linked to the PCB, which sought to change health care policy from within the state, and another that was more invested in participation and grassroots mobilization around health care reform and was originally linked to local health care movements and Catholic activists, especially in metropolitan areas (Abrantes and Almeida 2002: 24–5; interview, Kayano). Each of these two components prioritized different aspects of and strategies for reform, but both worked together on a common proposal for a single health care system for insiders and outsiders administered by municipal governments and enjoying broad levels of participation and social oversight.

As discussed in Chapter 3, public health doctors who would later form the HRM gained positions in the state in the mid-1970s, when the

---

[15] The movement is generally referred to as Movimento Sanitário, Sanitaristas, or Movimento da Reforma Sanitária. In order to highlight the fact that the movement was not formed only by public health doctors, or by *sanitaristas*, I call it the Health Reform Movement. See Abrantes and Almeida (2002); Arretche (2005); Avritzer (2009); Campos (2005); Escorel (1999); Escorel and Bloch (2005); Escorel et al. (2005); Fleury (1997); Labra (2005); Rehem (2003); Rodrigues Neto (1997).

military launched some basic preventive and primary care initiatives. As the democratic transition unfolded, and opposition parties could run in more competitive elections, public health doctors further tried to influence newly elected authorities and gain appointments in local governments to pursue their agenda for reform through institutional channels.

CONTAG and Social Assistance Movements

Two coalitions advocated pension expansion, the Confederation of Agricultural Workers (CONTAG) and a coalition of social organizations and social workers. CONTAG proposed the universalization of rural pensions, equal access for female rural workers, improvements in benefit levels, and lowering the retirement age. These requests were backed by the workers' confederation CUT, which demanded improvements in pensions for formal-sector workers. Both labor organizations formed a powerful lobby for pension reform. In the late 1980s, CONTAG comprised twenty-two rural workers' federations representing close to 10 million affiliates (Pereira 1997: 6), and had extensive experience interacting with public officials due to its role in service provision, as described in Chapter 3.

Associations of people with disabilities and social workers were fundamental promoters of the expansion of old-age and disability pensions.[16] These organizations engaged in intense lobbying to persuade legislators to universalize these benefits. Unlike CONTAG and the HRM, this coalition had not developed strong ties with powerful unions, which could have amplified their struggle for universal benefits. In the 1980s, social workers had not yet developed the influence they would acquire over the next two decades as a consequence of the gradual expansion of social services and the growth of public-service workers within the CUT (see Silva 2001).

4.3 DYNAMICS OF EXPANSION AND POLICY CHOICE: SOCIAL MOBILIZATION AND INCLUSIVE HEALTH CARE SERVICES AND PENSIONS

The writing of a new constitution in the late 1980s provided social movements with an invaluable opportunity to achieve the adoption of new social rights and benefits. Through mobilization of public opinion and information campaigns as well as lobbying, persuasion, and pressure on

---

[16] These included NGOs and professional associations of social workers.

legislators, SMCs were able to get their proposals approved. The implementation of new benefits and services was slow, however. Congress had to approve ordinary legislation to translate new social rights into specific programs, which was fraught with delays as well as with attempts by vested interests and their allied politicians to limit their reach. Through constant lobbying of legislators and policy makers, protests, and demonstrations, as well legal action to enforce new rights, SMCs managed to pressure the state to start implementing these new benefits in the 1990s. Next, I analyze how the politics of policy adoption and design across different administrations resulted in inclusive pensions and health care services, and I show how social mobilization played a fundamental role in motivating these policy changes.

The José Sarney Administration (1985–1990)

In 1985, President José Sarney, a former military supporter, assumed office after the sudden death of President-Elect Tancredo Neves of the PMDB. Negotiations in Congress had resulted in the selection of Neves and Sarney to lead the first democratic government after more than twenty years of military rule. Pro-democratic movements and politicians vehemently contested the absence of direct elections, launching mass demonstrations for direct elections in 1984. Facing a highly mobilized civil society, and concerned about his legitimacy, Sarney promised to address a multitude of political and social demands.

Sarney initiated major changes in health care policy in response to demands posed by the HRM. He established universal access to the existing social security health care system and announced the implementation of the Decentralized Universal Health System (SUDS), which would integrate services for insiders and outsiders under the administration of the states. Sarney also appointed key movement leaders to his administration, who advanced health care reform from their positions of power in the state. HRM's ties to the government were not new; some of its members had contributed to the elaboration of Neves' campaign program regarding health care policy (Rodrigues Neto 1997).

Both universal access to health care services and the SUDS were introduced through ministerial resolution, which limited resistance to these innovations. SUDS encountered several opponents, including the bureaucracy of the Institute for Social Security Health Insurance (INAMPS) – which would be transferred to the states for the implementation of

SUDS – and private hospitals, which preferred to negotiate contracts with the national government as decentralized negotiation with the states could reduce their bargaining power. SUDS also faced resistance from the PFL leadership, who had a strong preference for market provision and limited state intervention, and who feared that decentralization would empower its coalition partner, the PMDB, which governed all but one state and would therefore control implementation of SUDS.[17]

With these measures, Sarney sought to mitigate social activism for health care reform and gain support among social movements. The HRM was divided over SUDS, however. While some activists saw it as a first step in the establishment of the universal system, others considered it a potential obstacle toward municipalization, which the HRM promoted vigorously. Implementation of SUDS was nonetheless very slow moving, and the fundamental features of new health care system consonant with the HRM's goals were approved by the Constituent Assembly.

The Constituent Assembly
The most important institutional reform facilitating social policy adoption was the writing of a new constitution, which the Movement for Brazilian Democracy (MDB) had championed throughout the democratic transition. Social movements perceived the Constituent Assembly as a critical venue to achieve their social policy goals and participated actively (Michiles 1989). To maximize their capacity for influencing the new constitution, social movements pursued different strategies. As a result of intense lobbying, they were allowed to submit popular amendments to the first draft of the constitution backed by at least 30,000 signatures (Michiles 1989: 104). This provision allowed civil society groups not only to propose changes to the constitution, but also to show legislators existing support for a number of polemic issues, such as the agrarian reform.[18]

SMCs also engaged in intense lobbying in the assembly. Large organizations with offices throughout the country and with broad membership bases, such as the Conference of Bishops (CNBB), the CUT, and CONTAG, had permanent staff – including hundreds of activists – devoted to lobbying and attending sessions. Their capillarity, moreover, allowed these organizations to gather signatures and organize mobilization activities to pressure legislators in their own districts, a tactic legislators often feared. Lobbying

---

[17] See "O PFL pede revogação da portaria de Archer," OG, May 18, 1988.
[18] "Emendas populares obtem mais de 11.2 milhões de assinaturas," JdoB, August 16, 1987.

activities were often accompanied by informational campaigns about the movements' demands, as well as demonstrations.[19]

Two new actors emerged in opposition to the social and labor reforms SMCs advanced: the Rural Democratic Union (UDR), an association of big farmers, which mobilized actively in defense of the status quo regarding rural issues, and the Centrão (Big Center), a bloc formed by conservative legislators of the PMDB, PFL, and PSD. These parties opposed what they defined as the "manipulation" of the Constituent Assembly by organized groups and claimed to represent the people's "average will" (*vontade media*) (Rodrigues Neto 1997: 81).[20]

In the face of large-scale social mobilization for health care and pension reforms, legislators found it more costly to block these policies than to negotiate and approve reforms that satisfied movements' demands. Although these innovations were significant, it was clear for social movement leaders, legislators, and opponents to reforms that some aspects of new social policies would have to be determined by Congress in ordinary legislation, which left room for potential changes, and for implementation delays.

Health Care

By the time the Constituent Assembly convened, the HRM had already achieved substantial access to decision-making processes. The health care reform project that was debated in the assembly's committees had been previously elaborated by social movement and state representatives in the Committee for Health Reform established by Sarney, which largely endorsed the main features of the new system proposed at the massive Eighth National Health Conference convened by the state in 1986 and attended by 4,000 representatives of social movements, labor unions, service providers, and state officials (Escorel et al. 2005: 78).[21] These were fundamental antecedents to the debates for the approval of the SUS in the Constituent Assembly.[22]

The assembly provided ample opportunities for social movements to advocate the adoption of SUS through institutional channels. Members of the HRM held positions in health care agencies at different levels of

---

[19] See "CUT arma defesa dos itens pro-trabalhador," JdB, July 23, 1988. See also Michiles (1989).
[20] On the UDR's lobby, see *Jornal de Brasilia*, May 8, 1988, 3; *Jornal da Tarde*, May 13, 1988, 7; and *Jornal do Brasil*, May 8, 1988, 4.
[21] Health Conferences were regularly held in Brazil since the Vargas era. See Escorel and Bloch (2005).
[22] Activist Eleutério Rodrigues Neto quoted in RADIS (2008: 14).

government, which provided them with strong linkages to legislators. Moreover, some members of the movement ran for legislative office and pushed for health care reform from within the assembly. Particularly favorable to the proposals of the HRM were the left parties, PT and PCB – which had few representatives in the Constituent Assembly – and the leftist branch of the PMDB, the largest party at the time. Yet legislators were not always aligned to their party leadership or blocs within parties. They often held individual positions forming what Cardoso called "kaleidoscopes" within parties (2006: 112) that permitted the formation of unexpected coalitions. In the case of health care, the capacity of the HRM to establish linkages and mobilize support across partisan blocs facilitated the negotiations toward the approval of the SUS. In particular, the government leader in the lower chamber, conservative Carlos Sant'Anna, mobilized the support of dozens of Centrão legislators for SUS.[23]

Social movements also formed the National Plenary of Health Organizations for the Constituent Assembly, which was composed of 200 organizations that advised and lobbied legislators, attended meetings, organized information campaigns, and collected signatures for the amendment proposing the SUS (see Abrantes and Almeida 2002: 35; RADIS 2008: 18). Movement members also served as special advisors to legislators throughout the process of elaboration of the constitution's social chapter, which dealt with health care.

Opposition to the SUS stemmed from vested interests who benefited from the existing system, particularly the Brazilian Federation of Hospitals (FBH), and the association of private health insurance (ABRANGE), which principally complained about what they perceived as the "statist" nature of the initial SUS project, involving the state's ability to (a) expropriate private hospitals – a measure not agreed to within the HRM that was dropped from the project; and (b) regulate the private provision of benefits by making contracts between providers and the state a matter of public law. Another source of opposition came from Centrão politicians, who rejected the creation of corporate taxes to fund SUS.[24]

Private for-profit interests, which mobilized close to 1,000 lobbyists during the treatment of health care reform, developed strong connections with legislators in the Centrão through which they pushed for changes to

---

[23] See "Um aliado no Centrão," JdaT, May 17, 1988.
[24] See Assembleia Nacional Constituinte 1988; "Centrão negocia texto para a ordem social," FdSP, May 13, 1988; "Seis pontos provocam polemica no capítulo," GM, May 17, 1988.

the constitution's draft.[25] Their power increased substantially when the Centrão legislators managed to alter the rules by which the constitution would be voted and submitted their own alternative draft. In this version, they reduced the state's role within the SUS, rejected municipalization, and refused to decide on new sources of revenue for the new system.

In spite of opposition, and as a result of negotiations, legislators eventually approved the HRM's inclusive health care system. Not only was the HRM's cause more popular, but the HRM also appeared more powerful, well organized, and connected than the private health care sector's lobby in the eyes of legislators,[26] which discouraged them from blocking SUS. As Centrão's legislator, Andrada, stated at the time, his bloc's views did not prevail because Centrão's "base-level organization was lacking."[27]

The ability of the HRM to build new alliances also contributed to the passage of SUS. According to one of its leaders, Sergio Arouca, the HRM convinced governors who benefited from the SUDS to press their legislators to support the new health care system.[28] Ironically, although part of the HRM initially regarded the SUDS as an obstacle to the implementation of the SUS – as it did not municipalize the system but rather decentralized it to the states – its earlier adoption created an opening to find new allies who opposed the Centrão's attempt to alter the health reform proposal.[29]

The inclusive system that provided universal, uniform, and comprehensive (i.e., preventive, primary-care, inpatient, and high-complexity) health services and involved community participation was approved with the absence of one critical factor: adequate funding. Though the new constitution established that SUS would be funded with 30 percent of payroll contributions to social security, special taxes, and contributions of states and municipalities, funding proved a complex problem, as discussed ahead.

Pensions

CONTAG formed a powerful interest group, promoting and negotiating the reform of rural pensions.[30] Before the Constituent Assembly,

---

[25] "Como trabalham os lobbistas da medicina," JdaT, May 17, 1988.
[26] Legislator Carlos Mosconi (PMDB-MG) quoted in RADIS (2008: 16).
[27] "Foi alterada a atuação do estado," *GM*, May 18, 1988.
[28] Sergio Arouca, HRM leader quoted in RADIS (2008: 21).
[29] "Saúde ja começa a movimentar a constituinte," CB, May 5, 1988.
[30] See also Barbosa (2008) and Houtzager (1998). See "Projeto prevê extensão da Previdência a todos os trabalhadores rurais," JdB, January 22, 1986.

CONTAG had established fluid contacts with legislators and the president, who participated in CONTAG-organized meetings and conferences and promised to support its social policy demands. CONTAG pressed for reforms through institutional channels and occasionally resorted to contention. Its capillarity also allowed it to exert pressure on the ground, threatening to undermine legislators' support in their districts if they opposed social benefits for rural workers. For example, during the debates over agrarian reform, CONTAG's militants filmed legislators in order to broadcast their positions and votes in their districts. CONTAG also had a permanent staff of 1,200 militants participating in meetings, lobbying legislators, and organizing demonstrations to promote its demands.[31]

CONTAG joined forces with the CUT in the negotiation and promotion of rural benefits. As a result of incessant pressure on legislators, rural pensions were expanded and designed as inclusive benefits along the lines CONTAG advocated. They were universalized and benefit levels were increased. Changes reduced discretion in access, and favored female rural workers who previously could receive rural pensions only if they were heads of households. The value of the pension benefit was set equal to the minimum wage, which is the same value of the minimum pension for formal-sector workers, and the retirement age was lowered to fifty-five and sixty years for women and men, respectively.[32] The new pension program granted rural organizations the chance to participate in national and local pension councils – which played deliberative and advisory roles (interview, Schwarzer) – and local councils in charge of supervising policy implementation, a key concern of social movements pressuring for reforms.[33]

Pensions were approved because of the intense mobilization of CONTAG. However, the fact that pension reform as well as CONTAG's rather moderate land reform proposal constituted more palatable responses to demands from rural organizations than the more radical land reform the Landless Workers' Movement (MST) proposed, which was eventually not approved, undoubtedly helped in getting pension expansion approved without much resistance (see Weyland 1996a).

Another major change was the passage of noncontributory pensions for outsider seniors and for the disabled. A network of social associations,

---

[31] JdoB, June 12, 1987, 2.

[32] On these changes, see Schwarzer (2000).

[33] According to Section 3 of Law 8213/91, the national council has to "deliberate about social security policy and the administration of the system." Local councils were later deactivated on the grounds that pension policy was centralized (IPEA 2004: 30).

social workers and professionals, as well as church groups, pressed for this demand. Among the organizations promoting social assistance pensions was the Association of Parents and Friends of the Exceptional (APAES), a long-standing federation that advocated for the rights of people with disabilities and had chapters in every state of Brazil.[34] Together with the universalization of social assistance services (e.g., day care, nursing homes), these movements advocated the transformation of an existing small program of semi-contributory pensions for the disabled and for seniors over seventy years of age into a noncontributory, universal pension program.[35]

This coalition was influential but less powerful than the one promoting rural pensions (see Weyland 1996a). Moreover, the Ministry of Social Security was reluctant to extend disability pensions on the grounds that benefits would be vulnerable to fraud.[36] In response to lobbying, legislators nonetheless approved the social assistance reform, as well as the extension of disability and old-age pensions. As for other social policy areas, a participatory structure of national and local councils in charge of policy deliberation and oversight was also established for social assistance benefits.

Collor de Mello Administration (1990–1992)

After defeating the Workers' Party in the runoff for the 1989 presidential elections, Fernando Collor de Mello came to power with a conservative coalition led by the National Renovation Party (PRN). Collor was the first president elected in competitive and free elections after the elimination of literacy requirements, which granted the right to vote to at least 10 million illiterate.[37] As a candidate without a minimally established party or a vast political trajectory, Collor's victory in the first round, in which eighteen candidates competed, was unexpected. Scholars have attributed his ascent to power to an effective political campaign in which he ranted against the political class, claiming to represent the poorest sectors of society.[38]

In alliance with machine parties, Collor received massive support from outsiders in the runoff. Studies show that in that election, 71.7 percent of low-income primarily outsider voters supported Collor (see Singer

---

[34] See "Batalha começou na Constituinte," CB, December 25, 1993.
[35] *Folha de São Paulo*, May 19, 1988, p. A-5.
[36] See "Para Archer, Previdência não vai falir," CB, July 24, 1988.
[37] On the changes in literacy requirements, see Schneider (1995: 352).
[38] See Boas (2005); Weyland (1996a, 1996b, 2002).

1999: 170).[39] Ecological data further indicate that PT candidate Lula defeated Collor in only 14.25 percent of the country's low-income municipalities, and that electoral competition only took place in 22.27 percent of outsider municipalities (author's calculations).

Collor stalled the implementation of new social rights. The Collor administration had to pass legislation regulating the new rights to initiate their implementation. Despite having promised social policy expansion in his campaign, such as devoting 10 percent of the GDP to health care, and facing active social movements expecting swift responses, Collor sought to delay implementation.[40] In 1990, Congress passed a law establishing SUS, whose content had been negotiated among the HRM, private lobbies, and legislators (Rodrigues Neto 1997: 87). Collor vetoed several provisions in the law, hoping to preserve centralized control of funding allocations.[41] In particular, he vetoed automatic transfers for health care services to municipalities based on demographic criteria,[42] which allowed him to accommodate funding decisions to political needs and to the demands of private hospitals that had thrived under the old system (see Weyland 1996a: 171). This was further facilitated by Collor's veto of the creation of health councils, which was justified by Minister of Health Alaceni Guerra on the grounds that with health councils running, "the system would be handed to the extreme left" (quoted in Rodrigues and Zauli 2002: 410).

Due to intense pressure from the HRM and the local authorities that would be in charge of implementing SUS, some of these rules were reenacted (Arretche 2005: 293; Weyland 1996a: 171). Yet the Collor administration continued to transfer funds based on service provision instead of demographic criteria,[43] which allegedly introduced discretion in the distribution of resources and biased funding toward areas where hospital services were more developed. Collor, moreover, favored transfers to states vis-à-vis municipalities. In the words of the president of the National Council of Municipal Secretaries of Health, Collor's measures meant municipalities were "at the mercy of the states."[44] In short, the

[39] Respondents with household income below two times the minimum wage.

[40] See "Collor reafirma meta de elevar para 10% do PIB gastos com saúde até 95," GM, June 25, 1991. "Orçamento de 92 mantem a saúde em estado grave," OG, January 2, 1992.

[41] Chronology built with Data Set of Policy Making. See also Arretche (2005); Levcovitz, de Lima, and Machado (2001); Rodrigues and Zauli (2002).

[42] "Lei da saúde tem 14 itens vetados," OEdSP, September 21, 1990.

[43] See "Servicio de Saúde será pago por produtividade," FdSP, February 17, 1990.

[44] "Lei da saúde tem 14 itens vetados," OEdSP, September 21, 1990.

measures served vested interests and limited the expansion of health care services in areas with little infrastructure.

Collor's vetoes also affected the implementation of pension reforms. Once Congress had passed the two laws that regulated pension funding and the structure of benefits,[45] Collor vetoed critical provisions stalling their implementation.[46] To justify his decisions, Collor argued that the pension system was bankrupt, and proposed to raise payroll contributions to increase pension revenue. Because this initiative failed to gain support in Congress,[47] Collor then proposed pension privatization as a way to improve pension funding. Although this proposal found some supporters, it was not perceived as a solution to the pension system's alleged lack of revenue.[48] In response, pensioners and rural workers mobilized for the implementation of the new laws; they launched demonstrations and successfully sued the pension institute, obliging it to start honoring commitments in 1991.[49] Social assistance pensions, in turn, required a new law, which was passed by Congress and vetoed by Collor in 1991.

The president's approach to social policy and social movement demands was synonymous with his approach in other policy areas and can in part be explained by his lack of a strong support coalition. Collor's party was an electoral vehicle, and the president did not try to forge a legislative coalition, relying initially on temporary decrees to govern. Despite his support for pro-market policies, Collor did not build ties to business associations (Portugal Jr. et al. 1998: 10), which deprived him of support for his policies.

Economic strains compounded political problems. Collor faced high inflation, which he sought to contain with a harsh stabilization plan[50] enacted at the beginning of his tenure that eventually resulted in hyperinflation and a deep recession (Flynn 1993; Weyland 2002: 122–3). The disclosure of rampant corruption directly involving the president fueled massive anti-Collor demonstrations in 1992 and severely loosened the president's grip on power (Pérez-Liñán: 2007). These demonstrations

---

[45] "Oposição tenta aprovar plano da Previdência," FdSP, September 8, 1990.
[46] See "Collor veta projetos de leis da Previdência Social," JdeB, September 12, 1990.
[47] See "Câmara arquiva o aumento," JdaT, January 24, 1992.
[48] See "Objetivo e privatizar o sistema," JdeB, January 17, 1992; "Ministro insiste na privatização," OEdSP, November 21, 1992. See Stephanes (1998).
[49] See "Contag cobra a nova lei da Previdência," CB, March 3, 1990; "Trabalhadores Rurais Protestam no Sul," OG, February 12, 1992.
[50] Among other things, Collor had confiscated bank accounts, initiated state rationalization, and launched a privatization package – which did not take off – to ensure economic recovery.

were led by a core group of social and political organizations, including the CUT, CNBB, and several large NGOs, as well as the PSDB and PT, which coalesced into the Movement for Ethics in Politics (MEP) and demanded Collor's impeachment in May 1992.[51] In August 1992, demonstrations grew dramatically with the involvement of students and student associations. A survey by Datafolha in the main capital cities in the country then reported that 70 percent of respondents were in support of the president's impeachment.[52] Under pressure from massive demonstrations, the lower chamber voted for Collor's impeachment by the Senate and suspended him from office in September 1992 (Pérez-Liñán 2007: 17). Anticipating the Senate's approval of his impeachment, the president resigned.

The Itamar Franco Administration (1992–1995)

Itamar Franco (1992–5) initiated the implementation of social benefits. As Collor's vice president and successor, Franco assumed office in a scenario marked by hyperinflation, growing poverty, and high levels of social mobilization. Social movements and labor unions were empowered by the success of the impeachment campaign and expected transparency and decisive social policy responses from the new president. Aside from enjoying little legitimacy, Interim President Franco was therefore under strong pressure to address the economic crisis and appease social movement demands.[53]

Franco rapidly steered away from Collor's strategy of disregarding social policy commitments and promised to decisively address the social question.[54] Unlike Collor, Franco engaged in active consultation and cooperation with social movements, adopted proposals they advocated, and moved forward in the implementation of SUS and pension reforms established in the constitution, as discussed later. With these measures,

---

[51] See Landim (1998); Weyland (1993); pensioners' demonstrations included demands for the implementation of the constitution and for *Fora Collor* (out with Collor). The HRM also demanded Collor's expulsion. See "Conferência vai discutir falta de investimento para a saúde," JdB, August 10, 1992. See http://www.ibase.br/betinho_especial/com_a_palavra/o_novo_esta_nas_ruas.htm.

[52] See "70% acham que o Congreso debe aprobar o impeachment de Collor," FdSP, August 16, 1992.

[53] Media coverage from the time highlights such pressure. See "Pacote Social," JdeB, October 24, 1993.

[54] "Presidente aponta emergência social," OEdSP, March 19, 1993; "Itamar quer priorizar o social," FdSP, October 28, 1992.

Franco sought to gain legitimacy and to prevent social activism from turning into a destabilizing movement against his administration.[55]

Income Support and the Antihunger Program

The core organizations of the MEP hoped to channel the surge in activism surrounding Collor's impeachment campaign toward the achievement of social reforms. In December 1992, hundreds of organizations forming the MEP organized Citizens' Action against Hunger, Misery and for Life (Citizen Action),[56] to mobilize public opinion and put pressure on the government to address the social question, defined as one centered on hunger, with determination. As stated by an activist of the highly embedded NGO Brazilian Institute of Social and Economic Analysis, IBASE:

Citizen Action was the same coalition that had formed the Movement for Ethics in Politics ... When Collor left and Itamar assumed the presidency hundreds of civil society organizations met to see what could be done. ... People were on the streets and wanted change ... so we decided ... to talk about hunger. We thought that maybe hunger would attract public opinion and we would be able to form a movement around this topic (interview, IBASE).

In April 1993, Franco established CONSEA, a special advisory council on food security proposed by social movements and announced the adoption of a plan against hunger. With ten ministers and twenty-one representatives from highly active social movements, NGOs, labor unions, and religious organizations, who were appointed to the council by Citizen Action, CONSEA was expected to propose strategies, establish priorities, and supervise "measures aiming to reduce the problems of hunger and unemployment" (Decree 808, April 24, 1993). CONSEA served as a liaison between civil society and the state through which social movements could exert pressure and influence government decisions.

The plan against hunger embraced multiple initiatives ranging from the adoption of emergency alleviation measures (e.g., food distribution) to the decisive implementation of SUS, pensions, and land reform.[57] Food distribution became one of CONSEA's most visible activities. It assisted Citizen Action on a massive antihunger campaign that collected

[55] See *Folha de São Paulo*, November 24, 1992, pp. 1–6.
[56] Citizen Action also included the most prestigious and large-scale social organizations and coalitions of NGOs and community groups in Brazil such as INESC, IBASE, OAB, FASE, and ABONG.
[57] Reproduced in "Plano de Combate a Fome," FdSP, March 25, 1993.

and distributed food through informal councils formed by local organizations, individuals, and workers from state owned companies (Gohn 2003: 149).[58] A national survey in 1993 reported that 32 percent of respondents had participated in the campaign.[59]

Other proposals to reduce poverty such as the minimum guaranteed income (PGRM), an income support program promoted by PT senator Eduardo Suplicy, did not receive much attention. Suplicy met with the president and his cabinet to gain their support for the policy in 1993, and made unsuccessful attempts to get it approved in Congress.[60] The PGRM was not a central demand of the social movements in CONSEA, which primarily advocated land distribution and subsidized credit for small-scale agriculture. These movements believed that such measures would both reduce the price of foodstuffs for urban workers and help improve living conditions in rural areas. Although the PT proposed a cash-transfer program linked to education in the party's platform for the 1994 elections (Partido dos Trabalhadores 1994a), cash transfers did not receive broad support from social movements or within the party at the time (interviews, PT high official, Ruth Cardoso).

Pensions

Franco promoted legislation that enabled the implementation of the non-contributory pensions established in the 1988 constitution. Social movements representing people with disabilities, social workers, and labor unions successfully lobbied Congress to prompt the passage of the social assistance law (LOAS), collecting 600,000 signatures in support of legislation to regulate such benefits.[61]

Despite the fact that the constitution guaranteed social security benefits for all who needed them irrespective of contributions, LOAS extended disability and old-age pensions only to households with a per capita income below 25 percent of the minimum wage, and in the case of old-age pensions, to one senior aged seventy or older per household, to be expanded to people sixty-seven and over in the next four years. This was not as broad reaching as social movements had expected, yet because of high levels of destitution, together with rural pensions, actual coverage of

---

[58] "País Já tem 3 mil comitês pela cidadania," FdSP, September 5, 1993.
[59] IBOPE survey in FdSP, April 13, 1994, 1–3.
[60] "Suplicy defende o plano de renda mínima," JdoB, February 12, 1993.
[61] See "Batalha Começou na Constituinte," CB, December 25, 1993; FdSP, March 28, 1994, 2-2.

these noncontributory benefits called *Benefício de Prestação Continuada* (BPC), eventually reached a large share of outsider seniors.

Health Care

Franco launched and regulated the decentralization of health care services to initiate the full implementation of SUS (Arretche 2005). With input from the HRM and local authorities, the government established rules for municipalities with diverse capacities to gradually qualify for increasingly complex roles within SUS. A fundamental requirement for local governments to start implementation and receive national funding was the creation of a health council, which would be in charge of approving the municipal health care budget put together by the government.[62]

While fundamental institutions of coordination across levels of government were laid out to facilitate the implementation of SUS, funding became a major problem. Two critical sources of revenue for SUS could not be used: a corporate tax that was challenged in the courts and suspended on allegations of double taxation, and SUS's share of payroll revenue that was retained by the Ministry of Social Security on the grounds that SUS was not a social security program.[63] This sharp reduction of funding came at a time in which private hospitals were already demanding higher fees and delayed payments.[64]

To create more predictable sources of revenue for SUS, the minister of health who belonged to the HRM proposed and laboriously lobbied for a temporary tax on financial transactions, which Congress approved under Cardoso. In the meantime, Franco negotiated a loan from the Unemployment Fund (FAT)[65] – an entity administered by employers, labor unions, and the state – to reinitiate service provision, which had been interrupted by lockouts of hospital contractors and strikes of health care workers.[66]

Overall, social mobilization was critical to the social policy measures Franco pursued amid adverse economic circumstances. Social

---

[62] Health councils include representation from state officials and service providers (25 percent of total seats); users (50 percent of seats); and health care workers' unions (25 percent of seats).

[63] Lucchese (1996: 103–5); "Britto: Não ha como repassar verbas a saúde," OG, June 18, 1993.

[64] "Governo não paga e os hospitais podem parar," OG, June 18, 1993.

[65] "Itamar quer verba do FAT para salvar hospitais," JdeB, June 26, 1993; JdoB, July 6, 1993, 8.

[66] See OEdSP, April 30, 1993, 11.

mobilization pressured Franco to launch implementation of the social rights that had been approved by the Constituent Assembly in 1988. Social movements and labor union allies furthermore demanded participation in policy implementation and were included in policy councils as well as in the design of specific aspects of implementation.

The 1994 Election

Fernando Henrique Cardoso (FHC), Franco's minister of finance, was catapulted to the presidency by the success of the Plano Real adopted in July 1994, which ended rampant inflation a few months before the presidential election. Cardoso's landslide victory by twenty-seven points over the PT was also helped by the alliance he forged with two conservative parties, the PFL and the smaller Brazilian Labor Party (PTB), which, according to Ames (2002: 181), provided both the necessary electoral support for the PSDB in low-income areas and permitted approval of the Plano Real in Congress.[67]

The PT, the runner-up party in that election, could not win the support of outsiders in 1994 and was not a credible challenger. According to my data, the PT won only in 6.3 percent of the total outsider districts, while 19 percent of all outsider districts had electoral competition (author's calculations).

The Fernando Henrique Cardoso Administration (1995–1998)

Fernando Henrique Cardoso continued with the implementation of health care and pension programs, two areas in which social movements had gained institutional positions in councils and state agencies. The passage of the CPMF in 1996, a temporary tax on financial transactions initially devised under the Franco government, provided SUS with a more predictable source of revenue.[68] By 1998, 83 percent of the municipalities were already managing their primary health services and close to 10 percent were in charge of full administration of the health care system (Serra and Faria 2004: 156). Implementation of a preventive program for excluded populations, the Family Health Plan (PSF), which used

---

[67] The PMDB joined the government after the election.
[68] Some of CPMF's revenue was deviated away from SUS to the treasury (Serra and Faria 2004: 157).

community agents to control immunization and improve access to basic health care services, gained steam during this period and grew especially during Cardoso's second term. With significant delays and government resistance to paying a minimum wage per benefit, Cardoso eventually launched the implementation of the BPC in 1996, which reached close to 1.5 million seniors by 2002.

Soon in power, Cardoso renamed the CONSEA Solidarity Community (CS), and altered its structure in order to limit the high levels of direct access to the state social movements had enjoyed and the ease with which they could pressure the state from within under Franco (Cardoso et al. 2002: 8; interviews Ruth Cardoso, Chair of CS; Ana Peliano, Executive Director of CS). This was facilitated by the fact that several members of CONSEA resigned at the beginning of Cardoso's administration.

During Cardoso's first term, the incentives for expansion of new social benefits were not present, as the incumbent enjoyed broad electoral support from outsiders and social movements were not actively demanding social policy innovations. Cardoso, however, faced pressures from rural and social movements to implement the agrarian reform – which for these movements represented an adequate strategy to fight poverty – as well as the emergence of an increasingly salient debate on income transfers, as described next.

Income Support

Two main developments influenced the national government's agenda regarding income support. First, large-scale mobilization emerged around the agrarian reform. Its visibility and strength grew after two massacres of landless workers from the MST in 1995 and 1996, which triggered dramatic contention including land invasions, roadblocks, and marches, and afforded the MST and its demands broad public support (see Konder-Comparato 2001; Ondetti 2006). The Cardoso administration met with the MST leadership, opened up channels of negotiation, and promised to expand both credit and land distribution. Additional protests were launched to keep land distribution in motion, which were supported by the CUT, CONTAG and other social movements that pressed vigorously for the implementation of the agrarian reform.

In the face of wide mobilization, Cardoso addressed the question decisively. Between 1995 and 2002, 37.7 million hectares were distributed to 524,384 landless families, and whereas 30,400 families had been granted land in 1995, 66,800 and 98,700 were settled in 1997 and 1998, respectively. Overall, an average of 65,548 families per year was granted land during the two Cardoso administrations (1995–2002).[69]

The second major development that shaped the social policy agenda around poverty was the creation of cash transfer programs by local governments, which broadened the debate about a minimum income Suplicy had initiated in the early 1990s. The first initiative of this kind was introduced in the Federal District in 1995. Upon taking office, PT politician Cristovam Buarque followed through on his campaign promise and inaugurated Bolsa Escola, an innovative program that provided a minimum wage to low-income households with children conditional on school attendance (interview, Buarque). A similar scheme, Minimum Income, inspired by Suplicy's PGRM, was inaugurated by a major of the PSDB in Campinas in 1995.[70] From 1995 to 1998, twenty-three subnational units (three states and twenty municipalities) launched income-support schemes, many conditional on school attendance, covering around 130,000 households – still a tiny share of outsider households.[71] In 1998, bills proposing cash transfer programs were discussed in 170 local legislatures. Though not exclusively, most of these proposals were submitted by PT politicians and launched in relatively affluent cities, especially in the wealthy state of São Paulo.[72]

Amid the growing debate around conditional cash transfer programs, Cardoso supported a bill by PSDB legislators that allowed the national executive to provide 50 percent of the total funding for such programs launched by low-income municipalities. Called Renda Mínima, the new program was voted for by all blocs in Congress in December 1997. The bill raised questions, however, about how municipalities and states would come up with the resources to pay for the remaining 50 percent of the funding, and about the small grants that would be paid to families as compared with existing subnational cash transfers such as Bolsa Escola (Câmara dos Deputados, December 5, 1997).

The passage of this law indicated the government's intention to show some concern for the issue of poverty, but clearly evidenced a lack of commitment to the actual implementation of any meaningful initiative. This is because most low-income municipalities were expected to be unable

[69] Calculated with data from DIESSE and Ministério de Desenvolvimento Agrário (2006, 2008).
[70] Campinas is a middle-income municipality in the state of São Paulo. See FdSP, June 24, 1995, 7-3.
[71] Estimate built with data from Lobato (1998) and author's Data Base of Policy Making.
[72] Ibid.

to contribute their share of funds to launch their own schemes, especially where the eligible population was large. However, Renda Minima's design was flexible enough to accommodate different situations. As the minister of education noted at the time, municipalities "can establish criteria to restrict the total number of beneficiaries according to their own budgets."[73] With large numbers of families technically qualifying (about 10 million), most municipalities unable to launch benefits, others capable of covering some beneficiaries, and states able to choose to contribute some funding or not, the scheme was expected to be small and even vulnerable to discretionary implementation.

Prominent PFL legislators who represented low-income areas were enthusiastic promoters of the bill; they emphasized the importance of federal support for income transfer programs developed by low-income municipalities themselves. The law was moreover flexible enough to allow the national government to decide whether to extend the benefit, to extend it gradually to all low-income municipalities by 2002 and to every municipality afterward, and to be able to speed up implementation "conditional on the availability of resources." These resources could be determined in the annual budget, and also could be reallocated from other social or compensatory programs (Câmara dos Deputados, December 5, 1997).

As the 1998 elections neared, the PFL further submitted a set of proposals to Cardoso for his next term, which included the creation of an "exemplary" national income transfer program that would allow incumbents in poor municipalities to receive sufficient national funding to inaugurate such programs (PFL 1998: 48–9).[74] The PFL was a decisive promoter of cash transfers, and Renda Minima was the first step toward achieving national funding for initiatives launched by local governments. As discussed later, the national government was not determined initially to launch Renda Mínima and it was only in 2000, three years later, that its implementation began to gain steam.

The 1998 Election

In seeking reelection in 1998, Cardoso enjoyed broad support and high approval ratings. This generated little incentive to launch Renda Mínima

---

[73] "Programa Exclui 40% dos Municípios," FdSP, August 9, 1998. It was estimated that 10.2 million families qualified for the benefit. The federal government estimated that municipalities would actually enroll less than 20 percent of that number in 1998.

[74] "Tempo de Ideias," OG, May 26, 1998.

in order to appeal to outsiders before the elections. In his campaign platform, Cardoso primarily emphasized the positive effects of the Plano Real. Although he maintained that in his next term he would "implement cash transfer programs with municipalities according to the law already passed [Renda Mínima's law]" (Cardoso 1998: 94), publicizing this benefit was not a priority during his campaign. As expected in this book's framework, in the absence of electoral competition for outsider voters or mobilization for social benefits, incumbents may extend small benefits, or announce their intention to do so, to show concern for the poor when the question figures in the public debate.

One fundamental concern of the government at the time was the possibility that cash transfers would be manipulated on the ground (interview, Ruth Cardoso). Cardoso emphasized that cash transfers "could only be developed locally" to permit public control and "impede their clientelistic use" and to develop institutional and funding structures fit for Brazil's social diversity (Cardoso 1998: 93–4; interview, Ruth Cardoso). The idea of the national government itself administering a large-scale program that could be manipulated on the ground probably shaped the preference of the Cardoso administration for locally run, decentralized schemes. Local governance institutions – such as oversight councils – were not included in Renda Mínima, however, making the program's implementation vulnerable to discretion.

Despite high approval ratings and vote intention in polls, Cardoso's popularity declined before the elections. As measured with available polls from Datafolha, in December 1997 and from April 1998 to October 1998, Cardoso's overall vote intention stood between sixteen and twenty-three points above the second candidate, the PT's Lula, dropping to a small difference of four points between May and early July 1998.[75] The decline in popularity was mainly attributed to a drought in the Northeast, which generated high levels of contention by landless workers in 1998, and did not receive rapid policy responses. Land invasions jumped 29 percent and reached a record of 592 events that year.[76] Discontent with the absence of social policy innovations grew among Cardoso's allies in the Northeast, and the lack of response was strongly criticized by the PT and CUT, who argued that if Renda Mínima had been expanded more quickly, a safety net in place would have minimized suffering.

[75] Accessed in 2010 from Datafolha's website.
[76] Calculated with data from Comissão Pastoral da Terra, n/d.

In response to the decline in his popularity during the drought, Cardoso launched some emergency employment benefits and initiated massive food distribution through the existing Cesta Básica program, which the MST and subnational authorities had demanded but the Cardoso administration had tried to avoid given historic abuses in its distribution.[77] This fundamental concern with the political use of resources to palliate the drought (interview, Ruth Cardoso) probably delayed a prompt response by the national government in the face of grievances and large-scale mobilization in affected areas.

Cardoso's vote intention did grow as conflict around the drought declined, and he won reelection by a wide margin. Ecological data of electoral results in the 1998 presidential election show steady support for Cardoso in low-income municipalities where outsiders represented a large share of the population. Lula won in only 9.76 percent of the outsider municipalities and there was electoral competition in only 16.12 percent of those municipalities (author's calculations).

4.4 ELECTORAL COMPETITION FOR OUTSIDERS AND EXPANSION OF INCOME TRANSFERS

Electoral competition for outsiders emerged during Cardoso's second term. Pressured by declining popularity rates and growing electoral competition for outsiders in the 2002 presidential election, Cardoso initiated a broad income transfer program, Bolsa Escola, in 2001. The benefit was funded through an antipoverty fund championed by PFL leader Antônio Carlos Magalhães (ACM) and was approved by Congress in December 2000. Bolsa Escola had sizable coverage, but it was a restrictive benefit – reaching fewer than 50 percent of outsider children – and had no participatory structure.

After winning the 2002 elections with unprecedented support from outsiders, Lula created Bolsa Família to consolidate outsiders' support. The new transfer was inclusive owing to pressures from social movements and labor unions allied to the PT, who pushed for broad-reaching participatory benefits.

The Second Cardoso Administration (1999–2002)

In Cardoso's second term, the surge of electoral competition for outsiders and pressure from his coalition partners to consolidate outsiders'

---

[77] "FH Regulamenta Renda Mínima," OG, June 28, 1998.

support changed the incentives for expansion. If Cardoso's approach to the social question was probably the most criticized aspect of his first administration,[78] social programs for outsiders became a priority during his second term.

Cardoso's popularity declined immediately after taking office. The international crisis of the late 1990s badly hit Brazil's finances, and the government devalued the currency in early 1999. According to surveys by IBOPE, Cardoso's popularity plummeted in light of the devaluation of the Real, reaching a disapproval rate of 73 percent. This was a sharp contrast with his approval ratings from mid-1997 through 1998, which hovered between 60 and 54 percent.[79]

The declining popularity of the Cardoso administration and the cutbacks the government proposed to address the crisis raised fears among PFL politicians that discontent would translate into electoral decline for their party in the 2000 municipal elections and increase the prospects of alternation in 2002. In response to growing electoral competition for outsiders, Cardoso launched income transfer programs, which are analyzed next.

Income Transfers

In July 1999, ACM initiated a vigorous campaign for a national anti-poverty initiative, the Fund for the Eradication of Poverty, to be funded with an increase in the temporary tax on financial transactions (*contribuição provisória sobre movimentação financeira*) (CPMF). ACM was the president of the Senate and probably the most influential conservative politician in Brazil. As a key player in the articulation of legislative support in Congress, he was a fundamental component of Cardoso's coalition.[80] At first glance, ACM was an improbable promoter of large-scale antipoverty programs.[81] His electoral power stemmed from the PFL, a machine based in the low-income Northeast that governed three states

---

[78] See, for example, "Presidente se define como 'neo-social,'" OEdSP, August 26, 1995; "Cardoso defende a área social," *Jornal de Brasília*, August 2, 1995; "Críticas ao Presidente," JdaT, August 8, 1996. "FH repete programas já anunciados na área social," FdSP, May 7, 1996; "Líder do senado admite falhas na área social," OEdSP, August 7, 1999.

[79] IBOPE Survey data in *Veja*, April 4 2001, ed. 1694.

[80] Until his sudden death in May 1998, his son, Luiz Eduardo, played a similar role in the lower chamber.

[81] On ACM, see Ames (2002: 129–33).

and 1,191 municipalities, and had about 16,000 seats in local councils.[82] Throughout the Cardoso administration, the PFL had often delayed or voted against the expansion of taxes, including the approval of the CPMF, which would finance the antipoverty fund.[83] With the creation of the fund, ACM sought to gain full federal funding for municipalities to effectively launch cash transfer programs and social investments.

ACM's promotion of the fund was prompted by concern over the PT's growth on the ground and its potential victories in the 2000 local elections. With an eye on the future, the disapproval ratings of the incumbent government also indicated the potential defeat of the PSDB–conservative coalition in the 2002 elections. A national ally was key in order for discretionary economic resources to continue reaching machine governors and a PT victory did not augur well for such an alliance to be established (see Ames 2002; Borges 2011).

The national government initially did not mobilize support for ACM's antipoverty fund and did not decisively launch Renda Mínima either, which in December 1999 reached only 50,000 beneficiaries. This program lacked any significant funding until a couple of months before the 2000 municipal elections, when Cardoso announced IDH-14, a package of social programs – including Renda Mínima – for municipalities with low human development scores in the fourteen poorest states, all in the North and Northeast of Brazil.[84] After its announcement, IDH-14 was expanded to another nine states in response to complaints from excluded governors.[85] Although IDH-14 began implementation only after the municipal elections, providing transfers to close to 1 million families, the announcement of the new social investments sought to contain discontent and improve electoral support for the incumbent's allies.

As shown in Table 4.2, the PT grew significantly in the 2000 municipal elections. It won in 27 percent of the largest cities in the country – compared to 9 percent in the previous election – and attained the largest increase in vote share, 51 percent (Fleisher 2002: 95–7; Table 4.2).

Although the growth of the PT was most significant in large cities, it was especially important in the North and Northeast, two areas that had been particularly elusive to the PT. In fact, PT mayoral victories in

---

[82] "PFL investe em canal privado de televisão e vai fazer comícios eltrônicos em 150 cidades," OEdSP, July 6, 2000.
[83] ACM opposed an increase of the income tax rate in 1998. See FdSP, July 28, 1999, 5.
[84] *Jornal do Brasil*, July 29, 2000, 3–4.
[85] "FHC rebatiza IDH-14 e inclui 389 municípios pobres de 9 estados," FdSP, September 15, 2000.

TABLE 4.2 *Support for Main Parties in Local Elections, Brazil, 1996–2000*

	% Change in Vote Share 1996–2000	Number of Victories 100 Largest Cities, 1996[a]	Number of Victories 100 Largest Cities, 2000
PMDB	4.25	16	15
PSDB	3.47	21	16
PFL	28.79	8	9
PT	51.25	9	27
PPB	−30.32	11	3
Other Left[b]	24.5	23	15
Other	16.98	12	15

[a] Includes all state capitals and major cities in the country.
[b] PPS, PSB, PDT.
Source: Fleisher (2002: 95–7).

these areas almost doubled between 1996 and 2000.[86] PFL leaders were aware of the PT's expansion. Before the 2000 elections, the PFL leadership estimated that the PT would obtain the largest vote share in capital cities, followed by the PFL and the PSDB. As stated by PFL politicians and also noted by ACM before the elections, they expected the PT to grow significantly.[87] To diffuse the PT's promises of social policy, the PFL had launched an active campaign promoting the party's achievements, including ACM's proposal for an antipoverty fund.[88]

After the elections, ACM's antipoverty fund, which required a constitutional amendment, was approved with virtually unanimous support. A critical concern among legislators was the use of the funds. As a result of negotiations, Congress established that 44 percent of the antipoverty fund would be used for health-related investments and primary care plans, and the rest for income transfers.[89]

Despite Cardoso's initial reluctance to approve this fund and launch a large-scale program at the national level, the antipoverty fund provided him with resources to initiate a large-scale income program when electoral competition for outsiders increased. In January 2001, Cardoso transformed Renda Mínima into Bolsa Escola with a temporary decree.[90]

[86] Data from TSE (www.tse.jus.br accessed 2014).
[87] "Partidos de esquerda crescem nos grandes centros," GM, September 29, 2000.
[88] Ibid.
[89] The PT wanted to increase the share of income support. See statements in "Câmara aprova o fundo contra pobreza," OEdSP, December 14, 2000.
[90] MEP 2140, February 13, 2001.

Congress soon approved both the new program and the regulation of the antipoverty fund.[91] In contrast to Renda Mínima, Bolsa Escola was funded by the national government, which also played a greater role in the program's implementation, and was meant to effectively reach a larger number of beneficiaries, about 5 million families by 2002. The program would pay one grant per child up to three children per household with a magnetic card – which was meant to help prevent the manipulation of benefits.[92] As the minister of education in charge of implementing Bolsa Escola noted, "with a national-level program we have to minimize the risk of fraud."[93]

Bolsa Escola began implementation immediately in February 2001.[94] In contrast to his early reluctance to expand large-scale transfers, Cardoso became a strong promoter of Bolsa Escola.[95] One of the critical concerns of the Cardoso administration, and of incumbents facing intense electoral competition, was the potential manipulation of resources. The government repeatedly emphasized that the benefit was nondiscretionary[96] in order to counteract any accusations of clientelism that could discredit the incumbent coalition in the context of intense competition for outsiders. In the inaugural act of Bolsa Escola, Cardoso's speech centered on the program's audits and strongly condemned "corruption in social programs" as "unacceptable" and "disgusting."[97] The Ministry of Education, which was in charge of Bolsa Escola's implementation, further established that municipalities that registered mayors' friends or relatives to the program would get all federal funds blocked.[98]

Expansion in the context of electoral competition for outsiders was restrictive. Bolsa Escola reached fewer than 50 percent of outsider households with moderate benefit levels, and without participation in program implementation. Though the PT, which as noted had little institutional power with fewer than 10 percent of the seats in Congress, argued for more generous benefits comparable to those paid by Buarque in the Federal District, and wanted the benefit to reach all families in need, members of the Cardoso coalition in Congress, which was made up of

[91] Lei 10219, April 11, 2001; Lei Complementar 111, July 6, 2001.
[92] See "Cartão vai combater fraudes," JdoB, February 13, 2001.
[93] Quoted in FdSP, February 12, 2001.
[94] See "União espera beneficiar 5 milhões de crianças com Bolsa Escola," OEdSP, December 4, 2000.
[95] See "Íntegra do Pronunciamento do FHC," FdSP, June 3, 1998.
[96] See "A corrupção em programas sociais é nojenta," OG, February 13, 2001.
[97] "Presidente critica o uso político do programa," JdeB, February 13, 2001.
[98] FdSP, February 10, 2001.

conservative PFL, PMDB, and other machine parties, voted for the president's proposal, which stipulated a smaller scope of coverage.

The 2002 Elections

Seeking to win the presidency, the incumbent coalition's candidate, José Serra, and the PT's Lula competed for outsiders and both promised social policy expansion and ethics in government (see Boas 2010; Hunter 2007). The PT for the first time struck an alliance with a non-leftist party, the small Liberal Party (PL), in an effort to deflate concerns about its potential radicalization in office.

Growing electoral competition for outsiders incentivized the further extension of social programs and raised concerns over allegations of discretion in the distribution of benefits. Bolsa Alimentação, which provided support for children from birth to age six as well as pregnant women, was announced in February and inaugurated in September 2001; Auxílio Gás, which provided an extremely small subsidy for gas consumption, was initiated in 2002.[99] To avoid clientelism in the context of high competition, the government introduced Bolsa Renda, a temporary national-level transfer for families affected by a milder drought in 2001. As stated by the minister of agricultural development, this innovation in the way the government addressed the drought, promised to reduce corruption and clientelism as the government would not "stick with Cesta Básica, water trucks, and unemployment benefits because they engross oligarchic kleptocracy."[100]

Cardoso further launched a new magnetic card, Cartão Cidadão (Citizen Card), for beneficiaries of all social transfers, including noncontributory pensions. The introduction of the new card a few months before the elections was an attempt to claim credit for these transfers in the context of intense electoral competition for outsiders. As the 2002 elections drew closer, the number of income-transfer beneficiaries grew dramatically, jumping from 1 million in January 2001 to between 5.1 million Bolsa Escola beneficiaries and 6.07 million total beneficiaries in 2002.[101]

---

[99] It provided fifteen *reais* every two months, seven *reais* per month as a gas subsidy (more than two dollars). There were accusations of clientelism in the distribution of these benefits (see Draibe 2006: 13). See "Trabalho de Serra é extraordinario, elogia FHC," OEdSP, September 18, 2001.

[100] Quoted in FdSP, May 26, 2001.

[101] Data provided by Ministério de Desenvolvimento Social and Fight against Hunger (MDS).

One critical obstacle to the actual extension of benefits was the lack of capacity or political will of local administrations to register beneficiaries. As advanced in this book's framework, subnational authorities often fear that the national government will claim all the credit for expansion if they do not have a clear role in the new policy, potentially affecting their standing in local or state politics. When he launched Bolsa Escola, Cardoso emphasized that the national government had "no monopoly" on the benefit in order to encourage local authorities to cooperate with implementation.[102] According to Ruth Cardoso, rather than blocking new benefits, a sort of tradeoff would also work for subnational authorities concerned, at least initially, about the effects of large-scale national programs. In her words, "What they [mayors] want is that a little of the old [programs], what they already know how to use, remains in place" (interview, Ruth Cardoso). Although there were delays, virtually all municipalities had signed agreements to launch Bolsa Escola by 2002.[103]

Faced with the expansion of transfer programs by the Cardoso administration, the PT promised to unify these programs to reduce administrative cost and inefficiencies and also promised to launch Zero Hunger (FZ), a highly participatory program designed to eradicate hunger along the lines of the antihunger initiative Franco had adopted in 1993.[104]

A few months before the elections, the PT was well ahead in the polls, yet it only defeated the incumbent in the runoff. In both rounds, the PT managed to gain a share of the outsider vote away from conservative parties who supported the incumbent coalition. In the runoff, it won in 57 percent of outsider municipalities and there was overall electoral competition in 71.62 percent of outsider municipalities (author's calculations). This was precisely what regional machines feared when the PT became more competitive by the 2000 elections.

The Lula Administration and Expansion of Inclusive Income Transfers (2003–2010)

Luiz Inácio "Lula" da Silva (2003–10) assumed office after receiving unprecedented support from outsider voters, and quickly needed to consolidate this support base. His administration was further pressed to deliver because of the PT's campaign promises and historical commitments

---

[102] See "Presidente critica o uso político do programa," JdeB, February 13, 2001.
[103] O Globo, December 12, 2001, 2.
[104] "Texto final do Fome Zero exclui propostas polêmicas," OEdSP, October 16, 2001.

to fighting poverty, as well as due to the strong presence of social movements in the party itself. These movements were particularly involved
in the agrarian reform, as well as in the question of food distribution,
having influenced the design of Lula's antihunger proposal, Zero Hunger
(FZ),[105] which he launched upon taking office. However, facing difficulties in the program's implementation, Lula refloated another PT initiative involving a massive income transfer program and launched Bolsa
Família, as described next. This program became the flagship of Zero
Hunger and a cornerstone of Lula's popularity, which partly allowed him
to consolidate and even expand support among outsiders in the next election (see Hunter and Power 2007; Zucco 2008; Figure 4.2).

Income Support

On his first day in office, President Lula established the Extraordinary
Ministry of Food Security and Struggle Against Hunger (MESA) and then
launched Zero Hunger, framing the social question in Brazil as one centered on hunger. This program responded to the preferences of several
social movements allied to the PT, especially those movements linked to
the church or involved in agrarian reform or popular education, as well
as labor unions. Zero Hunger was created by temporary decree (*medida
provisória*) and was approved by Congress swiftly, like prior social policy
initiatives such as Bolsa Escola.

In line with the Plan Against Hunger of 1993, the mentors of FZ
believed the state had to implement "emergency" measures to combat
hunger – such as food distribution – as well as "structural" measures
such as agrarian reform, the establishment of water pumps in the semi-
arid regions, and support for small-scale family farms. Combining both
types of measures, FZ involved sixty different schemes. One of the main
innovations of Zero Hunger was a food stamp for low-income families,
Cartão Alimentação, which required beneficiaries to submit receipts for
expenses. Local participatory councils, which were involved in the selection of beneficiaries, were in charge of monitoring the implementation
of the program. FZ also engaged volunteers in literacy, health care, and
nutrition campaigns for low-income families, hoping to raise awareness
about hunger and food security. Promoters of FZ expected the mobilization of beneficiaries and the participation of civil society organizations in

---

[105] For a description of the program and its promoters, see Rocha (2004).

FZ councils to legitimate the program and prevent the misallocation of resources (interview, Paes de Sousa).

Critiques resurfaced immediately after Lula announced the adoption of FZ.[106] The centrality of hunger was contested by experts and opposition politicians who argued for prioritizing antipoverty over antihunger initiatives. The number of people with "food insecurity" identified by the program was also seriously challenged, which undermined its technical legitimacy. A number of shortcomings further compromised FZ and its centrality in Lula's social policy agenda. First, given the ambitious scope of strategies involved (e.g., agrarian reform, infrastructure development), progress was slow moving and it did not lend itself to producing immediate results.[107] Its inaugural measures consisted primarily of food distribution, which made FZ look outdated compared to Bolsa Escola and other transfers that had been launched by Cardoso and that had historically been promoted by PT politicians. Second, the fact that families had to submit receipts for their food stamp expenses was criticized as bureaucratic and unnecessary, since studies had already shown that Bolsa Escola allowances were spent on food.[108] Third, NGOs claimed that the state was competing with them by soliciting funding from NGOs and donors, as international and domestic donations were expected to constitute a source of revenue for the program (see Neri 2004: 37–8).[109]

At the same time, FZ generated resistance from politicians who questioned its implementation. Local authorities complained that there was a "partisan bias" in Zero Hunger volunteers and, as predicted in this book's framework, resented FZ councils' involvement in selection of beneficiaries.[110] In the face of critiques, FZ councils began to lose favor within the PT, as politicians saw them as a source of "political tension" in localities run by the opposition (interview, high official of PT). In Congress, the temporary decree that created FZ yielded similar reactions. PSDB Senator Sebastião Madeira proposed greater articulation between FZ and existing transfer programs and expressed concern about the PT colonizing FZ councils, noting that "nothing prevents ... that control in a given municipality be carried out by the local office of the PT or the CUT."[111]

---

[106] "Maior Vitrine do PT vira munição contra governo," OEdSP, April 6, 2003; "Mesmo insatisfeito Lula vai manter Graziano no governo," FdSP, March 14, 2003.

[107] "Social Estagnado," CB, June 24, 2003.

[108] See statements in "Com renda mínima, povo compra comida," OG, January 14, 2003.

[109] "Com Fome Zero, ONGs perdem doações," FdSP, December 25, 2003.

[110] See Draibe (2006:22), and Genoino for a discussion of FZ and the role of PT militants (2004: 14).

[111] "PT e PSDB Disputam o Fome Zero," FdSP, May 2, 2003.

Reactions against FZ and its slow-moving progress made Lula reconsider the initiative.[112] In response, he announced the consolidation of existing cash transfer programs into a single program in April 2003.[113] To get approval for unification and to guarantee the effective implementation of the new benefit, the Lula administration sought support from governors, the majority of whom belonged to other parties. The government perceived such support as critical for a number of reasons. First, Lula hoped to prevent governors from blocking critical reforms already under way – particularly tax and pension reforms – if they were dissatisfied with the launching of a new benefit. These reforms were critical to Lula's government, and the PT sought to gain legislative support from the PMDB, the largest bloc in Congress with which the PT could credibly form a legislative coalition.[114]

Second, given that some states already had their own income-support programs, the Lula administration wanted to offset governors' fears that a new massive program run by the national government would deprive them of their own tools for building electoral support and offered them the opportunity to share credit for the program. As noted by a government official working on the unification of transfers with the governors, the idea was that "credit [*protagonismo*] had to be divided."[115] Twelve states were running income-support programs at the time, none of which actually covered the entire population that would benefit from Bolsa Família (interview, high-ranking official MDS #2). Finally, Lula hoped that the new transfer would also be complemented with funding from the states.

Meetings involving governors, mayors of large cities, technocrats, and sometimes the president were held to discuss the new transfer program. Bolsa Família was launched by Lula through a temporary decree in October 2003, and the law that created the program was sanctioned in January 2004.[116] Bolsa Família was announced as the accomplishment of Suplicy's long-standing struggle for a guaranteed minimum income.[117] The new program provided a small allowance to low-income families and grants for up to three children per household. It aimed to reach 11 million families, and would be implemented in phases over the next

---

[112] "Graziano Ministro. Por enquanto," CB, March 14, 2003.
[113] "Conta Única para o Social," OG, April 20, 2003, 3.
[114] On the politics of pension reform, see Brooks (2009); Marques and Mendes (2004).
[115] Quoted in "Divisão do Bonus," OG, September 28, 2003, 2.
[116] "Emfin, o Bolsa-Família," OG, October 21, 2003.
[117] "Sancionada lei que cria o Renda Mínima," Valôr Económico, January 9, 2004.

three years.[118] Rather than dismantling FZ, Bolsa Família was introduced as the flagship of the FZ strategy.

Although governors refused to contribute funding to the program, they did not block the initiative and some even committed to establishing supplementary job training schemes for beneficiaries of Bolsa Família, as well as helping with the consolidation of beneficiary databases.[119] When Bolsa Família was launched, eleven states joined the program.[120] A critical concern for the national government was to coordinate the distribution of benefits so that no family would receive transfers both from national and subnational programs. Access to beneficiary databases, which was critical for the prevention of abuses, was gradually accomplished over the following years (interview, high-ranking official MDS #2).

Lula's policy shift from an emphasis on FZ to Bolsa Família reveals two groups with different proposals for income-support policies within the PT.[121] Both of these groups or social policy coalitions preferred broad-reaching programs and criticized Cardoso's cash transfers as too modest, but they differed on social participation, on how to build political support, and on the best tools to palliate poverty. Schematically, the first social policy coalition within the PT was a coalition of social movements and labor unions linked to agrarian issues, food security, and popular education. These groups pressed for highly participatory initiatives aiming at reducing clientelism by empowering beneficiaries through organization building and social participation, which would also contribute to empowering the social movement coalitions within the PT. In terms of income support, these groups emphasized agrarian reform, food production and distribution, and literacy and nutrition education campaigns, as well as infrastructure investments. These movements had a strong influence on the government (Paes de Sousa, secretary of evaluation MDS) and promoted the Zero Hunger strategy (interviews, MST and official MDS #1). The first team appointed to lead the newly created MESA belonged to this group (Graziano 2004).

The second social policy coalition was composed of politicians whose careers had generally not begun within the unions or social movements, and who were generally not close to them. Several PT politicians who implemented cash transfers subnationally before the PT won the

[118] "Lula Unifica Programas," CB, October 20, 2003.
[119] "Bolsa-Família terá só verba federal," JdB, October 1, 2003; "Reunião com governadores," OG, October 1, 2003.
[120] See "Unificação do social," OG, October 21, 2003.
[121] See essays in da Rocha (2004).

presidency can be grouped within this coalition. These politicians preferred broad policies that helped secure outsiders' support amid electoral competition for outsiders. A transfer program providing nondiscretionary and tangible individual benefits would better increase the chances of reaching out to outsiders and consolidating their support. Direct state implementation, moreover, would make the process of expansion quicker and more straightforward, and therefore these PT politicians who did not respond directly to social movements generally preferred nonparticipatory implementation in the programs they had launched at the local level.

Bolsa Família initially had nonparticipatory implementation. In spite of the fact that the law that created the program did establish a framework for community participation and community oversight, launching these councils was not a priority of the program's implementation. The aim of the government was to initiate an effective policy for outsiders and avoid critiques, such as those raised against the councils of FZ. Politicians involved in the design of Bolsa Família wanted to create accountability in a technocratic top-down way and sought to avoid any partisan bias in implementation that could harm the program's reputation.

As noted by the then-secretary in the Ministry of Social Development and Fight against Hunger (MDS),[122] Bolsa Família "generated a crisis with [FZ] councils" as it entailed a fundamentally different form of implementation. Social movements within the government pressured for Bolsa Família to be participatory, and some participation at the local level was later introduced (interview, Paes de Sousa) through pre-existing or new councils that local authorities could create to oversee implementation.

Yet, even if social movements achieved some participation in Bolsa Família, the highly participatory agenda pursued by FZ lost centrality.[123] As expected in my theoretical framework, this is generally the case when social movements participate in policy design as members of the incumbent coalition rather than from outside the government. Indeed, the backbone of the social policy agenda had to be agreed upon by other members of the governing coalition, who, not belonging to social movements themselves, preferred policy options that allowed for a more straightforward top-down implementation. At the same time, and as advanced in this book's framework, electoral competition generated pressures

---

[122] MESA was renamed Ministério do Desenvolvimento Social e Combate à Fome (MDS) (see da Rocha 2004: 8).

[123] See "Bolsa-família desmobiliza ação do Fome Zero," FdSP, April 4, 2004.

TABLE 4.3 *Bolsa Família Beneficiaries and Average Benefit Levels, 2003–2009*

	Number of Beneficiaries (Million Families)	Average Benefit Paid/ Poverty Line (Percent)	Average Benefit Paid/Extreme Poverty Line (Percent)	Average Benefit Paid/Minimum Wage (Percent)	Benefit for Family[a]/Poverty Line (Percent)	Benefit for Family[a]/Extreme Poverty Line (Percent)	Benefit for Family[a]/ Minimum Wage (Percent)
2003	3.6	13.4	32.0	30.0	14.9	35.3	33.3
2004	6.5	12.5	30.3	27.7	13.9	33.7	30.7
2005	8.7	10.3	26.1	21.6	12.8	32.1	26.6
2006	11.1	9.8	25.4	18.6	12.0	31.3	22.8
2007	11.1	11.5	28.8	20.2	14.1	35.2	24.7
2008	11.3	12.7	29.8	20.7	15.0	35.4	24.5
2009	11.1	13.8	31.3	20.4	16.3	36.9	24.0

[a] Family of adult/s and two children six to fifteen. If children are between sixteen and eighteen, the benefit is higher.
Sources: Estimates built with data from MDS and ECLAC. Includes beneficiaries of Bolsa Família only.

from opposition politicians who resented social movement involvement, out of fear that they would bias policy implementation. This generally occurs when movements are not powerful enough to trigger expansion themselves, and they are, instead, part of the incumbent government. By contrast, when social movements press from outside the governing coalition for social policy expansion, they generally demand policy designs that include participation to be able to monitor implementation. To reduce pressures, governments acquiesce to creating some policy councils engaged in policy deliberation or oversight.

By 2010, Bolsa Família reached more than 70 percent of outsider children (author's estimates). According to my scoring of benefit levels, Bolsa Família provided moderate benefits since its creation in 2003 through 2009. As shown in Table 4.3, the average benefit and the benefit paid to a family in extreme poverty with two children in school represented about 20 and 24 percent of the legal minimum wage, respectively, and about 14 and 16 percent of the poverty line[124] (see Appendix 1).

Although income transfers were the main policy innovation for outsiders under Lula, other innovations in pension programs that helped to effectively achieve broad coverage were also introduced. In 2004, noncontributory pensions (BPC) were extended to each senior instead of one senior per household, and the eligibility was set at age sixty-five instead of sixty-seven, as established in the social assistance law of 1993 (MDS 2004; interview, Cássia Tavares, chair of National Social Assistance Fund).

4.5 ASSESSING ALTERNATIVE EXPLANATIONS

This chapter has emphasized the importance of mobilization from below and electoral competition for outsiders for the expansion of social policies in Brazil. It has also shown that social movements were critical for the creation of inclusive benefits. When social movements were not involved in policy design, as in the case of the income transfers created under Cardoso, the resultant benefits were restrictive. Next, I analyze alternative explanations linking policy change to the partisan affiliation of the incumbent, to changes in socioeconomic conditions, or to diffusion effects.

Regarding partisanship, the expansion of health care and pensions cannot be explained by the presence of left-wing incumbents seeking

---

[124] The poverty line was estimated for a family of two adults and two children with per-capita poverty line data from ECLAC (2009).

redistribution through these reforms. As we have seen, governments that embarked on social policy expansion and legislatures that approved new benefits were dominated by conservative coalitions based on machine parties. The left-wing PT was not in office and it had little power in Congress – the two mechanisms through which partisanship is expected to affect expansion – at the time of these policies' adoption and implementation, with the exception of Bolsa Família. In the case of income transfers, it was initially ACM, the leader of the PFL, a machine party of the incumbent coalition, who demanded that the national government launch social policy innovations when his party began to face electoral competition at the subnational level from the PT, which promised social policy expansion if elected. ACM's negotiations and public promotion of a fund for antipoverty measures led Congress to eventually approve it after the 2000 municipal elections, when the PT substantially increased its vote share. As electoral competition for outsiders tightened, Cardoso utilized this funding to launch Bolsa Escola and other transfers in 2001 and 2002, hoping to increase the electoral chances of the incumbent coalition in the 2002 election. Overall, the only instance of expansion presided over by a left-wing incumbent was that of Bolsa Família in 2003, which unified the transfers expanded by Cardoso and dramatically increased coverage.

Changing economic factors such as crises, economic growth, or the commodity boom of the early twenty-first century were not critical triggers for decisions to expand social policy (Figure 4.3). From the Sarney administration through the end of the Franco administration, the economy was unstable, with high inflation and even hyperinflation. During that period of economic instability, the main health and pension innovations were adopted and some began implementation. Enjoying economic stability and growth thanks to the success of the Plano Real in 1994, the Cardoso administrations (1995–2002) continued with the implementation of health care and pensions (BPC was launched at this time), but did not embark on significant social policy innovations until electoral competition increased during the 2002 elections. In fact, the absence of new measures to deal with poverty was one of the main objections raised against Cardoso. Finally, Lula announced the gradual implementation of the broad-reaching Bolsa Família just before the commodity boom benefited Brazil's finances beginning in 2004 (see Campello 2015). During his administrations, Lula unified cash transfers and doubled their coverage, deepened health services, and reached more beneficiaries with noncontributory pensions, but the bulk of the reforms and most of the

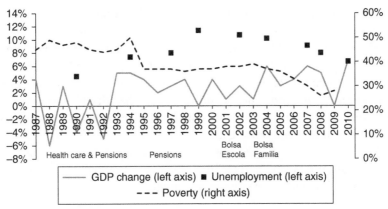

FIGURE 4.3 Economic growth, unemployment, poverty, and timing of expansion, Brazil, 1989–2010.
Note: health care and pensions were adopted and implementation took place between 1988 and 1993. BPC (pensions) was implemented in 1996.
Sources: GDP from IPEADATA, various years; unemployment rate from ECLAC (2009); poverty rate adapted from ECLAC (2009) and IPEADATA.

funding in these policy areas had already been established by preceding administrations.

These policy innovations are not consistently related to changes in poverty or unemployment rates either. During the 1980s and early 1990s, poverty – measured in terms of income – was high and declined significantly with economic stabilization. Income transfers were launched at the turn of the twenty-first century at a time when poverty rates were stable and lower than in the early 1990s. The unemployment rate followed the opposite trajectory, growing in the 1990s. Transfers were not launched when unemployment peaked in 1998, but rather throughout 2001 and 2002, in conjunction with the 2002 elections (see Figure 4.3).

Regarding the social policy model adopted, economic circumstances probably did hinder the rapid implementation of benefits, though delays in the implementation of health care and pension reforms can hardly be subsumed to financial issues, thus ignoring existing program stakeholders and the institutional transformations these programs entailed. An adverse economic situation did not determine whether inclusive or restrictive benefits were created. Inclusive programs were the choice in Brazil from the very first initiatives in the 1980s through the 2000s. The exception is Bolsa Escola, which was designed by a center-right executive in negotiation with a conservative-dominated Congress and with no social movement involvement.

Finally, the case of Brazil also shows that the diffusion of social policy models was not a critical factor for social policy expansion, or for the model ultimately adopted. A combination of participatory implementation and universal benefits was not strongly promoted within policy circles or by multilateral agencies in the 1980s and 1990s. In fact, Brazil was a pioneer in Latin America, universalizing health care assistance and pensions earlier than its neighbors, and creating the first renowned conditional cash transfer, Bolsa Escola, at the local level. The shape of these policy innovations emerged out of long-standing debates among social movements, politicians, and technocrats, and in negotiations among state officials and social actors over policy design.

4.6 CONCLUSIONS

Both factors causing expansion – mobilization from below and electoral competition for outsiders – have led to social policy expansion at different points in time and in different policy areas in Brazil. Mobilization from below propelled health care and pension expansion starting in the late 1980s. Incumbents responded to movement pressure to avoid declining popularity, even destabilizing mobilization in the case of rural issues, and to gain movements' support and claim credit for expansion. The creation of large-scale generous benefits such as the SUS and rural and non-contributory pensions was an outcome of social mobilization. Electoral competition for outsiders was not relevant in this period, as machine parties locked in low-income voters and the second-largest coalition, led by the PT, was incapable of reaching these voters in any significant way.

With the emergence of electoral competition for outsiders in the 2002 presidential election, income transfers for low-income families were launched by the Cardoso administration seeking the continuity of his coalition in power and hoping to offset the appeals of the PT, which campaigned on social policy expansion. When he assumed office, Lula expanded these transfers broadly with the goal of consolidating the support from outsiders who had voted him into office at an unprecedented rate. Owing to the alliance between social movements, labor unions, and the PT, these movements exerted influence over social policy design. Although they were not capable on their own of launching their preferred social programs when the PT was not in power, their involvement in policy design through the party ally accounts for the creation of the inclusive Bolsa Família program.

5

Social Mobilization and Inclusive
Social Policy in Argentina

5.1 INTRODUCTION

When Eduardo Duhalde of the Justicialista Party (PJ) assumed the presidency in 2002, he signaled his priorities by stating that he if we were not president, he might be an unemployed protestor.[1] Elected by Congress after four presidents resigned in late 2001, Duhalde sought to rebuild Argentina's collapsed economy and to dampen massive protests by unemployed workers and labor unions demanding jobs and social benefits. During his short tenure (2002–3), Duhalde initiated a dramatic expansion of social policy that continued in subsequent years.

Between 2002 and 2010, under the Duhalde and Néstor and Cristina Kirchner administrations of the PJ, large-scale income transfers, pensions, and health care services were extended to a large universe of outsiders. Aside from being broad and generous, these initiatives allowed for participatory implementation, especially in their early stages, and resulted in an inclusive policy model. As shown in Table 5.1, by 2010, a large share of the outsider population received social benefits: close to 74 percent of children accessed income transfers; 97 percent of seniors aged sixty-five and older received pension benefits; and free prescription drugs were extended to 15 million people, about 41 percent of the country's population. Beginning in 2005, a program to increase the demand for primary care services and improve mother and child health indicators was rolled out gradually.

---

[1] In Duhalde's words, "Mi responsabilidad es otra, si no, quizás, estaría en un piquete o con una cacerola" ("My responsibility is different; if [I were] not [president], perhaps I would be out in the picket or pot banging"). Quoted in *Clarín*, March 30, 2002.

TABLE 5.1 *Social Policy Expansion and the Inclusive Model in Argentina, ca. 2010*

Policy Area	Scope of Coverage	Benefit Level	Participation in Implementation	Dates of Expansion
Income Support	High 74% of school-age outsider children	High More than 20% of the poverty line for a family with two children	Low Organizations disseminate information and assist eligible population to enroll in the program	Workfare benefits: 2002 Family allowances: 2009
Health Care	High 100% of outsiders	High Free prescription drugs and primary care services	Moderate Organizations in charge of oversight in health centers; national oversight council	Free-prescription drugs: 2002. Primary-care improvements: 2002–4 (adoption and gradual implementation)
Pensions	High 97% of outsiders aged 65+	High Equal to minimum pension of insiders	Low National deliberative council with ceremonial role	2005–6 (adoption); 2005–7 (implementation)

Notes: Dates of Expansion refers to adoption and launching of implementation. Income Support: characterization refers to family allowances, which replaced workfare benefits.
Sources and Measures: See Appendix 1.

In contrast with the history of inequality in Brazil, Argentina was one of the wealthiest and more egalitarian countries in Latin America for most of the twentieth century, with broad public hospital services that were considered an anomaly in the region.[2] Despite having a smaller outsider population, which ranged from less than 50 percent to about 40 percent of the population,[3] initiatives to address the welfare gap were historically not successful beyond the adoption of broad health care services in the 1940s.

Scholars have often asserted that social policies for outsiders were neglected because labor unions did not mobilize outsider populations. After the democratic transition in 1983, and during the implementation of market reforms in the 1990s, labor unions negotiated the protection of their institutional prerogatives (Murillo 2001; Murillo and Schrank 2005; Torre 1998) instead of mobilizing the unemployed and informal sector workers (Etchemendy 2011). At the same time, scholars have shown that with the return of democracy, the PJ – which enjoyed loyal outsider support since its founding in the mid-twentieth century – turned into a patronage machine, prioritizing clientelistic linkages instead of expanding programmatic benefits for low-income voters (see Auyero 2001; Levitsky 2003).

In this context of union neglect and patronage politics, what explains the dramatic expansion of nondiscretionary social policy for outsiders in the 2000s? Why did incumbents create inclusive social policies? I argue that incumbents launched social policy expansion as a response to large-scale mobilization from below. This mobilization was led primarily by a social movement coalition (SMC) of unemployed workers and labor unions that emerged in the late 1990s and pressed for social policy expansion and jobs. As predicted in the analytic framework, when social mobilization pressing for expansion occurred at a large scale, incumbents responded with social provisions to contain instability, to prevent their popularity from declining, or to keep social movements from breaking up an alliance with the incumbent party. Incumbents sought to claim credit for the new benefits, but the most significant factor driving expansion was mobilization from below.

As the following sections demonstrate, social movements initially obtained small policy responses from the state until mobilization grew prior to the 2001 financial crisis. As analyzed in section 3, the government's

---

[2] See Chapter 3.
[3] See Figure 1.2 in Chapter 1.

initial failure to respond to the crisis and the overall turbulence produced by the country's economic collapse gave rise to wide protests that propelled incumbents to respond to organized demands from unemployed workers and labor allies. As shown in section 4, a combination of protest, pressure through institutional channels, and the alliance of some social movements with Néstor Kirchner's governing coalition beginning in 2004 allowed these movements to influence policy decisions, gain access to the state, engage in negotiations over policy design, and pressure incumbents to expand social policy along inclusive lines both from within and outside the state. As discussed in section 5, alternative explanations – such as the lack of economic resources during the 2001 crisis or their abundance during the commodity boom in the 2000s, the diffusion of models of social protection, or partisanship – do not better account for social policy expansion and the inclusive model adopted.

5.2 ELECTORAL COMPETITION FOR OUTSIDERS AND SOCIAL MOBILIZATION (1983–2010)

Electoral Competition for Outsider Voters

It is commonly understood that informal and unemployed workers have been the core electoral support of the PJ since the party's origins (Ostiguy 1998, chapter 5; see also Gibson 1997; Levitsky 2003: 105, 183, 226).[4] Since the return of democracy in 1983, electoral competition for outsiders has been very small with the exception of the 1983 and 1999 elections (see Figure 5.1). In 1983, Raúl Alfonsín, the candidate of the centrist, middle-class Radical Party (UCR), the second-largest party in the country, defeated the PJ in clean and fair presidential elections for the first time. Although there was some electoral competition for outsiders, according to this book's framework, it was not sufficiently high to motivate incumbents to trigger social policy responses.[5]

According to my data, electoral competition for outsiders only took place in the 1999 presidential elections. The end of the PJ administrations of Carlos Menem (1989–99) was marked by high unemployment and a deteriorating economy. Critical to the emergence of electoral competition was the formation of the Alliance for Jobs, Justice, and Education

---

[4] In his study of Peronism, Ostiguy refers to these sectors as "the lower third" (see Ostiguy 1998).
[5] Because I could not find national surveys for all elections since 1983, I am using only ecological data.

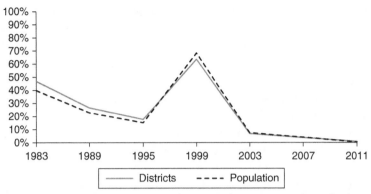

FIGURE 5.1 Electoral competition for outsiders in presidential elections, Argentina, 1983–2011 (% outsider districts and outsider population in outsider districts with electoral competition).
Source: INDEC, electoral data from Ministerio del Interior for most years and Abal-Medina and Calvo for 1999. See Appendix 3.

(Alliance), a coalition of the UCR and the Front for a Country with Solidarity (FREPASO) – a center-left offshoot of the PJ founded in the early 1990s. The Alliance obtained a large vote share in outsider districts that were bastions of the PJ, where it either defeated or challenged the party's electoral strength.[6]

The collapse of the Alliance government amid a political and financial crisis in 2001 contributed to the breakdown of the UCR and FREPASO.[7] PJ candidates won subsequent presidential elections comfortably and, as noted in Figure 5.1, they obtained remarkable support in outsider districts. In 2003, when the PJ did not hold a primary before elections, its three presidential candidates together won more than 60 percent of the vote and faced no competition from other parties in outsider districts.

Social Mobilization

Social movements of unemployed and informal poor workers emerged in the late 1990s[8] and forged alliances with labor unions, constituting a powerful SMC.[9] Several factors contributed to the unexpected emergence

---

[6] Outsider districts (municipalities) have at least 55 percent of the population classified as outsiders.

[7] See Lupu (2014); Roberts (2014).

[8] See Delamata (2004); Garay (2003; 2007); Silva (2009); Svampa and Pereyra (2003; 2005).

[9] For the sake of simplicity, I will refer to these movements and their allies as a single SMC, although at times there were marked divisions among blocs of unemployed workers' associations and labor unions.

of this coalition. In the face of high unemployment, which grew in the 1990s and peaked at 19 percent in 1995,[10] the government did not extend a safety net, leaving the plight of the jobless unanswered. The first organizations of unemployed workers emerged out of a wave of protest that unfolded in several provinces badly hit by unemployment in 1997. As described later, the distribution of workfare benefits by the national government to put an end to the very first protests unintentionally sparked a wave of contention in demand for these benefits that spread to different provinces. These early mobilization initiated a dynamic of protest for social benefits and state responses with social provisions that empowered the incipient unemployed workers' organizations and inspired new groups to form or to engage in protest as a way to access benefits. Workfare benefits, moreover, helped the organizations of the unemployed to grow, pose common demands to the state, and engage in coordinated action.[11]

Access to national workfare benefits was fundamental for the formation and consolidation of a movement of unemployed workers. These schemes financed small public works and social services provided by community associations and local governments, which hired unemployed workers for short-term assignments. The fact that popular associations could administer program benefits by setting up community projects in which the unemployed fulfilled their workfare obligations (i.e., soup kitchens, small manufacturing workshops, orchards) created allies and "co-beneficiaries" among existing community groups and new popular associations formed by unemployed workers, both of which sought to access program benefits. The associative administration of benefits empowered these movements of unemployed workers and the community associations linked to them. It increased their membership base, as benefits could be used as selective incentives to recruit members.[12] Moreover, it provided financial resources, as several of these associations began to collect membership dues from workfare beneficiaries to finance community projects and protest activity. These movements could therefore extend their organizational infrastructure with workfare benefits. At the same time, participatory institutions of decision making were established

---

[10] Data from INDEC, www.indec.gov.ar (accessed 2008).

[11] The unemployed workers' movement was composed of organizations with different views regarding partisan politics, but who mobilized together around social policy demands.

[12] On the importance of selective incentives for recruitment, see Olson (1965); Rothstein (1992); Tarrow (1998: 5); Western (1997).

to minimize conflict and prevent members from exiting, further strengthening these movements.

The movements of unemployed workers became appealing to labor unions. In 1998, the largest organizations forged alliances with the Argentine Workers' Central (CTA) and the Combative and Classist Current (CCC).[13] The CTA was a higher-level federation ("central") formed in 1992 by public-sector workers' and teachers' unions, which split from the historic General Labor Confederation (CGT) after its leadership supported market-oriented reforms. The CTA became a key ally of the unemployed. The CCC was a smaller coalition of public-sector and industrial workers' unions, which over the years came to control a number of internal factory commissions.

These alliances benefited both types of organizations in specific ways. The CTA saw in the movements of the unemployed a key ally to advance its own demands against state downsizing and for better salaries and public services, which had deteriorated as a result of economic adjustment in the 1990s. At the same time, these alliances allowed the CTA to represent a broader workers' movement rather than merely the formal-sector working class affiliated to labor unions (interview, Lozano, national board of CTA). Support for outsiders was therefore strategic – to increase the unions' own power to advance their agenda – as well as based on the CTA's view that the union movement should be organized as a broad democratic workers' movement. This stands in sharp contrast to the business-oriented structure of the CGT labor unions, which largely lacked internal democracy.[14] For the unemployed, alliances with labor unions became critical to expanding their movements geographically, gaining organizational skills, and increasing pressure on the state to expand social benefits.

As seen in Figure 5.2, a new wave of protest broke out in late 1999, after the Alliance's arrival to power. Protest intensified as social conditions deteriorated and the government failed to provide adequate responses to protestors' demands. With allied labor unions, unemployed workers' movements carried out nationwide roadblocks in demand for workfare benefits, social assistance, and jobs. The number of unemployed workers' organizations grew from six to thirteen, and protests took place in all provinces (Data Set of Protest). Unemployed workers' movements

[13] In 1998, these were the Federation of Land and Housing (FTV) and the CCC unemployed workers.

[14] On CGT unions, see Etchemendy (2011), Godio (2000).

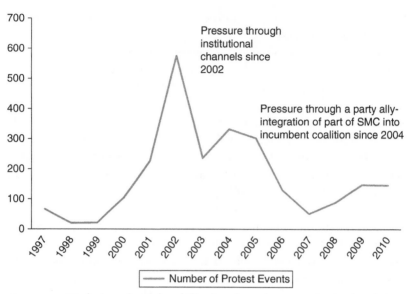

FIGURE 5.2 Evolution of social mobilization through protest, institutional channels, and a party ally, 1996–2010.
Source: Estimates from author's Data Set of Protest (1996–2010). See Appendix 2.

and the CTA also used institutional channels to advance and amplify
their demands. In coordination with a broad number of social organizations, this SMC demanded the establishment of universal pensions, family allowances, job-training schemes, and unemployment insurance.

Protest peaked in 2002. Demonstrations took place in coordination
with other organizations within a broader context of turbulence and
crisis that amplified the demands of the unemployed. By 2004, unemployed workers' movements mobilized at least 100,000 members in the
metropolitan area of Buenos Aires alone, and the largest groups spread
throughout the country.[15]

Various institutional channels of interaction and negotiation with the
state were opened up beginning in 2002. As shown in Figure 5.2, protest
in turn declined to some extent but remained high until late 2005, when
it began to decline significantly. Beginning in 2004, some of these social
movements integrated into the Néstor Kirchner administration (2003–7);
leaders joined positions in the state, while other groups remained separated from the government and resorted to contention to demand social

---

[15] For further information on the composition of these movements, see Svampa and Pereyra
(2003); Garay (2007).

policy, particularly in 2005, when protests jointly with labor unions grew significantly. Protest declined again, to grow in 2009.

5.3 EMERGENCE OF SOCIAL MOBILIZATION, ELECTORAL COMPETITION FOR OUTSIDERS, AND STATE RESPONSES

The first waves of social mobilization compelled incumbents to provide social policy responses and negotiate the distribution of benefits with protestors. However, policy responses under the second Menem administration (1995–9) were small scale, not amounting to what I define as "expansion," as movements exerting pressure for social benefits were still small; they were not operating nationwide, coordination with unions was still beginning, and though protests were intense in some localities, movement members and organizations were still few. Under the Alliance administration (1999–2001), social movements grew significantly and their protest activity expanded nationwide. In this context, the Alliance made several announcements of social policy expansion but failed to implement initiatives quickly, contributing to the erosion of the government's stability.

The following analysis traces the emergence and growth of social mobilization as well as the incentives of incumbents to respond to demands. It demonstrates that a dynamic of demand making by a growing social movement coalition and state responses to these demands were already under way before the 2001 financial crisis, and thus social policy expansion beginning in 2002 was not simply a direct consequence of the crisis. This dynamic of demands and responses is fundamental for understanding why (a) social policy expansion occurred and (b) why it resulted in an inclusive model, which is analyzed in section 4.

The Second Menem Administration (1995–1999)

The first wave of protests by unemployed workers broke out in 1997. The protest movement took shape after Menem's landslide reelection in 1995, in which outsiders voted massively for the incumbent. After the adoption of market reforms in the early 1990s, economic conditions began to deteriorate under Menem's second term. A recession triggered by the 1994 Mexican crisis and compounded by the international crisis of the late 1990s contributed to a dramatic surge in unemployment.[16] In

---

[16] On unemployment from 1974 to the present, see INDEC, www.indec.gov.ar.

response, the Menem administration only created a few targeted income-support programs, including the small workfare program Plan Trabajar,[17] to show concern for the plight of the unemployed.[18] According to a CGT labor leader, unemployment was then perceived as a "temporary" phenomenon produced by economic reforms, which would swiftly contract as the economy recovered (interview, Mastrocolla, board of CGT).

After the national government distributed benefits from Plan Trabajar to diffuse an isolated protest that had turned violent, unemployed workers and community associations organized roadblocks and marches to demand benefits from the plan in several provinces. In the context of skyrocketing unemployment, these benefits were seen as "jobs," and as a legitimate form of social inclusion. From April to June 1997, an average of 1.6 protests per day were held in demand for workfare benefits in seven of twenty-four provinces.[19]

This wave of protest was not strong enough to prompt the government to engage in large-scale policy expansion. However, the Menem administration made three important changes in workfare benefits, which allowed it to temper contention. First, it increased workfare beneficiaries of Plan Trabajar from 62,083 in 1996 to 126,246 in 1997.[20] Second, it created other workfare schemes, such as Community Services, with features similar to those of Plan Trabajar but governed by more flexible rules. These programs were inaugurated to have readily available provisions to allocate during protests (interview, high official, Ministry of Labor). As Minister of Labor Armando Caro Figueroa noted, these different workfare benefits "were meant to mitigate social tensions when there were roadblocks, but they also aimed at addressing the problem of people who had no income or who had lost their jobs" (interview). Third, the administration altered the federal distribution of workfare benefits to prevent contention in the densely populated province of Buenos Aires, which had largely been excluded from the distribution of targeted national programs before protests started (interview, Amadeo). In subsequent years the area became the largest bastion of the unemployed workers' movement.

---

[17] See Chapter 3. Plan Trabajar provided funding for NGOs and local governments to develop community projects and hire unemployed workers for three to six months. The distribution of the benefit on the ground was done by the provincial level and was highly clientelistic. See Garay (2007) and Giraudy (2007).

[18] On workfare programs, see Golbert (1998).

[19] Author's Data Set of Protest (Appendix 1). Twenty-three provinces plus the city of Buenos Aires.

[20] Average number of annual beneficiaries estimated with data from the Ministry of Labor. See Garay (2007: 312).

The emergence of unemployed workers' movements was consequential for party politics. First on their own, and then in alliance with the CTA, the organizations of the unemployed developed a new distributional structure on the ground. This affected to some extent the dominance of the PJ's local patronage networks[21] as it generated incentives for local PJ activists, especially those involved in community work, to exit party networks and enter the movements of the unemployed.[22] At the same time, facing competition from unemployed workers' networks, some local machines began to demand more substantial policy responses to prevent the exit of activists. Partly to respond to growing demands, several provinces established small workfare programs. By 2000, fifteen provinces ran twenty-four provincial workfare programs, nineteen of which had been created in the previous three years (Garay 2007: 325).

The 1999 Election

Electoral competition for outsiders was high in the 1999 presidential election. The midterm elections of 1997 had already shown declining support for the incumbent and the emergence of a unified challenger, the Alliance, which won the legislative elections in the province of Buenos Aires – the bastion of the PJ's future presidential candidate, Eduardo Duhalde.[23]

Competition for the vote of outsiders grew threatening to the PJ's continuity in power in 1999. Although the formation and ascent of the Alliance should have raised concern within the Menem administration about the potential defeat of the PJ in the 1999 elections, deep rivalries prevented Menem from supporting Duhalde's campaign. Divisions intensified as a consequence of Duhalde's opposition to Menem's tenacious and eventually unsuccessful attempts to run for another presidential term, which the constitution banned.[24]

Other factors further debilitated Duhalde's appeal among voters. First, in a highly uncertain electoral environment in which the PJ incumbent had low approval ratings, several PJ governors scheduled subnational elections separately so as to avoid being hurt by national electoral dynamics. This weakened Duhalde by depriving him of critical support. Second, Duhalde's critiques of Menem's policies made it hard for him to

---

[21] On patronage networks, see Auyero (2001); Levitsky (2003, chapter 6).
[22] See Garay (2007: 315); Svampa and Pereyra (2003: 92, 132, 186).
[23] Ecological data of outsider districts reveal some electoral competition for outsider voters, which was present in 39 percent of the outsider districts (author's estimates).
[24] See "Nada peor que otro Peronista" in *Pagina 12*, July 14, 1998.

forge a deal with the small right-wing party Action for the Republic (AR), which allied with the PJ in gubernatorial elections but entered Domingo Cavallo – Menem's former finance minister and the father of his stabilization program – for president. The PJ ultimately won several gubernatorial races, but obtained the lowest vote share ever for a PJ presidential candidate: 38 percent.

The Alliance candidate, Fernando de la Rúa, campaigned on job creation, programs to fight indigence, anticorruption measures, and macroeconomic continuity, a package that seemed appealing for both low-income and middle-class voters. At the same time, the alliance with FREPASO probably increased electoral support for de la Rúa among low-income voters (interview, high-ranking PJ politician). The Alliance won the presidential election comfortably, and gained unprecedented support from outsiders, with 63.52 percent of outsider districts experiencing electoral competition (see Figure 5.1).

The Fernando de la Rúa Administration (1999–2001)

Fernando de la Rúa came to power with an exceptional mandate. He had gained unprecedented support from outsider voters, and a decline in protest in 1999 was probably tied to the expectation that the new government would address joblessness and extend workfare benefits more effectively than the outgoing Menem administration. At first glance, this should have led the Alliance to respond to expectations in order to consolidate outsiders' support and prevent social mobilization from escalating. Although the incentives for expansion were present, the Alliance suffered from serious internal divisions among its component parties and coordination problems, which delayed responses. FREPASO was a "media party" without institutionalization,[25] and had a difficult time governing with the UCR, to the point that after launching strong accusations of corruption against part of the cabinet, the vice president and leader of FREPASO, as well as several ministers, resigned and informally terminated the coalition government by the end of its first ten months in office. Together with a lack of clear command on the part of de la Rúa, the breakup of the coalition weakened the president.

Overall support for the de la Rúa administration vanished rapidly.[26] At the same time, the incumbent made three crucial decisions that triggered

[25] On FREPASO, see Novaro and Palermo (1998).
[26] According to a survey by Gallup, in December 2000 only 11 percent of respondents reported to support the de la Rúa administration. "Persiste la mala imagen del gobierno," *La Nación*, February 25, 2001.

large-scale contention by the unemployed and labor union allies. First, he cut down workfare benefits and other small social programs, all of which were perceived as being distributed by PJ clientelist networks. The intention of the national government was to redesign these benefits to prevent their manipulation (interviews, Fernández Meijide and Cafiero, ministers of social development). Yet no new benefits replaced those that were being eliminated. Between March and August 2000, workfare beneficiaries declined from 150,000 to about 50,000, leading to forceful protests for the restitution of such benefits. Second, in an increasingly tight fiscal environment, the government reduced public expenditure with the intention to preserve the convertibility system, the exchange rate that had established parity between the Argentine peso and the U.S. dollar in 1991. In combination with other factors – such as the privatization of the pension system in the mid-1990s and the international financial crisis in the late 1990s – this exchange rate system spawned a large fiscal deficit and decreased the competitiveness of Argentine exports, which compromised economic activity. Finally, together with social policy retrenchment, the de la Rúa administration imposed a 13 percent cutback of public-sector salaries and pensions in an effort to reduce the public deficit in July 2001.

The new wave of protest that broke out under de la Rúa's administration was substantially larger and gained national scope. Sustained protests expanded geographically, taking place regularly in half of the provinces, and the number of federations in the movement of unemployed workers grew from seven to fourteen between 1999 and 2001. Aside from being backed by hundreds of community associations, the wave of mobilization by this SMC had a number of occasional allies, including labor unions in the most combatant faction of the CGT and the Agrarian Federation, which organized roadblocks of producers (Data Set of Protest 1996–2010).

Labor unions and organizations of the unemployed not only coordinated a series of nationwide protests to reinstate the benefits that had been cut, but also pressed for a Universal Child Allowance (AUH), pensions, and unemployment and job-training insurance. For example, in August 2000, the CTA marched for weeks, organizing acts in different localities with unemployed workers' organizations to publicize and press for these proposals and to gain popular support via the collection of signatures.[27]

In the face of growing demands from below for social benefits and jobs, the Ministries of Social Development and of Labor drafted several

---

[27] See "La Movilizacion de la CTA termina hoy en el Congreso," *La Nación*, August 9, 2000.

proposals to expand social policy. The proposals' scope of coverage increased as social pressure became higher. Despite contention, however, the president did not decisively launch any of these measures. In 2000, the Ministry of Social Development announced Solidarity and Heads-of-Household, two means-tested schemes for households in extreme poverty, which were estimated at about 300,000. Solidarity would provide a grant for children conditional on school attendance, while Heads-of-Household would provide a grant to single mothers to complete high school (interviews, Fernández Meijide and Isuani, secretary of policies for seniors). Solidarity was never implemented, and the Heads-of-Household program reached only 3,000 beneficiaries (interview, Isuani).

De la Rúa further advanced controversial measures that combined the retrenchment of existing benefits for insiders with some expansion. The first initiative concerned pension policy. To address both the pension system deficit and the lack of coverage of senior outsiders, the president issued a decree in 2000 that eliminated the basic state pillar for higher-income pensioners – those with a benefit equivalent to 4.3 times the minimum pension – and reallocated part of that funding to a very small pension for indigent outsiders over seventy years of age.[28] Several Alliance legislators rejected this reform on the grounds that its main goal was to contain costs rather than to seriously protect the poor, and the courts blocked its implementation, as it affected pensioners' acquired rights.

More ambitious proposals to respond to social protest were designed in 2001 as discontent mounted and the coalition crumbled due to the resignation of the vice president. After assuming office, the newly appointed minister of social development, Juan Pablo Cafiero, announced the gradual implementation of the Pact for Childhood, an all-encompassing initiative that included the Child Insurance – which provided support for households in extreme poverty – as well as the universalization of formal-sector family allowances, extending them to 3 million outsider children (interviews, Cafiero and Vinocur, secretary of social policy). According to Cafiero, upon accepting his appointment, the president promised that these measures would be implemented (interview, Cafiero).

Simultaneously, the Ministry of Labor proposed a different reform of family allowances: to reallocate existing family benefits to children in households with earnings below three times the minimum wage, thereby making them available only to outsiders and low-income formal workers

---

[28] Decree 1306/2000.

(interview, Patricia Bullrich, minister of labor).[29] Despite policy promises and growing social conflict, none of these initiatives was implemented. The president continued to focus his energy on the maintenance of the exchange rate parity, relegating other policy issues to this goal (interview, Cafiero).

Facing nationwide protests, some of which included close to 100 road-blocks at each event, the president made another announcement to contain destabilizing pressures. He passed by decree the "Argentine Plan," a package to reactivate the economy "with social justice," in November 2001. The plan sought to "strictly safeguard" the convertibility system and to introduce "completely revolutionary measures" to fight poverty.[30] It comprised a battery of social programs, including the Comprehensive System of Family Protection (SIPF), along the lines of the family allowances reform proposed by Minister of Labor Bullrich; school grants for 700,000 high school students; and a small pension for 60,000 indigent seniors aged over seventy-four (interviews, Bullrich, Caro Figueroa).[31] The SIPF's implementation would further replace existing workfare schemes. Despite the need for decisive action amid growing protest, implementation was scheduled for January 2002.

De la Rúa's reform of family allowances was strongly resisted by labor unions and by the movements of the unemployed. Family allowances are an important component of workers' income (interview, Mastrocolla and Rodríguez, national board of CGT), and CGT unions completely opposed transforming them into "social assistance" for "low-income workers" (interview, Rodríguez). Union leaders contended that the government had "invented a 'revolutionary system' of family allowances that takes money away from the poor and gives it to the poorest."[32] New benefits were not supported by the organizations of the unemployed either. In fact, some joined labor unions in protest against the reform. Minister Bullrich attributed the lack of support to the fact that "it was a time of political combat" (interview). Reflecting on the deterioration of the government's legitimacy, the secretary of social security at the time

---

[29] Both ministers sought funding from the World Bank, which favored the proposal of the Ministry of Labor.

[30] Decree 1382/2001. "El Mensaje Presidencial Completo," transcribed in *La Nación*, November 1, 2001.

[31] At the time there were about 500,000 people aged seventy and older without pensions (SIEMPRO 2002); "Claves de la Asignación Universal," *La Nación*, November 4, 2001.

[32] See "Movilización de la CGT rebelde por la soberanía y los jubilados," *La Nación*, November 21, 2001.

asserted: "No one supported the policy; times were too hard to find any partners" (interview, Jorge San Martino).

The CGT successfully contested the reform of family allowances in the courts.[33] Retrenching existing benefits and reallocating resources to the very poor had the same fate as de la Rúa's proposal to reform the pension system in 2000. As observed in other cases in this book, opposition from labor unions emerges when governments take away concrete benefits formal workers receive to reallocate them to outsiders. Otherwise, unions are likely to either support or remain indifferent to expansion.

A broad coalition led by the CTA, movements of the unemployed, human rights organizations, and other social and economic organizations such as the chamber of medium- and small-scale business (APYME) and the Agrarian Federation formed the National Front Against Poverty (FRENAPO) to demand universal benefits. To pressure the government to adopt its proposals, FRENAPO set out to mobilize broad public support by organizing a "popular consultation," a sort of nonbinding referendum on its policy agenda, in December 2001. More than 3 million people – close to 15 percent of the national electorate at the time – voted for the creation of universal family allowances, unemployment insurance, and pensions that would extend benefits similar to those received by formal workers (interview Lozano; Del Frade 2012).[34]

Ill-fated policy decisions triggered de la Rúa's resignation in December 2001. In a desperate effort to save the convertibility system and the banking sector, the national government froze bank deposits. A deep political and financial crisis broke out. Large-scale protests by bank depositors flooded the cities. With regards to outsiders, restrictions on bank withdrawals were particularly deleterious for the informal economy, which relied on cash payments. Together with the absence of any social policy measures and any clear indication on when bank accounts would be liberated, protests by the unemployed, labor unions, and bank depositors became incessant.

Within a context of growing discontent, de la Rúa ignored advice from part of his cabinet and produced no rapid alternative response to quell social conflict (interviews, Bullrich and Cafiero).[35] Bullrich contends, "On several occasions I warned de la Rúa that if we did not do anything for the extreme poor and if we did not provide a subsidy for the unemployed,

---

[33] See "Dos fallos favorables a la CGT," *La Nación*, December 13, 2001.
[34] See "Fuerte apoyo a un seguro de empleo," *Clarín*, December 18, 2001.
[35] To replace the SIPF, the government announced it would provide food stamps to 3 million low-income families in 2002.

the spiral of violence would be unstoppable."[36] Despite having the option to refloat the Pact for Childhood or to expand workfare benefits, which were not politically – and legally – controversial,[37] the de la Rúa administration delayed policy responses.

Facing widespread protest, de la Rúa declared a state of siege, thereby banning meetings and protests to contain conflict. Contrary to what the president expected, this measure immediately triggered massive antigovernment protests, provoking his resignation amid police violence and riots. In the following weeks, three caretaker presidents resigned until Duhalde – the PJ's candidate in 1999 – assumed power as the interim president in January 2002.

5.4 SOCIAL MOBILIZATION, SOCIAL POLICY EXPANSION, AND INCLUSIVE POLICIES

High levels of social mobilization compelled President Duhalde to launch unprecedented social policy initiatives to survive in office. Further expansion was carried out by the administrations of Néstor Kirchner (2003–7) and Cristina Fernández de Kirchner (2007–11) after Duhalde's short tenure. Facing high levels of contention, Néstor Kirchner managed to incorporate some of the largest movements in his broad coalition. After allying with the government, these movements of the unemployed advocated social policy expansion from within the state, while other groups continued to press for expansion through institutional channels and in the streets.

New policies were negotiated with social movement leaders and with their union allies, or were launched in direct response to their concrete demands for universal transfers, pensions, and health care services. Aside from being inclusive, these large-scale social programs were also nondiscretionary, which is striking given both the PJ's policies of state shrinkage in the 1990s and its reputation for clientelism (Auyero 2001; Levitsky 2003; Stokes 2005). Next, I analyze (1) why incumbents launched the expansion of nondiscretionary social policy starting in 2002, and (2) why they created inclusive benefits. I further refer to the ways in which they overcame resistance from entrenched interests in some policy areas and managed to fund the new policies.

---

[36] Quoted in "Combate contra la Pobreza," *La Nación*, December 18, 2002.
[37] The secretary of employment proposed to double the number of workfare beneficiaries.

The Eduardo Duhalde Administration (2002–2003)

Upon taking office, Duhalde made critical decisions to address the social and economic crisis. Facing dramatic levels of protest and lacking legitimacy due to his nonelected status, the interim president initiated a phase of rapid social policy expansion to both calm protest and stabilize his administration. On his first day in office, he passed by decree the expansion of income transfers for outsiders to mitigate protests, and established that the state's spending priority should be the payment of these transfers (interviews, Duhalde and Amadeo). At the same time, after one of his predecessors had defaulted on the foreign debt, Duhalde devalued the currency, ending the convertibility system and generating favorable prospects for agricultural exports in buoyant international commodity markets. The new exchange rate increased producers' profits and facilitated the reinstallation of export dues, which had been eliminated by the Menem administration in 1991.[38] While social policy expansion helped to contain protest, macroeconomic changes fueled economic growth, which reached levels above 8 percent of the GDP between 2003 and 2007.

To better address the economic and political crisis, Duhalde formed a plural cabinet and established several arenas of policy deliberation and negotiation. Of particular importance was the Argentine Dialogue (AD), a forum with representatives from government, business, agriculture, labor unions, and the federations of the unemployed that was set up by the president and sponsored by the United Nations Development Program and the Catholic Church. The AD discussed, agreed upon, and supported critical policy proposals. According to Cafiero, Duhalde established the AD to gain "strong backing" for his social policies because "at that time there were no political parties, nothing. Argentina had popular assemblies, pot banging, protest. There was nothing with some prestige, some authority, to hold onto" (interview). Informal meetings and consultation over social policy and labor-market issues also took shape. Duhalde and his ministers met with labor and social movement leaders to discuss social policy decisions and negotiate a "truce" whenever contention escalated.[39] Duhalde also established participatory oversight councils to supervise the implementation of his key social policy initiatives as a way to channel activism away from the streets and/or to contribute to policy implementation and oversight. Furthermore, he established a national council to discuss social policy proposals and oversee policy implementation. This

---

[38] See Decree 2284/91.
[39] Data Set of Protest (1996–2010).

council included representatives from social and economic organizations, such as business associations and agricultural producers.

Next, I trace the process of the adoption of specific policy initiatives, income transfers, health care, and pensions, and present the reasons why an inclusive model was chosen. It bears highlighting that, aside from their inclusive nature, these policies were nondiscretionary. Fearing discontent triggered by the biased distribution of benefits, or the potential discrediting of the new policies due to manipulation, the president adopted nondiscretionary benefits and aimed to enforce transparency mechanisms. Large-scale mobilization prompted subnational authorities as well as patronage networks to accept the implementation of nondiscretionary benefits by the national government.

Income Transfers

Soon after taking office, Duhalde passed by decree the creation of the Unemployed Heads-of-Household Program (UHHP), a massive workfare scheme for unemployed and informal poor workers with children under eighteen years of age or who were expecting a child. Given its broad-reaching coverage and the fact that it was established as a "right of social inclusion" and not as a temporary benefit, the UHHP represented a watershed in social policy for outsiders. The program was initiated in January at a small scale and expanded over the following months, when the second phase of the program was agreed upon by the Argentine Dialogue and institutionalized by decree in April. It reached more than 2 million households by the end of the year, about 20 percent of total households in the country.[40]

As Duhalde explained, the main goal of the program was to achieve "social peace," as high levels of conflict could severely compromise his government. In the words of his spokesman at the time, with the country "on fire" the president's main concern when launching the benefit was "survival" (interview, Amadeo). Despite the lack of state funding amid the crisis, payment of the UHHP became the number one priority of Duhalde's government, a completely unusual decision for the Argentine state, which had never prioritized these sectors before (interviews,

---

[40] Data from MTEySS and INDEC. See Decree 565/02 and Diálogo Argentino (2002). Note that Interim President Adolfo Rodríguez Saá of the PJ – who was in power for a week until he lost support from his party and resigned to allow Duhalde to assume office – had announced he would create 1 million jobs/workfare benefits.

Duhalde, Amadeo). In response to skepticism from politicians about his government's ability to pay the benefit, Duhalde notes:

I would tell them, "there is always money." The issue is whether you consider the UHHP a number one priority, and if you do, then there will be money, there won't be for other things... I established that the UHHP had to be paid first, then public salaries beginning with the lower-income employees. (interview)

Social movement leaders understood that the unprecedented provision of income transfers was a response to their mobilization. As described by an unemployed leader, the UHHP was "our conquest; [the conquest] of the 10 percent unemployed workers who are organized" (interview, unemployed leader #1). The program was not only perceived as beneficial to outsiders, but also as politically strategic for the incumbent to appease protests. As this activist explained, "Duhalde implemented the UHHP ... to disarticulate the movement. He tried to inundate the country with benefits to remove the motive to launch protests ... to internally demobilize the movements" (interview). Facing contention, the government could have expanded benefits on a smaller scale for those in the streets only. However, given both the level of activism and of deprivation, the small-scale distribution of benefits would have led to continuous levels of protest, as activists could have easily mobilized those marginalized by state policy. The response was therefore large-scale expansion.

The president himself, as well as government officials, met with unemployed movement leaders and the CTA, and the UHHP's design was largely a response to their demands. The features of the program were further discussed within the AD. Social movements and the CTA pressed for universal benefits and jobs, and understood that the massive scope of coverage of the UHHP was the fruit of their struggle (interview, Lozano, CTA).

The benefit level of the UHHP was initially high, established at 75 percent of the minimum wage paid to public employees by local administrations, and equal to the unemployment insurance paid to formal workers at the time. This was in line with the FRENAPO's proposal for a universal unemployment benefit. According to Cafiero, Duhalde's vice chief of staff, paying a higher benefit level would have created a conflict with mayors, who were expected to employ some workfare beneficiaries in municipal offices but could not pay them the same salary municipal workers received, as the workfare obligation entailed fewer hours of work (interview).

Social movements also pressed for participation in policy implementation as a way to remain involved in policy making and oversee implementation.[41] A national advisory council with representatives from business, labor, social movements, religious organizations, and the state was established to supervise the implementation of the UHHP, propose reforms, and issue monthly reports to the president. Local participatory councils were also set up to facilitate and oversee the implementation of the program in municipalities with more than 2,500 inhabitants. For the state, the inclusion of social movements in these councils was a good way to help curb contention by institutionalizing channels of communication with social activists, improving implementation of the workfare programs, and increasing accountability. The AD also promoted the establishment of councils as venues that could conduct oversight activities, as discretion in implementation was a major concern. Social movements and unions actively engaged in local councils and provided critical help to local offices swamped with large numbers of applications for social benefits. According to Duhalde and the public officials interviewed in this study, local councils helped contain social conflict (interviews, Duhalde, high official, Ministry of Labor).

Aside from demanding broad and participatory policies, social movements and participants in the AD further asked Duhalde to create benefits with clear rules. Government officials and social movement leaders interviewed for this project repeatedly mentioned the strategic importance for the incumbent of establishing benefits that would not be clientelistic or distributed through partisan networks. In this regard, the president's spokesman stated:

[T]he political class was terrified ... it was clear that this program [the UHHP] had to be administered with a *magnifying glass* and provided directly to beneficiaries. (interview Amadeo)

Discretionary and ineffective implementation was perceived as completely unfit for this context. Clientelism could easily be denounced by social movements and propel further destabilizing protest rather than the social peace that the government expected to achieve with massive social policy expansion.[42] In order to prevent the manipulation of benefits by local machines, the administration of the policy was centralized in the hands of the national government. The Duhalde administration

---

[41] After meeting with the minister of labor, leaders of the unemployed movement told the press that they had negotiated the participation of their organizations in the councils, Data Set of Protest (1996–2010).

[42] As a public official involved in the design of UHHP stated, "there was no room for clientelistic distribution in the crisis" (interview, high official, Ministry of Labor).

understood that provincial governments both lacked the capacity to quickly implement large-scale social policies (interview, top advisor, Duhalde administration) and could easily deviate program resources because they had traditionally "swallowed social expenditure" (interview, Cafiero). Given its bureaucratic capacity, the Ministry of Labor, which at the time administered social security benefits for formal workers and had run smaller workfare benefits in the past, was perceived as the best choice to embark on the implementation of the UHHP (interview, Feijoo, social policy advisor).

Provincial governments initially exerted strong pressure on the national executive to participate in the administration of the UHHP. Yet concerns about political survival and the national government's determination to keep a centralized policy design made them accept the new status quo. According to a key official involved in the implementation of the UHHP, "there was absolutely no negotiation with the provinces ... given the lack of administrative capacity of several provinces, it would have been suicidal to include them" (interview, top advisor, Duhalde administration). Therefore, in the context of large-scale mobilization, the involvement of partisan networks or delays and inefficiency in the distribution of social benefits could severely affect the legitimacy of the incumbent and trigger further conflict. Amadeo further asserted that "the central issue of the program [UHHP] was credibility. If the government failed to pay the benefit at 8 am [on pay day], you had a disaster" (interview Amadeo).

Lack of trust in the government's ability to effectively pay benefits also shaped the views of governors regarding the UHHP. According to Duhalde:

> There were governors who did not believe in the UHHP.... [T]hey were afraid.... [T]hey would say, "there's no money ... if you don't pay the benefits, the people will burn down the [provincial] house of government.' ... These were very difficult times... I never felt alone because I let them [governors] participate. Participation makes people feel well even if you don't adopt the decisions that come out of a meeting. (interview, Duhalde)

Despite the speed with which the UHHP was launched, the national government made important efforts to ensure its transparency by broadly publicizing its existence and the rules for accessing benefits, posting the database of beneficiaries online, emphasizing that the program should not be exchanged for any kind of support, and later facilitating the reporting of abuses to the national government. The high visibility of the program was a sharp contrast with previous food and workfare programs for the poor, whose distribution was characterized by high levels of opacity. A national survey carried out in 2007 found that 93 percent of respondents knew about the UHHP and 87 percent was familiar with the benefit's conditionality (Cruces and Rovner 2008: 60).

Just as in the early stages of cash-transfer programs launched in other countries, there were abuses and errors in the UHHP. As discussed in Chapter 2, the inclusion of ineligible beneficiaries (or leakage) and the difficulty of controlling implementation were huge challenges for governments when they initiated expansion in federal systems.[43] Regarding leakage, national officials could not correctly verify eligibility when governors failed to submit payroll information for provincial bureaucracies to the national social security agency. A widely cited problem in the early stages of the UHHP was the inclusion of police officers' dependents and some local employees, who through this loophole sometimes obtained benefits until the abuses were disclosed (interviews, Duhalde; Feijoo).[44] These errors did to some extent affect the reputation of the benefit. Aside from improving checks on beneficiaries, the Ministry of Labor created a commission to report and investigate abuses.[45]

If these inclusion errors were few and easier to solve, the main problem affecting the UHHP concerned the difficulty of monitoring the workfare obligation. This issue had been a bone of contention during discussions over the UHHP's design. While some policy makers were concerned about the potential manipulation of beneficiaries via the work requirement and preferred to create family allowances or a simple unconditional transfer, some of the AD participants proposed workfare benefits to enhance "work culture" despite the adverse economic context for the rapid creation of employment (interviews, Amadeo, Cafiero). The employment of beneficiaries by municipal governments was a source of concern among opponents of the work

---

[43] I focus more attention on the UHHP in this section given that it has been often defined as discretionary, overlooking several of the program's features and efforts to curb discretion described here, as well as significant problems initially found in other countries, as, for example, with Progresa in Mexico or Bolsa Escola in Brazil.

[44] Information on the UHHP provided by MTEySS. As reported in *Clarín*, November 9, 2005, data from the attorney investigating fraud in the UHHP indicates that, by 2005, 8,000 benefits had been withdrawn or investigated. Inclusion errors comprised 4,000 local employees, 1,148 policemen, 1,445 formal-sector workers and members of security forces and the military. This represents less than 0.5 percent of the total average annual beneficiaries between 2002 and 2005.

[45] See "Existen más planes que nunca," *La Nación*, December 1, 2003. Investigations used information on financial transactions, credit card consumption, and possession of motor vehicles.

requirement, who feared that it would make beneficiaries vulnerable to manipulation by partisan machines. A smaller share of beneficiaries ended up working for local governments. According to a survey by the Ministry of Labor, 20 percent of the UHHP's beneficiaries were employed by local governments, while the vast majority, 60 percent, worked in community-based projects (e.g., day care centers) (MTEySS 2004: 53).[46]

Other policy designs were considered, but were deemed too difficult to implement quickly. The difficulty of controlling the workfare obligation eventually limited the UHHP's political support and prompted government officials to try to replace it under the Kirchner administrations.

After a new round of intense protests in early 2003, the Duhalde administration launched two other smaller programs to complement the UHHP: Families for Social Inclusion ("Families") and the Community Employment Program (PEC). Families targeted households with earnings below the minimum wage. It paid a flat-rate allowance and granted additional benefits per child conditional on school attendance and health checkups. In 2004, the program reached 240,000 households. The PEC, by contrast, was a workfare program administered by community organizations, which hired unemployed workers for community service and public works projects and came to cover a comparable number of beneficiaries in 2003. Because the state had established a deadline to access the UHHP, these other two programs were instrumental for the extension of coverage to the newly unemployed or to people without young children who could qualify for the PEC.

A cash transfer targeting families with children had been in the pipeline for a few years. It was proposed and seriously discussed first by social development experts under the Menem administration, designed within the Ministry of Social Development during the de la Rúa administration, and began implementation under Duhalde (interview, Feijoo). In fact, at the beginning of the Duhalde administration, social development officials led by the president's wife, Hilda Duhalde, preferred Families over the UHHP as the former seemingly had "clearer and more transparent targeting mechanisms than the UHHP" at a time in which Hilda Duhalde "felt very threatened by potential allegations of corruption in the administration of social programs" (interview, top advisor). Yet Families did not lend itself to immediate implementation.[47]

---

[46] 81 percent of beneficiaries were required to carry out the workfare obligation. Exemptions were extended based on family and health issues (e.g., single parents with more than three children, adults in charge of a person with a health condition).

[47] Several officials from the social security agency and the Ministry of Labor voiced this in interviews.

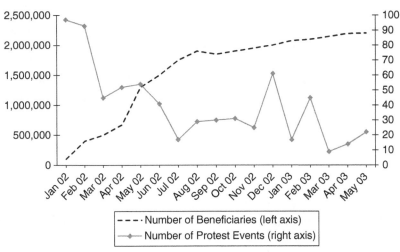

FIGURE 5.3 Protest for social benefits and workfare beneficiaries, Duhalde administration.
Source: Data on workfare benefits provided by Ministry of Labor; Protest Events from Data Set of Protest (see Appendix 2).

The PEC differed from Families and from the UHHP in fundamental ways. The PEC was established to have flexible, readily available benefits to curb contention after access to the UHHP was restricted by the government (interview, high official, Ministry of Labor).[48] Some organizations of the unemployed welcomed the inauguration of the PEC, which was considered "like Plan Trabajar" as it allowed associations to "hire and fire" beneficiaries who worked in their development projects (interview, unemployed leader #2). PEC benefits were granted to associations rather than to individual beneficiaries. In contrast, the UHHP provided a benefit to individuals, who could then choose where to do the workfare obligation. The design of the UHHP thus limited the institutional power of social organizations vis-à-vis beneficiaries, whereas the PEC (and previously Plan Trabajar) increased it. The PEC is a clear example of a club good, rather than of an inclusive benefit as it is defined here. These club-good benefits did not significantly reduce protest on their own, but they greased the wheels of negotiations with social organizations.

It was the creation of inclusive policies that ultimately helped reduce protest, as it drove the mass of participants away from the streets for two main reasons. First, benefits were often extended after negotiations had been reached with movement leaders, which led to a negotiated decline in

---

[48] The government had established a deadline for applications to the UHHP.

protest. At the same time, the extension of broad benefits simply made it more difficult for leaders to persuade protestors to keep on mobilizing in the streets. Figure 5.3 shows a decline of contention associated with the distribution of the UHHP during the Duhalde administration. As the distribution of benefits increased beginning in April 2002, when registration became effectively broad, protest – though it remained high – declined significantly, reaching between nine and thirty protest events per month under Duhalde in 2003.

Health Care

Health care was another important area of social policy expansion under Duhalde. Protests in demand for medical supplies and pharmaceuticals broke out early in the context of social mobilization surrounding the 2001 crisis, and pushed the government to decisively address problems in access to services.

After taking office, Duhalde declared a public health emergency to prevent the collapse of the health care system, especially of public hospitals serving outsiders, and adopted bold policy initiatives. In particular, Duhalde strengthened primary care services and created a free prescription drugs program for users of public health services. This unusual concern for the health care system, especially compared to previous crises such as the 1989 hyperinflation crisis,[49] responded to pent-up activism by health NGOs, labor unions, and organizations of the unemployed. In the first weeks of 2002, health workers and associations of patients with chronic conditions launched campaigns and engaged in protest activity to denounce the lack of pharmaceuticals and speculation on the part of pharmacies and labs. For example, several NGOs demanded that the state continue providing insulin and AIDS retroviral medications, and met with public authorities. Some of these associations further initiated legal action against the state to ensure access in the face of price hikes.[50] Due to the devaluation of the currency, and probably also to speculation, in the first quarter of 2002, the price of twenty-six leading medications grew 55 percent, limiting access (Ministerio de Salud 2006: 14).

---

[49] In the 1989 crisis, the government announced a voucher for low-income people to purchase pharmaceuticals, which was not implemented.

[50] See, for example, "El presidente declara la emergencia de salud," *Clarín*, January 10, 2002.

Hospital workers staged a number of strikes for improved labor conditions and to demand the uninterrupted provision of medical supplies. Their unions and associations launched a national campaign in support of public health, which mobilized thousands of people.[51] At the same time, federations of unemployed workers organized thirty-five protests in 2002 – compared to ten in 2001 – in which they demanded pharmaceuticals to distribute through their associations.[52] Demands for medications and health care services were thus another focal point of contention.

In the face of protests, and foreseeing declining access to medical supplies, medications, and worsening health indicators, Duhalde appointed a well-known public health specialist, Ginés González García, who advocated the use of generics and the creation of a free prescription drug program. Under his command, the government announced the allocation of 2 percent of the UHHP's allowance to create a prescription drug insurance system, yet the implementation of this program was immediately found to be impractical.[53] Upon revising the initiative, the Ministry of Health launched Remediar, a large-scale free prescription drugs program, to cater to the needs of nearly 15 million users of the public health care system. Concurrently, it channeled fresh funding to bolster primary care and guarantee the availability of medical supplies. Remediar was discussed and endorsed by the Argentine Dialogue.[54] At the same time, a law establishing the use of generic drugs, which allowed the state to reduce significantly the price paid for prescription medications, was passed first by decree to speed up implementation, and then approved by Congress in 2002. According to the head of Remediar, the generics law was critical for the program to take off (interview, Tobar). Both Remediar and primary care investments were initially funded with existing international cooperation loans for health infrastructure – which the Alliance had underspent (Ministerio de Salud 2006: 16).

Remediar was a fundamental innovation because the lack of access to prescription drugs on the part of outsiders was considered one of the most important inequities – if not the most – in the health care system (interview, top official, Ministry of Health). Outsiders could use state hospitals and health care centers for free, but they were generally unable

---

[51] Data Set of Protest (1996–2010).
[52] Ibid.
[53] See "Reemplazan el seguro de medicamentos," *La Nación*, June 20, 2002.
[54] Interview, leader of CCC; *La Nación*, January 25, 2001; Diálogo Argentino (2002).

to pay for prescription medications, which Remediar would provide for free. In this respect, a study found that in 1998, 90 percent of prescription drugs were issued for patients with social security or private insurance (Tobar et al. n/d: 5). Proposals to increase access to outpatient drugs had failed in the past. Together with the absence of political incentives to cater to outsiders; several factors were perceived as blocking innovation in the health care system: the highly decentralized nature of health care services, which left key policy decisions in the hands of provincial and some municipal governments, and the power of pharmaceutical labs that profited from unequal access to drugs.

Key public officials involved in the design and implementation of Remediar suggested that the political crisis and increased need to respond to the poor helped lift barriers to policy change in the health care sector in a number of ways. First, the dramatic levels of contention and the discrediting of the political class generated incentives for the national government to address the potential health care crisis that could result from the financial meltdown. The Ministry of Health indeed expected health conditions to deteriorate (Diálogo Argentino 2002). Within a context of social mobilization, provincial governments, which generally had a poor record in the administration of health care services, were forced to allow the national government to take on a larger role in order to strengthen service delivery and diffuse social conflict. According to Graciela Rosso, the vice-minister of health under the Duhalde and Néstor Kirchner administrations, provincial resistance was undercut by "the effectiveness" the government "needed to achieve with Remediar," "the speed with which we needed to implement the program," and "the severity of the crisis." As Rosso noted, "several things which would seem unthinkable in other moments were achieved in the context of the crisis" (interview).

Second, the crisis further facilitated the acquiescence of pharmaceutical labs to a new drug policy. Labs had typically opposed generics and regulations affecting medicines, as they considered them contradictory to their economic interests.[55] However, pharmaceutical companies came to see Remediar as an opportunity for making profits, for a number of reasons. On one hand, the consumption of medications (in medication units) had declined 53 percent between 1991 and 2002, plunging 30 percent

---

[55] The fight between the national government and pharmaceutical labs was particularly salient in national politics under the administration of Arturo Illia (1963–6). Conventional wisdom even imputes the active participation of labs in the overthrow of the president. Duhalde referred to this in his interview.

between 1998 and 2002 and 22 percent in 2002 alone (Ministerio de Salud 2006: 13–14). The status quo was therefore not kind to these companies' interests.[56] On the other hand, the state's strategy was to win over the companies by including them in the massive production of generics for outsiders (interview, Tobar). Therefore, labs had a real chance to increase their sales dramatically if the state became a large-scale provider of generics for a new market of 15 million people, about 40 percent of Argentina's population at the time (interviews, Remediar high official #2, Rosso).

If opposition to the adoption of a massive free prescription drugs program was overcome, a potential obstacle to the proper implementation of Remediar emerged from patronage-based local authorities. Studies of clientelism have shown that medications were often made available to poor people by local patronage networks (see Auyero 2001). As with other benefits, intense social mobilization and politicians' fears of accusations of clientelistic distributions discouraged the implementation of Remediar in a discretionary way. When the program was launched, officials in the Ministry of Health indeed feared that patronage networks could capture and distribute prescription drugs. Aside from the public health risk involved in distributing drugs without proper controls, health authorities perceived that if clientelist networks distributed free prescription drugs in exchange for political favors, or if the medicines were sold instead of distributed for free in health centers, Remediar would harm the credibility of the government and the program would be defunded. Manipulation did occur initially. Both Duhalde and the minister of health strongly emphasized the state's determination to implement the program correctly, which helped discipline local structures that sought to use prescription drugs in exchange for political favors. A high Remediar official recalled the beginning of implementation:

Mayors would go and take the boxes of medicines from health centers ... we told the minister that the party [the PJ] was destroying the program. The minister had a meeting with mayors of the Greater Buenos Aires in the headquarters of the Peronist Party, and told them, "I have the word from President Duhalde... if you touch the medicines I will cut your hands off." There was still some trouble initially ... but they did not do it anymore. (interview, Remediar high official #1)[57]

---

[56] Jacob Hacker argues that the Affordable Care Act received support from the pharmaceutical industry due to its declining profits (see Hacker 2010).

[57] This and other stories of legislators initially asking for boxes of medication to be delivered to their offices were told in interviews.

Technically, the program's design limited clientelist allocations. The fact that the national government purchased, stored, and distributed all pharmaceuticals on its own and through competitive bids, and that these activities had external oversight mechanisms, further shielded the program from abuse (interview, Remediar high official #2).

Remediar is an inclusive program, with generous, universal benefits to all outsiders and some social participation in implementation. Regarding the benefit level, Remediar met 80 percent of the demand for outpatient drugs free of charge to all users of the public health care system (Ministerio de Salud 2006). In October 2002, it provided free prescription drugs in 37 percent of existing public primary care centers, and in March 2003, it was extended to all 5,414 primary care centers nationwide (Ministerio de Salud 2006). The choice for universality responded to different reasons. Above all, in the context of the crisis, it was considered the best design to make a broad and quick impact. At the same time, officials in the Ministry of Health deemed universality the proper answer to elude the problems of clientelism. According to Remediar officials, if the program was massive and untargeted, it would be less susceptible to manipulation (interview, Remediar high official #1). As in other policy areas, nondiscretionary access was considered fundamental to the program's survival.

The inauguration of Remediar further expanded access to primary care. As a way to incentivize the use of health care services and reduce emergency room visits at public hospitals, the Ministry of Health established that pharmaceuticals would be available only in public health centers that assisted patients free of charge. An explicit precondition for health centers to participate in the free prescription drugs program was to forbid the request of "voluntary" contribution bonuses, which was thought to discourage access to medical assistance by the least advantaged. Although the collection of voluntary contributions was uneven across medical facilities, it had become quite relevant in the 1990s, both in hospitals and in health care centers (interview, Remediar high official #2). The adoption of Remediar therefore helped enforce free access to health care services. At the same time, it helped rationalize assistance by funneling demand from primary care services away from hospitals to health care centers, where free prescription drugs are provided. The proportion of checkups in health centers grew accordingly, from about 33 percent in 2003 to 54 percent in 2006 (Ministerio de Salud 2006: 46).

The creation of a universal health care program was not broadly supported. It ran counter to the preferences of the Inter-American Bank, which funded the program by allowing preexisting credits for public health to be allocated to Remediar in 2002 and wanted a targeted program (interview, Remediar high official #2). Health officials, however, defended the idea of universality and established a strategy to monitor whether pharmaceuticals ended up in the hands of higher-income people who already had health insurance (interview, Remediar high official #1). Surveys carried out in subsequent years showed that self-targeting worked, as there was no significant leak of medications to people with existing insurance. Specifically, 84 percent of beneficiaries were poor, and those who had medical insurance generally resided in remote areas, which made it difficult to obtain medication from pharmacies.[58]

Remediar also included social organizations in its implementation. This involvement entailed four different forms of participation. First, a council including representatives from NGOs, religious organizations, and the Medical Association, among others, was set up to discuss the evolution of the program and conduct oversight. Second, a partnership was established with the Red Cross and with the Catholic Church's Caritas, for these organizations to carry out oversight activities and control the distribution of pharmaceuticals. Third, the Ministry of Health launched participatory projects to engage local health centers and community organizations in addressing health issues. Finally, health centers relied on new or existing associations of patients and community organizations – similar to parent-teacher associations in schools – to work on service provision and general improvements to the centers.[59]

Collectively these initiatives demonstrated moderate levels of participation, as they entailed the active presence of social organizations in policy implementation, but participation was not a requirement, and participatory bodies were not asked to produce any specific outputs on a permanent basis, aside from the oversight partnership through which organizations issued reports regularly (Ministerio de Salud 2006: 20).

According to top Remediar officials, social and religious organizations that distributed medication in low-income areas initially requested to join Remediar's providers. In response, and to maintain control of the policy and prevent inefficiency, the Ministry of Health offered to some large organizations the task of monitoring the implementation of the program. A high official of Remediar recalled in an interview:

---

[58] See Ministerio de Salud (2006: 46); González García in "El problema no es la pobreza sino la equidad," *La Nación*, July 11, 04.

[59] See Ministerio de Salud (2004b; n/d).

Some of these associations used to distribute pharmaceuticals [before the creation of Remediar], and came to us to distribute Remediar medicines themselves... What we negotiated was that volunteers from these organizations would audit the distribution of pharmaceuticals in public health centers. In some places people believe that these organizations actually run the program.

Movements of unemployed workers also requested pharmaceuticals to distribute through their own community or local health centers.[60] Yet the Ministry of Health adamantly rejected their involvement. As the head of Remediar noted, if these organizations wanted to participate in implementation, they were encouraged to join the preexisting associations that cooperate with health centers (*cooperadoras*), which tend to be quite participatory, especially due to the fact that a large number of centers emerged out of community initiatives and were then absorbed and funded by the state (interview, Tobar).[61]

Pensions

Pension benefits were another central demand of social movements during the Duhalde administration. In January 2002, when Duhalde met with unemployed workers' movements and the CTA to negotiate a truce and discuss social policy innovations to address the crisis, the possibility of establishing universal pensions as advanced by the FRENAPO coalition was seriously considered. During 2002, however, the government's energy was placed on the expansion of workfare and health care benefits.

Acknowledging the severity of the financial troubles experienced by the existing pension system, two institutions proposed measures to extend coverage for outsiders. The Argentine Dialogue advocated the creation of a small, tax-funded, noncontributory pension for seniors without means. As the AD proposed, the means test had to be "strictly controlled" and transparency and accountability mechanisms had to be introduced to prevent abuse and clientelism (MTEySS 2003: 71–2). Following the example of the AD, and seeking to address pension reform promptly, the Ministry of Labor appointed a social security commission formed by government officials, representatives of labor unions and business, and experts to discuss the reform of the pension system. The commission elaborated a proposal that incorporated some of the AD's recommendations. It proposed that outsider seniors seventy and older without

---

[60] These demands were posed in meetings with public authorities and in protests (Data Set of Protest 1996–2010).

[61] On health centers, see Kalinsky, Arrúe, and Rossi (1993).

means would receive a pension lower than the contributory minimum pension, and that outsiders with some past contributions would receive a pension at sixty-five or seventy years of age depending on their contributory record. Pension payments would be lower than a minimum pension for beneficiaries with fewer than twenty years of contributions unless their pension savings were sufficient to pay for it (MTEySS 2003: ch. 4). Depending on an individual's years of contribution, age, and amount of savings in pension accounts, the universe of noncontributory and semi-contributory pensions would be segmented into multiple different benefits. To the commission, the critical point was that "non-contributory benefits should be set at reasonably lower levels to those of the minimum contributory pensions in order to foment work ethics and payment of contributions" (MTEySS 2003: 79). In those debates, the CTA advocated the nationalization of the private pension system and the creation of universal minimum pensions for all citizens.

As these different entities convened, protests demanding pensions for unemployed seniors broke out forcefully in 2003. These protests began after the largest federations negotiated pension benefits with the state in exchange for moderation in December 2002. A growing concern existed about unemployed workers who did not qualify for the UHHP because they did not have young children. In the absence of rapid policy implementation, protests for pensions grew intensely between January and February 2003. In response to heightened activism and to threats of "indefinite roadblocks" nationwide issued by unemployed workers' federations – especially the CCC and FTV – which had negotiated pension expansion in 2002, Duhalde promised movement leaders benefits for 1 million senior outsiders and extremely poor households, and launched a small pension scheme for unemployed seniors within the UHHP.[62]

In the next few months, the government implemented UHHP-Seniors as a new component of the UHHP, which reached fewer than 65,000 beneficiaries, and expanded as well an existing noncontributory pension program, which reached about 60,000 pensioners, a tiny share of those without pension benefits at the time.[63] UHHP-Seniors began implementation in 2003 and involved pensioner associations and other social groups in the supervision of the program.[64] Unlike transfers and health

---

[62] "Duhalde recibió a los líderes de las organizaciones piqueteras,"*La Nación*, February 13, 2002; Chronology built with Data Set of Protest (1996–2010).

[63] Elaborated with data from MTEySS and Pensions Commission, Ministry of Social Development.

[64] "Formosa: Lanzaron el Plan Mayores," *La Nación*, April 2, 2003.

care expansion, which Duhalde decisively expanded, the full expansion of pensions was left to his successor.

The 2003 Election

Despite Duhalde's efforts to stabilize his administration, he was forced to call for early elections after the brutal police repression of a demonstration that resulted in the death of two protestors. In response, massive protests – including arguably one of the largest demonstrations in the country since 1983 – broke out and demanded Duhalde's resignation, especially after the media broadcast images of the killings.[65]

The party system was highly fragmented in 2003. After the resignation of the Alliance, FREPASO and the UCR were in shambles. Three UCR politicians competed in 2003 with newly created parties or with the UCR ticket. The possibility that Menem would win the PJ nomination led Duhalde to persuade all PJ candidates to run simultaneously. Three Peronist lists competed in 2003; these included former presidents Menem and Adolfo Rodríguez Saá – who had been president for a few days in 2001 – and Néstor Kirchner, a little-known governor at the time. Duhalde sponsored Kirchner, who represented the opportunity to bring new blood to the presidential campaign and a loyal ally to the presidency. Although Kirchner ultimately chose another vice-presidential candidate, Minister of Health González García, whose policy innovations were showcased during Kirchner's campaign, was seriously considered as his running mate.[66]

The three PJ candidates won in all outsider districts but one, and together they obtained more than 60 percent of the vote nationally, 25 percentage points ahead of the three UCR candidates combined. Kirchner eventually won the presidency. Despite coming out behind Menem, polls anticipated he would score a smashing victory in the runoff, which persuaded Menem to step down.

The Néstor Kirchner Administration (2003–2007)

Néstor Kirchner campaigned on job creation, promising to reduce unemployment to single digits, and pledged to fix the pension system. Although

---

[65] According to the press, this was one of the largest demonstrations since democracy was restored in 1983. Unemployed workers' leaders coincide on the magnitude of this protest (interview, unemployed leader #1).

[66] See "El Ministro que quería conservar su cargo," *La Nación*, April 23, 2003.

Kirchner approached the federations of the unemployed and the CTA for support during his campaign, these movements initially mistrusted his relationship with Duhalde, as the outgoing president was associated with the PJ's sectors engaged in political confrontation with the movements of the unemployed.

Protest by unemployed and labor union allies in demand for social policy was high in 2003. Between January and May 2003, when Kirchner assumed office, unemployed workers' organizations performed eighty-nine acts of protest.[67] The number of federations had grown from fourteen to thirty-three between 2001 and 2003, and claimed to mobilize between 80,000 and 100,000 members in the metropolitan area of Buenos Aires alone.[68] Kirchner managed to reduce protest levels and even won the support of a large number of these organizations and part of the CTA, granting them access to meetings and decision making, incorporating some of the largest associations of the unemployed in his coalition, and extending social policy.

Kirchner sought to mitigate protests and forged a new relationship with social movements. As several informants mentioned, the idea of "controlling the streets" or reducing protest was critical for Kirchner. According to an unemployed workers' leader, Kirchner referred to incessant protest as "his greatest problem" (interview, crisis committee member #1) because, as a high government official pointed out, he believed that "when one government loses control of the streets it loses political control" (interview, Montoya). Under Kirchner, unprecedented access to the state, both through formal channels (e.g., policy councils) and informal channels (e.g., meetings and direct contact with government officials, and even with the president himself) grew for all the unemployed workers' movements, especially for the organizations that decided to forge a closer relationship with the government (interview, crisis committee member #1).[69]

A crisis committee set up at the office of the presidency in 2003 became particularly relevant. This committee was formed after a meeting between Kirchner and part of his cabinet with unemployed workers' leaders soon after he took office. Some of these leaders continued to participate in weekly meetings with the secretary of the presidency, ultimately forming the crisis committee. Committee members had direct access to ministers and occasionally met with the president himself. In these meetings, movement leaders discussed and

---

[67] Data Set of Protest (1996–2010).
[68] Ibid.
[69] Ibid.

advanced a social policy agenda that included broad policy changes, such as the expansion of pension benefits, as well as the demands and needs of specific movements and neighborhoods, such as funding for microenterprises and housing issues (interview, crisis committee member #1).[70]

In 2004, some of the groups in the crisis committee "integrated" themselves into the incumbent coalition, some of the meeting participants assumed positions in the state and in the office of the president, and the crisis committee ceased to exist as such (interview, crisis committee member #1). After joining the governing coalition, movements began to coordinate acts in support of the president, and although they still sometimes coordinated protests with movements outside the governing coalition, or threatened to exit the government to press for demands, these groups reduced their participation in protests (interview, crisis committee member #2).[71]

The organizations of the unemployed that were integrated into the Kirchner coalition achieved broader access to the state through two additional mechanisms: appointments in the public administration and inclusion in electoral lists. By 2006, at least fifty members of these movements held positions in such agencies as the Secretariat of Community Organization of the Ministry of Social Development and the Commission of Land and Housing.[72] That figure grew over time. According to some sources, there were representatives of these organizations in every national ministry. Appointments also grew in local public administrations. These movements gained especial access to the government of the province of Buenos Aires, where one leader of the unemployed became vice chief of cabinet, and members of his organization held positions in the Ministry of Health (interview, high official, provincial Ministry of Health). Ample access to the state resulted in these movements pushing for social policy change primarily from within the state or state-society channels.[73]

The inclusion of members in electoral lists was another form of integration, though one that proved less relevant than the incorporation of movement members into the state bureaucracy. In the 2005 midterm

---

[70] Five organizations participated in the crisis committee: Barrios de Pie, Federación Tierra y Vivienda, Movimiento Evita, Patria Libre, and Corriente Clasista y Combativa, which participated only initially.

[71] Data Set of Protest (1996–2010).

[72] "Cincuenta piqueteros cambiaron la calle por los sillones del poder," *La Nación,* September 11, 2006.

[73] For this reason, even if protest activity was a critical indicator of social mobilization until 2003, it ceased to be so thereafter.

elections, the Victory Front (FV), Kirchner's PJ faction, included several movement leaders in lists for municipal-level councils and provincial legislatures. At that time, the incumbent was competing with Duhalde's PJ faction in the province of Buenos Aires, which included most of the mayors in the metropolitan area. In his quest to defeat his former ally, Kirchner also extended links with smaller parties and with former UCR and FREPASO politicians. After his decisive victory, Kirchner negotiated with the defeated mayors, forming a broader base of support for his government. Despite their ability to mobilize large rallies, allied unemployed workers' movements were perceived as not having the capacity to mobilize voters in elections and were pragmatically marginalized from electoral lists in subsequent elections (interview, high-ranking politician, province of Buenos Aires).

In its quest to generate employment and entice unemployed workers' organizations, the Kirchner administration also launched social programs that responded to the interests of social movements as organizations. These organizationally targeted resources – or club goods – were small in scope. Some of these schemes had been adopted originally by Duhalde but were not fully implemented until Kirchner took office, such as a housing program rolled out through cooperatives and water and neighborhood improvement projects. These benefits were considered critical to gain support, moderate demands, and reduce unemployment among low-income sectors, a key concern of the government.

Protest remained high, however. Extending large-scale nondiscretionary social policy was a critical way to moderate protest from movements outside the governing coalition, and to respond to pressure exerted by allied movements in order to solidify their support. In 2005, demands increased for UHHP improvements and for the extension of pensions, among others. Coalition members also advocated for pension expansion through informal and institutional channels (interview, crisis committee member #1). The CTA, which was included in the Salary Council, an institution in charge of negotiating wages, employment, and productivity, further pressed for its social policy agenda, which included universal pensions.[74]

High levels of contention propelled Kirchner's decision to expand the pension system, a promise that had remained largely unmet by Duhalde. Together with economic growth and a decline in unemployment, this

---

[74] Consejo Nacional del Empleo, la Productividad y el Salario Minimo, Vital y Movil was created in 1991 and was inactive until 2004, when it was convened by Decree 1095/2004.

helped to mitigate protest in 2006 and 2007. Across the social policy areas analyzed here, the extension of pensions was Kirchner's most important social policy response to social mobilization.

The Kirchner government benefited from high levels of economic growth, which contributed to a reduction in unemployment and eased the financial burden of expanding benefits. Yet, under both the Néstor and Cristina Kirchner administrations, the partially privatized social security system for insiders – which was modified through several reforms, including its congressionally-approved nationalization in 2008 – was the primary source of funds for social policy expansion.

Pensions

Mobilization from below to extend pension coverage had begun in 1998 but gained prominence and grew during Duhalde's short tenure.[75] After he took office, Kirchner announced the Seniors' Plan, which would provide 350,000 noncontributory pensions to indigent people aged seventy and older.[76]

The National Council of the UHHP in turn advocated for the expansion of pensions for seniors seventy and older, and the unemployed pressed for universal pensions, which the CTA had been advocating since 1999.[77] Aside from being inadequate to cover existing needs, the implementation of the Seniors' Plan was slow moving, as the agency in charge lacked the infrastructure to distribute it nationwide (interview, social security expert).

The Kirchner administration understood that the provision of pensions to outsiders had to be linked to an overhaul of the contributory pension system for formal workers, which had been partly privatized in 1993. Private pension funds (AFJPs) had been negatively affected by the 2001 crisis and the public part of the system was not in better shape. It was running a large deficit, and benefit levels of existing pensions had deteriorated. Moreover, payroll contributions had been reduced prior to the 2001 crisis to stimulate employment, limiting savings. Eligibility

---

[75] Several demonstrations of the CTA beginning in 1998 sometimes included demands for pension for seniors, family allowances, and unemployment insurance. In 2000, these demands were advanced in some of the broad unemployed workers' protests (Data Set of Protest 1996–2010); materials about CTA's history available at www.cta.org.ar (accessed July 25, 2007).

[76] "Presentaron pensión para mayores de 69 años," *La Nación*, August 13, 2003.

[77] "Piden más planes sociales" *Clarín*, July 29, 2005.

conditions introduced in the 1993 reform extended the required years of contribution, making access to pensions harder for workers with unstable employment. A study showed that between 1994 and 2004, state lost 74.5 billion pesos (or dollars) due to the creation of the private pension system, reduction of payroll contributions, and centralization of provincial pension systems.[78]

The contributory pension system offered active workers a choice between a public, pay-as-you-go (PAYG) system, and a partially privatized scheme that included a basic pension and a funded scheme administered by private pension funds.[79] However, workers could not transfer from the privatized scheme to the public system. Under Kirchner, Congress passed legislation that strengthened the PAYG model, allowing workers to transfer from the private option to the PAYG[80] and encouraging older workers to do so by making its benefits more appealing to them. Furthermore, workers with minimal savings who were close to retirement age were required to transfer to the PAYG system as they were entitled to claim a small pension from the state, which had to be paid for with state revenue; therefore, transferring these workers' savings to the state was deemed appropriate. Collectively, these changes aimed at bringing savings back to the state to fund existing and future commitments.

FREPASO and CTA-related legislators had consistently and unsuccessfully advocated for similar changes in the 1990s, and these proposals inspired the subsequent pension reforms, which were supported by the CTA, allied legislators, and the opposition. The new legislation provided the PAYG fund with considerable resources.[81] Transfers from private pension funds and growing revenue from earmarked taxes and payroll contributions – which were consistently rising in a context of high economic growth and pro-employment policies under Kirchner – provided a stable source of funding to undertake the expansion of pension benefits to outsiders.

---

[78] Massa and Fernández Pastor (2007: 164). From 1994 through 2001, the peso was pegged to the dollar. About half the provinces transferred their pension systems to the national state in the 1990s.

[79] For a description of the system, see Alonso (2000) and Madrid (2003).

[80] The new law was voted for unanimously by the Senate and passed with broad support in the lower chamber, where 209 voted favorably and ten legislators from the right-wing PRO voted against it in February 2007. See "El Congreso aprobó fuertes cambios en las jubilaciones," *Clarín*, February 28, 2007.

[81] See MTSS (2006; 2009). See also, "Jubilacion: El beneficio real de los traspasos" in *Clarín*, April 22, 2007.

Together with this reform of the PAYG component of the system, resolutions issued by the social security agency (ANSES) and the tax agency (AFIP), as well as legislation passed by Congress, made access to pension benefits more flexible. These changes opened the door for the universalization of the system. In December 2004, Congress unanimously approved a bill put together by an ex-FREPASO legislator, which consolidated close to twenty existing bills aimed at providing early retirement to unemployed seniors. The new law allowed the unemployed who had completed the requisite years of contributions, but who had not yet reached retirement age, to claim a pension. At the same time, workers who had reached retirement age but did not have enough contributions could complete payments and claim a pension. Based on the new law, and more importantly, on a preexisting law that allowed independent workers to make payments in arrears spontaneously, the government established a generously subsidized moratorium renewable every two years. Given different mechanisms available in the law, as well as subsequent resolutions issued by the ANSES, people who had reached retirement age were able to obtain a minimum pension, the modal benefit in the system, and complete the years of contributions they owed by paying a subsidized moratorium out of their pension benefit.[82] Pressure to extend this benefit emerged immediately after the first law was passed in 2004, with demands for "expansion of the moratorium" even voiced in some demonstrations (Data Set of Protest 1996–2010).

Through these mechanisms, outsider seniors could gain the status of insiders, accessing contributory minimum pensions and ancillary benefits. These benefits included a food allowance, access to the health insurance scheme for formal-sector pensioners (PAMI), which provided full health care coverage, and family allowances for dependents. Therefore, instead of creating a separate pension program or a category of "noncontributory pensioners," or universalizing tax-funded minimum pensions, the Kirchner government made flexible and helped attain the status of insider for outsider seniors irrespective of their means. These reforms thus universalized access to contributory pensions, provided high benefit levels – comparable to those of low-income insiders – and also included some

[82] To apply for the benefit, people had to pay the first installment of the moratorium. Several subnational units agreed to pay the first installment for seniors in their districts. In this way, mayors and governors could claim credit for the new benefit together with the national government. See *Programa de Inclusión Previsional* in www.anses.gov.ar (accessed August 2009).

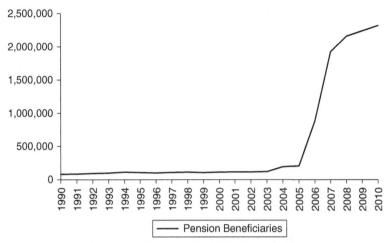

FIGURE 5.4 Outsiders 65+ with pension benefits, 1990–2010.
Source: Estimated with data from ANSES, MTEySS, INDEC, and other sources listed in Appendix 1.

measure of participation in implementation, yielding inclusive pensions for outsiders.

As shown in Figure 5.4, the number of outsiders with pension benefits jumped from 91,000 in 2001 to more than 2 million in 2008, reaching 97 percent of outsiders sixty-five and older by 2010.[83] The adoption of universal coverage can be understood as a response to the demands of the movements of the unemployed and the CTA for universal pensions for outsiders. Several technocrats in the social security agency and other former government officials criticized the broad access to contributory pensions (interview, Caro Figueroa). Aside from the fact that social movements advocated universal pensions, the government's choice can be explained by several reasons. First, non-poor outsider seniors were understood to be few at the time of expansion (interview, Arrigui, undersecretary of social security). With little operative capacity, discriminating across potential beneficiaries could be too complicated for the national government. Relatedly, social security experts argued that means-tested pensions were not only hard to implement, but could be vulnerable to manipulation and clientelism (interview, social security expert). The existence of discretion and clientelism in program implementation could make expansion backfire against the government. A universal program

---

[83] Disability pensions constituted less than 10 percent of total pension benefits.

was easier to implement and would be potentially more successful. Given the expectation that most seniors without pensions were low income in the first place, arguments against universality did not gain strong support. Opposition against broad expansion was not visible in the public debate at the time, either; pensions were a popular policy, and politicians and technocrats faced a tough time expressing vocal opposition to such programs.

One could also argue that by reaching some wealthier seniors, the government was seeking the support of middle-class beneficiaries, which tend to be a particularly volatile electorate. However, several government politicians and technocrats noted that pension expansion did not pursue such a goal. According to the head of the tax agency of Buenos Aires, pension expansion was a policy for the "hard-core" PJ support. In this official's view, even if they stood to benefit from these policies, "people with middle-class cultural views will have only short-term sympathy for this type of measure" (interview, Montoya). Finally, a key reason for creating new pensions as contributory benefits was that they could be easily funded with the public pension fund for formal-sector workers.

Aside from providing universal access, the new pensioners obtained exactly the same status as that of insiders earning a minimum pension, who represented about 60 percent of total pensioners when expansion began.[84] Although there were technocrats in ANSES who thought that the benefit level was too high, the fact that the new pensions were defined as "contributory" meant that they could not pay a benefit below the minimum pension. If pension payments were established at a lower level, then new pensioners could easily sue the pension system on the grounds of discrimination, which was a likely outcome given the tradition of litigation among pensioners and social security lawyers in Argentina (interview, Arrigui).[85]

The Kirchner administration did not add new formal participatory mechanisms to those that existed prior to pension expansion, an advisory council formed by representatives of more than 100 pensioner associations, some affiliated to the CTA, which had been a consistent supporter of pensioners' demands (see O'Neil 2006: 108). Organizations in this council disseminate information to pensioners and collect demands from their members. Yet its operation is quite limited; it holds meetings,

---

[84] Estimated with data from MTEySS (2006: 27–9).
[85] On pension policy in the 1980s and 1990s, see Alonso (2000) and Isuani and San Martino (1994).

though not regularly, and its involvement in the implementation of pension benefits (for example, advising pensioners on benefits) is not significant. Pensioner associations within the council are not highly active politically – although they did mobilize in the 1990s to oppose pension privatization and to demand higher pension benefits, which were frozen under Menem. According to O'Neil, the advisory council was set up in 1997 to reduce pension-related protest (O'Neil 2006: 153). Under Kirchner, this council did not operate as a venue from which associations have engaged in pension-related activism. This council has overall entailed low levels of participation in implementation.

The main links between the state and outsiders regarding pension policy worked through the social movements and the unions involved in the Kirchner coalition, rather than through this council. More informal ways of involvement in implementation did take shape. First, positions in ANSES offices were granted to movement members who could engage in policy implementation from within the state, especially at the local level. Second, social movements and local governments signed agreements with ANSES to disseminate information about pension expansion and to help seniors sign up for benefits. A leader from social movement Barrios de Pie recalls:

[W]e signed a partnership with ANSES to work with them... The idea was to prevent *gestores* [intermediaries] from deceiving seniors and collecting a fee for helping with the paperwork ... local governments and social movements participated this way. Our organization was the first to sign an agreement of this sort. (interview)

At the same time, the CTA was strongly involved in the dissemination of information concerning the option to switch from the partially privatized to the public PAYG component of the pension system. With support from ANSES, it set up posts in train and bus stations to inform and persuade workers to switch their pension contributions to the state, using the slogan "Come back to the state."[86]

Instead of new councils or other stable and formal structures of community participation, pension expansion opened up spaces for social organizations to operate more informally and to occupy positions in the bureaucracy. This form of involvement entails low levels of participation and is more likely to take shape when social movements are allied with the governing coalition, and it became the main pattern of participation in Argentina under the Kirchner administrations.

---

[86] "El sistema publico previsional ya sumo 1.200.000 jubilados," *La Nación*, May 3, 2007.

Health Care

In his inaugural speech, Néstor Kirchner emphasized Plan Remediar and the improved access to primary care initiated by Duhalde, which he further intensified during his tenure. Plan Nacer, announced in November 2003, became a critical component of the strategy to improve accessibility under the Kirchner governments.[87] Aiming to reduce mother and child mortality rates, Plan Nacer provided economic incentives for provincial governments and local health centers to improve coverage of pregnant women and children six years of age and under by ensuring that they obtained necessary medical checkups and adhered to the official vaccination schedule. Creation of a primary care plan was agreed upon between the government and the Argentine Dialogue in 2002 (see Diálogo Argentino 2002).

Together with Remediar, Plan Nacer was included within the Federal Health Plan established in 2004 to increase the effectiveness of health services for users of the public health care system, enable the national government to gain a stewardship role in the health sector, and increase the government's regulatory capacities.[88] The state of health emergency Duhalde declared in 2002 provided the impetus for these health initiatives and the national government's role in administering them. Provincial governments in charge of health services had few resources to assist outsiders, at a time when popular discontent put pressure on politicians to deliver and to take better care of state services (interview, Luis Pérez, World Bank official).

With the ultimate goal of reaching low-income populations nationwide, Plan Nacer was rolled out gradually, with priority given to the poorest provinces. While poor provinces were encouraged to sign up for the program, the timing of their response and the success with which they implemented new benefits varied subnationally and across health centers within provinces (interview, high official, Plan Nacer).[89] Although health officials pressed for Plan Nacer to finance health services directly, it ended up transferring resources to the provincial bureaucracies in charge of administering health care services (interview, Rosso). The national office, however, transferred such funding based on strict criteria and performance indicators, collecting data on services and monitoring

---

[87] See "La salud tiene que ser el motor del renacimiento de la Argentina," *La Nación*, November 25, 2003.

[88] See Ministerio de Salud (2004a).

[89] These differences are beyond the scope of this study to analyze.

their implementation. In this respect, Plan Nacer represented a break with the ways in which decentralized primary care assistance had been run in the past.

Although the development of health insurance programs to extend health services has been promoted by the World Bank since the 2000s – and Plan Nacer has received funding from the agency – the program's design differs from such insurance programs and was strongly influenced by officials in the Ministry of Health, who had long been committed to the creation of financial incentives to improve public infrastructure and coordinate, integrate, and strengthen subnational services under the stewardship of the national government. Officials considered involving private providers in Plan Nacer's implementation but they abandoned the idea in light of resistance within the Ministry and the broad scope of existing public-sector infrastructure.

Income Transfers

Under Néstor Kirchner, the bulk of the government's strategy to improve household income was centered on job creation and wage increases. Job creation was fostered by economic growth and·macroeconomic changes, especially a more favorable exchange rate, as well as specific policies, such as duties on imports, maintenance of reduced payroll contributions, and by the promotion of cooperatives and microenterprises – including some run by the organizations of the unemployed – through public works. These initiatives were also fundamental to enticing these movements' support.

Beneficiaries of the UHHP experienced important changes. Between 2003 and July 2007, 28.4 percent found jobs, about 27 percent of which were formal-sector jobs.[90] The rest saw their income decline relative to rising wages. This generated pressure from social movements to increase the UHHP's payments and expand coverage, demands which were voiced in persistent protest particularly between 2003 and 2005 and again in 2009. The universalization of income-support benefits was also demanded by the CTA, which kept on advancing its plan to create universal family allowances.[91] In response, the government offered beneficiaries of the UHHP an opportunity to migrate to Families – initiated under Duhalde – or to an employment-training scheme, both of which paid

---

[90] Estimated with data from MTEySS (2007).
[91] See Data Set of Protest (1996–2010).

higher benefit levels, though the latter was temporary.[92] The government also wanted to deactivate the UHHP owing to the difficulty in controlling the workfare obligation, and the discredit that affected the program when abuses were revealed.

By the end of the Néstor Kirchner administration, the percentage of Families' beneficiaries relative to the UHHP had grown significantly, with income transfers becoming "complementary income" programs for low-income households instead of "income replacement" programs, such as the workfare benefit (interview, Arroyo, Kirchner's vice minister of social development). With this growth in employment, the question became not only how to create jobs but also how to increase the incomes of outsider families, which tended to be low and unstable compared to formal sector wage earners. Government officials agreed at the time that a universal family allowance program was "in the pipeline," likely to come out in the late 2000s (interview, Arroyo).

The 2007 Election

Kirchner's popularity grew dramatically under his tenure. The FV came to dominate the PJ and it built broad legislative support. Kirchner's decisive victory against Duhalde in several districts in the 2005 midterm elections allowed the president to control the PJ machine, which pragmatically responded to his leadership.[93] Kirchner's popularity hovered over 70 percent,[94] which allowed his wife and successor, Cristina Kirchner, to win the presidential elections by a wide margin.

Electoral competition for outsiders did not take shape in 2007. The difference between the incumbent and the second party, a centrist coalition led by a former UCR politician, was more than twenty-two points. Cristina Kirchner in fact obtained almost twice the number of votes as the second candidate, and faced electoral competition in just 5 percent of outsider districts. In an attempt to expand the appeal of the FV among the middle classes,[95] a sector that has often proven more elusive to the PJ in metropolitan areas, the vice presidency was offered to Julio Cobos of the

---

[92] Presidential Decree 1506/04.

[93] For example, the day after the elections prominent "barons" of the local machine met with Kirchner to negotiate their support for the FV.

[94] Data from IPSOS-Mora y Araujo in *Infobae*, May 25, 2013.

[95] The second party was the Civic Coalition, an electoral alliance of former Radical politicians and the Socialist Party, which obtained 23 percent of the vote compared to the FV's 45 percent.

UCR.[96] Cobos' nomination was made possible by Kirchner's high level of authority, as the choice of a non-Peronist vice president was strongly resisted by some PJ governors and labor union leaders (interview, high-ranking PJ politician, province of Buenos Aires). After the elections, the pro-Kirchner bloc in the lower chamber was more than twice the size of the opposition combined, granting Cristina Kirchner strong legislative support (Levitsky and Murillo 2008: 24).

The Cristina Kirchner Administration (2007–2011)

Unlike her husband, Cristina Kirchner witnessed a sharp decline in popularity after taking office. An unsuccessful attempt to increase taxes on soybean exports, whose price had been growing since 2002, resulted in deep conflict with agricultural producers involving roadblocks, demonstrations, and lockouts, and producing a dramatic plunge in approval ratings from close to 70 percent to 30 percent in July 2008 (see Etchemendy and Garay 2011; Fairfield 2011, 2015).[97]

The international crisis of 2008 placed further challenges on the government. High economic growth from 2003 to 2007 stalled, reaching less than 1 percent in 2009. Unemployment also jumped moderately, from 8 percent to 8.8 percent, and fears of joblessness led labor unions and organizations of the unemployed to press for decisive responses to prevent employment and popular-sector income from contracting. Social movements advocated for increases in the benefit level of existing income transfers, which had remained almost invariable since 2002, and pushed for the CTA's historic proposal of extending universal child allowances. The CTA organized a one-day protest with 135 acts and strikes throughout the country in April 2009, calling on the state to declare an "occupational emergency" to prevent layoffs, grant salary and pension improvements, adopt the universal child allowance for outsiders, and threatening the government with a national strike. Several social movements participated in this day of action. In explaining its motivation for launching this massive protest, the CTA's secretary general pointed to the organization's unsuccessful "five months" of demands for the government to establish a "social shield ... preventing layoffs for six months" and "providing an income to the unemployed," arguing that

[96] The national leadership of the Radical Party did not endorse Cobos' alliance with the FV.

[97] Data from IPSOS-Mora y Araujo in *Infobae*, May 25, 2013.

without measures that "protect the most vulnerable, the workers ... the unemployed, pensioners ... the cost of the crisis will be shouldered by the workers."[98] Despite mounting pressures, the government did not make any major social policy announcement.

The combination of a weakening economic situation and low popularity undermined support for Cristina Kirchner in the 2009 midterm elections. The FV faced growing competition from a coalition of dissident PJ politicians and allies – which varied across provinces but included a rising local party, the right-wing Republican Proposal (PRO), which governed the city of Buenos Aires – and an alliance between current and former UCR politicians and the Socialist Party, whose composition also varied across provinces. Although no challenger posed a real threat in future presidential elections, support for the FV declined considerably; it lost the majority in the lower chamber and was defeated in the province of Buenos Aires, where the PJ–PRO alliance came out first with a slim margin. Despite the more competitive environment of 2009, the FV faced competition for outsider voters in 31.5 percent of outsider districts, below the level considered high in this analysis.

The main social policy innovation under Cristina Kirchner was the creation of the universal child allowance (AUH). The benefit did not reach many more families than the existing income transfers that it replaced (e.g., Families, UHHP, and PEC combined), but it paid a much higher allowance and reduced opportunities for discretion. As presented next, this innovation was the result of a new major wave of protest by the unemployed and labor union allies.

Income-Support Transfers

After the 2009 midterm elections, the Cristina Kirchner administration sought to consolidate the support of her PJ coalition in the metropolitan area of Buenos Aires, where several mayors who had endorsed the Kirchner list were hoping to be rewarded for their loyalty. In response, Kirchner launched Argentina Trabaja, a national workfare program that would be implemented only in the *conurbano* (districts surrounding the City of Buenos Aires). The new scheme was tailored to the preferences of mayors. As announced by the president, it would create 100,000 jobs in cooperatives that would carry out public works. The scheme granted municipal

---

[98] Yasky CTA's leader in "La CTA paralizo la ciudad con su reclamo," *La Nación*, April 23, 2009.

authorities ample discretion in the selection of beneficiaries. This feature clearly differentiated this policy from large-scale transfers, which had broad coverage and clear eligibility rules, thereby minimizing opportunities for local-level discretion.

The program's design met strong opposition from social movements. Movement leaders saw the small scope of coverage, the selection process, and the exclusion of social movement participation as allowing for discretion in the program's implementation. Finding no responses to their discontent, several movements initiated a wave of protests a few weeks after the announcement of the new benefit. As a leader of Barrios de Pie, a movement that had maintained an alliance with the government in the past, noted, what social movements strongly resisted was that mayors had the authority to decide on the composition of cooperatives. The movements feared that local machines would then manipulate workers by appropriating part of their salaries and by making them engage in political activity to maintain their jobs in the cooperatives.[99]

Protests by movements of unemployed workers broke out and peaked in September 2009, which, according to the press, became the "most contentious September since 1997."[100] One of the slogans of these protests was "Work for all, without clientelism." Besides jobs and transparency, protestors demanded the adoption of the CTA's universal child allowance.[101] In fact, in August and September, the CTA organized two days of demonstrations throughout the country to establish a "social shield" to protect jobs from the effects of the international financial crisis and extend family allowances to reach all low-income families "without intermediaries" (Hugo Yasky, head of CTA).[102]

Social movements organized protests and encampments outside the Ministry of Social Development. Although movements unaffiliated with the Kirchners' coalition launched these protests, government allies publicly expressed support for protestors' claims, putting some pressure on the government.[103] Protests were also coordinated with industrial workers who had taken over a plant in the *conurbano* in August 2009 to

---

[99] Debates in the Seminar on Transparency and Accountability organized by the CCC and NGO Poder Ciudadano, La Matanza, July 2011 (author's participation), interview, leader of CCC.

[100] "El septiembre con más conflictos sociales desde 1997," *La Nación*, September 28, 2009.

[101] See, for example, "Otra mañana de caos en los accesos a la Capital," *La Nación*, September 30, 2009.

[102] Quoted in "Fuerte Reclamo de la CTA," *La Nación*, August 8, 2009.

[103] See *Clarín*, November 4, 2009 and November 11, 2009.

denounce layoffs. On several occasions in September 2009, protestors blocked traffic access to the city of Buenos Aires for hours, producing chaos and frustration (Data Set of Protest, 1996–2010).[104]

After condemning sustained protests and roadblocks, though refusing to clear the streets out of fear that police intervention would result in violence, which would then trigger wider protests, the government promised to review registration to Argentina Trabaja and to establish local policy councils including representatives from social movements.[105]

Cristina Kirchner's response to heightened social conflict was the establishment of the universal child allowance (AUH), which was introduced by decree within the existing legislation of family allowances for formal workers.[106] The initiative was presented as a response to "the diverse political and social forces" who have "voiced their support" for the adoption of measures directed "to vulnerable children and adolescents."[107] The government further indicated that despite the ambitious nature of the policy, the AUH was only a "palliative measure" to address poverty that would only be reduced through growth and employment. The president maintained that because there was consensus about the "urgency to implement anti-poverty ... universal measures," the initiative was passed by decree instead of being taken to a vote in Congress. Given that at the time poverty rates were significantly lower than in previous years, the main urgency to launch the benefit was political, and the measure was driven by the goal of regaining control of the streets by placating social conflict.

Though protest continued occasionally around the workfare program, the expansion of the AUH contributed to a decline in contention by unemployed workers' movements. Beneficiaries of existing programs were automatically transferred to the AUH and qualifying families with children under the age of eighteen were enrolled. The design of the benefit did not raise suspicions of discretionary allocation, as it had clear eligibility rules and was administered by the technocratic social security institute, ANSES. The allowance provided a sum comparable to 12 percent of the minimum wage to each child up to the age of eighteen, and was paid to a maximum of five children per family. To improve health conditions and to expand school enrollment among adolescents, 20 percent of the benefit was conditional on school attendance and was paid as a lump

---

[104] See *La Nación*, September 22, 2009.
[105] See *La Nación*, October 2, 2009 and December 4, 2009; *Clarín* November 8, 2009.
[106] Decree 1602/2009.
[107] Ibid.

sum once a year. Consonant with the structure of family allowances paid to formal workers, the benefit was later extended to pregnant women starting in their third month of pregnancy.

As discussed earlier, the possibility of extending family allowances to outsiders was considered by policymakers in the Néstor Kirchner government (interview, Arroyo). The timing and the decision to adopt the policy had to do with the incumbent's political needs. As argued here, the policy was employed when protests got out of control for the first time since 2005, the last year of very high protest by social movements that had escalated since 2000. Contrary to scholars' suggestion that electoral competition in the 2009 midterm elections drove the decision to create the AUH (Pribble 2013: 157), no clear evidence points in that direction. Why would the government pass such a costly expansion of social expenditure four months after the contested midterm elections and two years before the presidential election? Why didn't the government expand the new benefit before the 2009 elections, when its low popularity was already evident? Why didn't it extend it in phases and reach the presidential election in 2011 with full coverage, as most incumbents did in Brazil and Mexico, if potential electoral competition was a concern? Why would the government want to reach outsiders, the electorate who *did* support the FV in 2009, with generous benefits? How would it improve its chances for 2011 if the contested electorate in 2009 were largely middle-class voters – formal-sector insiders and agricultural producers not necessarily reached by these benefits – some of whom had voted for the FV in 2007?

The government implemented the AUH quickly, reaching close to 2 million households in January 2010.[108] Rapid responses, rather than calculated and slow-moving decision-making processes, tend to be adopted by presidents responding to social conflict. The upsurge in protest and the combination of protest acts by SMCs raised credible fears of "losing the streets." According to a member of the crisis committee formed by Kirchner: "These programs are created in specific political junctures ... they are not about socioeconomic issues because then the AUH should have been created in 2003 ... The AUH is linked to social conflict; it is a defensive measure... It allowed the government to stop protests" (interview, crisis committee member #2).

The design of the program was inclusive and followed the CTA's long-standing proposal. The government could have opted for a scaled-back

---

[108] Coverage of this program was rather stable from February 2010 onward. See coverage data from ANSES, www.anses.gov.ar.

TABLE 5.2 *Income Support Programs[a] and the Minimum Wage Relative to the Poverty Line, 2002–2010 (percent)*

	Minimum Wage	Insiders' Family Allowances	Outsiders' Family Allowances	UHHP	Training Scheme	Families
2002	31.8	12.7	–	23.9	–	–
2003	28.2	11.3	–	21.1	–	21.1
2004	48.2	11.5	–	20.7	–	20.7
2005	65.9	15.5	–	19.4	–	25.8
2006	73.7	14.0	–	17.6	35.0	23.4
2007	86.7	15.6	–	16.2	32.5	21.7
2008	100.5	20.4	–	15.3	30.6	20.4
2009[b]	133.2[c] 102.5[d]	33.3[c] 25.6[d]	33.3[c] 25.6[d]	–	n/d	–
2010[b]	129.6[c] 99.7[b]	31.1[c] 23.9[d]	31.1[c] 23.9[d]	–	n/d	–

[a] Estimates for a household of four (two adults plus two children). Estimates correspond to May each year except for 2009, for which estimates correspond to December (see Appendix 2).

[b] Estimated poverty line for two adults plus two children. The poverty line measured by the government has been contested since 2008. I use two poverty lines to estimate the benefit levels for 2009 and 2010.

[c] Benefit levels are estimated with the poverty line built by INDEC (The National Statistics Agency).

[d] Benefit levels are estimated with a poverty line 30 percent higher than the one INDEC estimated.

Source: Elaborated by author with data from INDEC (poverty rate); Ministry of Finance (minimum wage); Ministry of Social Development, and ANSES (transfers).

policy reform, reaching fewer beneficiaries or providing fewer benefits, but it picked the more generous design that merged insiders and outsiders within the same policy, which social movements had requested. Under the AUH, a household with two children received a benefit that was slightly larger than the existing transfers at the time. Table 5.2 shows the ratio of the program's standard benefit to the poverty line. For reference purposes, I also estimate the ratio of the minimum wage to the poverty line. According to the data, the primary benefits paid since 2002 hovered around 20 percent to 24 percent of the poverty line. One important difference is that the AUH paid benefits relative to family size and thus payments larger families received were more significant under this program.

The AUH was less participatory than the UHHP, whose implementation was accompanied by national and local councils. By contrast, as with pension expansion, a network of organizations helped out in the registration process and accompanied its initial implementation, but their participation was mainly informal. As expected in this study's framework, when social movements are at least in part allied with the governing coalition, the chances of having participatory structures outside the state are reduced. Those structures can be easily identified as "partisan" and generate suspicions of bias in the implementation of large-scale benefits, or they can appear to confront with the state, creating resentment in other members of the government. Such an impression was shared by PJ politicians who saw participatory structures promoted by movements who had joined the Kirchner coalition as "confrontational … anti-democratic, operating against formal institutions" and viewed them as "something that has to disappear as the state takes over the activity of social organizations" (interview, high PJ official, province of Buenos Aires).

5.5 ASSESSING ALTERNATIVE EXPLANATIONS

This chapter has emphasized the importance of mobilization from below to the expansion of social policy in Argentina. Other potential explanatory factors, such as socioeconomic change, booms and crises, partisanship, and the diffusion of ideas, have not played a decisive, direct role in explaining policy expansion and variation in social policy models.

At first glance, economic crises may seem relevant to the expansion of social policy in Argentina. The first massive expansion in 2002 took place amid a dramatic financial collapse. However, it was not an interest in fighting poverty that drove the government expand social programs, but the goal of attaining social peace. Social policy expansion allowed

Duhalde to stabilize his administration and control protest. Eventually, his tenure was abruptly terminated not because of economic reasons, but because of the violent repression of a demonstration of unemployed workers, which compromised his continuity in power. After the murder of two protestors, massive demonstrations demanded Duhalde's resignation and called for new elections.

Economic crises had already occurred in Argentina in 1989 (which was particularly severe) and in 1994. These crises did not trigger expansion or even smaller-scale innovations to deal with their social effects. In the absence of mobilization from below in the context of these earlier crises, or of opposition parties that could mobilize the outsider electorate against the incumbent, the 1989 and 1994 crises did not propel social policy initiatives. As discussed in Chapter 3, fearing disorder, the government responded with a large-scale policy initiative that was eventually aborted in 1989 as the threat of lootings dissipated. The 1994 crisis produced a dramatic hike in unemployment, which peaked at 19 percent in the first half of 1995, but did not trigger immediate policy responses until Plan Trabajar – a very small clientelistic workfare program – was created in 1996 to show some concern for skyrocketing unemployment.

Economic growth – a simple measure of the absence of strict financial constraints – is usually understood as necessary for governments to launch new social programs. Income support and health care expansion were launched, as we have seen, in the context of dramatic negative growth in 2002, whereas pensions and the AUH were launched in better economic circumstances of the commodity boom – although 2009 was an uncertain economic environment of low growth (see Figure 5.5). In other periods of economic growth, expansion did not occur.

If social policy was launched in 2002 in the context of declining living conditions – measured by unemployment and poverty rates – the more recent expansion of pensions and family allowances did not take shape in a comparable context. Unemployment and poverty have gone down dramatically relative to 2002 (see Figure 5.5).

The model of social policy adopted was inclusive across these different economic contexts, the early 2000s of negative growth and during the boom. Policies were designed in negotiation with or in response to the demands of movements advocating policy expansion. These innovations did not copy models of social protection that diffused across the region or that powerful actors imposed. Benefit levels, scope of coverage, and participatory mechanisms were responses to concrete demands. The universalization of family allowances, pensions, and outpatient medications

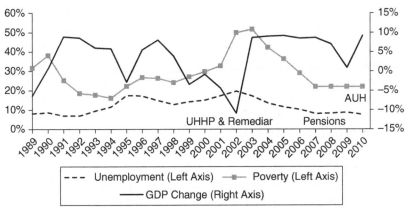

FIGURE 5.5 Economic growth, unemployment, poverty, and timing of expansion, Argentina, 1989–2010.
Sources: GDP 1989–92 from Murillo (2001b: 136), 1995–2008 from INDEC (www.indec.gov.ar), 2009–10 Ministry of Finance; poverty headcount, year average from EPH, INDEC (for 2008–10, I use 2007); unemployment from INDEC (1992–2006, 2009–10); and 2007–8 elaborated from Table 4, page 40 (http://www.mecon.gov.ar/peconomica/informe/informe64/version_completa.pdf, accessed August 8, 2009).

to outsiders had little resemblance to policy recommendations promoted by multilateral development agencies. These agencies have generally recommended targeted programs instead of costly benefits, as it was the case under the de la Rúa administration when the World Bank endorsed the proposal to reallocate formal-sector family allowances to the very poor, or when the IADB favored a free prescription drugs program that would be narrowly targeted. Moreover, the policy-making process in these areas was largely influenced by social movement demands and by the urgency of the political context. For instance, the massive workfare benefit launched in 2002 was not only extended quickly but also, according to a national government official, was in part designed "ex-post," as its implementation anteceded critical design decisions. Instead of adopting a particular, appropriate model, the goal was to respond quickly to demands. As we will see, this trajectory differs significantly with the cases of Mexico and Chile, where the policy process was shaped by other political dynamics and where policy implementation was top down in order to avoid the manipulation of benefits and discourage social demands, which were the sources of policy change in Argentina and to a large extent in Brazil.

Overall, it is clear that when incumbents face higher large-scale mobilization from below, this challenges their popularity and loosens their hold on power. Incumbents fear that their chances of survival will be further affected unless decisive measures are taken. Doing otherwise can compromise their administrations and contribute to the erosion of government support, as in the case of de la Rúa, whose lack of attention to low-income voters and lack of response to massive protest contributed to a dramatic political crisis. At the same time, and as the social movement literature has repeatedly shown, movements usually mobilize when incumbents are more vulnerable, either because there is a broader context of mobilization and antigovernment protest (as in 2001 and 2002) or because the government is losing popularity. In these cases, incumbents seem more prone to making concessions. This was the case of Duhalde's tenure and the first years of the Kirchner administrations, especially after Cristina Kirchner's intense confrontation with rural producers undermined her administration. These situations can be profitable for powerful actors with mobilization capacity and concrete demands who may perceive that government weakness is a propitious time to obtain concessions via mobilization.

5.6 CONCLUSIONS

This chapter has drawn on the analytical framework advanced in this study to explain (a) why Argentina expanded nondiscretionary social policy and (b) why it built inclusive programs. As predicted in the framework, high levels of mobilization from below led incumbents to expand large-scale, nondiscretionary social policy starting in 2002. Facing wide social mobilization, the Duhalde administration expanded large-scale policies in response to pressure by a powerful coalition of unions, unemployed workers' organizations, and other social movements. In the context of mass mobilization in 2001 and 2002, the coalition's demands were further supported by organizations with proximate interests, such as NGOs demanding pharmaceuticals and health workers' unions. Beginning in 2003, the Kirchner administrations further expanded social policies, granted fluid access to the state, and integrated some of these movements into the incumbent coalition to contain social mobilization.

Social benefits inaugurated since 2002 have been inclusive reaching a large pool of outsiders with generous, participatory provisions. This policy choice is explained by the active participation of social movements in the policy design process. The critical movements in these episodes of expansion – the unemployed workers' organizations and their union allies – demanded universalistic benefits similar to those of insiders. In fact, some benefits in Argentina (and likewise in Brazil) were eventually integrated into preexisting policies for insiders. This was the case of pensions and family allowances. Social movements further advocated participation in policy implementation to prevent manipulation of access and to empower their organizations. This participation was more significant in earlier policies, which were advocated by social movements from outside the incumbent coalition. When social movements and labor allies were at least partially incorporated into the governing coalition, then participatory institutions became less relevant and state society interaction operated through informal contacts and the appointment of movement members in the state.

6

Electoral Competition for Outsiders, Conservative Power, and Restrictive Social Policy in Mexico

6.1 INTRODUCTION

In the final months of Mexico's 2000 presidential campaign, Vicente Fox of the National Action Party (PAN), a conservative party that would soon govern the country after seventy-one years of uninterrupted rule by the Institutional Revolutionary Party (PRI), visited impoverished rural towns that had historically been the bulwark of the PRI. In explaining why he was pursuing an unusual strategy for a PAN candidate – and one that also implied a shift away from his earlier campaign – Fox stated:

> We have to break the PRI's wall in rural areas, we have to attract followers from other parties because there are virtually no more undecided voters to compete for ... [the goal is] to break the tie we have maintained with the PRI over the past three months and that is now beginning to cede. In the poll I received today, we are a little ahead, 40.7 percent vs. 40.5 percent of Labastida [the PRI's candidate]. We are in these towns because we are pursuing small gains in specific areas of the population, such as women and the peasants... [It is this new stage of the campaign] that will allow us to break the tie and leave Labastida behind.[1]

The emergence of intense electoral competition for outsiders after decades of PRI rule coincides with a period of large-scale social policy expansion in Mexico that constitutes an important effort to "include outsiders" and to temper the social policy divide between insiders and outsiders. After the inauguration of a smaller program of income transfers by PRI president Ernesto Zedillo in 1997, the expansion of large-scale health care services, income support, and pension benefits for outsiders began under the Fox administration (2000–6). By 2010, at least 36 percent of

[1] Quoted in "Busca Fox el voto rural en Huasteca potosina," *Reforma* March 25, 2000, p. 8.

TABLE 6.1 *Social Policy Expansion and the Restrictive
Model in Mexico, ca. 2010*

Policy Area	Scope of Coverage	Benefit Level	Participation in Implementation	Dates of Expansion
Income Support	Low	Moderate	None	2001-3
	36% of school-age outsider children	Less than 20% of the poverty line for a family with two children		
Health Care	Low	Moderate	None	2003 (adoption and gradual implementation)
	Free access for poor outsiders; about 40% of outsiders enrolled	Exclusion of some services and treatments		
Pensions	Low	Low	None	Oportunidades-seniors: 2006
	48% of outsiders aged 65+	33% of the minimum pension for insiders		70 y Más: 2006-7 (adoption); 2007 (implementation)

Notes: Dates of Expansion refers to adoption and launching of implementation. Pensions: characterization refers to 70 y Más, which replaced Oportunidades-seniors.
Sources and measures: See Appendix 1.

children received income transfers; 41 percent accessed subsidized health insurance, and about 48 percent of outsiders sixty-five and older had noncontributory pensions (Table 6.1).

At first glance, the expansion of social policy in Mexico is surprising given the political affiliation of the Fox government and the absence of large export revenues in the 2000s, as Mexico did not experience a commodity boom in this period in contrast to several South American countries. In this setting, why were nondiscretionary benefits launched for outsiders under the PAN administrations of Fox and Felipe Calderón (2006–12)? Why did the PAN, a conservative party with a core constituency in the economic elite, not launch small or even discretionary benefits, as the PRI had done in the past?

This chapter shows that the expansion of nondiscretionary, restrictive social policy began as a result of intense electoral competition for outsiders within a democratic regime. In this competitive electoral context, incumbents embarked on social policy expansion to consolidate the support of outsiders and to offset the appeals of credible competitors seeking to cultivate their support. Without reelection in place, the ultimate goal was the continuation of the incumbent party in office. Due to the absence of mobilization from below triggering and/or shaping the process of social policy design, these benefits were negotiated among political parties in Congress – especially the center-right PAN and the populist PRI, both of which had conservative social policy preferences – and resulted in more modest, nonparticipatory policy initiatives. Mexico therefore provides a good example of social policy expansion and social policy design under strong conservative power, a topic that remains understudied in the context of the regional turn to the left in the 2000s (see Levitsky and Roberts 2011; Weyland et al. 2010).[2]

In the next section of this chapter, I trace the evolution of electoral competition beginning in the 1990s, as Mexico democratized. I show how electoral competition for outsiders compelled incumbents to launch social policy expansion and why restrictive policies were created. First, I analyze the surge of electoral competition under Ernesto Zedillo (1994–2000) and the initial policy responses of the PRI president as democratization and electoral competition for outsiders deepened. When democratization intensified and support for opposition parties grew in the late 1990s, the Zedillo administration extended a still relatively small cash-transfer program which was nondiscretionary in an effort to avoid allegations of clientelism voiced by the invigorated opposition from PAN and the PRD. Next, in section four, I analyze social policy expansion after the defeat of the PRI in 2000. Having assumed power in a democracy with high levels of electoral competition for outsiders, Fox launched large-scale social policy expansion to solidify outsiders' support. Electoral competition for outsiders was intense at the end of Fox's tenure, with the ascendance of the left-wing Party of the Democratic Revolution (PRD) candidate Andrés Manuel López Obrador (AMLO), who campaigned on large-scale social policy expansion. Electoral pressure led Fox to embark on further social policy innovations to prevent the defeat of the PAN in upcoming elections, which were extremely close and in which outsiders supported both the PRD and PAN candidates in comparable shares. Given that some aspects of these policy innovations were either implemented or modified under the Felipe Calderón administration (2006–12), I refer to Calderón's government in the analysis of specific policy areas in section four. Finally, I assess the role of other explanations

---

[2] Forthcoming work by Estevez, Díaz Cayeros, and Magaloni on Mexico is an exception.

for social policy expansion, focusing on structural economic change, partisan politics, and the diffusion of new ideas of social protection.

6.2 EVOLUTION OF ELECTORAL COMPETITION FOR OUTSIDERS AND SOCIAL MOBILIZATION

Electoral competition for outsiders emerged as part of the process of democratization that resulted in the victory of PAN in the 2000 election and in the emergence of a three-party system with high levels of competition for national office. After decades of uncontested victories and legislative supermajorities for the PRI, voter de-alignment from the PRI began in the late 1980s and intensified in the 1990s, encouraging opposition parties to appeal to these voters and seek office.[3] When the vote share for the PRI declined, and the party lost its supermajority in the lower chamber, the Carlos Salinas administration (1988–94) negotiated with the PAN a series of electoral reforms in 1991 and 1993 in exchange for support for its economic reform agenda, which required constitutional changes. These reforms established the Electoral Tribunal and the Federal Electoral Institute (IFE) to oversee elections (Magaloni 2006: 90) and created a more auspicious environment for the growth of opposition parties. Although these reforms helped make national-level elections clean, the presidential election of 1994 was still not fair due to large incumbent advantages (Levitsky and Way 2010: 158).

Further institutional changes were carried out as competition increased in the mid-1990s. Comprehensive negotiations among parties launched by Zedillo materialized in reforms that guaranteed the independence of the IFE and introduced fundamental changes to electoral institutions in 1994 and 1996 – including rules on campaign finance (Levitsky and Way 2010: 159; Lujambio 2001; Magaloni 2006: 94). Analysts argue that these changes reduced the advantage the PRI had over opposition parties (Camp 2004: 28), allowing for opposition victories in municipal elections and the celebration of clean and fair elections at the national level in subsequent years (Lujambio 2001: 87). These opposition victories helped persuade voters that peaceful alternation was possible (Camp 2004: 27; Magaloni 2006: 94), facilitating the growth of both PAN and PRD in the 1997 legislative elections, which ended the PRI's majority in the lower chamber, and the PAN's victory in the 2000 presidential election (see Figure 6.1).

[3] See Bruhn (1997 chap. 3); Klesner (2005).

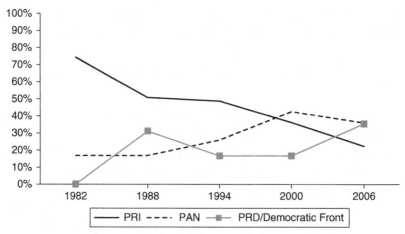

FIGURE 6.1 Vote share in presidential elections, Mexico 1982–2006.
Source: IFE.

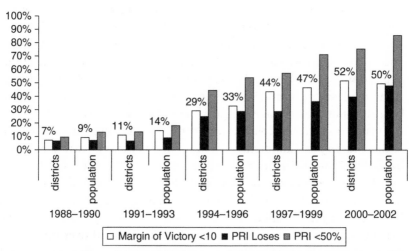

FIGURE 6.2 Electoral competition in municipal elections, Mexico, 1988–2002 (% outsider districts and population in outsider districts with electoral competition).
Source: Elaborated with data from INEGI and CIDAC.

Electoral competition for outsider voters also grew in the 1990s, particularly surrounding the 2000 presidential elections. Figure 6.2 provides a snapshot of these changing electoral dynamics. Given the absence of individual-level survey data on outsiders' electoral choices before the 2000s or ecological data on presidential elections at the district level, I work with results from municipal elections, for which systematic data since the late 1980s exists. As with the other cases in this book, I focus on "outsider" municipalities – those in which outsiders comprised at least 55 percent of the total population.[4] These districts totaled 1,908 of the 2,443 municipalities in Mexico, and comprised around 50 percent of the country's population and 65 percent of the outsiders as of 2000. Several of these municipalities were typically considered the bulwark of the PRI; in the heyday of the dominant party system, the PRI obtained victories with close to 100 percent of the votes in some of these districts. In the 1988–90 electoral cycle,[5] for example, the PRI obtained less than 50 percent of the vote share in only 9.5 percent of these districts.

Electoral competition in outsider municipalities began to grow in the 1994–6 cycle, when opposition parties expanded initially in urban areas, and was even higher at the end of the decade. I use three indicators to measure these changes in electoral dynamics: the percent of outsider municipalities and percent of the outsider population in outsider municipalities in which: (a) the margin of victory is less than ten points; (b) the PRI loses (any party other than the PRI is victorious); and (c) the PRI obtains less than 50 percent of the vote share. Given the PRI's smashing victories in previous years, these measures map the erosion of its electoral support and the expansion of the opposition.

In Figure 6.2 we see that close competition and opposition victories intensified at the end of the decade. Whereas in 1988–90, elections were close in around 7 percent of districts, by 1997–9, this figure had jumped to 44 percent. At the same time, the share of municipalities in which the PRI received less than 50 percent of the vote jumped from about 45 percent to 74.5 percent between 1994 and 2002, compared to 9.5 percent and 13.3 percent in 1988 and 1991, respectively.

Ecological electoral data of presidential elections in outsider municipalities are available for 2000 and 2006. As noted, I measure electoral competition looking at the share of outsider municipalities in which the challenger wins and/or the margin of difference between the first and second party in the presidential election is less than ten points. If electoral competition is present in at least 50 percent of outsider municipalities or the outsider municipalities experiencing electoral competition hold at least 50 percent of the outsider population in these municipalities, I score that presidential election as having electoral competition for outsider voters. In Figure 6.3, we see that in both elections there is competition

[4] This is based on the 2000 census.
[5] Municipal elections are carried out every three years. Because municipalities do not use the same electoral calendar, I grouped the years in which each municipality holds its election into three-year electoral cycles.

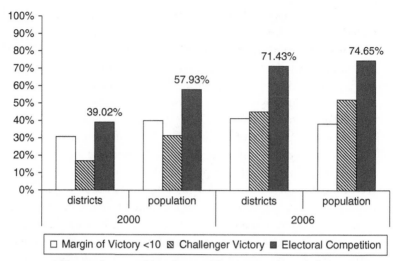

FIGURE 6.3 Electoral competition for outsiders in presidential elections, Mexico, 2000–2006 (% outsider districts and population in outsider districts with electoral competition).
Source: Calculated with socioeconomic data from INEGI and electoral data from CIDAC.

for outsiders. This competition concerns mainly the PRI (incumbent) and PAN (challenger) in 2000 and the PAN (incumbent) and PRD (challenger) in 2006.

A final systematic assessment of electoral competition for outsider voters consists of analyzing voting patterns with individual-level data, which are available for the 2000 and 2006 presidential elections. These data allow for an estimation of electoral competition for the vote of outsiders at a national scale. With postelection surveys carried out by CIDE-CSES, I classify voters into outsiders and insiders and estimate their vote choices (see Appendix 3 for measures). Two indicators are used to measure the presence of electoral competition for outsider voters with these data: whether the vote margin between the two most voted parties favored by outsider voters is less than ten percentage points and/or whether the challenger wins the most votes from outsiders.

Figure 6.4 shows that competition for these voters was high between 2000 and 2006. In 2000, the PRI faced a credible competitor in the PAN, which according to these data won the most votes among outsiders. By 2006, competition was further heightened. The PAN again received the most votes, but faced a rising credible challenge from the PRD, which

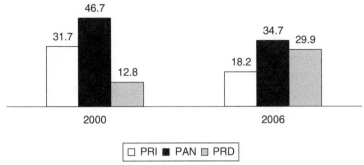

FIGURE 6.4 Reported vote of outsiders in presidential elections, Mexico, 2000–2006 (percent vote share).
Source: Elaborated with post-election surveys done by CIDE-CSES in July of 2000 and July and August of 2006 (elections took place each year in the month of July).

doubled its vote share among outsiders and narrowed PAN's vote margin, according to these data.

Social Mobilization

Social mobilization – understood as the sustained demand for social policy by a coalition of social movements and labor unions – did not take shape in Mexico in the 1990s and 2000s. Mexico did witness, however, the formation of an indigenous movement whose main component was the Zapatista Liberation Army (EZL) that emerged in Chiapas in the 1990s and staged an armed insurrection in 1994. The Zapatistas demanded better living conditions for indigenous peoples and made claims centered on the recognition of their rights as indigenous peoples alongside demands for democratization (see Trejo 2012; Yashar 2005: 26).

Despite the Zapatistas' political relevance, their movement does not fit the characterization of what is here defined as a social movement coalition (SMC), which leads national incumbents to respond with large-scale social policy provisions. The Zapatistas did not forge linkages with other political and social actors to form a national movement advancing a social policy agenda. The Zapatistas remained quite isolated from national-level actors, as well as from other rural movements. The Chiapas conflict remained geographically bounded, and over time became increasingly identified with cultural claims for indigenous autonomy, rather than with its initial economic demands (see Trejo 2004).

The government sought to prevent the movement from expanding beyond Chiapas and responded to the Zapatistas with development programs directed specifically to that state and often administered by the movement itself.[6] The wide-reaching mobilization demanding social benefits that triggered expansion in Argentina and Brazil was not present in Mexico at the national level or coordinated across rural areas throughout the period.

6.3 THE DEMOCRATIC TRANSITION AND SOCIAL POLICY RESPONSES

Electoral competition grew dramatically during the Zedillo administration. After winning the presidency comfortably, the PRI lost every major subnational election in 1995. In 1997, the PRI lost its majority in the lower chamber, inaugurating the first divided government in Mexico's post-Revolutionary history (see Lujambio 2001). Facing electoral decline, and also considering the possibility that subsequent elections would involve growing levels of competition for outsiders (local-level elections in 1994 and 1995 showed inroads by the opposition into areas in which outsiders represented the majority of the population, as shown in Figure 6.2), Zedillo initiated social policy reforms. He dismantled PRONASOL, which was perceived and criticized as highly discretionary, by transferring its infrastructure and social investment funding to states and municipalities, and initiated PROGRESA, a social program that granted nondiscretionary, individual social transfers. PROGRESA constituted the basis on which expansion under democracy would be built, but owing to its limited scope it does not constitute a large-scale expansion as here defined. The goal of this section is to lay out the drivers of social policy change as competition heightened.

The Ernesto Zedillo Administration (1994–2000)

A deep political and economic crisis contributed to the discrediting of the PRI and the rapid growth of electoral competition after Zedillo assumed

---

[6] Several interviews with PRD, PRI, and PAN politicians and technocrats involved in social programs such as Oportunidades, PRONASOL, and PROGRESA denied the insurgency's impact on the state's decision to launch PROGRESA in 1997. The benefit was extended to Chiapas in 1998. Several interviews also noted the importance of resources being directed to Chiapas specifically to prevent the conflict from expanding or escalating. On the Zapatistas and the state, see Eisenstadt (2009).

office.[7] A succession of events in the last year of the Salinas administration unleashed the crisis. In January 1994, the peasant-led Zapatista uprising in Chiapas challenged the PRI government. Among a battery of demands, insurgents expressed opposition to the North American Free Trade Agreement (NAFTA) that Salinas had signed, initiating a rebellion the day the agreement went into effect. The Chiapas conflict revealed deleterious living conditions among indigenous populations and was accompanied by episodes of violence.

Political turmoil incentivized capital flight, showing the vulnerability of Mexico's financial policy, which was based on an overvalued exchange rate and high interest rates (Kessler 1998). The uprising was further followed by the assassination of PRI presidential candidate Luis Donaldo Colosio at a campaign rally in March 1994. Political instability produced further capital flight, which Salinas managed to check by spending reserves to control the exchange rate (Kessler 1998: 58) and by appointing Zedillo, a technocrat and Colosio's campaign manager, as presidential candidate. In a bleak scenario, Zedillo won the election, largely benefiting from Salinas' popularity, who at that time still enjoyed high approval ratings of about 63 percent, and from the enormous advantages and access to state resources that the PRI still enjoyed over its competitors.[8] However, more political assassinations,[9] disclosure of corruption in Salinas' clique, and a new round of armed conflict in Chiapas induced further capital flight before Zedillo's inauguration. After assuming office in December 1994, Zedillo launched a devaluation that triggered the peso crisis and produced a dramatic economic downturn, causing a 6 percent drop in the GDP and rising unemployment in 1995 (see Kessler 1998; Wise 2003).

The discrediting of Salinas and the PRI, along with the dramatic collapse of the economy, undermined electoral support for the party. In the months following Zedillo's inauguration, the PRI lost key urban areas to the opposition (Lujambio 2001: 85–6). As noted in Figure 6.2, competition grew between 1994 and 1999 in outsider municipalities as well. Moreover if we break up the 1994–6 electoral cycle, we see that whereas in 1994 the PRI lost in 23.1 percent of local elections, in 1996 this figure jumped to 34.4 percent (author's estimate). At the state level, the

---

[7] On democratization, see Levitsky and Way (2010); Magaloni (2006); Wise (2003).

[8] Approval ratings from CIDE 2008 in Murillo (2009: 206).

[9] These events include the murder of José Francisco Ruíz-Massieu, Salinas' former brother-in-law and secretary general of the PRI and charges against Raúl Salinas, the president's brother, for alleged involvement in the crime.

opposition won fourteen of the thirty-one gubernatorial races between 1994 and 2000 (Magaloni 2006: 54).

The growth of the opposition put pressure on Zedillo to initiate social policy reforms. A target of criticism was PRONASOL, the social program strongly identified with the Salinas administration.[10] PRONASOL lacked clear rules for benefit distribution, and was perceived as a fundamental pillar of Salinas' strategy to perpetuate the PRI in power. Empowered by the president's declining backing, legislators and subnational authorities of the opposition advocated the decentralization of social expenditures to both reduce the manipulation of resources by the national government and increase the power of local governments (interviews, Boltvinik, Vélez).[11] They further promoted the passage of a Social Development Law as well as other mechanisms that would limit discretion in social policy allocations from the national government.[12]

Pressure to decentralize social expenditures also came from the president's own party. Just as the opposition was winning subnational elections, subnational PRI politicians began to gain power vis-à-vis an enervated president. Like the opposition, subnational PRI authorities hoped to administer more funds themselves and limit discretion in the allocation of resources on the part of the federal government in a political environment of unprecedented levels of competition (interviews, Marván, Vélez, Boltvinik).

In response, the Zedillo administration initiated two changes regarding social policy: (a) the gradual establishment of the Program of Education, Health, and Nutrition (PROGRESA), a nondiscretionary cash-transfer program that would be the backbone of his antipoverty strategy, and (b) the decentralization of PRONASOL's funding, which culminated in the dismantling of the program.

In 1994, Zedillo assigned two technocratic teams to design an alternative social program to PRONASOL. One team was led by José Gómez de León, head of the National Population Council (CONAPO). The other team, in charge of designing the financial structure for the new benefit, was led by Santiago Levy and was based within the Secretariat of Finance. Both teams operated independently from secretary of social development Carlos Rojas, the architect of PRONASOL.

---

[10] See Chapter 3.
[11] See Cámara de Diputados (1996; 1997).
[12] See *La Jornada*, July 8, 1995. The 1997 and 1998 congressional debates of the annual budget in the lower chamber are indicative of these concerns.

Contributions from both teams of experts resulted in the design of a nondiscretionary scheme that provided grants to low-income families with children conditional on school attendance and health checkups. The new program had nonparticipatory implementation. Wary about the potential identification of the program with the political targeting of PRONASOL under the Salinas administration, key officials claimed that the new benefit had to be "the antithesis" of PRONASOL, excluding all community participation that could open the door to manipulation of benefits (interviews, Székely).

PROGRESA, then called the Nutrition, Health, and Education Program (PASE), was piloted in 1995 and 1996, which provided evidence of its technocratic credentials, the program's future impact, and the way it would reach beneficiaries. The program was launched after the 1997 midterm elections. Although the PRI majority in Congress approved funding for PROGRESA in the 1997 annual budget, the Zedillo administration waited to launch the program until after the competitive midterm election in order to prevent legislators and public opinion from associating the new scheme with electoral calculations[13] and clientelism. Zedillo's advisors feared public opinion would consider PROGRESA "Zedillo's PRONASOL."[14] Allegations of discretion in social programs were voiced by the opposition in Congress within the debates over the 1997 budget, whose approval was not endorsed by the PAN or the PRD (Cámara de Diputados, December 11, 1996).

PROGRESA started out with 300,000 beneficiaries in 1997 and was expanded over the next years to reach close to 2.47 million households and 2.48 million children before the 2000 presidential election. In 1998, when the PRI lacked a majority in the lower chamber – which is in charge of approving the budget – the PAN supported the expansion of PROGRESA (Cámara de Diputados, December 13, 1997). The PRD opposed it. Legislator Demetrio Sodi sustained that funding for PROGRESA had increased "550%" and criticized what he said was a "totally clientelistic" program (Cámara de Diputados, December 13, 1997). Fears and allegations of benefit manipulation still affected its implementation.

Although PROGRESA represents an innovation in Mexico's social policy for outsiders, its design borrowed from PRONASOL's Children in Solidarity scheme, which had been established to combat child labor

---

[13] See "Pide Rojas apoyar programas sociales," *Reforma*, August 8, 1997.
[14] See Levy (2006: 108 fn 35).

in rural areas (interviews, Hernández, Rojas). According to Rojas, "PROGRESA [was] the continuation of Children in Solidarity," which provided a small grant in exchange for school attendance and medical checkups for children selected by Solidarity Councils (see Chapter 3; interview, Rojas).

PROGRESA differed from Children in Solidarity in two fundamental ways. A distinctive feature of Children in Solidarity was the presence of social participation, which was avoided in PROGRESA out of concerns about discretion in the program's allocation. As Rojas noted in an interview:

[Children in Solidarity] was an individual benefit but it nonetheless had an important community-involvement component. By contrast, in PROGRESA what you see is the criterion of … killing social participation … of individualizing everything. (interview, Rojas)

At the same time, PROGRESA's beneficiary selection process involved technocratic teams who based decisions on clear eligibility criteria, whereas in the case of Children in Solidarity, community councils determined access. In the words of a former director of PROGRESA:

"Mexico had a package [of school grants] that was called Children in Solidarity… There were thousands of communities that received forty school grants each. Who received those grants within those communities? Who knows. The idea was to provide a more or less fixed number of grants to each community and then leave the community … to decide how to distribute those grants the best possible way. This was a festival of criteria. (interview, Hernández)

With respect to PRONASOL, the administration's goal was to dismantle its structure. By 1996, Zedillo had begun to increase PRONASOL's direct transfers to municipalities. When the PRI lost the majority in the lower chamber in 1997, a more plural legislature pushed for further decentralization. Funding for infrastructure investments was decentralized according to a revenue-sharing formula defined by Congress, which made allocations more transparent. Other smaller schemes included within PRONASOL, such as Enterprises in Solidarity, were either kept within the Secretariat of Social Development (SEDESOL) or transferred to other national-level agencies. Opposition parties in Congress vigorously promoted decentralization. The PAN voted favorably for the annual budget in 1997 to a large extent owing to these concessions.[15]

---

[15] See Cámara de Diputados, December 13, 1997. On decentralization, see Sour et al. (2004).

The new rule-based automatic allocation of former PRONASOL funding to subnational units eliminated national-level discretion and negotiations over these funds.[16] However, states and municipalities in charge of spending those resources enjoyed ample room for discretion.[17] The key point, however, is that the national executive, pressured to reduce discretion, decentralized PRONASOL – and other national programs – through clear criteria and implemented PROGRESA, which was highly targeted and technocratic.

When PROGRESA began implementation, opposition politicians worried about how benefits were actually distributed, especially whether beneficiaries were deceived by patronage networks that required them to work for local authorities in order to maintain their benefits or that scared them away from voting for opposition parties on the grounds that they would lose their benefits if the opposition won. As seen in other countries analyzed in this book, such problems emerged in the programs' early years, when new benefits were inaugurated against a background of entrenched clientelistic relations. Although these practices were not pervasive with respect to cash transfers, and the distribution of benefits was largely nondiscretionary, national officials still acknowledged their existence in the 2000s and made significant efforts to prevent them (interview, Gómez-Hermosillo, director of Oportunidades).[18]

Overall, although PROGRESA does not amount to an expansion as it is defined here given that it reached less than 35 percent of the relevant outsider population, it represents the groundwork on which subsequent expansion of income transfers would be based. In terms of transparency, efforts to reduce discretion, and nonparticipatory implementation, the contrast between PRONSASOL and PROGRESA is stark. Although both programs were launched by PRI administrations as their main social policy strategy for outsiders, their differences can be attributed to the political environments of electoral competition and democratization in each administration. Zedillo faced high levels of competition in a democratizing environment, as well as unprecedented competition for outsider voters when a credible challenger made more aggressive

---

[16] In the first years of the new fiscal law, however, some studies report biases in the federal allocation of resources (see Sour et al. 2004).

[17] Interviews, Székely; Rojas; Escobedo-Zoletto. For the use of resources by subnational units, see Benitez Iturbe (2009); Díaz-Cayeros, Estévez, and Magaloni (forthcoming).

[18] These concerns appear repeatedly in newspaper articles and interviews. Informants argued that external evaluations of PROGRESA helped highlight the efforts and achievements at creating a nondiscretionary program. On these allegations, see, for example, "Bloquean campesions un accesso a Tapachula," in *El Universal*, January 14, 2000.

attempts to mobilize their support as the 2000 elections neared. By the end of the Zedillo administration, about 50 percent of the population in Mexico lived in municipalities governed by the opposition, in contrast to 2 percent when Salinas inaugurated PRONASOL in 1988 (Lujambio 2001: 85). Under Zedillo, moreover, the incumbent party did not control the lower chamber of Congress, and electoral laws passed in 1996 limited the restrictions on the opposition and the advantages of the incumbent. By contrast, under Salinas, opposition parties competed on a much less favorable basis. The PRI's campaign spending far outstripped that of the opposition, and the party was able to use the state apparatus to ensure its continuity in power (see Greene 2007, Magaloni 2006). Moreover, it was able to manipulate electoral results and use repression against the opposition (interview, Cárdenas, PRD presidential candidate, 1988–2000, Magaloni 2006: 92), raising the cost of opposition party building (Greene 2007).[19]

The 2000 Election

The July 2000 presidential election was marked by intense electoral competition, and unlike the 1994 presidential election, it was not only free but fair. Until a few months before the election, PRI candidate Francisco Labastida was the frontrunner. In November 1999, when Labastida won the PRI's first primary elections, polls showed that he held a lead of 20 points with 53 percent of vote intention against 32 percent for Fox and 10 percent for the PRD's candidate, Cuauhtémoc Cárdenas (Lujambio 2001: 88). In January 2000, this difference had shrunk to 10 percentage points and polls showed a potential PRI victory or a technical tie since February 2000.[20]

In the last few months of the campaign Fox, who had launched a "catch-all" strategy appealing to voters around the issue of democracy and regime change, achieved decisive support to win the election. Fox

[19] Magaloni notes that political confrontations emerged in several local elections in which the PRD competed against the PRI, resulting in close to 500 PRD activists murdered in these electoral confrontations under Salinas (Magaloni 2006:92).

[20] Lawson (2004) notes that in January 2000 Labastida led the polls for 15 points. In the next months, polls showed Labastida's support eroding but even coming out first until the end of the campaign; see "Fox: Sólo aspiro a gobernar bien," in *La Jornada*, February 26, 2000. Others reported Labastida winning by a wide margin; see "El PRI bien posicionado para ganar las elecciones," *La Jornada*, March 22, 2000. Even a poll in June 2000 showed Labastida three points ahead, "Mantiene Labastida ventaja mínima," *Reforma*, June 22, 2000.

invited all Mexicans to cast a *useful* vote "to get the PRI out of government," appealing to strategic opposition voters[21] who would support the candidate with the highest chance at defeating the incumbent (Greene 2007; Lujambio 2001: 88–9). At the same time, Fox's campaign targeted outsider voters and especially sought to reach out to the countryside, seeking to mobilize the rural vote away from the PRI.

To mobilize support from low-income outsiders, Fox promised to maintain existing programs such as PROGRESA and to embark on further social investments. Social policy issues gained ground in the campaign agenda as competition tightened. Fearing an increase in vote intention for Fox in the context of a virtual tie between the candidates, Labastida promised to strengthen PROGRESA.[22] As the election neared, Fox further pledged to double the funding for social programs and to expand health care services, stating, "my commitment is that every Mexican will have access to primary care and hospital services."[23]

Analysts of Mexican politics note that as voters became increasingly less attached to parties in the 1990s, the three main parties adopted catch-all strategies to gain votes outside their social bases (Greene 2007; Klesner 2005). As Klesner argues, even if opposition parties had distinct social bases that conditioned their ideological or programmatic orientation, they tried to reach voters broadly. In this context, Fox managed to gain support among outsiders.

Based on the data presented in Figures 6.3 and 6.4, we see that electoral competition for outsider voters was high in the July elections. Starting in 2000, under a democratic regime, outsiders were willing to support different parties across elections, rather than throwing their support primarily behind a single party as they had done in the past. Such levels of volatility among outsiders generated high incentives for reaching them via social policy to consolidate their support, as discussed later.

6.4 ELECTORAL COMPETITION FOR OUTSIDERS AND SOCIAL POLICY EXPANSION

Fox's victory in the 2000 presidential elections inaugurated the first PAN government and the first alternation of parties since the creation of the PRM, predecessor to the PRI, in 1929. As president, Fox faced

[21] "Llama Fox a hacer *útil* el voto de la oposición," *La Jornada*, March 6, 2000.
[22] Quoted in "Se definen sobre UNAM, Fobaproa, el IVA y Chiapas," *Reforma*, May 26, 2000.
[23] Ibid fn 21.

the challenge of consolidating the broad electoral coalition that had brought him to power. This coalition comprised voters seeking regime change and alternation, historic PAN supporters, and low-income voters mobilized by the PAN through promises of change and social improvement.[24] Regarding outsiders, a large majority of whom were poor,[25] the PAN faced the dilemma of retaining their support through social policy appeals while simultaneously catering to its constituency in the economic elite, who preferred modest government intervention and market mechanisms in social policy.

When proposing and negotiating social policy for outsiders, PAN politicians therefore designed large-scale though restrictive social programs, reaching a relatively small pool of beneficiaries with modest benefit levels, especially compared to programs for insiders and provisions extended to outsiders in the inclusive models created in Argentina and Brazil. Specifically, the PAN proposed benefits that despite attaining unprecedented coverage were targeted to the poorest of outsiders.

As in other cases in which social policy expansion was propelled by electoral competition for outsider voters, the new policies and/or funding for these initiatives required negotiations with parties in Congress. The shape of the resulting policies depended on these parties' social policy preferences and their balance of power. In this regard, the PRI did not have a consistent social policy agenda for outsiders in the 2000s. The party had supported high levels of state intervention in programs for the formal sector until the 1990s, when it embraced pro-market policies (see Brooks 2009; Madrid 2003; Murillo 2001). The Salinas administration pursued sweeping market-oriented reforms but kept social security systems virtually intact, while the Zedillo administration privatized the pension system run by the Mexican Institute of Social Security (IMSS) and tried, unsuccessfully, to liberalize health insurance. Social policy for outsiders promoted by the PRI in turn largely consisted of rural benefits: land distribution, which was executed unevenly until the 1980s, and food programs and price subsidies, which benefited outsiders but often channeled more resources toward higher-income consumers.[26] In the 1990s, some PRI politicians preferred a more subsidiary role for the

---

[24] On the 2000 elections, see essays in Domínguez and Lawson (2004).
[25] Note that in 2000, when outsiders represented 58 percent of the population, the poverty and indigence (extreme/food poverty) rates in the total population were 53.6 percent and 24.1 percent, respectively (see CONEVAL 2006:7).
[26] See Chapter 3.

state while others sought higher levels of state intervention in policies for low-income populations. Both of these sectors were relevant under Salinas, but the pro-market PRI politicians became more prominent during the Zedillo and the Fox administrations.

The PRD initially lacked a clear social policy agenda aside from opposing the pro-market reforms introduced by PRI politicians and advocating nondiscretionary provisions. This changed with the rise of AMLO, who sought to actively mobilize outsider support during his campaign. Programs for outsiders then became a key topic in the party's social policy agenda. Just like the PRI and the PAN, in a highly competitive environment, the PRD advocated nondiscretionary social policies with unmediated state implementation.

As advanced in this book's analytic argument, when political parties face electoral competition, they generally prefer to establish social policies with nonparticipatory implementation, both to avoid empowering organizations that may engage in demand-making, and out of concern that the involvement of social groups may generate allegations of patronage or benefit manipulation, which could discredit the incumbent administration. Despite the fact that some PRI legislators strongly preferred participatory social policies under Salinas, when facing a competitive environment, the PRI bloc in Congress did not actively promote participation in policy implementation in the social policies introduced in the 2000s.

During the period under examination, the president lacked a majority in both chambers. The distribution of power in the lower chamber was split between the PAN and PRI, and the PRI also had the largest bloc in the Senate and controlled several governorships. The PRD had a small share of seats in Congress and therefore little influence on policy design (see Table 6.2). To pass new social benefits or to obtain funding in the annual budget for social programs, which requires approval of the executive's budget proposal from the lower chamber only, the PAN needed backing from other parties. Fox especially needed PRI support until the last few months of his administration when the PRD became the second largest party in Congress.

Next, I characterize the social policy innovations of the Fox administration and discuss the reasons why restrictive designs were chosen. Because some of these innovations – especially those concerning pensions – were either more fully implemented or changed under Calderón, I refer further to his administration in the discussion of each policy area.

TABLE 6.2 *Composition of Congress, Mexico, 2000–2009*

	2000–2003		2003–2006		2006–2009	
	Chamber	Senate	Chamber	Senate	Chamber	Senate
PRI	211	60	224	57	104	33
%	42.2	46.9	44.8	44.5	20.8	25.8
PAN	213	46	151	47	206	52
%	46.6	35.9	30.2	36.7	41.2	40.6
PRD	51	16	97	15	158*	36
%	10.2	12.5	19.4	11.7	31.6	28.1
PVEM	11	5	17	5	19	6
%	2.2	3.9	3.4	3.9	3.8	4.7
Other	14	1	11	4	13	1
%	2.8	.8	2.2	3.1	2.6	.8
Total	500	128	500	128	500	128

* Includes sixteen from Convergencia and sixteen from Partido del Trabajo.
Note: 2000 alliance between the PAN and PVEM (Ecologist Green Party of Mexico); 2006 alliance between the PRI and PVEM.
Source: IFE-Sistema de Consulta de las Estadísticas Electorales 2000–12 (www.scieef.ife .org.mx).

The Vicente Fox Administration (2000–2006)

After taking office, Fox sought to solidify the support of outsiders through social policy. Fox transformed PROGRESA into a new income-transfer program, Oportunidades – which by 2003 reached more than twice the number of its original beneficiaries – and inaugurated health insurance for outsiders, a key innovation of his administration. Facing intense competition for outsiders surrounding the 2006 elections, when the PAN's continuity became threatened by the rise of AMLO, the Fox administration inaugurated means-tested pensions in an effort to offset the appeals of this credible challenger who promised large-scale pension expansion.

One major concern of the Fox administration was avoiding allegations of benefits manipulation, such as the ones that had characterized prior programs like PRONASOL.[27] PAN legislators submitted a social development bill to Congress to create clear rules, transparency, and accountability mechanisms in social programs.[28] Among other measures, the new law established an evaluation system and provided guidelines to

---

[27] This concern about avoiding discretion in the selection of beneficiaries was particularly highlighted in interviews with Székely and Hernández.
[28] The PRI and PRD had also submitted bills, and Congress discussed all three projects.

inform the population about existing benefits.[29] This law was approved unanimously in the lower chamber. As advanced in this book's argument, both the incumbent and the opposition faced a highly competitive environment and therefore had incentives to support a law that established clear criteria and rules for social policy. As PRI legislator Sonia Rincón noted, "We need to keep on making progress on the institutionalization of public policies, even more now that alternation is a reality."[30] In explaining both the decision to pass the law and the PRI's support for it, former president and legislator Felipe Calderón noted:

Social expenditure is so relevant that it has to be conceptualized as state policy not as the policy of a specific administration. With that in mind ... the legislators promoted the Social Development Law in 2004. The issue is that the opaque and discretionary administration of social programs can become your worst enemy because it creates divisions among and confronts political parties, levels of government, and beneficiaries themselves... Obviously, the PRI, an opposition party, then became interested in generating the transparency grounded in the law. (interview)

Income Support

The first innovation under Fox was the reform and expansion of the cash transfer program launched by Zedillo. Although Fox promised social policy expansion during the 2000 presidential campaign, there were doubts as to whether a PAN victory would keep PROGRESA in place, and there was profound mistrust among several PAN politicians toward the program, which they associated with the PRI (interviews, Hernández, Calderón).[31] Before assuming office, the Fox transition team announced that the president-elect would maintain PROGRESA, noting, "on inauguration day we cannot tell 2.6 million families they will lose their benefits."[32] Fox himself assured constituents he would maintain PROGRESA,[33] and suggested that PROGRESA would be transformed into "PROGRESA Plus" and would grant every family in Mexico a

---

[29] Some of those mechanisms already governed PROGRESA and Oportunidades, but were not present in other social programs (e.g., obligation to publicize the fact that benefits were accessible without political intermediaries and that receiving a benefit did not imply exchanging it for political support).

[30] Quoted in SEDESOL (2005: 8).

[31] "Candado Electorero al Progresa," *El Universal*, May 9, 2000.

[32] Carlos Flores, social policy expert of the president-elect's team in "Fox preservará el Progresa, anuncia equipo de transición," *La Jornada*, July 21, 2000.

[33] See also "Evaluan retos de la política social," *Reforma*, July 21, 2000.

minimum income, guaranteed health treatments, pensions, and some savings for contingencies.[34]

In the next two years, and with an eye toward consolidating support, the Fox administration introduced important changes to PROGRESA. In 2001, Fox announced its extension to semi-urban areas, incorporating 800,000 beneficiaries, and increased the budget for social development, foreseeing a broader expansion of this program in following years. In 2002, Fox changed the name of PROGRESA to Oportunidades – partly to differentiate his approach from that of the PRI – and expanded the benefit to another million households.[35] As an indicator of transparency in the distribution of benefits, Fox appointed Rogelio Gómez-Hermosillo, the head of Alianza Cívica, a nongovernmental organization involved in monitoring elections, as the director of Oportunidades.

By 2003, the number of beneficiaries of Oportunidades had reached 4.3 million, almost twice as many as at the beginning of the Fox administration. A year later, the number of households covered was extended to 5 million, and school grants were provided, on average, to one child per family conditional on school attendance (see Figure 6.5). The expansion of Oportunidades to urban areas was not only championed by the PAN, but also requested by legislators from the opposition in congressional debates over annual budget allocations.

The program's design was restrictive. Despite its meaningful reach, Oportunidades covered only 36 percent of the outsider school-age children by 2010, a scope that is here classified as low.[36] Aside from targeting families in extreme poverty only, enrollment was further limited in a number of ways. As stated in several interviews with top officials of the program, at the end of the Fox administration Oportunidades had a wait list of families who qualified for the benefit. At the same time, several children in households reached by Oportunidades did not receive fellowships. These restrictions on the reach of the program to potentially eligible families and children operated through several mechanisms. First, the government established a quota of beneficiaries of 5 million households, which was increased to 5.8 million in 2010. Even if people qualified for the benefit, they were not included until a spot opened up. Second, conditionality was strictly enforced and families who lost their

---

[34] In "Ofrece 'progresa plus' que asegure sustento," *El Universal*, November 22, 2000.

[35] The expansion of Oportunidades was decided by the executive. The lower chamber in Congress voted to provide funding for the program.

[36] In the present study, a "low" scope of coverage is defined as between 35 percent and 50 percent of the population.

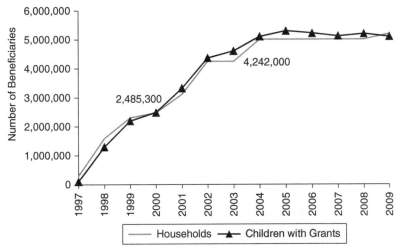

FIGURE 6.5 Beneficiaries of income transfers (Progresa and Oportunidades), 1997–2009.
Source: SEDESOL.

benefits faced a wait period if they wished to reenter the program. Third, Oportunidades did not encourage children to go back to school if they had already dropped out. When asked about the low ratio of children with grants to protected families, especially compared to other cases under investigation, one top Oportunidades official suggested that mothers did not want all of their children to be enrolled in the scheme, and another noted that these figures reflected children who had dropped out of school and who therefore did not receive the benefit. Understanding household choices is beyond the scope of this project. The low number of recipients may be attributed to the difficulty of getting dropouts to return to school, but it also reflects the government's intention to reach many households while also keeping the program small. In Brazil, a country whose socioeconomic characteristics most resemble Mexico among the cases here analyzed, the ratio of children with grants to protected families has been consistently higher than one on average. Finally, it is worth noting that program officials at some point seriously considered the possibility of making the benefit conditional on academic performance. Yet that proposal was discarded, as it would potentially limit access even further (interview, Escobedo-Zoletto, director of Oportunidades).

Under the Fox and the Calderón administrations, the benefit level of Oportunidades was moderate. The program provided a grant to children in school, a food supplement to families in extreme poverty, and a

TABLE 6.3 *Benefit Level of Oportunidades, 2010*

	Total Amount in Pesos	As Percent of Extreme or Food Poverty Line[a]	As Percent of Poverty Line[b]	As Percent of Minimum Wage
Benefit Household with Two Children[c]	906	35	17	53.10
Minimum Wage[d]	1706.5	66	32	100

[a] Average of urban and rural *línea pobreza alimentaria* calculated by CONEVAL for 2010 times three (the equivalent of two adults and two children).

[b] Average of urban and rural *línea pobreza carencias* calculated by CONEVAL for 2010 (similar to poverty line defined by ECLAC) three times (for two adults and two children).

[c] Average benefit paid to households with one or two adults plus two children – one in primary and one in secondary school – provided they fulfill the conditionality (food support, food supplement, two average grants for primary and secondary school). Note that grants are provided ten months a year.

[d] Average of minimum wage (estimated with "Area A," 57.46 pesos per day and "Area C," 54.47 pesos per day times 30.5.

Sources: Estimates built with data from Oportunidades, CONEVAL (available at www .coneval.gob.mx), Servicios de Administración Tributaria (www.sat.gob.mx) and SEDESOL for July–December 2010.

small subsidy for electricity (which in Brazil and Argentina was provided separately). With the crisis in the late 2000s, a food supplement to compensate for food price hikes was added. The amount school grants paid varied according to grade level and, beginning in secondary education, varied according to gender to foment women's education. Although benefits could be high for older children, reaching over the minimum wage by the final year of high school, the average benefit paid to households (including fellowships, food support, and electricity subsidies) was lower. In 2010, the benefit paid to a hypothetical household with two children (including food support and two average grants for children in primary and secondary education) was equivalent to 36.3 percent of the cost of the food basket and 17.5 percent of the poverty line (see Table 6.3). Based on this last measure, the benefit level of Oportunidades is here considered moderate, as it stands between 10 percent and 19 percent of the poverty line (see Appendix 1). The coverage and benefit level of Oportunidades reflect a preference for limited government intervention, which the PAN and Zedillo administrations shared.

The PRD had different preferences with respect to income support. It contested the use of conditionality and advocated broader transfers, which were rejected by the PRI and PAN (interviews, Laurell, secretary of health and welfare, Mexico City; and Pérez-Bejarano, head of social welfare of the PRD's 2006 campaign). However, it could not influence the design of income transfers under Fox for a number of reasons. First, the PRD did not have enough power in Congress to affect policy making during the Fox administration. Second, the PRD prioritized other policy areas, such as pensions and health care, for which it had alternative policy proposals. PRD administrations in Mexico City in the 2000s showcased the party's policy proposals and helped AMLO place social policy issues on the national agenda, but they did not launch any massive income-support program for children. In fact, the PRD did not have a specific policy proposal that could replace or significantly overhaul Oportunidades, as it did in the case of pensions and health care. According to the candidate for the Ministry of Social Development, in the event of a PRD government in 2006, Oportunidades would have been kept in place (interview, Pérez-Bejarano).

Just like PROGRESA, Oportunidades was administered directly by the national state and did not include social organizations in the program's implementation. In the absence of strong social movements that could demand involvement in participatory arrangements, political parties in a highly competitive party system preferred nonparticipatory implementation of large-scale income transfers. For PAN technocrats, the idea was to have "zero" community involvement (interview, high official of SEDESOL) to avoid what they perceived as unnecessary intermediation that could result in abuses.

Health Care

In 2003, the Fox administration formally launched its most ambitious social policy initiative, Seguro Popular (SP), which aimed to expand health insurance for outsiders. Due to its relevance and visibility, and the fact that it was an innovation introduced by Fox rather than an initiative inherited from the Zedillo administration, SP was undoubtedly the signature social program of the administration.

With the goal of gaining the support of outsiders, Fox promised to guarantee access to health services for those without formal social security coverage in his presidential campaign. After the elections, a transition team led by Julio Frenk – an internationally renowned public health expert and future secretary of health – began to work on a proposal for health care expansion that culminated in SP. At the time, outsiders could use health services through clinics and health posts run by the states, as Mexico's health care system had been decentralized in the 1980s and 1990s. Access to these services was limited due to inadequate infrastructure, especially outside of large cities, uneven provision of services, and lack of funding. User fees were collected at the point of delivery, raising barriers to the poor – almost half of the population of Mexico at the time.[37]

To promote SP and make its approval more likely, the executive followed a strategy similar to the one Zedillo used with PROGRESA. While working on the draft bill, the Secretariat of Health launched the pilot of what would ultimately become SP, covering 295,000 families by 2002 (Ortiz 2006: 43). The pilot program helped show that despite the dearth of funding and infrastructure in many localities, the implementation of SP was feasible, and provided PAN legislators with ammunition to defend the policy. According to Frenk, the pilot "included baseline surveys to see the health conditions of the families, their propensity to pay [for health insurance] … a large number of studies… It was very important to have not just an abstract proposal but an annex that said: we have been doing this in several states and it is working."[38] Once the pilot had been evaluated, Fox submitted the bill creating the System of Social Protection in Health Care – within which SP would operate – to Congress in November 2002.

SP was passed in April 2003 with support from the PAN and the PRI, which introduced few modifications to the original bill. The PRD had a different proposal for health care reform and opposed the initiative in the lower chamber. Yet given the party's small share of seats in both chambers, this had no impact on the policy's approval or design.

SP was designed as a restrictive health insurance for outsiders. According to the law, SP offers a package of basic health services contracted out from state, social security, or private providers. Affiliation is voluntary. While SP fully subsidizes the extremely poor, all other outsiders – most of whom were poor at the time – are required to pay an insurance premium according to their household income. Aside from premiums, SP is funded with resources provided by the national and state governments.[39]

---

[37] Poverty data for 2002 from CONEVAL (2006: 7).

[38] Quoted in Ortiz (2006: 44), my translation.

[39] Households were initially exempted from paying premiums if they were among the poorest 20 percent of the population. In 2010, families with incomes up to the fourth-poorest decile were exempted.

In order to gain support for the program and raise enough funding, implementation was agreed to be gradual. One of the biggest challenges facing SP was persuading households that would have to pay premiums to enroll. When the program was approved, it was estimated that about 55 million Mexicans lacked health insurance. SP established the goal of reaching more than 45 million people in 2010.[40] Coverage grew significantly between 2004 and 2010, when SP affiliated 26.23 million people, about 41 percent of outsiders.[41] Out of this pool, the vast majority had fully subsidized insurance premiums.[42]

Regarding health treatments and/or interventions, SP guarantees basic rather than comprehensive coverage. The number of treatments included grew gradually from 90 in 2005 to 266 in 2008.[43] High-complexity interventions, some of which were included within a fund for catastrophic expenses, were not fully covered by SP at the time. In this respect, SP resembles Chile's FONASA, which leaves some treatments uncovered or provides partial coverage. As in the case of pensions and income support, SP is implemented without the participation of organizations representing users or affiliates.

The structure of SP reflects the preferences of conservative politicians within the PAN. In expanding health services to consolidate support among outsiders, the PAN hoped to make the new policy compatible with the preferences of its core upper-income constituency – and the party's historic program – for a subsidiary, small role of the state and market expansion. This resulted in a program with rather modest reach and coverage in which affiliates, excluding the very poor, are required to pay an insurance premium to access services.

At the same time, the Fox administration pursued to a greater or lesser extent other goals with the expansion of health services. First, it sought to make more room for a private market of health care providers, and second, it aimed to reduce the power of the main social security institutions that provided health services to private and public formal workers, the IMSS and the Civil Servants' Social Security Institute (ISSSTE),

---

[40] Estimated with data from INEGI's 2000 census. See Secretaría de Salud (2004: 3); "En marcha, El Seguro de Salud," *La Jornada*, May 14, 2003.

[41] Estimate based on 2010 census data from INEGI. See discussion about discrepancies in coverage, which vary significantly depending on the source. The Secretariat of Health claims a much larger number of affiliated individuals than the data coming out of the census and other surveys, which all yield much smaller affiliation rates to SP. See CONEVAL (2014), INEGI-ENESS (2014), and Secretaría de Salud (2013).

[42] See Secretaría de Salud (2004) and CONEVAL (2014).

[43] Secretaría de Salud (2004: 3) and (2008: 62).

respectively – as well as that of their powerful unions. These goals were also in line with the preferences of the core business constituency. In fact, the basic guidelines of SP coincide with the proposal for health reform put together by Funsalud, a foundation supported by the business community, which advocated the creation of public insurance for low-income people and a plural health care market that would foster the private provision of health services (Funsalud 2001).

Regarding the private provision of services, promoters of SP believed that because the IMSS and ISSTEE delivered services exclusively through their own facilities, they both discouraged the development of private provision, competition, and user choice, resulting in less effective services. In the words of Frenk, "social security of the twentieth century created a monopoly of providers without incentives to satisfy users' needs."[44] The expansion of health insurance for outsiders offered an opportunity to address such perceived distortion. Unlike the IMSS and ISSSTE, SP can contract out services from diverse private, public, and social security providers (e.g., hospitals, labs, clinics) and foster the growth of private contractors.[45]

Another transformation more or less explicitly pursued through this reform was the erosion of the power of the social security institutions, which could potentially facilitate their overhaul in the future. There were several serious attempts at reforming the IMSS and ISSSTE since the 1990s, which did not prosper largely owing to opposition from their labor unions (interview, Genaro Borrego, director of IMSS, 1992–2000). Essentially, these reforms aimed to reduce IMSS expenditures by contracting out services to private providers (interviews, Borrego and high IMSS official) and by scaling back labor contracts and pensions of IMSS employees (interviews, Vega-Galina, IMSS union secretary-general), which were particularly generous relative to the rest of the formal workforce.

Some labor union leaders saw the expansion of private providers fomented by the SP as a threat to the survival of the IMSS. While not opposing the protection of outsiders, they were wary of the potential effects of the new program. According to Francisco Hernández-Juárez, head of the National Union of Workers (UNT), private interests supporting SP were "working to dismantle the IMSS so that they capture that population [it serves] and benefit economically" (interview).

---

[44] Frenk in Gómez Dantés (2005: 22).
[45] Confidential interview.

Promoters of SP initially considered the possibility of integrating it within the IMSS.[46] Interviews with officials from the IMSS and from SEDESOL revealed that the government explicitly refused to expand services to outsiders through the IMSS because that would mean empowering IMSS and its workers' unions.[47] In contrast to the government, union leaders believed the IMSS should manage the expansion of services to outsiders as it had some infrastructure and the capacity to administer a new large-scale program (interviews, Hernández Juárez, Vega-Galina). The IMSS already ran a program, IMSS-Coplamar, later called IMSS-Oportunidades, which provided very basic primary care in some rural areas and could be used as a platform to expand services (interview, director of IMSS-Oportunidades).

SP was approved in Congress with broad support from PAN legislators and from the PRI. Support from opposition senators was deemed critical for its passage and to enable its implementation, as senators largely responded to governors who would have to contribute to the program's funding and guarantee its operation (see Ortiz 2006). The PRD opposed SP. In the congressional debate, Senator Elías Moreno-Brizuela suggested the PRD had "discussed intensely the proposal" and had "contradictory views." He advocated voting against the policy because although SP would give more resources to the states and governors might see that as "a carrot," it would end up "impoverishing many states" because they would have to pay for part of the services extended by the program without adequate resources (Cámara de Senadores, April 24, 2003). The PRD also maintained that the new health care law opposed "universality" and "free access" by guaranteeing a reduced package of services and establishing premiums for low-income families. These two features, universal coverage and free access, were key aspects promoted by the party's alternative health policy proposal (interview Laurell, PRD's leading expert and secretary of health of Mexico City).

Close to half of the PRI's legislators supported the initiative in the lower chamber, which guaranteed its passage.[48] In opposition, some PRI legislators argued that the measure would undercut IMSS-Oportunidades (legislators Victor Infante; Francisco López-González, Cámara de Diputados, April 29, 2003). The PRD, in turn, voted against the policy. PRD legislators rejected SP's separation from social security institutions,

---

[46] Noted by Frenk interviewed by Gómez Dantés (2005: 17).

[47] Interviewees requested confidentiality.

[48] See http://gaceta.diputados.gob.mx/Gaceta/Votaciones/58/tabla3or2-48.php3 (accessed August 2009).

arguing that universality had to be achieved by funding existing health care facilities (subsidizing the supply of services) to ensure free access for all. At the same time, and in line with PRD senators, others rejected the fact that SP provided access to "essential" rather than comprehensive services (statements by Adela Graniel-Campos, Cámara de Diputados, April 29, 2003). PRD experts furthermore believed that SP would segment access among low-income populations, providing only a limited set of treatments to people enrolled in the plan, and neglecting those not enrolled and/or seeking treatment for non-SP conditions. As we will see in Chapter 7, similar concerns emerged with the AUGE in Chile.

SP began implementation gradually. As skeptics had predicted, the lack of infrastructure proved decisive for the evolution of implementation in different localities (see Coneval 2014). As Lakin noted, one critical aspect of SP that did not work as expected was the actual payment by the states of their required contributions. The national government in turn did little to modify this situation, hoping instead to strengthen the program and keep it in motion (see Lakin 2010). According to Calderón, who saw an important expansion in coverage during his tenure as president, the role of the states in SP's implementation was its weakness (interview, Calderón).

The other aspect of the program that did not take off was the collection of family premiums. In fact, initial reports showed non-indigent families being fully subsidized (Lakin 2010). Under Calderón, these requirements were eased and families within the four poorest income deciles were exempted from paying premiums, which helped expand the program's reach and avoid misclassification of beneficiaries or selective application of eligibility criteria.

In sum, SP was probably the most relevant expansion in Mexico and also the most challenging one given the infrastructure and funding required to accomplish its goals. This expansion was done in a top-down way in the context of electoral competition for outsiders. Its main programmatic features were discussed and designed by experts and negotiated in a Congress dominated by conservative politicians. The absence of social mobilization pressing for expansion and participating in the program's design helps account for the restrictive model adopted.

Pensions

Pension expansion was closely intertwined with the 2006 presidential election and the rise of AMLO, who posed a credible threat to the continuity of the PAN, and who promised to create a large-scale pension program. Well before the presidential campaign, in 2004 and 2005, opinion polls showed that if AMLO ran for president, he would win comfortably (see Lawson 2009: 7). During the 2006 race, the margin of difference narrowed, with AMLO having a ten-point lead (Lawson 2009: 1).

The PRD and PAN competed intensely for the support of the low-income electorate. The PRD-led coalition, with the slogan "For the Good of All, the Poor First," promised social policy expansion in its attempt to reach out to low-income voters nationally. AMLO had a strong record of social policy innovation. As Mexico City's head of government (2000–5), he launched a universal pension for people seventy and older – reaching 400,000 people in 2006 – access to free health services and medications, and pensions for people with disabilities and for orphans, which benefited 86,000 people (interview, Encinas, PRD mayor of Mexico City).

According to key PRD advisors and the opposition, these social policies amassed dramatic electoral support for the PRD in Mexico City, where the party won by a landslide in the midterm election of 2003.[49] In particular, old-age pensions were widely recognized as a fundamental source of popularity for AMLO (interview, Boltvinik). A key social policy expert and PRD politician highlighted the "political brilliance" of AMLO when he decided to launch pensions, and suggested:

His political intuition enlightened him... There is an obvious thing: each senior is at the peak of a pyramid with a large base. If you assist all the seniors then everyone is happy because everybody has a parent, a grandparent. It is impressive the number of people who came to admire a political leader who launched a program reaching seniors. The increase in popularity attained with this program was impressive. Why wouldn't I vote for this candidate who did so much for my grandpa? (interview, PRD policy expert)

Under AMLO, social policy became a fundamental source of competition between the national and city governments. For example, PRD legislators representing Mexico City voted against SP in Congress, and AMLO initially refused to start its implementation in the district.[50] Although he claimed to support SP,[51] his was the last state to eventually agree with the

---

[49] Interviews, Boltvinik, Encinas, confidential interview.
[50] "La Salud sin colores ni partidos, señala Frenk," *La Jornada*, January 14, 2005; "Sin acuerdo formal Fox pone en marcha el Seguro Popular en el DF," *La Jornada*, April 6, 2005.
[51] "Con austeridad viable en todo el país la pensión universal," *La Jornada*, March 14, 2005.

national government to start rolling it out, on the grounds that it had a different health care policy that provided free universal health care.

Tensions between Fox and AMLO surged surrounding a failed attempt by the PRI and the PAN to remove AMLO from office in Mexico City on the grounds that he had allegedly violated an injunction by opening a road on expropriated land. As Wuhs argued, this move "not only ultimately failed but also aggravated existing tensions along the parties and gave AMLO a significant bump in his approval ratings and overall political profile" (2008: 143).

Facing a real challenge to the PAN's continuity in power, President Fox initially discredited AMLO's programs. In particular, he dismissed noncontributory old-age pensions as "populist" and in criticizing the policy, stated:

Workers in firms, civil servants – all save to have a pension when they retire. I believe it is terribly unfair that just for being seniors, others are protected with precisely the money of those who work.[52]

In response, AMLO noted that the pension program was "an act of justice" and suggested that social benefits could be paid for with a reduction of discretionary government expenditures and their reallocation toward social policy.[53] In a public rally in Mexico City in which AMLO formally granted 2,700 new pension benefits, he argued that "an austerity plan of the national government" that reduced politicians' expenses and cut high salaries and privileges could spare enough to "guarantee the right to a food pension ... scholarships for people with disabilities, more housing, schools, and hospitals."[54]

Soon after his critiques of AMLO's pension program, and aware of the difficulty that the PAN faced in the coming elections, Fox announced that his government was planning to launch a pension program for people sixty-five and older without social security coverage that would be funded with a "solidarity contribution from the national government" and with savings from beneficiaries.[55] He further pledged that his government

---

[52] Public statement quoted in "Fox vs. los programas sociales del DF," *La Jornada*, March 18, 2005. This statement was noted in a number of interviews with PRD politicians.
[53] "Con austeridad viable en todo el país la pensión universal," *La Jornada*, March 14, 2005.
[54] Ibid.
[55] "Pronto habrá un plan de jubilaciones para mayores de 65 años, anuncia Fox," *La Jornada*, April 17, 2005.

would establish "three pillars of social justice" involving education, pensions, and the social security system, especially Seguro Popular.[56]

In late 2005, Fox's administration formally announced the extension of pensions for seniors in households receiving Oportunidades. In January 2006, the Fox administration began the distribution of close to 800,000 pensions to the poor through Oportunidades-Seniors to offset the momentum of the PRD's candidate. Oportunidades-Seniors provided a pension equivalent to 17 percent of the minimum wage, well below the benefit AMLO had promised, which was equivalent to half of a minimum wage. The choice of Oportunidades as the structure through which the pensions would be distributed responded to the fact that it had operative capacity to implement a large program quickly. According to the director of Oportunidades, "clearly the intention was to create out of nowhere the capacity to put together a list of beneficiaries and extend the transfer" (interview, Gómez-Hermosillo, director of Oportunidades). At the same time, Fox requested a technocratic team to design a pension program out of which adults in households receiving Oportunidades could save for a future pension (interview, Székely).

Fox made further announcements that emphasized his commitment to consolidating social policy for outsiders in an effort to ensure their support for the PAN. In 2006, he inaugurated the Council of Social Protection (CPS), which sought to integrate different programs for outsiders (Oportunidades, Seguro Popular and Oportunidades-Seniors). The first meeting of the CPS was held on March 2006, three months before the national elections. On that occasion, Fox, who had previously rejected universal policies launched by the government of Mexico City, stated that: "To universalize social security is not only a mandate but an ethical and human imperative that cannot be procrastinated. Democracy is equity and equity means inclusion and opportunities to all Mexicans."[57]

Facing a technical tie in the final months of the campaign, Calderón launched an increasingly aggressive attack against AMLO, portraying him in the media as a radical populist and a danger to Mexico. Coupled with campaign mistakes made by the PRD candidate, such as declining to participate in the presidential debate, the dirty campaign tactics helped

---

[56] See also "Fox planteará sistema de pensiones para los comerciantes informales," *La Jornada*, October 10, 2005.

[57] "Fox insta a evitar el uso electoral de programas," *La Jornada*, March 24, 2006.

pull Calderón ahead as the election neared, awarding him a razor-thin victory of less than half a point.[58]

AMLO disputed the election results and claimed that the PAN had stolen the presidency. The PRD launched protests and an encampment in Mexico City, which lasted for months. Calderón took office in December 2006 in the context of political challenges to his legitimacy.

The pension program Oportunidades-Seniors Fox launched in the months prior to the elections was widely recognized by the PRD as well as by PAN politicians and policy makers as motivated by the centrality of pensions in the public agenda promoted by AMLO (interview, Encinas) and initiated to keep up with his candidacy (interview, Pérez-Bejerano). In the words of Gómez-Hermosillo, director of Oportunidades at the time:

Evidently the issue was brought into the public agenda by the subnational programs that started in Mexico City but in other states as well. It became an issue on the agenda, so it was necessary to find options and the government did not want to extend a universal pension. Fox's government did not believe that [a universal pension] was a good, progressive, solid measure… [One goal was to] give the message [that] the country would move towards a non-contributory pension. It had to be well targeted, it should not be a broad-reaching thing, universal in the false populist sense, but [it had to] really provide for the needs of those who do not have minimum income in old age. (interview)

Because this last-minute program expansion was regarded as polemic and, more importantly, given pressure from the PRD to create an institutionalized benefit in the context of high electoral competition and post-election conflict, the executive adopted a new pension program with clear eligibility rules in 2007.

As soon as the new Congress assumed office in in September 2006, PRD legislators submitted a bill for a universal pension for seniors seventy and older and began to negotiate funding for this benefit within the 2007 annual budget law. The PRD was now the second-largest party in Mexico's Congress and the PAN hoped to win its support to govern and to get the annual budget approved. The PRD's proposal for pension expansion was discussed in the Commission for Vulnerable Groups, where legislators agreed to the PRD's initiative to create a more institutionalized benefit. At the same time, however, PAN legislators favored a more modest program and significantly lower funding than the one the PRD proposed. In explaining why conservative politicians agreed to extend pensions, Marta Pérez-Bejerano maintained that while they find it

[58] See an analysis of the campaign in Wuhs (2008: 143–6).

hard to oppose to a popular policy, what they do is to "reduce the funding, lower the benefit level" (interview).

Instead of moving forward with the pension bill, funding for a pension program was negotiated among legislators of the PRD, PAN, and PRI, and was introduced within the 2007 annual budget. When Calderón assumed office in December 2006, Congress approved the 2007 budget, which included pension funding, with support from the PRD and the PRI (Cámara de Diputados, December 23, 2006).

Aside from seeking to court outsiders through pension expansion – and to avoid blocking a popular proposal – PAN legislators supported the initiative as a fundamental concession to the PRD in exchange for its support to approve the annual budget (Velez, interview). For the PRD, the passage of the new program was an important achievement despite the post-electoral confrontation they maintained with the PAN. It signaled not only the PRD's influence on the national agenda, but also the accomplishment, at least in part, of its promise to create pensions for outsiders. As noted by PRD legislator Pablo Trejo, "A politics of dialogue, concertation, agreement ... is possible. We did it [negotiated] to achieve a social program that was our campaign commitment" (Cámara de Diputados, December 23, 2006). In the words of Perez-Bejerano, the new pension "was our victory ... there was opposition against it ... but after a long time we made them approve it" (interview). It is likely that PRD legislators expected voters to identify the pension program with their party, given AMLO's emphasis on pension expansion in his attempt to win the presidency.

The shape of the new benefit was restrictive. This resulted from negotiations among conservatives of the PAN and PRI with left-wing politicians of the PRD at a time in which conservatives had significant power. The PRD advocated a universal benefit for people seventy and older that would be implemented gradually. This pension would pay a benefit equivalent to 50 percent of a minimum wage (interview, Perez-Bejerano).[59] The PAN, by contrast, supported a smaller benefit, reaching only the extreme poor aged seventy and older in low-income rural localities (interviews, Pérez-Bejerano and Navarro-Quintero, PRD legislator and proponent of the bill).

Despite their differences, legislators of all parties within the Social Development Commission voted unanimously for the program's guidelines, which were approved by Congress and adopted by the Calderón

---

[59] See the government program of the Coalition for the Good of All, the Poor First.

administration in 2007. This benefit provided pensions of 500 pesos per month, equivalent to about one-third of the minimum wage, to the extreme poor in localities with fewer than 2,500 inhabitants. As in other policy areas in Mexico, benefits were implemented in a state-centric way without social participation. As expected in the analytical framework, in the absence of social movement involvement in policy making, benefits tend to be nonparticipatory. Political parties did not foster the involvement of social organizations in policy implementation in order to avoid empowering social groups, and to limit potential allegations of clientelism. In the following years, the scheme was extended to localities with up to 30,000 inhabitants. Despite these extensions, coverage remained low, as the program reached only about 48 percent of outsiders over sixty-five in 2010 (author's estimate, see Appendix 1).

Note that prior to this policy, Fox had launched a small noncontributory pension, Program for the Assistance of Seniors (PAAM), for the extreme poor in rural areas in 2004, which involved the participation of rural organizations. PAAM was sparsely implemented and died out in the following years.

This small pension scheme was launched in the context of the National Agreement for the Countryside, in which the government negotiated agricultural policy with rural organizations (interview, Vélez). This renegotiation provided an incentive for rural organizations to coordinate joint action.[60] Although the demands of rural organizations centered primarily on agriculture, the agreement signed in 2003 established a pension benefit for rural seniors in extreme poverty aged sixty and older.

In 2004, the number of beneficiaries was 241,000 and later declined.[61] Benefits were very small, representing about 12 percent of the minimum wage. A particularly interesting feature of this program was that rural organizations were involved in its administration, thereby benefits represented selective incentives more than nondiscretionary provisions. Although this scheme could have empowered the organizations involved, it was replaced with new pensions created in 2007, which did not involve social participation. The fragmentation of interests regarding social policy among rural organizations and their focus on agriculture in their negotiations with the state probably made this small program much less important to them and limited its growth.

[60] Acuerdo Nacional para el Campo (2003: 16); interview, Vélez.
[61] Data from SEDESOL.

6.5 ASSESSING ALTERNATIVE EXPLANATIONS

This section assesses the role of competing factors such as partisanship – especially regarding the decision to expand social programs for outsiders – structural and economic change, and the diffusion of social protection models in social policy expansion and the model adopted.

As in the other cases under study, the partisan affiliation of the incumbent did not decisively shape decisions to expand – or not expand – social policies. The conservative PAN launched major social policy innovations. Therefore, although Mexico did not form part of the "left turn" in the region – that is, the arrival of left, or populist politicians governing on the left, to the national executive – it did experience dramatic social policy expansion.

Partisanship did matter, however, for the social policy model adopted. Negotiations about policy design involved the PRI and PAN – and later on the PRD – and resulted in restrictive benefits, which reflected the preferences of conservatives for small state intervention. The PRD advanced universal and more substantial policy initiatives compared to the PAN and the PRI. A greater role for the PRD in Congress starting in 2006 facilitated the approval of a pension program for outsiders that was restrictive, but slightly more generous than the scheme proposed by PAN legislators and the one launched by Fox in 2006. Thus, although partisanship does not account for why expansion happened, it does help explain why different benefit levels and/or coverage levels are chosen.

An assessment of the role of economic crises on policy change is particularly relevant in the case of Mexico, as this country suffered two important financial crises: the debt crisis of 1982 and the 1994 peso crisis. As discussed previously, the 1982 crisis did not trigger social policy expansion to deal with its immediate negative effects. The expansion of nondiscretionary policies began incipiently in 1997 after the financial and political crisis of 1994–5 had badly eroded support for the PRI during the Zedillo administration. These policy changes were not launched immediately after the economic downfall of 1994, even though they would have helped contain the negative social effects of the crisis and increased the legitimacy of the incumbent amid the financial collapse.

During the Fox administration, expansion occurred at different moments and in a context of economic stability. Despite the dramatic effects of the 2008 international crisis on the Mexican economy, health care and pension expansion continued their gradual implementation begun in 2004 and 2007, respectively. As discussed in the Argentine case,

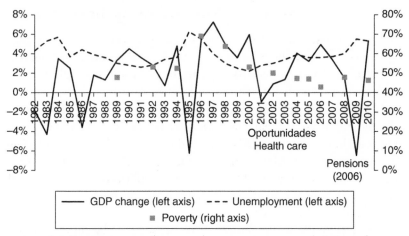

FIGURE 6.6 Economic growth, unemployment, poverty, and timing of expansion, Mexico, 1982–2010.
Sources: GDP and unemployment rate 1994–2009 from INEGI; 1982–94 from Murillo (2001); poverty rate from CONEVAL.

crises may contribute in certain ways to social policy expansion when they intensify either the chances of parties competing for outsiders or the scale of mobilization from below. However, based on the analysis of the policy process and the chronology of policy expansion, crises by themselves do not have a direct systematic effect on policy expansion.

Economic prosperity and the lifting of tight fiscal constraints could also be factors that account for policy expansion. Looking at the evolution of GDP growth since 1982 (see Figure 6.6), we can see the absence of a clear pattern of social policy expansion linked to the evolution of GDP. Innovations began forcefully in 2001, 2003, and 2006. The gradual implementation of these policies made the whole period starting in 2001 through 2010 one of a phased extension of benefits. This period in turn witnessed significant changes in GDP growth, which are not linked to decisions to expand. Indeed, 2001 and 2009 experienced negative growth, and both saw either new social policy initiatives, such as the expansion of income transfers, or the continuation of pre-established gradual expansion of health care and pensions, respectively. From 2002 through 2008, moreover, the economy grew at levels similar to those of the early 1990s, when nondiscretionary social policy expansion did not take shape.

Figure 6.6 also shows the evolution of poverty rates. We can see that Mexico has had high poverty rates throughout the whole period, particularly compared to Argentina and Chile. Available data show a sharp increase in poverty levels surrounding the 1994 crisis, when at least 70 percent of the population was poor. However, the Mexican state did not respond until a few years later with highly targeted direct transfers to low-income families, and it did so at a time when poverty was declining. In 1997, Zedillo launched PROGRESA, which reached 10 percent of the households in the country in 1999, a small share given the level of deprivation. The increase of poverty in the 1990s was thus not a major concern driving social policy innovations. Moreover, despite having a larger share of the population in poverty, the scope of transfers was relatively small, and reached only the rural poor until 2002.

Finally, the diffusion of policy models has not been a major factor shaping policy adoption and design. Even if specific policy tools, such as transfers for low-income families or a particular insurance system in the health care sector, have been popular in certain policy circles by the time of adoption, the decision to expand in the first place has been related to political needs. Responses to the question of how to appeal to outsiders led governments to look for policy tools and to reach out to experts in order to launch policies that would help them gain or consolidate outsiders' support in ways acceptable to the parties' core constituencies and compatible with their programmatic commitments.

6.6 CONCLUSIONS

Social policy expansion in Mexico occurred in the context of electoral competition for outsiders, which formed part of the broader process of democratization that ended the dominant party system based on the PRI. Electoral competition for outsiders drove incumbents first from the PRI, and then from the PAN, to respond to the emergence of credible challengers, that is, the emergence of parties that could defeat the incumbent by mobilizing electoral support among outsiders. Challengers seeking to win the vote of outsiders in turn promised social policy expansion to appeal to that constituency.

As suggested in the analytical framework, social policies created in the context of electoral competition are nondiscretionary. Incumbents fear that new policies will be considered clientelistic and will favor opposition parties competing intensely for outsiders. Opposition parties in turn strive to prevent incumbents from using social policy in discretionary ways, or to create temporary programs that would benefit the incumbent and the incumbent's party in the short term. Nondiscretionary policies are better in a context of intense competition and accusations of voter manipulation by the opposition. These dynamics were clear under the Zedillo administration, which dismantled PRONASOL and created the highly technocratic PROGRESA in response to accusations of clientelism and pressures from subnational authorities within highly competitive environments. PRONASOL was terminated due to its association with the Salinas administration, and was perceived as highly discretionary by subnational authorities and opposition parties pressing for decentralization. Under Fox, Congress passed the Social Development Law and institutionalized rules to avoid the manipulation of benefits. In this sense, the strategic goals of the incumbent and opposition parties led to the adoption of rule-based national social policies.

The resulting social policies in Mexico have been restrictive. In the country's new multiparty system, incumbents had to negotiate social policy expansion with the opposition in Congress. Because these innovations were popular measures, opposition parties had little incentive to block them, especially if they were competing for the vote of outsiders. Therefore opposition parties in Congress supported incumbents' proposals to expand social programs, and they also shaped the process of policy design. Given the large and powerful conservative presence in Congress, these social benefits have a smaller scope and lower benefit levels. In the absence of coalitions of social movements and labor unions pressing for large-scale expansion and participatory arrangements, political parties facing intense electoral competition opted for direct, state-centric implementation.

7

Electoral Competition for Outsiders, Conservative Power, and Restrictive Social Policy in Chile

7.1 INTRODUCTION

Despite being one of the welfare pioneers in Latin America, and exhibiting high levels of economic growth and stability since democratization in 1990, Chile initiated expansion of social policy for outsiders in selected areas only under the administrations of Ricardo Lagos (2000–6) and Michelle Bachelet (2006–10) of the Concertación. In designing social programs for outsiders, policy makers in Chile followed a similar path to that of Mexico. In contrast to the inclusive policies seen in Argentina – another welfare pioneer – and Brazil, restrictive ones were established in Chile. These programs provide relatively modest benefits to a smaller pool of outsiders and are implemented in a top-down way without involving social organizations.

Social policy innovations in Chile were initiated with the passage of Plan AUGE,[1] which strengthened and expanded health care coverage to outsiders in 2004.[2] In 2007 and 2008, respectively, the Bachelet administration embarked on a significant expansion of family allowances – reaching close to 60 percent of outsider children – and extended noncontributory pensions to about 55 percent of outsider seniors (Table 7.1).

Although the Concertación – an alliance that included conservative politicians of the Christian Democratic Party (DC), the left-wing Socialist

---

[1] AUGE stands for Acceso Universal de Garantías Explícitas (Universal Access to Guaranteed Health Treatments).
[2] At the time, the public health scheme FONASA provided contributory-based services to lower-income insiders, free health services to the extreme poor, and partly subsidized health services to the rest of outsiders

TABLE 7.1 *Social Policy Expansion and the Restrictive Model in Chile, ca. 2010*

Policy Area	Scope of Coverage	Benefit Level	Participation in Implementation	Dates of Expansion
Income Support	Moderate	Low	None	2007
	58% of school-age outsider children	Less than 10% of the poverty line for a family with two children		
Health Care	Moderate	Moderate	None	2004 (adoption); 2005 (implementation)
	Free for indigent and some low-income outsiders	Effective free services for the indigent and some low-income sectors		
Pensions	Moderate	Moderate	None	2008 (adoption and gradual implementation)
	54.3% of outsiders 65+	50% of the minimum pension for insiders		

Note: Dates of Expansion refers to adoption and launching of implementation.
Sources and Measures: See Appendix 1.

Party (PS), and the centrist Party for Democracy (PPD) – had been in power since the return of democracy in 1990, it initiated expansion only in the 2000s. What explains this shift? Why did incumbents not create broader, inclusive benefits given that Chile had a smaller outsider population to protect than Mexico and Brazil? Finally, in light of the dramatic decline of labor union power since the dictatorship,[3] why did Chile not do more for outsiders if labor unions – who, according to some scholars, tend to block policies for outsiders – were so weak relative to their counterparts in Argentina and Brazil?

In this chapter, I show that social policy expansion in Chile was initiated in the context of intense electoral competition for outsiders, which

[3] See Collier and Collier (1991); Etchemendy (2011); Hipsher (1998); Oxhorn (1995); Posner (2008); Roberts (1998); Valenzuela and Valenzuela (1986).

began in connection to the 1999 presidential elections. The intense courting of outsiders by a credible challenger, the Alliance formed by the right
parties Independent Democratic Union (UDI) and National Renewal
(RN), drove the Concertación governments of both Lagos and Bachelet
to embark on social policy expansion to secure outsiders' support and the
continuity of their coalition in power.

In the absence of social mobilization for expansion, which was a feature of Chile's democracy until the emergence of a large-scale student
movement in 2011, policy design was shaped by negotiations among parties in Congress.[4] Within an environment of competition for the vote of
outsiders, the Alliance feared electoral punishment if it blocked popular
social policy initiatives proposed by the Concertación. As expected in my
analytic framework, instead of blocking proposals, conservative parties in
Congress sought to shape policy design. The presence of conservative politicians within the Concertación and the power of the Alliance in Congress
placed limits on the more redistributive ambitions of the center-left politicians in the incumbent coalition, producing a restrictive model of social
protection. Concertación presidents often sought to avoid the rejection of
some aspects of their policy proposals by the right, which had substantial
power in Congress, and thus they submitted initiatives that seemed politically feasible. The Alliance – and sometimes the DC – in turn sought to
limit the scope and cost of these policies to align such initiatives with the
preferences of their core upper-income, business, and/or middle-class constituencies in order to court outsider voters without alienating their base.

As in the other cases of policy expansion analyzed here, the resulting
benefits were nondiscretionary. Aside from the historically high bureaucratic capacity of the Chilean state (see Luna and Mardones 2014; Soifer
2015), incumbent parties were concerned about allegations of clientelism
that could discredit them, and the opposition feared that incumbents
might gain an advantage from clientelistic expansions. Both coalitions in
Congress thereby strategically avoided discretion in policies for outsiders.

In the next section of this chapter, I trace the emergence of electoral
competition for outsiders in the late 1990s and the absence of mobilization from below demanding social policy expansion, the two factors that
in my framework shape the occurrence of expansion. I briefly analyze the
lack of initiatives to expand social policy during the first Concertación
governments until the surge of electoral competition for outsiders in the
late 1990s. In the fourth section, I show that in the context of intense competition for outsiders, the Lagos and Bachelet administrations expanded

---

[4] On the student movement and education and tax policy, see Fairfield and Garay (2013).

social programs for outsiders to secure their support and the continuity of the Concertación in office. Through process tracing of policy-making processes, I further analyze the reasons why restrictive policies were established. The final section assesses alternative explanations to account for the adoption of social policy for outsiders and for the design of a restrictive model.

7.2 ELECTORAL COMPETITION FOR OUTSIDERS AND SOCIAL MOBILIZATION (1990–2010)

Electoral Competition for Outsiders

The democratic transition in Chile was inaugurated with the defeat of the Augusto Pinochet dictatorship in the plebiscite of 1988, which determined whether elections would be held in 1989 or Pinochet would stay in power for another eight years.[5] Two party coalitions formed in the new democracy. The parties that had mobilized against Pinochet's continuity formed the Concertación de Partidos por la Democracia, which embraced seventeen parties with heterogeneous ideological views ranging from social conservatism to the left. The Concertación was led by the DC, PS, and the PPD – an "instrumental" party PS politicians established to register electors for the plebiscite when the PS was not legally operating.[6] Owing to its electoral success and its appeal among independent voters, the PPD remained in place after the plebiscite (see Angell 2007: 39–40). The right and center-right parties UDI and RN in turn formed the Alliance for Democracy and Progress, later known as the Alliance for Chile.[7]

Aside from ideological differences, the regime question alienated the parties in the Concertación, especially the Christian Democrats – whose views and whose supporters often did not differ substantially from those of right-wing parties – from the Alliance. While the Concertación parties came together for democracy and were particularly opposed to the military dictatorship, several Alliance politicians had endorsed the dictatorship and the UDI had a significant number of leaders who had been in government positions under Pinochet.

---

[5] See Chapter 3 and Angell (2007) for further reference.
[6] See Angell (2007); Joignant and Navia (2003: 130).
[7] The Alliance was initiated as Democracia y Progreso in 1989; in 1993, it became the Unión por el Progreso de Chile; in 1999, it was renamed Alianza por Chile (Angell and Reig Salinas 2007: 13).

The formation of these two coalitions was incentivized by the binomial electoral system the Pinochet dictatorship established after its defeat in the 1988 plebiscite. This electoral system had majoritarian features that generated strong incentives for coalition building and rewarded the second party in legislative elections, which the military expected to be the right bloc based on the results of the plebiscite.[8]

In the new democracy, the Concertación won the first two presidential elections of 1989 and 1993 by large margins, gaining 55.7 percent and 58.9 percent of the vote against the Alliance candidates' 29.4 percent and 24.4 percent, respectively. Yet electoral competition grew significantly in the 1999 presidential election when the Concertación candidate barely won the first round and the runoff election by small margins of less than one and three percentage points, respectively. Electoral competition was intense again in 2005. This time, the Alliance split and each party ran its own candidate. The Concertación won the runoff election again by a close margin of seven percentage points.

Electoral competition for outsiders also emerged beginning in the 1999 presidential election. Ecological data of the share of outsider districts[9] with electoral competition in each presidential election show a pattern of changing support (Figure 7.1). Whereas in 1989 and 1993, 21 percent and 6 percent of outsider districts, respectively, experienced electoral competition, those figures grew to nearly 75 percent and 60 percent in the 2000 and the 2006 runoffs. The leap between the 1993 and the 2000 elections, when Lagos defeated Alliance candidate Joaquín Lavín by a slim margin, is particularly pronounced.

Pre-election survey data of reported vote intention of respondents here classified as outsiders reveal a similar pattern (Figure 7.2). The difference in vote intention for the Concertación and the Alliance was greater than ten percentage points until the 1999 elections, when competition intensified and the margin narrowed significantly. In 2005, the UDI and RN fielded their own candidates. Here we see that vote intention for these two candidates together was similar to and even slightly higher than that for the Concertación candidate before the first round of elections, raising threats of replacement in the likely event of a runoff, when UDI and RN voters were expected to support the most-voted right candidate in the first round.

---

[8] For a discussion of the binomial system, see, among others, Angell (2007), Navia (2006), and Siavelis (2005). Congress approved a new electoral system in 2015.

[9] In which outsiders were at least 55 percent of the population; see Appendix 3 for further reference.

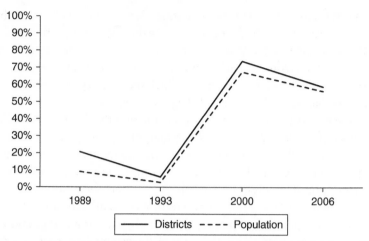

FIGURE 7.1 Electoral competition for outsiders in presidential elections, Chile, 1989–2006 (% outsider districts and outsider population in outsider districts with electoral competition).
Note: 2000 and 2006 are runoff elections.
Source: Calculated with Historical Data Set of Elections elaborated by Observatorio Político-Electoral, Universidad Diego Portales, and socioeconomic and population data from Observatorio Social, Gobierno de Chile for 2011.

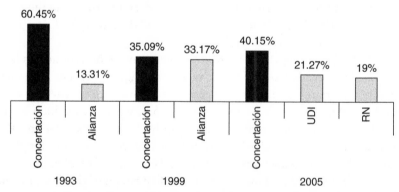

FIGURE 7.2 Reported vote intention of outsiders in presidential elections, Chile, 1993–2006.
Source: Author estimates with surveys from Centro de Estudios Públicos, Encuestas N° 23, 38, and 51. Note: 1999 and 2005 are first-round elections. In 2005, UDI and RN each ran its own candidate. According to these data, UDI and RN together obtained a slightly higher vote share among outsiders than the Concertación.

The decline of the Concertación particularly affected the DC, which lost a significant amount of support and ceased to be the largest party in the Chilean Congress. The UDI, by contrast, gained ground dramatically. The expansion of the UDI was related to the party's effective territorial and organizational development and its active campaign to mobilize low-income voters. This became more pronounced in the late 1990s, when the *gremialista* faction gained more influence within the party[10] and the UDI successfully captured broad support among the poor. The growth of the Alliance occurred at a time of economic recession influenced by the international crisis that began in 1997, but it cannot be circumscribed to these events. This coalition had been mobilizing more actively since before the crisis, attaining higher electoral support in the 1997 midterm election. As discussed later, the Alliance sought to conquer low-income voters through promises of welfare expansion and territorial organization – measures especially undertaken by the UDI.[11]

Social Mobilization

Chile's democracy lacked social mobilization – a sustained process of demand making by social movements and labor unions – since the return of democracy in 1990 until 2011, when large-scale, sustained protests led by students emerged for the first time around education reform.[12] Despite episodes of social mobilization during the 1980s, as well as high levels of poverty and inequality in the new democracy, social mobilization was hindered by different political and institutional factors in the 1990s and 2000s.[13] First, the mobilization capacity of labor unions – which are fundamental components of the social movement coalitions (SMCs) that triggered social policy expansion in other countries – declined dramatically in the 1970s and 1980s. The military dictatorship changed labor laws to reduce the power of labor unions through plant-level organization and decentralized negotiation, and adopted more flexible labor contracts that facilitated hiring and firing – a critical concern of labor unions (see Etchemendy 2011). In the 1980s, thousands of weak and small firm-level labor unions with little capacity for coordination emerged. Indicative of

---

[10] This faction was particularly adept at organizing low-income groups (see Chapter 3). On the UDI, see Joignant and Navia (2003).

[11] See Luna (2010; 2014).

[12] See Fairfield and Garay (2013).

[13] On social participation and mobilization in Chile's democracy, see Delamaza (2010).

these unions' diminished power and coordination, a general strike took place for the first time in 2003 – thirteen years after the democratic transition. Coordinated national protests by labor unions were rare during this period. Protests were mainly organized by public-sector workers' unions and little activism took shape among private-sector workers (interview, Etiel Moraga, national board of CUT).

Another factor contributing to the absence of social mobilization was the decision of the Concertación parties to actively demobilize social organizations linked to its parties in order to avoid potentially destabilizing conservative reactions. This stood in sharp contrast to these parties' choices in the late 1960s and early 1970s, when they vigorously mobilized labor unions and promoted the formation of grassroots organizations. As noted in Chapter 3, left-wing parties and the DC at the time both sought to mobilize outsiders and formal workers in competition for their vote and to gain support for policy proposals. This process of party mobilization was terminated with the military coup of 1973. Although protest emerged during a deep economic crisis in the early 1980s and some mobilization also flourished during the transition, especially around the No campaign for the 1988 plebiscite, it died out in the new democracy. Political parties did not open up institutional or party channels for social movements to exert pressure, and they dissuaded them from mobilizing in the streets on the grounds that such activity might destabilize the political system to the advantage of the right (see Hipsher 1998). The fact that the DC – which held more moderate views about the role of social mobilization in the new democracy – was stronger than the left within the governing coalition in the 1990s further discouraged potential activism promoted by Concertación parties (see Hipsher 1998). When the left gained more power within the coalition in the 2000s, this situation was not reversed.

This state of affairs in which social actors were not present in social policy making, save for ceremonial roles, changed with the remarkable emergence of the student movement in 2011. This movement's demands focused on education and tax reform, which by 2013 had undergone substantial changes in response to contention, though this did not seriously affect the policy areas under consideration. Without active mobilization from below operating through protest, institutional channels, and/or party allies, the policy-making process regarding health care and pensions was dominated by politicians and lobbies connected to private providers that operated through right-wing party allies, as discussed later.

7.3 DEMOCRACY WITHOUT ELECTORAL COMPETITION FOR OUTSIDERS OR SOCIAL MOBILIZATION

The first two Concertación administrations did not undertake social policy expansion across selected areas. As predicted by the argument advanced in this book, despite high poverty levels and in a context of economic growth, the absence of electoral competition for outsiders or mobilization from below meant that social policy expansion did not figure prominently in these governments' agendas.

The Patricio Aylwin Administration (1990–1994)

The Aylwin administration primarily strove to consolidate Chile's democracy after almost two decades of military rule, and to preserve the economic stability achieved at the end of the dictatorship – which was perceived as a fundamental requirement for political stability. This was particularly relevant because the military extended its power in the new democracy in different ways, affecting policy making particularly through the presence of nine non-elected senators in Congress. According to the constitution the military passed in 1980, designated senators were selected by the chief of the army – a position Pinochet occupied until 1998, when he became senator for life until his resignation in 2002. Designated senators generally sided with the Alliance, and owing to the distribution of power in Congress, their presence limited the capacity of the executive to introduce major reforms (see Siavelis 2000: 40).

Facing no incentives for expansion, Aylwin did not launch any major social policy innovation for outsiders aside from reversing some of the severe budget cuts the dictatorship had introduced. In particular, Aylwin increased health care expenditures, which had deteriorated under the military, by raising them by 40 percent within his first three years in office (MIDEPLAN 1994: 205). Priority was given to strengthening primary care services by making them effectively free to the extreme poor and to improving the salaries of health care workers, which had lagged behind since the dictatorship (interview, Jiménez de la Jara, minister of health under Aylwin; Boeninger 2008: 161; MIDEPLAN 1994: 205).[14] These changes helped temper some of the transformations that had made access to medical services more difficult for outsiders. The Aylwin administration also introduced a very limited increase in the quota of beneficiaries

---

[14] This was pursued through the creation of emergency primary care rooms.

of noncontributory old age and disability pensions established by the military dictatorship, which grew 5.2 percent,[15] reaching 25 percent of outsiders sixty-five and older in 1992.[16]

The main innovation for lower-income outsiders under Aylwin was the Social and Solidarity Investment Fund (FOSIS), which was implemented starting in January 1991.[17] FOSIS provided support for microenterprises and community development projects with the goal of creating jobs and skill-building opportunities for lower-income workers. The main mechanism for allocating resources involved the selection of projects submitted by microenterprises, associations (e.g., cooperatives, communal soup kitchens), and recently created local governments in poor areas (FOSIS 2006: 7). Despite being highly publicized, and having been initially introduced as the star program of the Aylwin administration, FOSIS was extremely small (see Repetto 2001: 258). Due to its limited coverage, this new program does not constitute an expansion as it is defined here.

The Eduardo Frei Administration (1994–2000)

Aylwin's successor, Eduardo Frei, also came to power with a landslide victory. Under his administration there was an attempt to expand FOSIS and to include it within the National Program to Overcome Poverty (PNSP), which intended to channel social investments through local governments.[18] However, this initiative failed to gain sufficient support and FOSIS remained largely unchanged. According to several analysts, the PNSP had a complex institutional design, which undercut the political backing needed to launch it (see Raczynski 2000; Repetto 2001: 274–5).[19] Besides the technical design of the program, and as predicted in this book's argument, in the absence of electoral competition for outsiders or demands from below, the PNSP was not deemed a priority within the incumbent coalition and it thus failed to be launched.[20]

---

[15] Built with data from MIDEPLAN and CASEN. See MIDEPLAN (2006).
[16] Data on pension coverage is presented in Table 7.4.
[17] See MIDEPLAN (2001: 1); FOSIS (2006: 7). Created by Law 18.989 of 1990.
[18] Around 32.7 percent of the population was poor at the time. See Angell (2007: 62); MIDEPLAN (www.mideplan.cl), and Arellano (2004).
[19] Although some analysts emphasize technical issues explaining the lack of implementation of the PNSP, Concertación's social policy expert, Clarisa Hardy, quoted in Repetto (2001), emphasizes the lack of political support for a more decisive struggle against poverty.
[20] On the evolution of FOSIS and PNSP, see FOSIS (2006: 8).

Support for the Concertación began to wane under Frei. The first sign of change occurred in the midterm election of 1997, which showed a significant drop in voter turnout and the growth of the right-wing UDI. Voter turnout as a share of the adult population declined from 73.68 percent in the presidential election of 1993 to 53.38 percent in 1997 (Angell 2007: 90). The rise of both rates of abstention and of the opposition occurred especially at the expense of the DC (Huneeus 2007b: 81). Despite the fact that overall results for the Concertación in the 1997 election were auspicious, concern among Concertación politicians began to mount due to an increase in voter dissatisfaction with political parties, growing disbelief in their capacity to solve everyday problems, and a more pessimistic view about the country's progress, all of which were revealed in opinion polls (see Angell 2007: 91).[21] For example, a 1998 survey quoted by Angell (2007: 91) showed that only 23 percent of the poorest quintile of the population believed the country was progressing, compared to 58 percent in 1991 (Angell 2007: 91). A final sign of discontent was Frei's declining popularity at the end of his tenure. According to surveys by the Center for Public Studies (CEP), Frei's disapproval ratings reached about 40 percent, which contrasted with Aylwin's disapproval rate below 20 percent at the end of his presidency.[22]

The 1999 Election

Concertación candidate Ricardo Lagos was initially the frontrunner for the 1999 election. As the election approached, however, the Alliance candidate, Joaquín Lavín of the UDI, gained more support and began to challenge the Concertación's continuity in power. Much of Lavín's gains were obtained by mobilizing lower-income voters, for whom Lavin promised to expand effective antipoverty programs and to create jobs. In response, social policy expansion assumed a more prominent position in Lagos's agenda.[23] This was especially important before the runoff, which resulted from the Alliance's dramatic showing in the first round, in which Lagos obtained a razor-thin victory of half a point over Lavín.

To gain outsiders' support, Lavín promised pensions for all indigent outsiders, job creation – his campaign slogan was "one million new jobs for Chile" – and health care reform – including an expansion of services

---

[21] See essays in Huneeus et al. (2007).

[22] See Centro de Estudios Públicos. Available at www.cepchile.cl (accessed 2009) .

[23] See Lavín, Joaquín. 1999. Programa de Gobierno. Available at www.archivo-chile.com (accessed 2009).

for the poor. In addition, the Alliance attempted to conquer low-income voters through the UDI's intensive work in low-income neighborhoods and with a decisive territorial electoral campaign.[24]

Inroads made by the UDI in low-income neighborhoods intensified in the mid-1990s (see Luna 2010; 2014). Building on the *gremialistas*' historical approach of mobilizing support in lower-class neighborhoods through territorial organization (Etchemendy 2011; Huneeus et al. 2007),[25] the UDI launched "UDI on the Ground" when this faction gained further power within the party (Pollack 1999: 129). The UDI's territorial work focused on establishing mothers' centers, youth clubs, and neighborhood organizations to reach communities effectively and to identify community leaders who could better connect them with the party (see Barozet 2003: 44). Pollack notes that this strategy led the UDI to create "as many neighborhood groups as possible" and to "set up rival organizations to compete with those [*juntas*, neighborhood organizations] which it has been unable to infiltrate successfully" (1999: 130). As covered in Chapter 3, this approach was similar to that of the DC in the 1960s, when the party spread in these areas in its quest to conquer the support of low-income voters (Pollack 1999: 131). Note that aside from UDI's intense work on the ground, scholars have pointed out that the Concertación's explicit demobilization of community associations and the moderation and pragmatism of these groups have also contributed to the influence of right and center-right parties in low-income areas, particularly within the historically well-organized shantytowns (see Hipsher 1998: 160).

Finally, seeking to mobilize support and win the presidency in 1999, Lavín launched an intensely territorial presidential campaign (Boas 2010: 145). According to Boas, Lavín "visited all 345 districts [*comunas*] in the country, and various neighborhoods in each, for a total of over 1,500 distinct locales." To increase his closeness to low-income voters, and to sound credibly committed to improving their fate, Lavín would occasionally spend the night in the house of a shantytown dweller during his visits (Boas 2010: 145).

Scholars suggest that other factors may have contributed to the decline in support for the Concertación in 1999 (see Angell 2007).[26] First, Chile

---

[24] See Luna (2010, 2014) and Boas (2010).

[25] Note, for example, that 75 percent of UDI legislators elected in 1989 had been mayors under Pinochet (Joignant and Navia 2003).

[26] See Angell (2007) for an analysis of the Chilean elections from the 1988 plebiscite to 2005–6.

was badly hit by the international crisis in 1998, which triggered low growth compared to the average 6 percent GDP growth of the first two Concertación administrations. In these circumstances, and lacking a solid safety net, unemployment rose to about 11 percent, increasing dissatisfaction with the Frei administration. Second, there was mounting discontent within the Concertación. Divisions separated politicians who prioritized the market model and economic growth over redistribution, and those who sought higher levels of economic equality. By 1998, income distribution in Chile was similar to that in 1987, at the end of the dictatorship. Because of these divisions, the coalition found it "increasingly difficult to speak with a unified voice and share a common vision" (Navia 2006: 45). Finally, the Concertación's presidential candidate, Lagos, represented the PS and PPD but was not initially supported by sectors of the DC who aspired to a new presidency but had lost the coalition's primaries. Traditional DC voters were furthermore reluctant to support a PS candidate. According to Huneeus, some of the electoral support for the DC in fact migrated to the UDI in the 1999 elections (2007b: 82).

The growth of the Alliance raised fears of replacement among Concertación politicians. In this highly competitive environment, Lagos emphasized social policy expansion and job creation to secure the vote of low-income outsiders and offset the appeals of his competitor, especially as the election neared. According to Marco Enríquez-Ominami, one of Lagos' campaign managers, Concertación politicians believed they had "lost the poor to Lavín" (interview), which motivated Lagos to make promises of social policy expansion to win them back.

After Lagos' razor-thin victory in the first round, health care reform took on a larger role in the candidate's agenda. Aside from appealing to outsider voters, Lagos sought to explicitly mobilize health care workers behind his candidacy, meeting with union leaders, asking them to support his campaign, and promising a reform that would provide greater access and solidarity within the health care system. According to the leader of the municipal health workers' union, Lagos's unexpected appeals to the health unions were motivated "precisely because of Lavín's growth" (interview, head of CONFUSAM). Social policy expansion thus became an important component of the campaign as competition for outsiders tightened.

Overall, Lavín obtained the highest vote share of any right-wing candidate in Chile's history of full enfranchisement (Navia 2006: 46). The growth of the Alliance was especially marked among low-income sectors. Lavín won a majority in nine of the fourteen poorest districts in Chile in the first round (Angell 2007: 102), and nearly 75 percent of outsider districts had electoral competition in the runoff (author's data).

7.4 ELECTORAL COMPETITION FOR OUTSIDERS
AND SOCIAL POLICY EXPANSION

Electoral competition for outsider voters propelled social policy change under the Lagos and the Bachelet administrations. Lagos addressed two issues that loomed large in the public opinion: improvements in access to health care services – one of the top three concerns cited in polls throughout the 1990s – as well as measures to overcome extreme poverty, which had remained stable since the mid-1990s.[27] The stubbornness of extreme poverty had deepened divisions in the incumbent coalition among those who demanded higher levels of redistribution, and those who defended more moderate spending with the idea that it would better preserve economic and political stability. As discussed later, after assuming power in a highly competitive environment, Lagos' successor, Michelle Bachelet, launched a pension reform – an issue that was more controversial than health services – as well as the expansion of the Family Subsidy (SUF) allowance program, originally established by the military dictatorship in the 1980s, which, thanks to this expansion, reached between 55 percent and 60 percent of outsider children by 2010.

Despite the fact that both Lagos and Bachelet belonged to center-left parties within the Concertación, their social policy proposals during this period were restrictive for two reasons. First, the coalition comprised parties with different approaches to social policy. While the DC generally advanced conservative positions close to those of the Alliance, PPD and PS politicians generally preferred to increase access and benefits more broadly.[28] Aiming to satisfy and gain support from both sectors within the Concertación, policy proposals were moderate. The second reason for the Concertación's rather moderate proposals was that the Alliance was strong in Congress. Together with conservatives in the Concertación, the Alliance had the ability to restrict the approval of more generous and more comprehensive benefits. Anticipating conservative legislators' preferences within and outside the Concertación, both presidents – who have the monopoly on the submission of social policy bills in Chile[29] – sent

[27] See surveys from the Centro de Estudios Públicos 1990 through 2004, www.cep.cl.
[28] Although preferences varied across parties as described, note that some politicians of the PS and PPD also had moderate views regarding social policy expansion.
[29] On the president's powers, see Siavelis (2006: 35).

policy proposals to Congress that were largely palatable to conservative legislators, and they faced defeat on aspects of proposed legislation that affected insider benefits administered by private agents (i.e., pension funds, health insurance companies).[30]

The Ricardo Lagos Administration (2000–2006)

The reform of health services was Lagos' star social policy initiative and the only expansion for outsiders as here defined during his tenure. The antipoverty Chile Solidario program, which aimed to help families in extreme poverty access existing services and transfers, gained significant visibility, but given its limited reach it does not constitute an expansion.

The content of these two initiatives was shaped by negotiations in Congress among the parties of the Concertación and the Alliance. As shown in Table 7.2, the Concertación had a larger legislative bloc under Lagos in the first two years of his administration and one comparable to that of the Alliance during the rest of his tenure. Designated senators in turn traditionally sided with the Alliance (see Siavelis 2000: 40).[31] The DC, which had more moderate social policy preferences than the center-left PS and PPD, had more than half of the Concertación's legislators in the first two years of the Lagos administration, but its power declined after the 2001 election to the advantage of the UDI, which became the largest party in Congress.[32] Owing to the large presence of legislators with a conservative social policy approach, resulting policies featured rather limited state commitments, as analyzed later.

Health Care

During the 1999 campaign, Lagos announced his intention to launch a comprehensive reform to address the problem of "unequal access to health care," which he considered "one of the worst injustices in Chile."[33] The new system would guarantee quality and prompt access to services to all affiliates, including access to "costly" treatments, and would end "the sinister institution of payment guarantee (*cheques en garantía*)," blank checks people had to write in advance of receiving assistance at the point of delivery

---

[30] See Fairfield (2010, 2015) for an analysis of tax policy that identifies this dynamic.

[31] Designated senators were eliminated in 2006.

[32] Composition of the senate available at www.senado.cl.

[33] Lagos, Ricardo. (1999). "Programa de Gobierno." Available at www.archivo-chile.com (accessed 2009).

TABLE 7.2 *Composition of Congress, Chile, 2000–2006*

	Deputies 1998–2002	Senators 1998–2002	Deputies 2002–2006	Senators 2002–2006
Concertación	69	20	62	20
DC	38	14	23	12
PPD	16	2	20	3
PS	11	4	10	5
Other	4	0	9	0
Alliance	47	17	57	17
UDI	17	5	31	6
RN	23	7	18	6
Independent	7	5	8	5
Other	4	1	1	1
Designated	0	9	0	9
TOTAL	120	47	120	47

Sources: Election data from Ministry of Interior (www.elecciones.gov.cl), and Angell and Reig Salinas (2007: 13).

in case they could not pay once the treatment had been provided.[34] Health care reform was undoubtedly the star program of the Lagos administration and the most complex social reform the Concertación had undertaken since the return of democracy. It would benefit outsiders and insiders, all of which were affected by problems to access health services in a timely and economical way.

The health care system at the time was the outcome of a substantial overhaul the Pinochet dictatorship carried out in the 1980s. After a radical privatization of health services was discarded as unfeasible, the dictatorship designed a two-tier system, one run by the state and the other by private agents.[35] Starting in 1985, formal workers could choose among health insurance plans administered by private health funds (ISAPRES) or by the public fund (FONASA). The new health care system segmented users by income level, as choice of plans was largely determined by payment capacity. Additional services and greater choice of providers required higher premiums. Regarding outsiders, the reform established free access to a FONASA health care plan for the extreme poor. The remaining outsiders could choose

[34] Note that in 1999, Frei eliminated these payment guarantees for emergency services, and subsequent legislation in the 2000s banned them. Despite their legal elimination, as of 2013 the Superintendence of Health reported that some private clinics still required them. See *La Tercera*, July 30, 2013.

[35] On this reform, see Castiglioni (2005); Medlin (1998); Raczynski (2001).

to pay into private health insurance or, based on their household income, they could enroll in one of FONASA's plans that required monthly contributions and copayments.

Despite renewed health funding in the early 1990s, health services continued to be a major concern of the public. Owing in part to inadequate public infrastructure, users of FONASA – between 63 percent and 74 percent of the population in the 1990s[36] – experienced long wait lists, crowded facilities, and often expensive copayments.[37] For example, affiliates of FONASA with chronic conditions reportedly had to wait years to get surgery procedures.[38] Similar plights affected beneficiaries of ISAPRES, as the health funds used cream skimming (risk selection) procedures and often charged expensive copayments to high-risk patients and increased the premiums of seniors, pushing them to transfer to FONASA.[39] Because of this, risk was more concentrated in FONASA (see Titelman 2000), which therefore subsidized the private funds (interview, health care reform advisor to the president). Furthermore, in 2003, the superintendence overseeing the system found that ISAPRES, which served at the time about 20 percent of the population, offered more than 47,000 different health plans with an average of twenty-six affiliates each.[40] This situation raised concerns about transparency and fairness.[41] At the same time, between 8 percent and 12 percent of the population was estimated to have no health care coverage in the 1990s and early 2000s.[42]

Upon taking office, Lagos requested two teams to work on a proposal for health reform. One was based in the Ministry of Health, then headed by Michelle Bachelet, and the other constituted the Commission for Health Reform. Bachelet's team consulted with labor unions and other health care actors and drafted a proposal "along the lines of Lagos' campaign promises" (interview, leader of CONFUSAM). However, the

[36] Coverage from Titelman (2000: 17).
[37] On the problems of the health system, see Lagos (1999). Programa de Gobierno. Available at www.archivo-chile.com (accessed 2009); Boeninger (2008: 161-2).
[38] "Gobierno lanza las primeras medidas de la reforma del sistema de salud," *El Mercurio*, January 4, 2005.
[39] See "Isapres se defienden de lluvia de críticas del mundo político," *El Mercurio*, December 15, 2005.
[40] "Reportan existencia de 47.000 planes de salud vigentes," *El Mercurio*, March 4, 2005. By 2011 the Superintendence of Health reported that there were 12,000 health plans offered by 13 ISAPRES funds (Romero Strooy 2011).
[41] See Boeninger (2008: 165).
[42] Estimated with coverage data from FONASA, www.fonasa.cl, accessed 2009. Note that aside from ISAPRES and FONASA, members of the armed and security forces use services provided by their own systems.

president made cabinet changes and chose to pursue the Commission for Health Reform's proposals. Among other proposals, this team devised Plan AUGE, which aimed to guarantee timely access to 80 percent of the most prevalent conditions treated in Chile's health care system. In order to fund AUGE, the government proposed a Solidarity Fund (FS) with three-sevenths of the contributions affiliates paid to FONASA and ISAPRES, and later on also proposed to increase the value-added tax (VAT) by one percentage point.[43] The Solidarity Fund would help finance equal access to AUGE on the part of both ISAPRES and FONASA members by establishing cross-subsidies from the private to the public system.

Anticipating resistance from the left – which expected more encompassing reforms – and especially from the right – which favored a less solidaristic reform – the Ministry of Health divided the reform project into five different bills to facilitate the approval of at least part of the package (interview, health care reform advisor to the president) and submitted them to Congress in 2002. The government in turn initiated an aggressive public information campaign in the media about the reform and launched a pilot project of AUGE in August 2002 (see Lenz 2007: 17). These measures aimed at gaining credibility and support for AUGE by mobilizing public opinion and showing the expected positive results of the new program (see Boeninger 2008: 163).

In a tight electoral environment, both the Concertación and the Alliance acknowledged the need to embark on health care reform to fix existing deficiencies and to address citizen's concerns regarding health services. Both coalitions, moreover, knew that the reform process would gain visibility and that a reasonable proposal had to be approved if they were not to pay electoral costs.[44] However, they had especially contradictory views about how to fund the new benefits for outsiders and low-income insiders and launch implementation.

Congress was the site of intense negotiations over AUGE and funding for health care reform. DC and Alliance legislators – who held conservative social policy views – initially opposed new taxes to pay for the system. Both Alliance and most DC politicians also rejected the Solidarity Fund on the grounds that it would create cross-subsidies from the private to the public sector, as FONASA users presented a higher risk profile and

---

[43] Because ISAPRES offered segmented and optional services, their plans charged higher fees. The average payroll contribution for members of ISAPRES was 8.5–9 percent.

[44] Lenz contends that the government ran opinion polls to measure support for the health reform and for AUGE in particular (2007:17).

thus would more likely use AUGE at higher rates (interview, Jiménez de la Jara; see Boeninger 2008: 165). In contrast with the left's support of the FS and the increase of the VAT, DC politicians advocated the sale of public companies and the leadership of the UDI proposed the reduction of public spending to fund AUGE.[45] Both DC and right-wing parties represented middle- and upper-class constituents who, politicians feared, would be upset if the reform transferred their contributions to the poorest sectors.[46] The UDI was also particularly proximate to the ISAPRES lobby, which pushed against this aspect of the reform.

Although tax creation and the pace of AUGE's implementation were also highly debated issues, the FS was undoubtedly the most controversial aspect of the reform. Using their ties to Alliance legislators, ISAPRES lobbied Congress vigorously to block the FS's creation. Summarizing their position vis-à-vis the Solidarity Fund, the director of Colmena ISAPRE asserted: "We rejected it from day one because we found it unfair to have to provide the money of our affiliates to the state so that it would end up in the hands of FONASA affiliates."[47] Alliance legislators supported ISAPRES's claims and threatened to block the reform, arguing that the FS was unconstitutional as it allegedly limited choice on the part of ISAPRES users and interfered with private property, entailing an "expropriation" of social security contributions of higher-income workers (interview, high official, superintendence of ISAPRES).[48]

Given that politicians from the DC, which supported all other aspects of the health care reform, also rejected the FS, this mechanism compromised the approval of the reform. Aside from dropping the FS, conservative politicians proposed a slower implementation of AUGE to guarantee its funding in a more gradual way.[49] They also proposed a measure that was soon discarded, which consisted of the "portability" of subsidies that would allow low-income and indigent FONASA affiliates – whose health

---

[45] Former minister and DC legislator Alejandro Foxley and UDI senator Evelyn Matthei quoted in "Subir los impuestos para financiar gasto público no convence a expertos," and "Senadora rechaza anuncio de aumento impositivo," *El Mercurio*, May 23, 2003.

[46] On the DC, see Boeninger (2008: 164).

[47] "Duro Informe cuestiona reparto de platas del Fondo Solidario Interisapres," *El Mostrador*, August 25, 2004.

[48] See also "Reforma de salud: Peligro de naufragio," *Qué Pasa*, April 16, 2003.

[49] This was also proposed by the Association of ISAPRES, the Liberty and Development Foundation linked to the UDI, as well as the Medical Association. See "Gremio médico defiende aplicación del plan Auge," *El Mercurio*, April 21, 2003 and "Hacienda descarta tener mayor déficit fiscal para 2003," *El Mercurio*, April 17, 2003.

assistance was subsidized in public hospitals – to enroll in ISAPRES and use private providers that did not operate with FONASA patients.[50]

Labor unions representing health care workers also sought to influence the reform. Among other issues, they proposed to fund AUGE with the establishment of royalties on transnational mining companies, which was not seriously considered by legislators.[51] Labor unions especially wanted to negotiate with the government directly – outside Congress – but the Lagos administration rejected that option. Largely excluded from negotiations, the CONFUSAM maintained that the absence of deliberation with the unions was "a trigger to mobilization."[52] Unions worried about potential discrimination of patients treated for non-AUGE conditions as well as about the growing role of private health care firms, which would be contracted out by the state to guarantee prompt access to services under AUGE. Instead they advocated more public investment in health facilities to be able to meet the demand for AUGE treatments by patients of FONASA (interview, head of CONFUSAM). Despite their pressure, which materialized in a few strikes during the negotiation of the bill in 2002 and 2004, unions had little influence on the reform (interviews, head of CONFUSAM, CONFENATS, and Moraga). As the head of CONFUSAM noted, during the reform process, "the politics of consensus (negotiation of parties across the ideological spectrum) was stronger and we had to recognize that we were defeated" (interview). As we will see in the case of pension reform under Bachelet, the fact that unions were so weakened and that – to a great extent owing to this weakness – they had tenuous ties with the Concertación meant they were not a great concern or interlocutor of the government in any major social policy reform (interview, Moraga).[53]

As the health care reform faced gridlock in Congress, some members of the Concertación feared for the survival of the project. However, it was clear for government officials that blocking health reform would negatively affect the Alliance electorally.[54] Health care reform was a salient issue in the public debate, one of the top concerns of the population, and

---

[50] See proposals from the Liberty and Development Foundation. This proposal was also backed by some DC legislators, though not all (see Boeninger 2008: 166).

[51] See "Trabajadores de la Salud niega intención de privatizar hospitales," *El Mercurio*, June 4, 2003.

[52] Esteban Maturana, President of Confusam in "Sector salud aplicará medidas contra plan de reforma," *El Mercurio*, December 5, 2002.

[53] The only consultation mentioned in interviews was with the Ministry of Health under Bachelet (interview, CONFUSAM).

[54] See "La Reforma de Salud: Peligro de Naufragio," *Qué Pasa*, April 16, 2004.

AUGE would not only benefit outsiders with limited access to health services but also affiliates of ISAPRES and FONASA undergoing difficulties to access treatments in a timely manner. Even if it sought to respond to the priorities of its core business constituency, the Alliance was seeking to mobilize the support of outsiders in order to reach office, and blocking the proposal for AUGE could hurt such prospects.

In April 2004, with the support of right-wing legislators, ISAPRES threatened to initiate actions to declare the bill unconstitutional if the Lagos administration continued to consider the FS. At the same time, legislators of the Alliance proposed that if the state insisted with the FS, then it would also have to pay the cost of AUGE to beneficiaries of ISAPRES.[55] President Lagos refused to subsidize ISAPRES. In the government's view, a key problem with ISAPRES was the "unacceptable" fee that they charged their affiliates, and suggested that improvements in efficiency rather than subsidies should allow ISAPRES to spend more on their clients.[56]

After two years of negotiations, the Lagos administration eventually dropped the FS, which was challenged in the Senate. AUGE's implementation was further agreed to be gradual; the plan would guarantee prompt access to medical services at a reasonable cost to treat fifty-six conditions by 2007. As Concertación politicians expected, the Alliance did not oppose the entire package because of the electoral risks it posed, but instead limited its redistributive reach by rejecting the FS and clearly emphasizing that point in negotiations over the bill. For instance, when he voted for AUGE, RN legislator Leandro Bayo stressed that his party – and the Alliance – had supported AUGE "from the first minute" even "before knowing the content of the bill," as it constituted "an aspiration of the executive and of all Chileans."[57]

AUGE was finally passed in 2004 with almost unanimous support in the Senate, and the support of the right-wing parties of the Alliance and the DC in the lower chamber. Several legislators from the PPD and PS, by contrast, abstained from supporting the entire bill as a protest against the Solidarity Fund's removal, and some voted against the bill.[58] The Lagos administration managed to prevent those PS and PPD legislators from voting against the project, but could not persuade them to

[55] Ibid.
[56] Ibid.
[57] Cámara de Diputados, Legislatura 351, sesión 26, August 10, 2004, p.15.
[58] "Plan Auge da paso final y ahora es ley," *El Mercurio*, August 11, 2004. See Cámara de Diputados, Legislatura 351, sesión 26, August 10, 2004.

support it.[59] For some legislators, elimination of the solidarity component had changed the nature of AUGE's design.[60] The FS was eventually created for ISAPRES only, which helped limit discrimination against high-risk patients.[61] According to a functionary of the Superintendence of ISAPRES:

> It was expected that there would be opposition to the reform. ISAPRES and the right said that the FS affected private property. They said that creating a risk pool was an expropriation... They claimed it was unconstitutional. So when [the bill] was gridlocked, it was negotiated. What was agreed? Something unexpected: that the fund would only be created for ISAPRES. And those who negotiated the reform thought that it was better to introduce the idea ... in order to discuss it again in the future... The issue is that the fundamental logic [of the reform] was the solidarity between the public and the private sectors. (interview, top official, superintendence of ISAPRES)

The health care policy resulting from this reform was restrictive. AUGE provided coverage of select treatments to outsiders who were beneficiaries of social transfers such as the SUF or the noncontributory pension (discussed later) and to those categorized as indigent and low income, with earnings below the minimum wage or between 1 and 1.4 times the minimum wages, respectively. The rest of the outsiders had to pay 7 percent of their income in order to participate in FONASA or to join an ISAPRES, in addition to copayments. My estimates with data from 2007 indicate that about 27 percent of the outsider population was not formally covered by any system and thus could not access health care services beyond primary care at the time. This figure went down to about 20 percent in 2009.[62]

Despite improving health care access significantly, AUGE is compatible with conservatives' preferences for limited state expenditure on the poor, benefits segmented by income level, and limited restrictions on

---

[59] "Gobierno juega sus cartas tras amplia aprobación del AUGE," *El Mercurio*, August 10, 2004.

[60] Guido Girardi, PPD, quoted in "Gobierno elimina el fondo de compensación para lograr reforma a la salud," *Mercurio*, May 13, 2004. See Cámara de Diputados, Legislatura 351, sesión 26, August 10, 2004, p. 36-7.

[61] Introduced in a law that reformed the ISAPRES.

[62] Calculated with data from FONASA. The size of the population classified as "indigent" by FONASA far exceeds that classified as such by the MIDEPLAN. In 2007, about 15 percent of the population apart from beneficiaries of cash transfers were considered indigent by FONASA, while the 2006 household survey from MIDEPLAN measured indigence as just 3.4 percent of the population. This indicates that there is a broader ad hoc inclusion of outsiders, which may be curtailed if eligibility conditions are more strictly enforced. Data accessed June 2010, www.fonasa.cl.

market mechanisms. That said, AUGE's creation lowered copayments – except for non-AUGE treatments – and it reduced, though it did not eliminate, the long waitlists that plagued the system and hindered access." As in other policy areas in Chile, health care services lacked consistent user participation. In the absence of social mobilization for health care reform, social groups were not invited to participate actively in the implementation of the new program.

Income Support

In conjunction with AUGE, the Lagos administration launched Chile Solidario, a very modest scheme, to reach out to extremely poor families, estimated at about 225,000 households (5 percent) in 2004. It received funding from the VAT increase that Congress had approved to fund both AUGE and Chile Solidario (see Fairfield 2010; 2015). The new scheme aimed at helping households in extreme poverty access existing public services such as education, health care, and housing programs, apply for existing subsidies such as family allowances for low-income families, and obtain noncontributory pensions, which were not easily accessed by those on the margins. Access to job training and employment in turn would be facilitated via FOSIS (interview, FOSIS official; FOSIS 2006). Chile Solidario employed social workers who contacted eligible households and helped them achieve these goals. The scheme further provided a bonus, a monthly payment of decreasing value for two years, to incentivize families to join the program. Families would then remain monitored by regular contact with social assistants for a period of five years.

Both the Concertación and the Alliance had promised to inaugurate effective antipoverty measures if elected, and supported the creation of the new benefit proposed by Lagos. Yet changes were made to the original layout of the program. These included the use of highly technical procedures on the part of the national government to determine the number of families that would benefit within each district, and the conditions under which social workers would be hired to prevent them from conducting party-related activity in their work with low-income families (Boeninger 2008: 148). As an official of the Ministry of Development and Planning (MIDEPLAN) stated, the main concerns the Alliance raised against Chile Solidario referred to "the fear that it would be used in electoral ways" (interview, Chile Solidario official).

Besides discussing the rules governing the program and how to prevent manipulation in the selection of beneficiaries, the UDI pressed for local governments to be in charge of selecting beneficiary families. The Alliance had proposed a communal antipoverty fund if it won the elections and privileged decentralized implementation of social benefits. This point was particularly controversial and resulted in a compromise across parties and national and local political interests (Boeninger 2008: 148). It was agreed that MIDEPLAN would identify the number of beneficiaries per district, but those beneficiaries would be verified by mayors (interview, Chile Solidario official). Thus, the final word on *who benefits* became a matter of local decision making, whereas the number of beneficiaries – or quota assigned – by *comuna* was determined by the national government using technical criteria (interview, Chile Solidario official).

Because of its scope, temporary nature, and goals, Chile Solidario does not exactly fit the characterization of an expansion of social transfers, or social policy expansion more broadly as here defined. It differs significantly from other income-transfer programs as it primarily constitutes a "bridge" for beneficiaries to access other benefits, such as pensions and SUF, which are the focus of this research. Unlike the scholarly treatments of Chile Solidario as comparable to the UHHP and the Universal Child Allowance (AUH) in Argentina, or Bolsa Família in Brazil and Oportunidades in Mexico, this study finds SUF to be the key income-support program in Chile and the only one that covers at least 35 percent of the outsiders, as discussed later.

The 2005 Election

Despite Lagos' high approval ratings during his tenure, the competitive environment the Concertación had faced in the 1999 elections remained a source of concern in 2005.[63] The parties of the Alliance had obtained more than 40 percent of the vote in the 2000 municipal and legislative elections, and the UDI was still the largest party in Congress (Joignant and Navia 2003: 137–8). In the 2004 municipal elections, the Alliance obtained a significant vote share of 38.7 percent against the 44.8 percent garnered by the Concertación (see Gamboa 2007: 60).

In this competitive environment, the Concertación selected Michelle Bachelet as its presidential candidate. She was the choice of the coalition because of her popularity and high approval ratings as Lagos' minister of health and then minister of defense (Angell and Reig-Salinas 2007; Navia 2008: 192). The parties of the Alliance in turn suffered from internal

---

[63] See, for example, Gamboa (2007: 58).

divisions. After the UDI and Lavín's rise in previous years, the RN faced the dilemma of either supporting Lavín's second run for the presidency – and thereby continuing to play a secondary role in the coalition and even risking being completely overpowered by the UDI – or seeking to reshape internal dynamics by proposing its own candidate. The RN followed the second strategy, partly facilitated by a decline in Lavín's popularity, and its leading politician, Sebastián Piñera, ran against the UDI and the Concertación in the 2005 presidential election (Gamboa 2007: 58–61, 77).

Tight electoral competition resulted in a runoff between Bachelet and Piñera, which Bachelet won by a margin of seven percentage points. The runoff also saw high competition for outsider voters, with close to 60 percent of outsider districts experiencing competition, as illustrated in Figure 7.2.

The Michelle Bachelet Administration (2006–2010)

In the face of high electoral competition for outsiders, the Bachelet administration embarked on a reform of the pension system, which she had announced during the campaign. As stated by an advisor to the president, pension reform was a "taboo" in Chilean politics, and therefore had never before been prioritized among the Concertación's social policy initiatives (interview). The pension system was a symbol of market reforms and Chile was held as a worldwide pioneer of pension privatization.[64] Piñera also campaigned on pension expansion for housewives, which signaled that the right was not only using pension policy in its attempt to reach out to outsiders, but also that an expansion of the pension system could find support from opposition parties. Although pension reform was undoubtedly the main social policy innovation under Bachelet, her government also launched an important expansion of SUF – the family allowance program – in 2007; by 2010 it reached 58 percent of outsider children with transfers conditional on health care and education requirements.

These social policy initiatives were negotiated in Congress. Despite some changes in the distribution of power among parties within the governing coalition favoring center-left parties, the Concertación's majority

---

[64] There is a large body of literature and consultancy reports about the Chilean model of pension policy. See, among others, studies of pension reform that note the visibility of the Chilean model: Alonso (2000); Brooks (2001); Madrid (2003); Weyland (2004).

TABLE 7.3 *Composition of Congress, Chile, 2006–2010*

	Deputies 2006–2010	Senators 2006–2010
Concertación	65	20
DC	20	7
PPD	21	3
PS	15	8
Other	9	2
Alliance	54	17
UDI	33	9
RN	19	8
Independent	2	1
Other	1	1
Designated	0	0
TOTAL	120	38

Source: Angell and Reig Salinas (2007: 23).

in the lower chamber, and the elimination of designated senators, politicians with conservative social policy views – within and outside the Concertación – were still strong enough to affect the content of social policy proposals by the president, which resulted in adoption of restrictive benefits (see Table 7.3).

Pensions

The government's pension reform bill affected not only benefits for outsiders, but also the regulation of insiders' benefits administered by private pension funds (AFPs), which had ties to the Alliance. Specifically, the Bachelet administration sought to achieve three major goals. First, it attempted to facilitate access to pension benefits for outsiders who lacked contributions or had inadequate contributions to qualify for a pension. At the same time, it sought to increase the pension benefit of those with low-wage jobs whose contributions only allowed them to reach a small, state-subsidized minimum pension. Finally, Bachelet sought to improve individual account savings for insiders. To this end, she proposed to reduce the administrative fees charged by the AFPs, and to promote competition among the different funds.[65]

---

[65] See Gobierno de Chile (2006a, 2006b).

With these reforms, the Bachelet administration also aimed to make transparent the Chilean state's financial commitment to sustaining the existing pension system. Contrary to predictions made by proponents of privatization, state expenditure had remained high after pension privatization in 1981. Since then and through 2004, the Chilean state spent on average 5.7 percent of its GDP annually to support the pension system (Gobierno de Chile 2006b: 2). State funding was directed to a number of items. First, the state had to pay for the "transition cost" of switching from a pay-as-you-go to a fully funded private system – meaning payments to current pensions once the state no longer received revenue from current contributors. Given the large size of the pay-as-you-go pension program before privatization, the transition cost was sizeable. At the same time, the state also subsidized some pension funds that were not privatized – such as the military's – that required additional support in order to meet their commitments.[66]

Third, the state subsidized minimum pensions and noncontributory pensions for workers who lacked sufficient contributions to qualify for a pension at retirement age but who did qualify for a minimum state-subsidized pension after twenty years of contributions or who might be able to obtain a noncontributory pension (PASIS).[67] Inadequate contributory records responded to a number of causes: (a) tighter eligibility conditions to access pensions introduced at the time of privatization, (b) the instability of the labor market – particularly in the 1980s – and (c) the fact that more than 40 percent of the workforce was outside the formal labor market since the 1990s.[68] Last, the dictatorship eliminated employers' contributions, which obviously reduced workers' savings significantly and increased the need for state-subsidized pensions.[69]

Government officials expected that noncontributory commitments would remain stable or grow, but at the same time, they also knew that the number of pre-privatization pensions benefits – the transition cost – would decline significantly as pay-as-you-go pensioners passed away. In light of this, the government sought to channel an increasing share of these resources toward noncontributory pensions and subsidized pension benefits.

---

[66] See Gobierno de Chile (2006b). The pensions of the armed forces and the police represented 1.4 percent of the annual GDP on average between 1981 and 2004.

[67] Ibid.

[68] See Gobierno de Chile (2006b) for an analysis of the pension system and problems affecting coverage.

[69] On the privatization of the pension system, see Mesa-Lago (1994).

To increase savings in individual pension accounts, Bachelet aimed to reduce fees charged by private funds. This was a particularly strong concern among politicians of the left and labor unions. The private pension funds charged a fixed monthly fee that punished low-income workers and represented on average 20 percent of their monthly contributions, reducing their savings (CENDA 2006; CUT 2006). The method the government proposed to limit high fees was to allow banks to enter the pension fund market. This would permit the state-owned Bank of the State of Chile (Banco del Estado) to create a state pension fund, which would charge a lower fee and regulate competition.

Anticipating reactions from the Alliance and the powerful AFP lobby, and in an effort to gain leverage for her reform, Bachelet established the Advisory Council for Pension Reform. The council included fifteen experts who would advise the president and listen to proposals and views from civil society associations, labor unions, pension funds, and other experts.[70] By consulting with civil society actors, the government sought to grant visibility to the reform process and to the different interests involved, as well as to create a veneer of participation in decision making, one of the greatest perceived weaknesses of the Chilean political system (see Delamaza 2010).

Lacking political influence and capacity for coordination, labor unions and other social organizations representing street vendors and technical NGOs did not put together a joint proposal for the council, which could have helped them influence the government's agenda. The actual absence of social mobilization around pension policy resulted in this body primarily serving the government's purpose and playing a ceremonial role. According to a CUT leader, the consultation was "a fiasco" given that "none of the proposals of the social and labor movement was included in the government's project" (interview, Moraga).

The CUT's proposal differed from the government's acknowledging that "the private funds will not disappear," the CUT hoped to "create the conditions for actual competition, allowing new workers to sign up for the public pension system" that the Pinochet dictatorship had eliminated for active workers (interview, Moraga). For unions, the government's project placed the burden to finance the system on the state and "shielded the private system with subsidies, while workers also have to pay both contributions and subsidize the private pension system" (interview, Moraga). Labor unions also wanted employers to reinitiate the payment

---

[70] See Consejo Asesor Presidencial para la Reforma Previsional (2006).

of payroll contributions, which had been eliminated in the 1980s, and they wanted the government to allow for the participation of beneficiaries in pension administration (CUT 2006). None of these features made it into the reform bill.

Even if it did not serve social actors, the council made the reform process and the positions and interests of all parties involved more visible and transparent to the public. Given this visibility in a context of high competition, blocking expansion or advocating very low benefit levels would thus be a harder task for conservatives and other vested interests in the existing system.

The Alliance quite easily agreed with the creation of new benefits for outsiders, and with the main features of these benefits as proposed by the government. However, strong disagreement revolved around the issue of the public pension fund, which was rejected by Alliance legislators and the AFPs.[71] According to UDI legislator Julio Dittborn, this was "undoubtedly one of the most polemic aspects of the project."[72] When the bill was discussed in the Committee of Finance in Congress, Alliance legislators asked the executive to split the bill into two proposals, one concerning new benefits and another dealing with the regulation of the AFPs. Dittborn stressed that such division "would have allowed us to discuss more quickly the solidarity pillar because there is wide agreement to approve it. If the government had accepted ... benefits would have been paid earlier ... The rest of the bill could have been left for discussion later"[73] The government rejected the separation of the bill – probably hoping to get the two pieces approved. As noted by Minister of Labor Andrade, "we reiterate it clearly: it is the political will of the government of President Bachelet to create, abiding by the legal requirements, an AFP in the Banco del Estado.[74]

AFPs at the time constituted a powerful interest group. Aside from their strong ties with Alliance legislators, their financial power was impressive. The investment portfolio managed by AFPs represented more than 60 percent of Chile's GDP in 2007.[75]

As in the case of health care, the reform process was stalled by intense lobbying by the AFPs and by the Alliance against the state-run

[71] Interview, high official of the Asociación de AFP; Asociación de AFP (2006); Cámara de Diputados, Legislatura 355, Sesión 68, August 28, 2007.
[72] Cámara de Diputados, Legislatura 355, Sesión 68, August 28, 2007, p. 22.
[73] Ibid p. 18.
[74] Ibid p. 26.
[75] Data from OECD pension statistics (www.stats.oecd.org).

pension fund. The reform was eventually passed in 2008 only after the public pension fund had been dropped from the bill. Like AUGE, pension expansion was set to roll out gradually. The reform increased the benefit level received by low-income formal-sector beneficiaries through state subsidies, and created a larger noncontributory pension program called Solidary Pension (PS) that absorbed existing PASIS beneficiaries. Concerns about transparency in the selection of beneficiaries of PS emerged, but they were not a central aspect of the debates.

Note that at the same time that the government was initiating the pension reform process, Bachelet submitted a bill to Congress to increase the budget for the existing noncontributory pensions (PASIS), in order to expand the number of beneficiaries.[76] PASIS had remained relatively stable since the Pinochet administration created this benefit in the mid-1970s. This resulted from the fact that the state had established a quota of benefits, regardless of the number of seniors who qualified. This quota had created wait lists of potential beneficiaries who lacked pension benefits. In 2006, Congress approved increased funding and removed the quota. While the number of old-age noncontributory pensions grew 10 percent between 1990 and 2004, it grew 38 percent between 2004 and July 2008.[77]

Due to the strong presence of conservative policymakers in Congress, both from the Alliance and within the Concertación, the features of the Solidary Pension (PS) for outsiders were restrictive. The scope of coverage was moderate, barely reaching 54.3 percent of outsiders sixty-five and older according to data from CASEN (2013). Yet, this is an important contrast with the situation of outsiders in 1992, when 25 percent of this group received pension benefits, and in 2006 – the year the reform process was launched – when pensions reached slightly more than 40 percent of outsiders due to the expansion of PASIS. Table 7.4 presents the percentage of the outsider population sixty-five and older – which represented close to 37 percent of the senior population in 1992 and 40 percent in 2006 – who received noncontributory pension benefits.

As shown in Table 7.4, the Solidarity Pension's benefit levels were moderate. In 2009, the pension represented 50 percent of the minimum benefit paid by the contributory system and 43.6 percent of the minimum wage.[78] PASIS – the previous pension program for extremely poor

[76] See Gobierno de Chile (2006a).

[77] Estimates calculated with data from MIDEPLAN, and Instituto de Previsión Social (INP).

[78] Built with data from Instituto Nacional de Estadistica (INE), Consejo Asesor para la Reforma Previsional (2006), and Superintendecia de Pensiones (SP).

TABLE 7.4 *Outsiders with Pension Benefits, Selected Years*

	1992	2006	2013
Outsiders 65+ with benefit	25%	43%	54%

Estimates built with data from MIDEPLAN (2006 and 2013) based on CASEN surveys.

TABLE 7.5 *Benefit Level of Pensions, Selected Years*

Pensions for Outsiders/ Minimum Pension		Pensions for Outsiders/ Minimum Wage	
PASIS (2004)	Solidarity Pension (2010)	PASIS (2004)	Solidarity Pension (2010)
51.5%	50%	33%	43.6%

Source: Estimates based on data obtained from Superintendencia de Pensiones and INE (various years) and Consejo Asesor de la Reforma Previsional (2006). For 2010, benefit levels correspond to July.

outsiders – provided a similar benefit level. In 2004, it represented on average 51.5 percent of the minimum pension paid by the contributory system and 33 percent of the minimum wage. Note that PASIS was segmented by age group, with higher benefits for seniors aged seventy and older and seventy-five and older,[79] while the SP was a flat-rate benefit (Table 7.5).

As in the case of health care reform, in the absence of a powerful SMC demanding outsiders' participation in policy implementation, mechanisms such as councils or the inclusion of associations in monitoring the implementation of pension benefits were not established.

Income Support

The most important innovation in income support since the Concertación took office in 1990 was the expansion of the preexisting allowances program for low-income outsiders (SUF). This benefit, which consisted of the provision of formal-sector family allowances to low-income outsiders, had been extended by the Pinochet dictatorship in the early 1980s.

---

[79] See Reports of the Consejo Asesor Presidencial para la Reforma Previsional (2006).

As discussed in Chapter 3, the 1983 economic crisis produced massive discontent in the face of more than 30 percent unemployment and triggered protests by popular sectors that had been mobilized by parties before the coup. Income transfers for the unemployed were massively extended to dampen such discontent. However, they were rapidly discontinued as unemployment dropped from 31.3 percent in 1983 to 14 percent in 1987 (see Raczynski 1994: 48, 75). As the dictatorship also faced electoral challenges, family allowances for low-income families were extended gradually throughout the 1980s, reaching an estimated 29 percent of outsider children at the end of the decade.[80] The plebiscite of 1988 and the 1989 elections, which marked the democratic transition, created strong incentives for the dictatorship to focus on social policy to boost its own electoral support first as well as that of right-wing parties in the new democracy when the transition began. As discussed in Chapter 3, because these programs were either small, temporary, and/or selective (see Etchemendy 2011; Graham 1991; Pollack 1999), they did not constitute expansions as here defined.

Given that the SUF was a means-tested program, the number of beneficiaries declined in the early 1990s as the economy improved. The first Concertación governments did not significantly modify the SUF, but increased the reach of the benefit to children up to eighteen years of age in 1996. This change in the eligible population did not mean a significant increase in the scope of coverage, which, according to my estimates reached about 25 percent of outsider children below eighteen years of age in 1999. The SUF was distributed through a quota system that the Ministry of Finance and the Social Security Agency determined every year. This system established eligibility criteria and a fixed number of benefits for distribution in each municipality, which selected beneficiaries according to these criteria but often left many eligible families in wait lists due to the restrictions imposed by the quota.

In 2007, the Bachelet administration sent a proposal to Congress to eliminate the quota system and make the benefit automatic for eligible low-income families.[81] It framed the reform of the SUF as a change involving little additional expenditure but that would make access more transparent and less bureaucratic. The new procedure would eliminate

---

[80] Calculated with data from MIDEPLAN, Superintendencia de Seguridad Social, and Instituto de Previsión Social (IPS).

[81] Eligible means those families with a specific poverty score measured with a standardized social protection instrument (ficha de protección social).

wait lists, which were understood to open the door for discretion in the selection of beneficiaries from the pool of eligible families in each municipality.[82] With the new system, access would be granted for a three-year period, at which point a means test verifies families' vulnerability scores. The bill did not establish concrete eligibility conditions. The ministries of finance and labor would determine the SUF's budget and accordingly set the level of household vulnerability at which households qualify.[83]

Both the Concertación and the opposition in Congress voted for the SUF's expansion unanimously. The Alliance was seeking to mobilize outsiders' support, and thus blocking SUF, which the president announced soon in office, would have been an unpopular strategy. Moreover, the initiative had a small financial cost, as the program represented less than 0.1 percent of GDP before expansion. At the same time, members of both chambers across party lines widely recognized the existing quota system as "cumbersome,"[84] and one that made SUF vulnerable to "political considerations" in the distribution of benefits.[85]

One concern raised against the reform was the fact that the annual eligibility conditions are determined largely based on budget considerations (Jaime Orpis, UDI).[86] Senators from the Alliance stressed the need to define the benefit's reach (Evelyn Matthei, UDI) and to establish precise, clear eligibility conditions to help "depoliticize" social assistance (Pablo Longueira, RN).[87] This issue was not modified. As summarized by Viera-Gallo, Secretary General of the presidency, in response to senators' concerns, "you cannot establish legal obligations of this type [fixed eligibility conditions] if the state tomorrow does not have the resources to fund them."[88] In turn, PS Senator Juan Pablo Letelier noted that every year he would expect that "social criteria instead of the criteria of the budget office prevail."[89]

---

[82] See Biblioteca del Congreso de Chile (2007). Reform of SUF formed part of a broader package of legislation for children.

[83] Reports of the congressional committees that sponsored the bill and the congressional debates are available at Biblioteca del Congreso de Chile (2007). The level of household vulnerability is based on a household's scores measured by the standardized social protection instrument.

[84] Felipe Salaberry of UDI, Cámara de Diputados, legislatura 355, sesión 10, April 4, 2007.

[85] Pablo Lorenzini of DC, Cámara de Diputados, legislatura 355, sesión 10, April 4, 2007.

[86] This was especially contentious because the government claimed it would reach 40 percent of the most vulnerable population, which sounded unclear and that universe was not defined in the bill.

[87] Senado, legislatura 355, sesión 19, May 15, 2007.

[88] Ibid.

[89] Ibid.

TABLE 7.6 *Benefit Level of SUF, Selected Years*

	SUF/Poverty Line (%)	Minimum Wage/Poverty Line
2000	3.25	73.64
2006	5.23	85.60
2009	9.08	80.09

Note: Estimated SUF for a family with two children. Estimated poverty line for two adults and two children.
Source: Estimates with data on minimum wage from INE (www.ine.cl); poverty data from MIDEPLAN; SUF data from IPS and MIDEPLAN.

In explaining why the opposition supported the measure, a high-ranking official of MIDEPLAN suggested:

In concrete terms, to keep your hand pressed on financial resources may generate in the public opinion a negative impression. When we have lean cows we don't spend because there is no money, and now that there is money we don't spend because we have to keep on saving for the times of lean cows. So citizens perceive that... It is not an organized thing, but they perceive it... And the opposition benefits if the state is not seen as the one that blocks these resources from being used. The opposition is working hard to win the next election. (interview)

With the elimination of the quota, beneficiaries almost doubled, from about 30 percent before expansion to 58 percent of children in "outsider" households by 2010.[90] The SUF's reform resulted in a restrictive transfer that by 2009 paid a small benefit level in exchange for school attendance and medical checkups. Although the benefit level was equal to that of family allowances for low-income insiders, its value was low compared to the poverty line. For a household with two children, it represented 3.25 percent of the poverty line in the early 2000s and more than 5 percent in 2006. When the SUF was expanded in 2007, the benefit level was raised and a grant was systematically extended to mothers as well – this provision existed in SUF legislation but had not been implemented full scale. The benefit level for a household with two children came to represent 9.08 percent of the poverty line in 2009 (Table 7.6).

The implementation of the SUF has not involved the participation of social organizations representing outsiders in national or local councils. As demonstrated in this book's framework, in the absence of social movement coalitions pressing for expansion and/or engaging actively in policy design, benefits are implemented in a top-down way.

[90] Estimates with data from MIDEPLAN, Seperintendencia de Seguridad Social, and Instituto de Previsión Social (IPS).

7.5 ASSESSING ALTERNATIVE EXPLANATIONS

This chapter has emphasized the importance of electoral competition for outsiders for the expansion of social policy in Chile. Unlike the cases of Argentina and Brazil, mobilization from below was not significant in Chile in the 1990s and did not emerge around the demand for social benefits until the surge of the student movement in 2011 pressing for education reform. After the transition to democracy, political parties in Chile sought to prevent the intense mobilization of the 1964–73 period, concerned that this might generate reactions and affect regime stability. Since the democratic transition, the parties of the left, in particular the PPD and the PS, formed the Concertación with the DC, and developed direct linkages with voters, without involving social organizations. Labor unions, which had been significantly disarticulated through repression and changes in the labor laws, were marginalized by their historic party allies.[91]

The partisan affiliation of the incumbent was not a good predictor of decisions to expand new policies in Chile during this period. The Concertación initiated expansion beginning in 2004, after a decade in which such initiatives were off the agenda under Concertación governments. Even if center-left politicians (Lagos and Bachelet) occupied the presidency at the time of expansion, both left- and right-wing parties competing for low-income voters promised social policy expansion in their campaigns in 1999–2000 and 2005–6.

Even if partisanship was not a decisive motive for expansion, it was important for the kinds of social programs that parties preferred in terms of their scope of coverage and benefit levels. While the right-wing parties generally advocated smaller policies for the poor, the left-wing in the Concertación preferred broader coverage and benefit levels. A major difference among the left and the conservatives concerned, as it did in Mexico, the role of the state and the market in the administration of social programs. We have seen that conservatives advocated the interests of ISAPRES in Congress during health care reform, whereas the left-wing parties in the Concertación hoped to achieve higher levels of solidarity across income groups by subsidizing the public system with resources from higher income affiliates. These cross-subsidies were strongly resisted by the parties in the Alliance and generally by the Christian Democrats.

---

[91] See Hipsher (1998), Oxhorn (1995), and Schneider (1995) on social movements. On the mobilization of the electorate by the Concertación, see Angell (2007), Boas (2010), and Navia (2006).

Higher levels of state regulation that could affect the profits of private agents were other aspects on which social policy preferences of the left and the conservatives differed.

Due to higher levels of economic stability in Chile compared to the other countries under investigation, it is worth assessing its effect on social policy. According to some authors, lack of crises should generate a more auspicious environment for policy expansion (see Haggard and Kaufman 2008). Yet, in Chile, the inauguration of new policies for outsiders began only under Lagos. These reforms did not come as a result of stability, which had been a feature of Chile's economy throughout the 1990s.

A similar argument can be made about the role of economic growth. As seen in Figure 7.3, the economy grew in Chile since the late 1980s. Despite high levels of growth in the 1990s in particular, there were no serious attempts to expand social policy until the 2000s. The absence of economic restrictions may help advocates of expansion, but it does not straightforwardly motivate politicians to launch expansion. The same parties that refrained from expanding benefits to outsiders for a decade did engage in or promised expansion in the new millennium. These innovations, as here suggested, were triggered by competition for the vote of outsiders.

The lack of expansion – despite the absence of economic crises and of financial constraints produced by low growth – is surprising, given the high poverty rates in Chile during the 1990s. When the Concertación came to power, poverty was about 40 percent, and remained high even after Frei's landslide victory in a context of economic stability and growth. Frei's administration witnessed relatively high levels of unemployment, yet no serious attempts were made to address joblessness (see Figure 7.3). The only innovation before the Lagos administration was the highly targeted FOSIS, which does not qualify as an expansion as I here define these policy innovations. As seen in Figure 7.3, the poverty rate was indeed lower when policy expansion began than it was during the years in which no innovation was carried out.

These reforms were not substantially shaped by international agencies or policy blueprints that dictated how to address high poverty or the plight of low-income outsiders. The features of pensions for outsiders and low-income insiders and the expansion of the SUF have little resemblance with comparable initiatives for outsiders in the region. Perhaps the closest in terms of policy design to Chile's SUF are the family allowances in Uruguay, though Chile's are much smaller in scope. Overall, it is hard

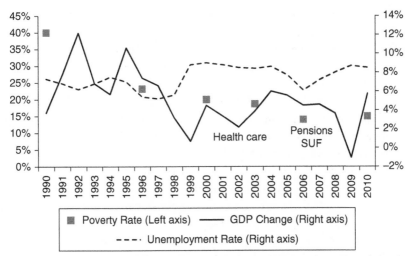

FIGURE 7.3 Economic growth, unemployment, poverty, and timing of expansion, Chile, 1990–2010.
Sources: GDP (1996–2009) and Unemployment from Banco Central de Chile (www.bcentral.cl); poverty from MIDEPLAN.

to say that these reforms were based on or created in response to international models of social protection that diffused within the region through emulation or imposition by a powerful institutional actor.

7.6 CONCLUSION

In this chapter, I have drawn on the analytic framework advanced in this study to explain (a) why Chile embarked on social policy expansion in the 2000s, and (b) why restrictive social policies for outsiders were extended. As expected in the framework, electoral competition for outsiders led incumbents to expand social policy to offset the appeals of credible competitors seeking to win support among outsiders. Moreover, these challengers mobilizing the outsider vote campaigned on social policy expansion to win away that constituency from the incumbent Concertación. Fearing electoral defeat – especially after the dramatic showing of Alliance candidate Lavín in the 1999 presidential election – the Lagos administration and then Bachelet initiated social policy expansion to ensure the support of outsiders and the continuity of the Concertación in office.

These innovations resulted in restrictive policies with moderate or limited coverage, low or moderate benefit levels, and no participation of organizations representing outsiders in policy implementation. This policy outcome is explained by the negotiations involved in the process of policy design. These negotiations were carried out among political parties without social movement involvement, which constitutes a critical condition for the creation of inclusive benefits. Moreover, these negotiations involved, as they did in Mexico, conservative politicians with significant power in Congress. In contrast with Mexico, however, institutional power in Congress was not accompanied by the presence of a conservative incumbent. Chile illustrates a scenario in which center-left incumbents faced high conservative power in Congress – from within and outside of their governing coalitions – and advanced and negotiated policy proposals that were acceptable to conservatives in order to ensure the success of their policy projects.

As in all the other country cases, new benefits were nondiscretionary. In the context of intense electoral competition for outsider voters, concern about accusations of clientelism and manipulation made incumbents particularly attentive to creating institutions that limit discretion in new policies. The opposition in turn pressed for rule-based policies to prevent the incumbent from manipulating benefits and taking advantage in the short term. Because Chile has a tradition of relatively lower levels of clientelism and discretion (see Luna and Mardones 2014; Soifer 2015), particularly compared to the other country cases in this study, fears of discretionary use of resources did emerge but did not loom large in policy debates.

8

Social Policy Expansion in Comparative Perspective

This book has documented a dramatic and unanticipated expansion of nondiscretionary social policy for outsiders in Latin America beginning in the late 1980s. Despite the focus in recent literature on privatization and on targeted, clientelistic benefits for the poor as the dominant trends in social policy, I have documented episodes of large-scale nondiscretionary social policy expansion in three policy areas that historically displayed a marked divide between insiders and outsiders – pensions, health care, and income support – in Argentina, Brazil, Chile, and Mexico. These transformations have had important welfare implications by providing stable – albeit modest – income for poor households that previously lacked such means, by helping to combat infant mortality rates, and by contributing to the containment or reduction of income inequality in a region marked by the highest levels of inequality in the world.[1] Unlike benefits for insiders, these programs have also reached women in greater proportions, establishing a direct connection between them and public policy. While men have been the primary targets of insider benefits due to their larger presence in the formal workforce, women are the main recipients of pensions and income transfers, the latter granted primarily to mothers. These issues are central questions for further comparative research.

In this chapter, I first summarize this book's argument, connect it with the four cases studied in preceding chapters, and extend the argument to another four cases within and outside the region. I then discuss three theoretical implications of this study that refer to fundamental debates in comparative politics addressing both critical real-world and normative

---

[1] On inequality see Lustig (2015), among others.

questions: the relation between democracy and welfare, the role of social mobilization and alliances across insider-outsider cleavages in social policy development and interest representation, and the political conditions necessary for the adoption of discretionary as opposed to nondiscretionary benefits in unequal societies.

8.1 THE ARGUMENT AND MAIN CASES COMPARED

Large-scale programs for outsiders were expanded in several Latin American middle-income countries beginning in the 1980s. In all cases, governments undertook expansion under democratic regimes. In some cases, expansion advanced slowly and gradually, most notably in Brazil, while in others, rapid policy changes occurred after decades of neglect of the outsider population, as in Argentina. These initiatives had been preceded by failed attempts to extend benefits to outsiders at different moments starting in the 1920s and 1930s, when programs for formal-sector workers were first implemented. The earlier successful attempts included the remarkable free public hospital services in Argentina in the 1940s and the expansion of health care services, particularly primary care, in Chile during the 1960s and early 1970s. Other innovations were also introduced for outsiders before the 1980s, but unlike the institutionalized social policies that are the focus of this book, these initiatives were either small or temporary and/or clientelistic, such as the unemployment benefits and the rural pensions that military dictatorships launched in Chile and in Brazil, respectively, in the 1970s.

I have identified two models of social policy, which I term *restrictive* and *inclusive*. Restrictive policies have more limited scope of coverage, provide lower benefit levels, and do not include the participation of social organizations in implementation. Inclusive policies, by contrast, are broad reaching – achieving often universal or near-universal coverage of outsiders – provide higher benefit levels, and include social organizations in policy implementation to some extent.

I have shown that incumbents expanded social policies in response to factors opened up by democratic politics: (a) electoral competition for the vote of outsiders, and (b) social mobilization from below. When incumbents face credible challengers competing for the vote of outsiders, they have strong incentives to solidify outsiders' support to secure their or their parties' continuity in power. Incumbents expanded social policies to that constituency in order to offset the appeals of credible challengers who often tried to mobilize outsiders by promising social policy expansion. When incumbents face social mobilization from below demanding expansion through protest, institutional channels, or from a movement ally within the governing coalition, they are likely to try to curb this social pressure by responding to demands. Across cases, when social mobilization occurred it was sometimes intense, to the point that it could destabilize or seriously weaken the incumbent's hold on power. Other times, social movements gained the support of public opinion, which threatened to undermine the incumbent administration's popularity if it remained unresponsive to the movements' demands. Under these conditions of social mobilization, incumbent presidents responded to movements' demands for social policy expansion in order to restore social order and ensure their parties' continuity in office.

The choice of policy model is related to the actors involved in negotiations around policy design, their preferences, and institutional power. In Latin American multiparty systems, incumbents facing electoral competition for outsider voters have to negotiate policy design – policy features and/or funding for new benefits – in Congress. Given that new social programs tend to be popular and that electoral competition often makes social policy expansion a salient issue of public debate, opposition parties have few incentives to block these measures, particularly if they are competing with the incumbent for the vote of outsiders. However, the opposition may still affect policy design, depending on the balance of power in Congress.

Across the examined cases in which electoral competition drove expansion and social movements were not involved in policy design – Chile and Mexico – social policy initiatives were either proposed by conservatives or negotiated with conservative parties with substantial power in Congress. As documented in the literature on the welfare state, conservative parties generally prefer reduced state intervention and targeted social programs. As a result, these negotiations across congressional parties produced relatively more modest policy initiatives. At the same time, in the absence of mobilization from below, politicians prefer nonparticipatory implementation to avoid deviating from program goals and to discourage social demands around new policies. In the cases under investigation, congressional negotiations involving conservative parties resulted in policies that were *restrictive*, with smaller coverage, lower benefit levels and nonparticipatory implementation.

Powerful social movements may engage actively in policy design because they have either propelled expansion in the first place or they are linked to the incumbent party and acquire influence in decision making through formal or informal channels. Incumbents often negotiate the policies' design with social movement leaders or respond strategically to movement demands when social movement coalitions are large in scale. Social movements generally demand generous, broad-reaching benefits equivalent to those benefiting insiders, as well as participation in policy implementation in order to contribute to policy deliberations, ensure organizational survival, and monitor implementation. Across the cases examined, incumbents generally responded with broad policies and participatory implementation in order to limit pressures from below and channel activism into policy implementation. These negotiations and strategic responses generally resulted in *inclusive* policies.

In explaining the remarkable creation of nondiscretionary policies in environments with high – though variable – levels of clientelism, informal institutions, and weakly enforced rules, I have argued that this relates to the strategic interests of politicians and social movement leaders who participate in policy design.[2] In the context of intense electoral competition for outsiders, opposition politicians are likely to worry that incumbents will gain substantial credit among outsider voters with new policies and may even manipulate beneficiaries into supporting the incumbent. Opposition politicians would prefer to be the ones launching benefits to court outsiders, but they often cannot block expansion due to the electoral cost it may bring. In this situation, they try to influence policy design and to ensure benefits are nondiscretionary so that incumbents do not manipulate them to their advantage during elections at the expense of the opposition.

A critical priority for the opposition competing for outsiders then consists in ensuring that new benefits are nondiscretionary and that the policies reflect their preferences to some extent. Across cases, when incumbents announced a new benefit – even if they were copying opposition proposals to court outsiders – opposition politicians would often denounce the proposed benefits as potentially clientelistic, a source of manipulation, or "electoral" spending, and they would fight to make sure resulting provisions were nondiscretionary.

When social movement coalitions advocate and press for benefits, a similar logic is observable. Coalition leaders pursue nondiscretionary policies to prevent the incumbent from manipulating access, sometimes out of fear that movement members will be excluded from receiving

---

[2] The exclusion of activists from program benefits is a typical tool political machines employ.

benefits, and that patronage party structures will benefit from the distribution of discretionary resources that social movements have managed to get expanded. Social movement coalition leaders thus wanted benefits to be distributed to all beneficiaries both to ensure higher levels of welfare and to limit potential selectivity that may result from targeted benefits.

Incumbents in turn are not prone to rely on clientelism when expanding large-scale benefits in the strategic environment of high competition for outsiders and social mobilization. Facing electoral competition, incumbents fear allegations of clientelism that may discredit them and favor the opposition. For this reason, they want benefits to be nondiscretionary and designed and implemented in a way that minimizes clientelism. In the context of mobilization from below, incumbents fear that clientelistic benefits may trigger further mobilization for nondiscretionary benefits instead of appeasing pressures, which is generally the goal they seek to achieve with social policy expansion. Incumbents launching large-scale expansion also make sure eligibility is determined by a technocratic agency, and they embark on wide dissemination of information on the programs and of the eligibility conditions.

Despite their different socioeconomic characteristics and partisan histories, Argentina and Brazil both created inclusive policies. In Argentina, by 2010, pensions and family allowances covered a large share of outsider seniors and children, respectively. Health care services, which were already significant in Argentina, extended access to primary care and pharmaceuticals via a free prescription drugs program.

The expansion of protection for outsiders was propelled by mobilization from below led primarily by a social movement coalition (SMC) formed in the late 1990s by unemployed workers' movements and social movement unions. The movements of unemployed workers comprised federations of organizations that included hundreds of community-based associations. Despite partisan political divisions among unemployed workers' groups, they formed the basis for coordinated, large-scale mobilization. Ties with labor unions, particularly public-sector unions in the Argentine Workers' Central (CTA), helped this movement grow and expand geographically. At times, alliances with other organizations and NGOs helped amplify and expand their demands around specific programs. This SMC put together demands and policy proposals, such as expansion of income transfers and the universalization of family allowances and pensions, which were addressed by different administrations beginning in 2002 in response to pent-up mobilization. These efforts resulted in large-scale expansions that strongly resembled this SMC's demands. In the case of health care, the state responded to demands posed by the SMC and health-related NGOs for pharmaceuticals, medical supplies, and health care services, which were lacking and severely affected by the 2001 crisis, with a comprehensive plan to strengthen primary care services and extend free prescription drugs.

Part of this SMC forged an alliance with the Victory Front (FV), a Justicialista Party (PJ) faction led by Presidents Néstor and Cristina Kirchner starting in 2004. Groups allied with the incumbent coalition and from outside the government put pressure on the state to expand generous nondiscretionary programs and to allow for participation in implementation, and they also received selective benefits to empower their organizations.

Electoral competition for outsider voters was not intense during this period, with the exception of the 1999 elections that brought the Alliance for Jobs, Justice, and Education – a coalition of the Front for a Country with Solidarity (FREPASO) and Radical Party (UCR) – to power. The Alliance announced expansion on several occasions but delayed policy responses despite large-scale protest. Fernando de la Rúa's government collapsed after ill-fated financial policy decisions and the breakup of the coalition within the first year in power. During his tenure, he did not implement any of the announced social policy benefits.

In Brazil, social policy expansion began in the late 1980s with the inclusion of social rights in the 1988 constitution. In the early 1990s, Brazil implemented a universal health care system as well as pensions for rural workers and low-income outsiders. Beginning in 2001, the government expanded cash transfers to low-income families, which were later integrated into a single program and extended massively starting in 2003. By 2010, Brazil had built a universal health care system, pension benefits reached around 80 percent of outsiders aged sixty-five and older, and about 70 percent of outsider school-aged children accessed cash transfers.

The first wave of expansions in the late 1980s was propelled by mobilization from below. Social movements promoting health care reform, rural workers, labor unions, church groups, and other social movements pressured the José Sarney administration (1985–90) and the Constituent Assembly to create universal policies with benefits similar to those of low-income insiders and participatory implementation. These movements were more or less closely connected and supported each other's demands for social policy change. Through lobbying, persuasion, and sometimes protest and demonstrations, social movements managed to accomplish the adoption of their proposals for pension and health care expansion.

The implementation of new rights did not occur immediately, and only began after a new wave of social mobilization during the Fernando Collor de Mello administration (1990–2). Facing pressures and lacking legitimacy after Collor's collapse, his vice president, Itamar Franco (1992–5), negotiated social policies with movement leaders and initiated the implementation of social rights. Electoral competition for outsiders was not high during the first years of democracy. Despite attempts to mobilize low-income voters by the Workers' Party (PT), these voters remained locked in by partisan machines allied with incumbent presidents and conservative coalitions.

Electoral competition began to grow subnationally with the expansion of the left at the local level in an increasingly institutionalized party system, culminating in high electoral competition for outsiders in the 2002 presidential elections. Municipal governments of the PT expanded income-support benefits – among other popular policies – to win support in areas of recalcitrant conservative presence. In response, conservative machines pressured the national government to approve an Anti-Poverty Fund championed by the Liberal Front Party (PFL), which would fund social transfers and health care programs in subsequent years. Despite its initial reluctance to expand large-scale national benefits out of fear of their clientelistic use by local machines allied to the government, the Fernando Henrique Cardoso administration eventually launched income-transfer programs before the 2002 elections to offset the credible challenger. Designed by conservatives, these benefits were restrictive, with relatively limited coverage, low benefit levels, and no participation in implementation.

In 2003, after a failed attempt to implement a participatory anti-hunger program promoted by social movements linked to the PT, the administration of Luiz Inácio da Silva (Lula) unified all income transfers into a large program, Bolsa Família, to consolidate unprecedented outsider support for the electoral coalition that had brought him to power in 2002, and expanded the new benefit significantly. Empowered by their access to the state, social movements allied to the party demanded broad policies – an historic commitment of the PT – and participation in implementation, like in Argentina. Although income transfers resulted into much less participatory implementation, Bolsa Família did eventually include some mechanisms that gave a voice to social organizations. As predicted in my analytic framework, participatory mechanisms are more relevant when movements that pushed for their adoption were not allied to the party in office (as in the case of health reform and rural pensions in Brazil) than when social movements advocating their adoption accessed the policy design process as members of the governing coalition (as in the case of Bolsa Família and several social programs in Argentina).

Mexico and Chile, on the other hand, expansion was propelled by electoral competition for outsiders. In both cases, policies were either launched or negotiated with conservatives in Congress, resulting in restrictive social policies. In Mexico, expansion began under the Vicente Fox administration (2000–6) of the center-right National Action Party (PAN), which came to power defeating the Institutional Revolutionary Party (PRI) after seventy years of that party's consecutive rule, inaugurating the first democratic government. Fox transformed an income-transfer program previously established by the outgoing PRI president, Ernesto Zedillo, into a large-scale nondiscretionary program, and he established health insurance and pensions for outsiders. By 2010, more than a third of outsider school-aged children received transfers; health care benefits reached about half of the outsider population; and around 48 percent of outsiders aged sixty-five and older received pensions.

The expansion of social protection was propelled by electoral competition for the votes of outsiders, which grew dramatically in the late 1990s, particularly surrounding the 2000 elections as voters de-aligned from the PRI and the regime became more democratic due to institutional reforms. In power, Fox sought to consolidate support among the outsider population and established the foundation for a set of social protection policies for outsiders. These programs were designed by the executive and negotiated in a conservative-dominated Congress, which resulted in restrictive benefits. As the 2006 elections approached, the rise of the left-wing Party of the Democratic Revolution (PRD) candidate Andrés Manuel López Obrador, who had campaigned on social policy expansion – particularly on extending universal pensions – increased pressure on the incumbent to expand pensions or on the PAN candidate to promise expansion if elected. Fox managed to launch a pension program rapidly during the presidential campaign to offset the appeals of López Obrador. After the new Congress assumed power in 2006, the PRD – with stronger institutional power as the second party in Congress – negotiated with the PAN the creation of a larger – though still limited – pension program in exchange for supporting the PAN's 2007 budget law. In the absence of social movements demanding benefits, parties preferred nonparticipatory implementation, fearing allegations of clientelism or opening the door for social groups to influence social policy.

Chile also implemented restrictive policies, although some were broader than those in Mexico. The expansion of health care services and income support began in 2004 with the approval of Plan AUGE. Between 2006 and 2008, pensions and family allowances were extended to low-income families. By 2010, about 60 percent of outsider children received family allowances, and 55 percent of outsiders aged sixty-five and older received pension benefits. A large share of outsiders had access to health care, which, as we have seen, had been broad since the 1960s, but many suffered from high copayments and excessive wait lists, while others remained excluded from any insurance."

These changes were propelled by heightened electoral competition for outsider voters that started around the 1999 presidential election, when the right-wing Alliance, in particular the Independent Democratic Union (UDI), was on the rise. The Ricardo Lagos administration (2000–6), which assumed power after a razor-thin victory in the runoff, expanded health care after long negotiations in Congress with conservative politicians within the Concertación and the Alliance. With the arrival of Michelle Bachelet in 2006 after another election with high competition for outsider voters, pension reform was negotiated and approved in 2008, and a small preexisting program of family allowances was extended to twice as many children. As in the case of Mexico, these policies were restrictive, featuring a moderate scope of coverage, low or moderate benefit levels, and nonparticipatory implementation.

8.2 EXTENDING THE ANALYSIS: LATIN AMERICA AND SOUTH AFRICA

Does the argument on the centrality of social mobilization and electoral competition for outsiders developed around these cases help explain social policy expansion elsewhere? Is the presence of social movement coalitions in policy making a fundamental factor contributing to the adoption of inclusive policies? And are incumbents and congresses with conservative power more likely to approve restrictive policies?

In Chapter 3, I assessed the evolution of social policy for outsiders in Argentina, Brazil, Chile, and Mexico prior to the occurrence of expansion during the third wave of democracy. This historical analysis uncovered few episodes of expansion taking place under the rather unique conditions of democracy and electoral competition for outsiders. Other policies created for outsiders during these decades do not fit the description of nondiscretionary social policies. The analysis helped distinguish different types of such policies for outsiders and identify the political conditions under which they emerged. We saw that authoritarian regimes facing high levels of mobilization or electoral competition expanded rather large, discretionary, and/or temporary provisions in response to protest or to the rise of a potential challenger disputing outsiders' support. Authoritarian regimes that experienced none of these pressures extended no benefits, while democracies without electoral competition or mobilization from below created rather small programs – some of which were discretionary – to show some concern for the poor but avoid engaging in the more costly and laborious process of including outsiders with large-scale, nondiscretionary benefits.

Acknowledging that a similar analysis to the one conducted in this book requires a substantial amount of fieldwork and data on mobilization and electoral dynamics, which exceeds the scope of this study, my goal is to provide an assessment of whether the argument advanced here contributes to our understanding of other third-wave democracies in Latin America and beyond. Selected cases include three middle-income countries in South America – Peru, Uruguay, and Venezuela – as well as South Africa. These cases demonstrate considerable variation in their outcomes, including the establishment of large-scale but highly politicized and often discretionary social programs (Venezuela), restrictive benefits in only one policy area (Peru), and inclusive benefits across all (Uruguay) or some (South Africa) policy areas. At the same time, these cases exhibit broad cross-country and cross-temporal variation in the explanatory factors identified in this study as relevant to the expansion of nondiscretionary social policy: the presence of democracy with (a) electoral competition for outsiders – together with stable parties or consecutive reelection provisions – and/or (b) social mobilization from below.

Briefly, Venezuela and Peru saw the collapse of their party systems in the 1990s and the emergence of nondemocratic regimes at some point during this period. Under democracy, the absence of stable political parties and consecutive reelection in both cases made incumbents' continuity in power unlikely and attenuated the incentives for expansion that electoral competition for outsiders typically creates. Protest emerged at some points, but social mobilization for social benefits – as mobilization is here defined – did not take place. By contrast, in Uruguay, probably the strongest democracy in the region,[3] electoral competition for outsiders propelled expansion, and social movements eventually engaged in

---

[3] On levels or quality of democracy, see Pérez Liñán and Mainwaring (2013).

policy design. In South Africa, social mobilization pushed for expansion across specific policy areas, and electoral competition did not emerge at all throughout the period under investigation.

Venezuela: Regime Instability, Political Conflict, and Broad Discretionary Expansion

Venezuela offers an interesting case for assessing this book's argument. After a period of economic decline beginning in the 1980s, which was followed by party system collapse in the 1990s, Venezuela saw dramatic economic growth propelled by soaring oil prices under the left-wing administration of Hugo Chávez in the 2000s. Although substantial social policy expansion did take place, it resulted in social programs that differ from the nondiscretionary, large-scale income transfers, pensions, and health care services for outsiders adopted in the main cases analyzed in this book.

The absence of the key factors identified in my theoretical argument helps account for this different policy trajectory. In the 1990s, support for Venezuela's traditional parties eroded dramatically, ultimately resulting in party system collapse by the end of the decade. In the 1993 elections, the incumbent embarked on social policy expansion in the face of declining support, high levels of electoral competition for outsiders, and spontaneous protests. In the context of sharp economic restrictions and conservative policy preferences, the resulting benefits were restrictive. Party system collapse and the absence of consecutive reelection provisions (until 1999), both of which created little prospects for politicians' continuity in power, generated no incentives for expansion as the 1998 elections neared. As advanced in this book's framework, the presence of either minimally stable parties or reelection provisions is necessary in order for electoral competition to motivate incumbents to expand social policy for outsiders. With the arrival of Chávez to the presidency in 1998, the disarray of the opposition and Chávez's strong appeal among low-income voters curtailed the emergence of electoral competition for outsiders. Social mobilization by a national coalition demanding expansion did not take shape either. Collectively, these features disincentivized large-scale social policy expansion. By contrast, the deterioration of the political regime and growing political conflict, with an eventually unsuccessful coup in 2002 and the development of a competitive-authoritarian regime (Levitsky and Loxton 2013), created incentives for the adoption of large-scale albeit discretionary provisions for outsiders. Without a party organization or strong movements on which to rely in the context of deep political conflict, Chávez launched highly participatory social programs associated to his presidency to help him organize and mobilize a base of support. This kind of social policy could be launched precisely because electoral competition was low in presidential elections, the regime was becoming nondemocratic, and Chávez was not accountable to the opposition, which was at times ready to dramatically destabilize the government, as described next.

Unlike the other cases under study, Venezuela was a stable democracy founded on an institutionalized two-party system since the late 1950s, until the system collapsed in the 1990s. Democratic Action (AD) and the Committee of Independent Political Electoral Organizations (COPEI) governed since the signing of the Punto Fijo agreement of 1958. These parties penetrated and co-opted civil society organizations, weakening and demobilizing autonomous movements and constituting a party cartel or "partyarchy" (Coppedge 1994; Lander 1995).

Severe economic troubles beginning in the 1980s resulted in the erosion of popular support for these parties (see Roberts 2014).[4] In 1989, after failed stabilization plans, the newly elected AD administration of Carlos Andrés Pérez (1989–93) announced a drastic package of market reforms, known as the "great turnabout" due to its departure from existing policies and Pérez's campaign promises. Spontaneous protests emerged following the announcement of the reform package, which included spending cuts, privatization, and the elimination of subsidies, and intensified dramatically after sharp increases in gas prices and public transit fares, triggering a wave of lootings known as the Caracazo (see López Maya 2005; Stephany 2006). The government responded to the lootings with repression by police and military forces, resulting in about 800 people killed in the popular neighborhoods of Caracas alone (López Maya 2005: 85–9; Stephany 2006: 82). The state's response to the lootings, and the fact that both the AD and COPEI were seen as implicit supporters of this unparalleled level of repression under democratic rule, seriously undermined popular support for the two parties and the political system as a whole (see López Maya 2011: 219). These protests did not spawn an organized social movement, but remained

---

[4] AD won the two presidential elections in the 1980s comfortably (see López Maya 2005: 114).

spontaneous manifestations of collective discontent (see López Maya 2005; Stephany 2006).

In response to these spontaneous protests, and facing dramatically declining popularity, the Pérez administration initiated a series of temporary targeted social programs known as the Plan to Combat Poverty (PEP), which increased social expenditures for the poor from 0.69 percent to 1.13 percent of the GDP in 1990 (see Carvallo 1999: 142; Michelina 1999: 95). The most important benefit was the Food Grant (*Beca Alimentaria*) (BA), which provided allowances to up to three children aged six to eleven per family in low-income areas, conditional on public school attendance (Lima 1995). The BA attained broad coverage of the target population, reaching close to 2.5 million low-income children in the early 1990s. Initially the allowance was relatively generous, representing close to 20 percent of the minimum wage for a family with two children. However, its value remained fixed, and it eroded with inflation (Lima 1995). Despite some economic recovery in the early 1990s due to rising oil prices, the Pérez administration's legitimacy crumbled, and hostility to the incumbent's policies grew within the party. Pérez faced two coup attempts by nationalist military officers, one of them led by Chávez in 1992, and he was eventually removed from office in 1993 amid a corruption scandal.

Within a highly unstable institutional environment, Rafael Caldera, who had broken with COPEI when he failed to win the party's presidential nomination, ran on a newly formed party, Covergencia, and won the 1993 elections.[5] Marking the end of Punto Fijo's two-party system, four parties obtained rather similar vote shares (all between 21 and 30 percent) in this election, which also featured high abstention. Support for Caldera declined rapidly. Despite campaigning on a pro-state discourse, he was prompted by the 1995 financial crisis to switch tracks and implement orthodox adjustment measures. Coupled with declining oil prices in 1998, the economic situation deteriorated dramatically (López Maya 2011: 219). To preempt upheavals, Caldera maintained and strengthened social programs targeted to the poorest populations (see Briceño 1999: 132). Aside from food distribution, the largest scheme was the BA, which Caldera renamed the Single Family Subsidy (SUF), and which reached about 1.5 million households in 1997,[6] providing them with the

---

[5] Levitsky and Loxton (2013: 124).
[6] Estimated coverage from Cavallo (1999: 145), and population data from the National Statistics Agency (INE) (available at http://www.ine.gov.ve).

equivalent to about 10 percent of the minimum wage for a family with two children.

In 1998, the party system had eroded to the point that traditional parties did not field candidates for the presidential election. Their discrediting boosted support for rising left-wing parties and new political organizations, such as the Bolivarian Movement led by Chávez – who had become for many a national hero in the 1992 coup attempt and had engaged in political organizing since he was released from prison in 1994. Chávez formed the Fifth Republic Movement (MVR) with the Bolivarian Movement and other small parties, and won a landslide victory in 1998, obtaining 56.2 percent against 39.97 percent of the vote by the second-most-voted candidate (López Maya 2005: 229).

During his first years in office, Chávez convened a Constituent Assembly – his main campaign promise – that wrote a new constitution including mechanisms of direct democracy, reelection provisions, and transformation of the National Assembly from bicameral to unicameral. Another presidential election in 2000 after the passage of the new constitution granted Chávez a smashing victory by a vote of 59.8 percent to 37.5 percent against the main opposition candidate. As López Maya noted, in this election, as well as in 1998, support for Chávez was high among the low-income population and he obtained landslide victories in all but the wealthier states of Venezuela.[7]

Despite facing high levels of poverty, Chávez initially eliminated – or cut back – the Caldera government's main social programs, as well as the Ministry of the Family that administered them, and launched very few social policy innovations (Penfold-Becerra 2008). In 1999, Chávez established Plan Bolívar 2000, a scheme with a modest budget that distributed food and vaccines in very poor areas of the country via the military, and in 2001, he established the Unified Social Fund to manage social funding, a program that was also under the control of high-ranking military officers. Both initiatives suffered from administrative problems and discretion, which resulted in corruption scandals (Penfold-Becerra 2008: 70).

Political conflict escalated in the early 2000s, severely deteriorating the political regime and prompting a shift in Chávez's policy agenda. Scholars have pointed out that agricultural and business elite sectors, as well as workers from Venezuela's oil company (PDVSA), believed that the Land Law passed by decree in 2001, as well as the government's increased

---

[7] Electoral data from López Maya (2005: 242).

political control over PDVSA, threatened property rights. This precipitated the political confrontations that culminated in a coup in 2002 (see Penfold-Becerra 2007: 71; Dunning 2008: 191; Roberts 2006: 142). The coup was short-lived, as Chavez's supporters in the military and in lower-class neighborhoods rapidly managed to reinstate him, removing the head of the fedecamaras business association who had assumed the presidency (López Maya 2005; Roberts 2006: 142). Following the unsuccessful coup, a two-month general strike and lockouts by business associations and labor unions demanding Chávez's resignation produced a sharp economic decline and a spike in poverty levels (López Maya 2011).

In response to these episodes of political conflict and regime breakdown Chávez strengthened the formation of Bolivarian Circles and launched a more ambitious set of social funds known as Bolivarian Missions to reach low-income populations. Missions were created parallel to the existing bureaucracy and funded land reform, health care services, and education programs, among others.

While missions helped address deteriorated social conditions, they also helped Chávez connect with his loose support base and mobilize it behind his project. Missions promoted the formation of local councils, encouraged high levels of participation in program implementation, and were strongly identified with the president. The Bolivarian Circles were critical to the formation of new organizations that participated in some of the missions and operated as sources of mass support for the incumbent (see Roberts 2006: 142–3; D'Elia 2008). Other grassroots organizations that were formed to coordinate activities around the missions also engaged in mobilizing voters (Roberts 2006: 143).

Among the missions, Barrio Adentro, which first provided primary health care services in Caracas and later throughout the country, is particularly relevant (López Maya 2005: 357). By 2005, the program was run by 20,000 Cuban doctors, community agents, and nurses, some of whom were recruited from the new higher education programs provided through other missions (López Maya 2005: 358). In an AP-IPSOS poll taken in 2006 and quoted by Dunning (2008: 188), 42 percent of respondents in the country reported benefiting from Barrio Adentro. Other missions provided school grants to teenagers and adults, yet the number of grants extended was negligible, reaching about 200,000 recipients per year by 2010.[8]

---

[8] See Misión Robinson, www.misionrobinson.gov.ve, accessed 2010.

Missions furthermore suffered from little institutionalization, a lack of clear rules for accessing benefits, as well as from the absence of oversight mechanisms (see D'Elia 2006: 208; D'Elia 2008: 15; López Maya 2005: 362–3).[9] These features, combined with the partisan nature of the missions, likely resulted in high levels of discretion in the distribution of benefits, alienating non-Chávez supporters.

Aside from the missions, the government extended pension benefits through a number of temporary decrees starting in 2006. Through these decrees, non-contributory benefits paid by the social security system were offered to specific categories of workers (e.g., low-income fishermen, housewives) according to a pre-established quota. The chance to apply for benefits was often temporary, and the social security agency itself was in charge of identifying qualifying beneficiaries. This method of expansion lacked clear rules for determining eligibility, and access was subject to discretionary, opaque criteria. Decrees providing such benefits were issued in 2006 and 2007. According to my estimates, by 2010 about 20 percent of outsider seniors had pensions through these short-term mechanisms.[10]

In the 2006 presidential election, Chávez won a remarkable 62.8 percent of the vote against the opposition's 36.9 percent. His coalition also won all the governorships. A critical factor explaining Chávez's electoral performance was a voter turnout of 74.7 percent of the electorate, a sharp increase relative to prior elections (see Hawkins 2010; López Maya 2005). In subsequent years, and within a political regime characterized as competitive-authoritarian (Levitsky and Loxton 2013) in which growing polarization led to strong clashes between the president's partisans and the opposition, Chávez continued to enjoy broad support among the outsider population.

In 2012, Chávez, who had managed to amend the constitution and end term limits in 2009, ran again for the presidency. Although this time the opposition was better organized, and the economy was deteriorating with growing inflation, Chávez won the election comfortably by a margin of victory of eleven points and faced no electoral competition for outsiders.[11]

---

[9] For example, social organizations have denounced that credits are not granted to cooperatives that do not form part of Chavismo or that criticize the government (López Maya 2005: 363).

[10] Calculated with data from the social security institute based on analysis of relevant decrees. See Fernandez (2012).

[11] Note that because outsiders are a large share of the population in Venezuela, reaching more than 60 percent of the population during this period, I consider electoral

With respect to social policy, the government launched new missions that extended family allowances for low-income households, covering about 14 percent of outsider children in 2013, and introduced a new scheme providing non-contributory pensions for poor seniors. With this new pension scheme, coverage of outsider seniors jumped to 40 percent.[12] The criteria for targeting these new pension benefits remained, as with previous extensions, nontransparent. As expected in this book's argument and discussed in Chapter 3, incumbents facing growing contestation in nondemocratic regimes, even if competition is not yet high, use different tools to prevent it from growing into a serious electoral challenge (e.g., discretionary deployment of state resources, intimidation of opposition, and other means). Unlike incumbents in democracies, incumbents in these contexts are likely to create benefits that are strongly identified with them and are politically targeted in order to mobilize recipients in their favor. In an environment of intense political conflict, incumbents may seek to discourage the opposition from disputing outsider voters and/or to counterbalance the opposition's attempts to destabilize the government.

Overall, the theoretical argument in this book highlights the lack of incentives for the expansion of large-scale, nondiscretionary social policies in the Venezuelan case. In the 1990s, the absence of a coordinated social movement coalition pressing for expansion, together with party decomposition and no reelection provisions, offered few incentives for large-scale expansion beyond the 1993 election. During Chávez's governments, the absence of bottom-up social mobilization pressing for benefits that would ordinarily lead an incumbent to respond to demands, or the absence of electoral competition for outsiders within a democratic regime that would typically prompt leaders to promise and extend social benefits, created no incentives for the expansion of broad, nondiscretionary provisions.[13] The deterioration of the political regime after the unsuccessful coup instead motivated Chávez, who lacked an organization to mobilize support for his government, to use social programs with highly participatory and politicized designs to try to build such networks of supporters. These benefits were highly discretionary, often lacking clear

---

competition for outsiders present if competition is high (characterized by a margin of victory below ten points) in general elections.

[12] Calculated with data from the social security institute based on analysis of relevant decrees. See Fernandez (2012).

[13] As noted before, this assumes that those demanding benefits are excluded from existing protections reaching insiders.

access rules and alienating those who did not share the mobilizing nature and discourse of Chavismo. Instead of providing permanent, broad-based pensions, transfers, and medical services organized within a more institutionalized state policy, Chávez extended social provisions through missions that contributed to organizing and mobilizing his base of supporters to better confront strong polarization and protests by the economic elite and middle-class sectors challenging his legitimacy and his continuity in an increasingly nondemocratic polity.[14]

Peru: Attenuated Incentives for Expansion

Peru stands out for the absence of meaningful social policy innovations. The only initiative that qualifies as an expansion is a restrictive health insurance program initiated under the Alejandro Toledo administration (2001–6) of the Peru Posible party and expanded more broadly under the administration of Alan García (2006–11) of the American Popular Revolutionary Alliance (APRA). Like Venezuela, Peru saw dramatic economic decline followed by the deterioration of the political regime and the collapse of the party system in the 1990s, which in part helps explain this outcome. Yet the absence of significant expansion in Peru in the 2000s compared to its neighbors in Latin America is puzzling in light of the return of democracy and high economic growth, as well as Ollanta Humala's ascension to the presidency in 2011 after running on a redistributive platform.

In this context, why has expansion not happened across policy areas as it has in Bolivia or Ecuador – the other Andean countries in which outsiders represent at least 70 percent of the population? Given the technocratic features of the Peruvian national state, why has Peru not "emulated" Chile's social policies and made an effort to protect a larger share of outsiders?

The main factors identified in this book as creating incentives for incumbents to expand social policy were not strong in Peru since its democratization. Peru saw an authoritarian reversal in the 1990s led by Alberto Fujimori (1990–2000), as well as the decomposition of its party system, which began in the 1980s (Levitsky 2013; Levitsky and Cameron 2003). The absence of consecutive reelection in the 2000s, together with the lack of meaningful party organizations that could get successors elected or even allow incumbents to effectively run for nonconsecutive

---

[14] Roberts (2006) explains when populist leaders build organizations and when they do not.

reelections, made the prospects of continuity in power unlikely and attenuated the incentives for expansion, even if candidates competed intensely
for the support of outsiders in presidential elections.[15] At the same time,
without a national social movement coalition pressing for social policy,
incumbents did not find strong incentives to engage in large-scale expansion to respond to demands.

In this context, incumbents seeking nonconsecutive reelections, as
Toledo and García did since 2000, initiated small-scale cash-transfer,
health care, and pension schemes to demonstrate their concerns for
poverty. These initiatives did not amount to expansions as they are here
defined, but cumulatively resulted in modest but growing coverage. The
only innovation that passed the threshold of expansion was health care
reform, a policy area in which stakeholders – namely a coalition of doctors and NGOs – did press for broader expansion and helped produce
a more decisive response, though they were not as strong as the social
movements in Argentina or Brazil. The evolution of this dynamic is
traced next.

When Peru returned to democracy in 1980, the incentives for expansion were not strong. The Popular Action Party (AP), which had held the
last democratic government before the dictatorships of the 1960s and
1970s, defeated the APRA with a large margin of victory in 1980. Facing
a deep recession triggered by the debt crisis and the surge of a guerrilla
movement, Shining Path, the Fernando Belaúnde Terry administration
(1980–5) initiated market-oriented policies unsuccessfully and launched
indiscriminate repression against the Shinning Path. With annual inflation reaching three digits (125 percent) and GDP falling by 12 percent in
1983 (Arce 2003: 574), the AP government lost any chances of continuation. At the same time, the armed conflict and state repression discouraged the emergence of large-scale mobilization.

García won the presidential election by a landslide in 1985, with the
opposition AP receiving only 5.6 percent of the vote. Although electoral
competition was high due to alternation, García did not adopt meaningful social programs for outsiders. The most visible and costly program
for low-income outsiders was a temporary workfare program (PAIT)
that reached 500,000 beneficiaries among a vast pool of potentially
eligible low-income workers on a three-month basis by 1988 (Graham

---

[15] Note that given the size of the outsider population, which includes throughout the period
from 80 percent to 75 percent of the total population, electoral competition for outsiders
is present in any election with high competition as here defined.

1992: 181). According to Graham, misuse of PAIT's funds was widespread and program administrators built reputations for using benefits to establish their support bases on the ground. Over time, and as the economy worsened, PAIT was defunded amid strong allegations of political manipulation (Graham 1992: 182).

Facing a deep crisis, García pursued heterodox economic measures that resulted in hyperinflation and economic collapse. Between 1988 and 1990, the country's GDP fell 25 percent (Arce 2003: 575). Profound economic deterioration severely weakened established parties, which were massively rejected by voters (Levitsky 2013; Levitsky and Cameron 2003: 2). In this context, Fujimori, a political amateur running on an electoral vehicle, made it to the 1990 runoff presidential election against a center-right coalition with a broad privatization agenda and led by another political amateur. Pledging redistributive policies and with an anti-politics discourse, Fujimori won the runoff by a wide margin.

In power, Fujimori soon abandoned his redistributive discourse, adopted market-oriented reforms, and launched relatively small discretionary social programs, especially for the urban poor. Importantly, Fujimori produced an authoritarian reversal, which made the expansion of nondiscretionary social policy for outsiders unlikely. On the grounds that he was unable to advance on further institutional reforms, Fujimori closed down Congress with a military-backed self-coup in 1992 and called for legislative elections to reform the constitution, inaugurating one of the very few authoritarian reversals of the third wave in Latin America (see Conaghan 2005). After his second reelection – which generated a constitutional controversy over its legality and occurred under allegations of fraud – Fujimori's participation in a deep web of corruption was disclosed, propelling his escape to Japan and subsequent resignation.

Fujimori's ten years in power were marked by the existence of an authoritarian regime, party system decomposition, a confrontation with the Shining Path that resulted in human rights abuses, and strong support until his government's collapse. All of these factors play against the expansion of nondiscretionary social policies for outsiders by suppressing democratic competition and the emergence of mobilization. In this context, Fujimori initiated rather small and selective targeted programs. He launched a social investment fund, Foncodes, which served as a tool to mobilize electoral support with politically targeted discretionary allocations (Roberts 1995; Schady 2000). Fujimori also launched some minor primary care initiatives, such as the Basic Health

Program for All (PSBT), which provided a small package of primary care services in low-income communities and a free health insurance plan for children in public schools (SEG). As analyzed by Ewig (2010), the PBS charged fees for services and used means testing to grant reduced fees or fee waivers. Each health care facility determined the eligibility criteria, which created discretion in implementation. On paper, the SEG was a broader scheme, exempting children in public schools from paying fees in public facilities. In 1998, the government further created a maternal and infant health insurance (SMI), whose funding and coverage proved negligible (see Ewig 2010).

With new elections celebrated in 2001, Alejandro Toledo (2001–6), a vocal opponent of Fujimori's reelection in 2000, won on the ticket of Peru Posible, a new improvised party (see Levitsky 2013). After the Valentín Paniagua caretaker administration merged the SMI and SEG, Toledo launched the Integrated Health Insurance (SIS) plan in his first year in office, extending free health care services to children, pregnant women, and indigent adults, and promising to reach 100 percent of those without coverage by the end of his tenure.[16] Although the SIS was initially small in scale, it represented a marked improvement compared to the previous neglect for decisive health care responses, as it enrolled about 24.2 percent of the outsider population by 2007.[17] Toledo also launched JUNTOS, a conditional cash transfer program for children in rural areas, which also reached a very small number of beneficiaries.

Why did Toledo not expand more benefits, given high growth rates averaging 5 percent during his tenure and a campaign based on a commitment to the poor and democratization? Toledo faced few incentives for expansion: he did not belong to an established party, there were no consecutive reelection provisions that could guarantee his continuity in power, and no large social movement demanded social policy expansion. Therefore, despite the existence of competition for outsiders in elections and the presence of nonconsecutive reelection, the conditions for creating large benefits, establishing the requisite funding, and embarking on implementation were seriously attenuated during his tenure. In fact, Toledo did try to benefit specific groups – such as shoe shiners – by expanding SIS initially on a group-by-group basis, probably to build more enduring organized support. In this context of attenuated incentives given the low prospects for tying benefits to a future nonconsecutive reelection, the

[16] "Anuncia presidente peruano SIS para los pobres," *El Comercio*, January 28, 2002.
[17] Calculated with data from Wilson, Velazquez and Ponce (2009: 209).

creation of smaller-scale innovations was the strategy he pursued to show concern for the poor but avoid committing his administration to launching the more dramatic reforms seen in other cases.

Former president García returned to power in 2006, winning the run-off election by a small margin against Humala, a left-wing former military member who campaigned on redistribution with a newly created party. In his tenure, García increased coverage of JUNTOS – which nonetheless remained very small – and initiated Gratitude, a pilot pension program for seniors seventy-five and older in extreme poverty that paid a very small benefit. These extremely modest initiatives contrast with the abundance of export resource wealth during García's tenure (see Cameron 2011; Figure 1.2).

García did implement a larger expansion of health care services by transforming SIS into a broader health system. In 2005, political activists and large NGOs promoted health policy expansion (see Ewig 2010: 185). As the presidential elections neared, domestic and international NGOs as well as think tanks led the formulation of the Political Agreement in Health,[18] in which political parties and presidential candidates agreed upon to expand health care services. According to Ewig, the Medical Association and other NGOs also advocated expansion and continued to lobby for it under García's administration (2010: 185). Despite not leading a broad movement, these actors could put the question of badly needed health care services – and the outstandingly low health care expenditures in Peru – on the candidates' agendas. In fact, politicians agreed on the goals of achieving universal coverage and increasing health care expenses to match the average level of expenditures in the region. In line with his campaign commitments, García promised to work on expanding health care coverage in his first address to Congress as president (Ewig 2010: 185). In 2009, Congress passed a law agreed to by all parties and initially sponsored by the APRA to guarantee health access and funding for every Peruvian, which permitted the SIS to reach between 40 percent and 50 percent of outsiders in 2010.[19] Given the institutional power of conservative politicians, and the absence of powerful social movements pressing for broader health care expansion, the resulting program was restrictive.

[18] See "El seguro universal en salud será tarea de nuevo régimen," *El Comercio*, May 16, 2006.
[19] Estimated with data from the national statistics agency INEI, and surveys it conducts: Essalud, and ENHAO.

Subsequent administrations featured similar dynamics of small improvements in existing benefits and the initiation of new, small-scale programs. After a tight race with Keiko Fujimori, who also campaigned on a non-institutionalized party, Humala won the runoff election in 2011. As García was barred from running a consecutive term, the APRA in turn did not field a candidate, but Toledo made an unsuccessful attempt at reelection. Both leading candidates made social policy promises in the campaign. While Humala promised to extend pensions to all low-income outsider seniors through Pension 65, Keiko Fujimori had a more conservative platform, pledging to expand JUNTOS.[20]

Although Peru at the time enjoyed high levels of economic growth, Humala's Pension 65, which was passed by decree in 2011 and reached 23 percent of outsider seniors in 2013 and 28 percent a year later, was important but not large in scale, reaching below the threshold here considered to be an expansion.[21] JUNTOS coverage also experienced a modest increase, from 12 percent to 17.5 percent of outsider children by 2013. The benefit levels of these two programs were very low. In 2013, JUNTOS provided an allowance equivalent to 11.4 percent of the basic basket for a household with two children, and the value of Pension 65 represented 30 percent of the minimum pension for formal-sector workers.[22]

Although one could argue that reaching more people would be too costly for a country with at least 70 percent of the population outside the formal labor market, other countries, such as Bolivia, with comparable outsider populations and levels of economic growth did embark on more generous expansion. The argument advanced in this book helps explain why incumbents did not embark decisively on expansion in Peru and why the modest initiatives accumulated in a piecemeal way, adding some small additional coverage and providing low levels of benefits over time. The only initiative amounting to an expansion was health care, which occurred when attenuated incentives of electoral competition and a social movement coalition that was much less powerful than the other SMCs analyzed in this book pressed for more decisive responses, collectively moving Peru's health care system past the threshold of expansion in the late 2000s.

---

[20] "El Debate Técnico," *El Comercio*, May 27, 2011.

[21] Estimated with data from JUNTOS (accessed December 2014), Pension 65 (accessed 2014), and INEI.

[22] The basic basket of food and services is the measure with which the poverty line is calculated. Estimates with data from JUNTOS, Pension 65, and INEI.

Uruguay: Electoral Competition, Social Mobilization, and Social Policy Expansion

Uruguay offers a contrasting example of high party system institution-alization and of probably the strongest democracy – and democratic record – among higher middle-income countries in the region, thus serving as a good case to assess the applicability of the argument advanced in this book. It specifically helps us to identify the factors that lead incumbents in a strong democratic regime to decide to expand social policy for outsiders.

Together with Chile during the period under examination, Uruguay had one of the most institutionalized, programmatic party systems in Latin America (Mainwaring 1999; see Luna 2014). Similar to Argentina and Chile, in Uruguay outsiders represented 40 percent and 45 percent of the total population. Historically, Uruguay developed a broad system of social protection with some public health services available to the poor and pensions reaching low-income outsider seniors over sixty-nine. After the return of democracy in 1985, expansion in Uruguay began in the late 1990s when competition for low-income voters intensified with the rise of the left-wing Broad Front (FA), and incumbents launched child allowances. When the FA took power, it expanded protections across policy areas and developed an inclusive policy model.

At first glance, as traced later, the argument developed in this book helps account for these innovations. While electoral competition for outsiders triggered expansion in all of these different moments, the model adopted varied according to whether conservative politicians designed these innovations, which resulted in largely restrictive benefits, and whether labor unions and social organizations linked to the FA participated actively in policy making, which resulted in the adoption of inclusive programs. Despite the similarities with Chile's party system generally highlighted in the literature, Uruguay developed more comprehensive, inclusive programs for outsiders across selected policy areas comparable to those of Argentina and Brazil.[23]

The Broad Front (FA) party's victory in 2004 ended the electoral dominance by the traditional Colorado (PC) and Blanco (PB) parties since the nineteenth century (Luna 2007: 1). These were two "elite parties" that cleaved the electorate vertically, mobilizing voters across social classes (Collier and Collier 1991; Lanzaro 2004; Roberts 2002: 12). Historically,

---

[23] On variation in policy models between Chile and Uruguay, see Pribble and Huber (2011) and Pribble (2013).

the labor movement was not organizationally linked with either of these parties and was not a stable partner in governing coalitions, although working-class voters tended to support the Colorados (Collier and Collier 1991). The National Party, or Blancos, in turn, particularly mobilized voters in rural areas. Both of these parties were highly fragmented organizations and were tied to constituencies through clientelistic arrangements (see Collier and Collier 1991: 125). Until the late 1950s, the Colorados had a dominant position, which reflected low levels of interparty competition for outsider voters.

In the 1960s and 1970s, new political forces challenged this stable party system. At a time when labor conflict escalated and a guerrilla movement formed (Collier and Collier 1991: 640–1), small left-wing parties without previous significant electoral support (the Communist Party, Socialist Party, and Christian Democratic Party) formed the FA and made an important showing in the 1971 presidential elections (Lanzaro 2004: 36; Luna 2007: 5). A conservative military coup in 1973 interrupted these transformations. With the restoration of democracy in 1985, the Colorados won the first presidential election, and the FA began to amass a larger electorate, appealing to middle- and working-class voters, and seeking to reach low-income outsiders historically mobilized by traditional parties especially the Colorado Party in urban areas (see Lanzaro 2004; Luna 2007: 5).

Social policy expansion began during this period of electoral growth for the FA. After coming to power in an extremely tight election, in which it defeated the incumbent Blanco party, the administration of Julio Sanguinetti (1995–2000) of the Colorado Party initiated a transformation of family allowances for formal workers first and an expansion for outsiders at the end of his tenure.[24] Early in 1995, it doubled the value of the allowances received by low-income formal-sector workers and capped access to exclude high-income workers. An expansion for outsiders was approved in July 1999, a few months before the October presidential elections. Family allowances that previously reached only formal-sector workers were extended to all children in households with incomes up to three times the minimum wage that were headed by a single female adult or an unemployed male or in which there was a pregnant woman. This program reached only 37 percent of low-income outsider children with a small benefit that was half of that low-income formal workers received, and had no social participation in implementation.[25] It

---

[24] At the time presidential elections were won by a simple plurality.
[25] Estimated with data from Caristo (2005).

was thus a restrictive program as here defined. The government launched this expansion to curb the momentum of the rising FA, which had not only grown significantly in urban areas, but had also expanded its reach among the poor in the interior of the country in the late 1990s.[26]

Competition intensified in 1999. The FA won the first round with 40 percent to 32.8 percent against the Colorado candidate, Jorge Battle, but the latter ultimately won the presidency in the second round, with the support of the Blancos.[27] The newly created majority runoff system was used for the first time in 1999 and, according to Luna (2014), was adopted precisely to prevent the rising FA from displacing traditional parties, which were ready to form a coalition with the goal of preserving power. This election featured high competition for outsiders, as polls show low-income voters reporting their intention to support the three parties in almost equal shares (see Moreira 2004: 50). The composition of Congress also began to change; in the lower chamber the FA became the largest party with about 45 percent of the legislators, compared to 55 percent from the Colorados and Blancos together. It was also the largest party in the Senate with close to 40 percent of the senators, but Colorados and Blancos together had a legislative majority.

In 2004, the Batlle administration (2000–5) initiated a much more significant expansion as the presidential election drew near. Electoral competition for outsider voters had increased dramatically, with the rising FA severely threatening the Colorado Party's hold on power. In 2003, the executive submitted a bill to Congress for a more significant expansion of family allowances in order to offset the FA's appeal among outsiders. This new expansion targeted low-income children who remained unprotected, about 62.8 percent of total children aged eighteen and younger in households with incomes below three times the minimum wage and who were not covered by the previous expansion in 1999.[28]

Opposition parties in Congress suspected that the initiative was motivated by electoral concerns and noted that the Colorado Party had dismissed similar proposals submitted by the FA to expand these benefits since 2001.[29] Congress nonetheless supported the proposal. As summarized by a legislator of the FA, "Is this initiative electoral? Is this motivated

---

[26] On the FA and its electoral evolution, see Luna (2007: 7–8; 2014).

[27] Blancos obtained 22 percent and Colorados 32.8 percent of the vote in the first-round election.

[28] Estimated with data from Caristo (2005).

[29] Legislator Pablo Mieres (Independent Party), Cámara de Representantes, December 30, 2003.

by awareness of a social problem? If these are the questions, then let's support the measure and hold the government accountable..."[30]

The timing of this expansion is important for two reasons. First, the initiative was launched right before the elections and after virtually no innovations during the Batlle administration. Legislators of the Colorado Party emphasized that the executive wanted a speedy implementation, which indicates the president's electoral concerns.[31] Second, Uruguay experienced a recession following Brazil's currency devaluation in 1999 and a dramatic financial collapse after the Argentine economic crisis in 2002.[32] Unemployment grew in 2002 to levels comparable to those of Argentina at the time (see MIDES 2009). Despite these dire economic circumstances, the incumbent party considered social policy innovations only in the face of the highly competitive elections of 2004. With this expansion, family allowances reached at least 80 percent of low-income outsider children.[33] However, these allowances provided only half of what formal low-income workers received, and the program did not include participation in implementation (see Caristo 2005).

The 2004 elections marked the victory of FA candidate Tabaré Vázquez and a dramatic collapse of support for the Colorado Party, which obtained a historic low of 10 percent. Aside from winning in the first round, the FA amassed a legislative majority, which no party had attained since 1985 (Luna 2007: 1). In office, the Vázquez administration (2005–10) created the Ministry of Social Development (MIDES) and launched the emergency plan PANES in 2005, which provided food support and monetary transfers to households below the extreme poverty line.[34] In 2007, the government designed the Social Equity Program (PES), a more institutionalized plan to fight poverty. The PES entailed a battery of innovations, such as improvement of the family allowances program, which was already broad-reaching but provided small benefits; the creation of the National Integrated Health System (SNI) to improve access to health insurance among children, which was approved in 2008; and a 30 percent increase in the number of noncontributory pensioners, with the extension of the benefit to low-income people aged sixty-five and older in poverty.[35]

---

[30] Legislator Brum Canet (FA), Cámara de Representantes, December 30, 2003: 67.
[31] Cámara de Representantes, December 30, 2003: 67.
[32] On the effects of the Brazilian and Argentine economies on Uruguay, see the discussion in Castiglioni (2010).
[33] This includes 80 percent of all outsider children in households with earnings below three times the minimum wage.
[34] See Arim, Cruces, and Vigorito (2009) and MIDES (2009).
[35] This benefit existed for people aged seventy and older.

The FA, moreover, set up participatory roundtables with social organizations and labor unions to discuss these initiatives. It opened up spaces of deliberation about pension reforms with pensioner associations and included social organizations in permanent channels of consultation, at both the local and national levels.[36] These initiatives corresponded with Vázquez's participatory policy making approach as mayor of Montevideo (see Goldfrank 2007). More particularly, the design of these new programs was influenced by allied social movements, such as the Movement for Popular Participation, labor unions, and social organizations who could access decision-making venues also through the party. These movements were not powerful enough to propel expansion on their own, but they could and did influence the shape of the resulting programs under Vázquez.

Acknowledging that further research is necessary to explore the process of policy making and the resulting policies in greater detail, a brief period of initially restrictive innovations occurred under the Colorado governments in 1999 and 2004, though only in one policy area, that of family allowances, propelled by electoral competition for outsider voters. The 1999 expansion of family allowances neatly fits the characterization of restrictive benefits, but the 2004 innovation had a broader reach, though its benefits were smaller in scale and no social movements participated in the policy design or implementation. Yet, taken together, the initiatives for outsiders were still limited during this period; there had been no improvements in noncontributory pensions – which reached seniors over seventy years of age only – or health care services, despite the harsh economic environment of the early 2000s.

The arrival of the FA to power in the context of intense electoral competition for outsiders led to the creation of inclusive social policies. Under the Vázquez administration, the left-wing FA had a majority in Congress and opened up channels for consultation and participation with social organizations allied to the party, which influenced the social policy model adopted. As a result of these innovations, family allowances achieved a slightly broader coverage of outsider children with benefits comparable to those of low-income formal-sector workers, pensions were extended to virtually all seniors over sixty-four years of age, and access to health services was expanded and improved.[37] Social policies also incorporated

---

[36] For example, the National Dialogue on Social Security was a channel for discussing reforms to the social security system. See MIDES (2009) and MPP n/d.

[37] See Arim et al. (2009). Data on Pensions from Pereira (2010) and on family allowances from Caristo (2008).

participatory mechanisms in policy implementation advocated by social movements and labor unions. The formation of councils such as the National Board of Health (JUNASA) accompanied the expansion of the health care system and included labor unions, organizations of users of health care services, and participatory health councils. The implementation of income programs, such as PANES and PES, also entailed social participation, and social organizations formed local councils in order to foster policy deliberation and oversight of the programs launched by the MIDES (Movimiento de Participación Popular n/d: 6; MIDES 2009). In 2009, there were twenty-two social councils – one per district – and thirty-one councils in small localities, with about 280 community associations participating (MIDES 2009).

South Africa: Mobilization from Below and Social Policy Expansion

Does the argument presented here travel beyond Latin America? Despite differences in colonization, a history of exclusionary racial institutions, and a parliamentary as opposed to the presidential systems of Latin America, similarities in terms of high inequality, insider-outsider cleavages, and recent democratization make South Africa a good and challenging case for this book's theory.

Reversing the absence of significant social policy innovations immediately following the new democracy in 1995, South Africa's government expanded transfers for children in the 2000s. The adoption of broad-reaching child allowances was propelled by a coalition of social movements and labor unions (SMC) that pressed for a basic income grant (BIG) in the face of extremely high unemployment and poverty (see Makino 2004; Seekings and Nattrass 2005: 364). Despite the fact that outsiders have been loyal supporters of the African National Congress (ANC), it was only under social movement pressures that the government initiated the expansion of a small preexisting benefit, expanding the Child Support Grant (CSG).

The African National Congress has governed South Africa since the end of the apartheid system. Allied to the Congress of South African Trade Unions (COSATU), the party has won by a landslide with more than 60 percent of the vote in every parliamentary election since 1994. The vast majority of low-income voters in South Africa strongly support the ANC. The second-largest party for most of this period, the Democratic Alliance (DA), is a conservative coalition that obtained a maximum vote share of 16 percent in the 2009 election and has a core constituency within the economic elite.[38] Although the DA's support for broader social policies (see Makino 2004: 28) raised concerns from the ANC and the COSATU about the DA's "attempts to woo voters" in "disadvantaged communities," it did not gain support to the point of becoming a credible challenger competing for the vote of outsiders.[39]

In the new democracy, the ANC faced high unemployment – which hovered between 20 percent and 30 percent of the economically active population[40] in the 1990s and 2000s – as well as weak social infrastructure, especially for providing health care services.[41] Although pensions reached low-income seniors broadly, as discussed later, there were no meaningful benefits for low-income families. In 2009, informal-sector workers, the unemployed, and home and agricultural laborers represented 47 percent of the total workforce.[42]

Upon taking power, the ANC set up the Lund Committee to analyze existing social assistance programs and provide advice for future reforms. This committee proposed the replacement of a preexisting child support benefit for single parents with a cash grant for all low-income children up to nine years of age conditional on health checkups in 1997. The proposed grant would provide a lower benefit level but reach a much larger number of households (see Lund 2008).

Community associations, NGOs, and the COSATU were not satisfied with the recommendations of the Lund Committee (Lund 2008: 91). NGOs put pressure on the government to increase the benefit level, and they demanded participation in decision making (Lund 2008: 103–4). After setting up hearings and meetings with NGOs, the government increased the benefit level and included social organizations in the implementation and monitoring of the Child Support Grant (CSG), which began in 1998 (see Lund 2008: 104–5). As the take-up rate of the allowance grew slowly due to complicated registration procedures (Makino 2004: 22), social movements pressed for further changes to the program.

---

[38] Data from the Electoral Commission of South Africa (accessed May 2012).
[39] COSATU (2003: 5) documents are available at www.cosatu.org.za (accessed May 2010).
[40] ILO employment database (accessed May 2012). See also Seekings and Nattrass (2005).
[41] Mayosi and Benatar (2014:1346). Immunization data, which is often taken as a measure of state capacity, as well as infant mortality rates, are also used to make this claim. Data from World Health Organization (WHO) (www.who.org accessed May 2012).
[42] Author's estimates with data from International Labor Organization (ILO) Database (www.ilo.org accessed May 2012) and Statistics South Africa's (StatsSA) Statistical Release (2011) and Quarterly Labor Force Survey (2011). Unfortunately I do not have more precise data on the share of outsiders within the population.

The COSATU, a coalition of NGOs, and social movements joined forces to form the BIG coalition, advocating the creation of a universal basic income grant (BIG). The coalition finalized the BIG proposal in 1998 and the COSATU included it in its platform in 2000. By 2002, a large number of NGOs, human rights organizations, and the South African Council of Churches lobbied for BIG's adoption (Makino 2004: 18). In response, the government set up a new committee – the Taylor Committee – that proposed the adoption of BIG and presented it as a constitutional obligation of the state (see BIG coalition 2002; Reports of Taylor Committee 2002).[43] Despite support from the Taylor Committee, the government refused to create a basic income grant, which propelled campaigns and protests in favor of the proposal (Makino 2004: 18).

The ANC government responded to these pressures by extending the CSG to children up to age fourteen and then to eighteen years of age in 2008. It also launched a broad registration campaign, with the support of NGOs, to reach the eligible population. Coverage increased substantially. From 2002 to 2009, it jumped from 2 million to more than 9 million children, representing about 47 percent of the total children in the country, likely covering the vast majority of outsider children.[44] As here measured, the value of the CSG for a household with two children was high. In 2010, it represented 30 percent of the average wage of the country's 25 percent lower-income wage earners and 40.6 percent of the minimum wage for farm workers.[45]

Pensions were already available for low-income outsider seniors before the democratic transition. In 1944, South Africa established a means-tested noncontributory pension that reached low-income beneficiaries of all races but paid blacks with a substantially smaller allowance (Sagner 2000: 535; Seekings 2000. Under apartheid, labor and social policies were racially biased. Starting in the 1970s, disparities in benefit levels of noncontributory pensions began to shrink until their eventual elimination. On the eve of the democratic transition in 1993, benefit levels were set to be equal for all (Seekings and Nattrass 2005: 341).

---

[43] Materials of the BIG coalition submitted to the Taylor Committee, available from http://www.sacc-ct.org.za/BIGCoal.html.

[44] Coverage from SASSA (2009). Estimated with population data from South Africa's statistics agency, StatsSA (www.statssa.gov.za).

[45] Despite the fact that South Africa has low wages for low-skilled workers, the idea is to see how the benefits compare to other forms of income. Data from StatsSA (www.statssa.gov.za accessed 2014) and DSD-SASSA-UNICEF (2012).

According to Seekings (2000), these pensions were originally introduced at a time of welfare expansion in which radical liberals, inspired by welfare developments in postwar Europe, pursued universal policies. Comparable proposals, including universal health care services, were advanced at the time but not approved. Old-age noncontributory pensions have constituted an important form of redistribution from wealthier taxpayers to the poor, positively affecting the welfare of seniors and of children in households with senior members (see Seekings 2007). The value of the old-age pension was relatively high. In 2010, it represented almost 100 percent of the minimum wage for farm workers, and 80 percent of the average wage of the country's bottom 25 percent of wage earners.[46]

In contrast with the provision of old-age pensions – whose expansion predated the new democracy – and the child grant, health care services did not see significant innovations since the democratic transition until 2010, the end of the period under examination. This is observable in high and stagnant infant mortality rates between 1994 and 2010 – especially compared to the other countries under investigation – low child immunization rates, and the high prevalence of HIV and tuberculosis (Mayosi and Benatar 2014).[47] Although the right to health care was established in the constitution and health care services were made free for mothers and children, the implementation of these innovations was limited, especially in low-income areas. Aside from spending cuts in the late 1990s, health care scholars have attributed this to the "infrastructure-inequality trap" by which health care funds are allocated in South Africa according to output and thereby benefit areas with more developed infrastructure. This pattern of resource allocation, which is common in other developing, highly unequal countries, and has in part perpetuated pre-apartheid inequalities in South Africa (Stuckler, Basu and Mckee 2011), was one of the key issues Brazilian activists fought against in the 1990s, especially under the Collor government, as discussed in Chapter 4.

At first glance, this book's theoretical framework helps account for the evolution of social policy initiatives by the national government in South Africa since the installation of democracy in 1994. The ANC, an undeniable promoter of excluded interests in South Africa, did not proactively launch social policy for outsiders. During the period under examination,

---

[46] Calculated with data from Sassa (www.ssasa.gov.za) and StatsSA, monthly earnings release available at www.statssa.gov.za.

[47] Data from WHO's database (accessed May 2012).

electoral competition for outsider voters as it is here defined was not present. Incumbents in South Africa initiated social policy expansion as a response to pressure from below around concrete social policy demands posed by a coalition of social movements and labor unions, some of which are allied to the ANC. As expected in this book's analytical argument, it is likely that without such pressures, income transfers would have not reached a meaningful number of beneficiaries with high allowances and involving NGOs and social movements in implementation.

8.3 THEORETICAL IMPLICATIONS

Democratic Politics and Social Policy Expansion

One of the main implications of this study concerns the importance of democratic politics for the creation of large-scale, nondiscretionary social policies for outsiders in middle-income countries of Latin America. The role of democracy deserves particular attention because earlier literature has suggested that democracies in Latin America did not provide the requisite environment for social policy expansion.[48] While it is true that democratic governance alone is not enough to motivate incumbents to expand social policy, this study identifies additional factors that are likely to yield expansion in middle-income democracies: the presence of high electoral competition for outsiders and/or large-scale social mobilization pressing the state for benefits, which rarely emerge or grow in authoritarian regimes. When some meaningful level of electoral competition or social mobilization does emerge within authoritarian regimes, these factors do not yield the same kind of broad-reaching, stable, nondiscretionary social policy responses.

A broad comparative literature has addressed whether democracies or authoritarian regimes have greater welfare effects. Because democratic regimes treat citizens as political equals, they are expected to provide greater opportunity for citizen influence on public policy; therefore, democracies should be relatively more welfare-enhancing political systems. However, the empirical association between democracy and redistribution or the welfare effects of democracy is far from settled within the literature. While democracy is more prevalent than authoritarianism among more equal countries (see Boix 2003; Haggard and Kaufman 2012), the effects of political regime on social service provision and welfare outcomes remain subject to debate (Lake and Baum 2001; Mulligan

[48] For example, see Weyland (1996a).

et al. 2004; Ross 2006). Scholars found that democracies are less likely to reduce social spending during economic slowdowns (Brown and Hunter 1999) and tend to produce better welfare outcomes (Lake and Baum 2001). Lake and Baum's comprehensive analysis (2001) found a battery of social improvements associated with democracy (e.g., higher literacy, access to running water, and lower infant mortality rates). Focusing on infant mortality rates, Ross by contrast has found that infants, the most vulnerable population, do not fare better in democratic regimes as compared to authoritarian ones (Ross 2006).

A number of elements have been identified as accounting for the dissonance across these studies. Measurement problems undermine several large-N analyses due to the unavailability of good comparable measures. Furthermore, quantitative studies have sometimes had a hard time identifying *who* benefits from social expenditure as well as establishing the causal mechanisms accounting for the posited relationship between regime type and welfare.

The theoretical framework of this book seeks to contribute to this debate by identifying the circumstances under which incumbents in democracies invest in welfare policies that reach those historically excluded from social protection in Latin America. When incumbents compete intensely for the vote of outsiders, and when they face large-scale mobilization for social policy expansion, they are likely to respond with broad-based benefits and services. The new enfranchisement of outsiders in some countries and the emergence of electoral competition for their votes in democratic regimes have increased outsiders' political relevance. Social mobilization has moreover placed crucial issues on the public agenda, leading governments concerned about stability and their popularity to address demands. Critical institutional dimensions of a political regime long highlighted by Robert Dahl – the level of inclusiveness and of public contestation – thus foster, though do not determine, the emergence of more extensive party competition and social mobilization that may lead governments to become responsive to their low-income citizens (see Dahl 1971).

Authoritarian regimes may in turn appear responsive to outsiders by creating policies that reach them. Even if these policies may positively affect welfare outcomes, this study has found that within the main cases investigated, such interventions are more likely to be selective, unstable, or temporary. Authoritarian regimes have lacked the stable commitment to outsiders' welfare that democracies were able to develop under propitious political circumstances. They may expand in the face of mobilization for social provisions or in the face of a challenger seeking office. But these benefits, as noted, are likely to be selective, temporary, or small in scale. Authoritarian incumbents have a large menu of tools at their disposal to deal with competition and social mobilization, including repression, intimidation, and institutional changes that bias electoral results and make mobilization less likely. It is only under democratic regimes facing electoral competition for outsiders and/or mobilization from below that incumbents have incentives to adopt and implement stable, large-scale, and nondiscretionary policies reaching this sector.

Social Mobilization and Insider–Outsider Coalitions

Another major implication of this study concerns the importance of social mobilization on two fundamental questions: a) the creation of broader and participatory social policies, and b) for understanding the reactions of labor unions vis-à-vis social policy expansion for outsiders. Regarding the first question, in the cases in which social mobilization emerged, notably Argentina and Brazil, large and coordinated movements included alliances between organizations representing outsiders and labor unions, which pressed for the creation of inclusive policies. Although the literature generally views outsiders as unable to advance their own interests, achieve state concessions, or form insider–outsider alliances, social mobilization within these cases has been able to propel the adoption of large-scale policy initiatives.

Social movement leaders advocating social policy expansion have not simply acted out of self-serving interests or to seek clientelistic exchanges with the state, extracting resources for their organizations. On the contrary, they promoted universal nondiscretionary policies in part out of fear that the new schemes would be manipulated. Several of the individual organizations in these movements had indeed emerged or engaged in coordinated action in part with the goal to challenge existing clientelistic arrangements that either excluded or manipulated their (members') access to benefits. Institutionalized social policies were perceived to more effectively prevent partisan machines from capturing policy benefits while excluding social movement members. Social movements generally demanded participation in implementation with the goal of perpetuating their influence and ensuring oversight over policy implementation. The involvement of social movements in policy design represents the main reason for the creation of inclusive policies in Argentina and Brazil.

Several groups did receive programs that provide selective benefits, which are fundamental for organizations to grow as well as to retain members. Club goods help organizations consolidate and remain a meaningful presence in members' lives, especially when their main social policy agenda regarding policy expansion has been addressed, as it was the case with several of the social movements studied here. Keeping membership alive was often made easier by the administration of smaller, more selective programs, such as support for microenterprises, funding for education programs, and housing projects.

Labor unions that formed part of these coalitions viewed cross-sectoral alliances as an opportunity to grow, represent a broader workers' movement, and extend their influence to advance their own agendas. A social policy agenda promoting universal benefits facilitated labor unions' redefinition of who they represented and what they advocated, and helped consolidate labor unions' alliances with organizations of outsiders. Instead of representing the worker, as a leader of Brazil's Unified Workers' Central (CUT) argued, social movement unions tried to represent citizens, and instead of wages, they also sought to discuss income. A shift in focus from workers' wages and working conditions to citizens' income formed part of the transformation that these labor organizations underwent more or less successfully in their struggle to join with broader forces for social change and to pursue their own agenda. Divisions within union movements had deepened before these alliances were formed, separating those unions that remained tied to old forms of representation and new ones that clearly identified with a broader set of demands and causes, and joined social movements.

A critical, and second question to highlight, is that beyond the transformation that social movement unions experienced and their ties with a broader universe of associations, this study has shown that labor unions historically did not proactively block initiatives to cater to outsiders within selected policy areas and country cases. The empirical record of the cases analyzed in selected policy areas contradicts a literature that views unions as preventing the expansion of social policy for outsiders. Rather than simply opposing policies for outsiders, unions typically adopt one of three positions: (a) *opposition* to expansion if this entails reductions in existing benefits for formal workers; (b) *indifference* to expansion if measures do not imply any tangible immediate reduction of benefits for union affiliates, even if expansion may involve cross-subsidizing provisions for outsiders; and (c) *support for expansion* if they are allied with the movements promoting it. Among the examined countries, unions in Argentina in 2001 opposed an attempt by de la Rúa's government to eliminate family allowances for formal workers earning more than three minimum wages and reallocate funds to family allowances targeted to low-income outsiders. Examples of the second strategy include the indifference of the Argentine labor movement affiliated with the powerful General Confederation of Labor (CGT), the business unions, to the creation of pensions and family allowances for outsiders funded with payroll contributions of formal workers in 2006 and 2009, respectively. Finally, instances in which labor unions have supported the creation of benefits for outsiders include most of the policies inaugurated in Argentina and Brazil, which were supported by unions affiliated with the CUT in Brazil in the 1980s and 1990s, and with the CTA in Argentina, which are social movement unions.

At a more general level, the coalitions of insiders and outsiders and their impact on social policy in Latin America provide interesting insights about diverging modes of interest representation within the region. In the cases of Argentina and Brazil, the interests of outsiders are being expressed not exclusively in the electoral arena, but also through institutionalized spaces of organized influence within the state. This has important ramifications for the evolution of these new policies and for politics cross-nationally. Specifically, in line with studies of institutional evolution and change (Pierson 2004; Thelen 2004), we can expect institutionalized participation to increase the difficulty of scaling back these policies and to speed up the pace of welfare expansion. The presence of organized participation within the state, and the pace of welfare reform over the past decades, suggests that the inclusive model may become a site of greater experimentation and policy innovation in the coming years. At the same time, the creation of institutionalized spaces of organized representation for outsiders may further strengthen these organizations and potentially affect the coalition bases of future political parties and party systems in fundamental ways.

The restrictive model in turn will probably face pressure to expand benefits, as many outsiders still remain unprotected. The question of expanding coverage and benefit levels in outsider policies – which are lower than those provided by insider policies – may emerge as an important theme in the public debate.

Nondiscretionary Benefits and Clientelism

This study also speaks to the literature on clientelism, which figures prominently in the research agenda on Latin American politics and social policy.[49] The party systems in the countries analyzed here, with

---

[49] See Kurtz (2004a) and Weyland (1996a), as well as Kitschelt and Wilkinson (2007) and Stokes (2005).

the exception of Chile since the 1990s, have been considered exemplars of political clientelism and state patronage. Yet the large-scale policies inaugurated for outsiders in all of the cases established clear eligibility rules and were implemented in ways that explicitly sought to prevent the manipulation of benefits, even if some abuses initially existed. This is striking given the pervasive view in the literature that non-machine parties are the only ones capable of creating such policies.

The argument advanced in this study to explain nondiscretionary expansion contributes to the literature on clientelism in two ways. First, it helps identify the conditions under which institutionalized policies, rather than clientelistic provisions, are created for low-income populations. These conditions include the presence of intense competition for outsider voters and large-scale mobilization from below demanding social benefits. As discussed in the empirical chapters of this book, social movements demanded expansion despite the presence of clientelism (and often to avoid clientelism). These movements, as well as politicians facing intense electoral competition and incumbents concerned with their parties' continuity in office, strove to enact policies with institutional features that could minimize abuses. Under these conditions of intense competition and mobilization from below, the manipulation of social benefits was perceived as detrimental to the strategic interests of the actors involved in the process of social policy expansion.

Second, the argument in this book also contributes to a recent debate on the effects of quality of government – understood as impartiality in the use of public power – on social policy expansion (Rothstein 2011: 129). According to recent work by Bo Rothstein, we should not expect proposals for social policy expansion to have broad appeal in countries with high levels of clientelism and corruption (Rothstein 2011: 128–9). As Rothstein suggests, perceptions about the competence and trustworthiness of institutions in charge of implementing policies affect individuals' expectations and support for expansion. This study shows, by contrast, that quality of government is not exogenous to the process of expansion, but rather an outcome of the strategic interests of the actors involved in the creation of new policies.

Despite perceptions in public opinion that corruption permeates several states of Latin America, social movements have pushed for expansion, and citizens have often supported the new benefits established. This process resonates with Peter Evans' conceptualization of state capacity for economic development as uneven within "intermediary states." Intermediary states lack the capacity to launch comprehensive projects for economic development, but they have not succumbed to the disorganizing logic of predatory states, which plunder society and cannot advance a minimal agenda for collective interests. Intermediary states, by contrast, possess some highly capable and autonomous agencies that can operate competently within a sea of clientelism, so long as politicians are interested in retaining these agencies (see Evans 1995). Thus, the creation of these large-scale policies does not presume the complete absence or elimination of clientelism. Similarly, this study recognizes the obstacles clientelism creates for the development of rule-based and universal policies, but highlights specific political dynamics and strategies that lead incumbents to launch large-scale social policy expansion and strategically avoid abuses and discretion within these programs. As one leading Mexican politician noted in Chapter 7, discretion in these types of programs "can be your worst enemy," as it thwarts the goals incumbents seek to achieve with large-scale expansion.

Appendix 1

Measuring Outsiders, Social Policy, and Data Sources

To measure outsiders (Figure 1.4), I estimate the share of the population without social security.

For **Argentina**, I use census data of the population without social security health insurance (years 1991, 2001, 2010). For earlier decades, I employ figures from Feldman et al. (1988) for 1940 and 1950. For 1970 and 1980, I use estimates of health coverage from Neri (1982).

For **Brazil**, I use information on workers with social security contributions from the *Anuário Estatístco* from IBGE (several years since the 1960s). I also estimate the share of the population sixty-five and older without pensions with data from IBGE and *Anuário Estatístico da Previdência Social*, several editions from 1980–2008, Ministério da Previdência e Assistência Social, and Ministério da Previdência Social.

For **Chile**, I use data of the economically active population with social security contributions. Historical data come from Mesa-Lago (1978) and from Arellano, José Pablo.1989. "La Seguridad Social en Chile en los 90s," *Colección Estudios CIEPLAN* 27. Santiago de Chile: CIEPLAN; as well as government sources of the Institute of Social Security (INP), MIDEPLAN and the Consejo Asesor de la Reforma Previsional (2006).

For **Mexico**, I use information from Zorrilla Arenas (1988) and historical statistics from INEGI. For 2000 and 2010, I referenced INEGI census data of population and social security health coverage.

MEASURING SOCIAL POLICY

Scope of Coverage

Share of outsider population that receives social benefits or health services. Pensions: outsiders sixty-five and older; Income transfers: outsider school-aged children (children without social security health insurance); Health care: all outsiders. When I do not have the exact number of children without social security coverage, I estimate it with population data and the size of the outsider population overall.

The scope of coverage is **high** if it reaches at least 70 percent of the relevant outsider population; **moderate** if it reaches between more than 50 and less than 70 percent of the relevant population; **low** if it reaches between 35 and 50 percent of the relevant outsider population. Note that programs that cover less than 35 percent of the outsider population are not considered "expansions."

With regards to health care, if beneficiaries who are not in extreme poverty have to make insurance payments and/or copayments for all or some treatments, coverage is moderate or low depending on what proportion of this population the program enrolls for free. Copayments and premiums are here considered barriers to access.

Benefit Level

Pensions. Benefit level is **high** if equal or similar (above 75 percent) to the low-income informal sector benefit, such as the minimum pension. It is **moderate** if it is between 50–75 percent of the minimum pension, and **low** if it is below 50 percent of the minimum pension.

Income Support. I measure the average benefit of families with two children. **High:** at least 20 percent of the poverty line; **Moderate:** between 10 and less than 20 percent of the poverty line; **Low:** below 10 percent of the poverty line for such family.

Health Care. High: Comprehensive coverage of hospital services, including high-complexity operations. **Moderate:** coverage of hospital services but exclusion of some interventions and presence of important copayments and fees. **Limited:** coverage of hospital services but exclusion of significant interventions and presence of relevant copayments and fees.

Participation

Inclusion in national and/or local-level policy councils, policy boards, advisory boards, and/or information campaigns involved in implementation.

Participation is:

High if the participatory arrangement is a requisite for the policy to start rolling, it is a permanent structure, and it has to produce some output (i.e., oversight report).

Moderate if the council does operate and meets frequently but does not fulfill one of the foregoing conditions (to be a requisite for the implementation of the policy, to be a permanent structure, and to produce an output).

Low if the policy is an informal (even if active) or ceremonial arrangement that meets infrequently.

No Participation: no participatory arrangements in place, even if they are included in legislation.

MEASURING POLICY MODELS

A policy is:

Inclusive if the scope of coverage and benefit level are high or moderate with one being high, and has some level of participation in implementation.

Restrictive if the scope of coverage and benefit level are moderate or low, and has no participation in implementation.

Models are:

Inclusive if the majority of the policies at a given time are inclusive.
Restrictive if the majority of the policies at a given time are restrictive.

DATA SOURCES

Pensions

Pension Coverage

Argentina. Estimates built with pension data from Cipoletta and Archaga (1997) for 1990; *Informe de la Seguridad Social* (several years), *Panorama de la Seguridad Social* (several years), *Boletín Estadístico de la Secretaría de Seguridad Social* (several years) all from the Ministerio de Trabajo, Empleo y Seguridad Social (MTEySS), as well as documents from provincial pension funds (Buenos Aires, Santa Fe, and Córdoba). Population data from INDEC (www.indec.gov.ar). I also contrasted my data with data of total pension coverage (1990–2006) estimated by social security expert Carlos Gruska.

Brazil. Estimates built with data from *Anuario Estatístico da Previdência Social*, Ministério da Previdência e Assistência Social and Ministério da Previdência Social (several years). Estimates of total pension coverage available for some years (contributory and noncontributory benefits) from the statistics institute, IBGE. Population data also from IBGE (www.ibge.gov.br).

Chile. Estimates built with pension data from MIDEPLAN (2006, 2013), and *Anuario Estadístico* from Instituto de Normalización Previsional and Instituto de Previsión Social. Population data from the statistics agency INE (www.ine.cl).

Mexico. Estimates built with data of pension benefits from the Secretariat of Social Development, population data from INEGI (www.inegi.gov.mx) and from CONEVAL (www.coneval.gov .mex).

Benefit Levels/Implementation

I used the same sources as well as government documents and legislation. I complemented those data with information from newspapers clippings and interviews.

Income Support

Coverage of Income Support Schemes

Argentina. Data on workfare and employment programs as well as on the AUH was provided by the Ministry of Labor. Data for some years is available from *Estadísticas laborales* of the MTEySS. Data on *Familias por la inclusion social* provided by Ministry of Social Development. Population Data from INDEC (www.indec .gov.ar)

Brazil. Estimates built with data on transfers provided by the Secretariat of Evaluation of the Ministry of Social Development (MDS) from

2002–6. For 2007–10, data from documents of the MDS (www .mds.gov.br). Population data from IBGE.

Chile. Estimates built with data from *Anuario Estadístico*, Instituto de Previsión Social (2000–10), MIDEPLAN and Superintendencia de Seguridad Social (1984–99). Population data from INE (www .ine.cl).

Mexico. Estimates built with data on Progresa-Oportunidades from the Secretariat of Social Development, available at www.sedesol .gov.mx and from Levy (2006). Population data from INEGI (www .inegi.gov.mx)

Benefit Levels/Implementation

I consulted the same sources as well as government documents and legislation. I complemented those data with information from newspapers and interviews.

Health Care

Coverage/Benefit Levels/Implementation

To characterize health care policy, I consulted the secondary literature, gathered information in interviews, and used data from the following sources:

Argentina. Information provided by Ministry of Health on Remediar and Plan Federal de Salud. See Ministerio de Salud (2006), and *Boletín Remediar* (several editions) available at www.remediar .gov.ar.

Brazil. Documents from Ministry of Health on SUS. See Ministério da Saúde (2009).

Chile. AUGE's legislation and statistical information on FONASA's coverage and services available at (www.fonasa.cl).

Mexico. Information from Secretaría de Salud, *Informes de avance del Seguro Popular* (several years), CONEVAL and INEGI.

Measuring Outsiders in Latin America

The estimated size of the outsider population in middle-income countries of Latin America in the 1990s, which is mentioned in Chapter 1, is calculated with data of social security health coverage that comes from different government sources.

Bolivia: social security coverage in the 1990s available from the Instituto Nacional de Estadística (INE) (http://www.ine.gob.bo, accessed March 2014).

Colombia: the share of outsiders in 1994 comes from data on social security coverage from Agudelo Calderón, C.; Cardona Botero, J. Ortega Bolaños, J. and Robledo Martínez, R. 2011."Sistema de salud en colombia: 20 años de logros y problemas," *Ciência & Saúde Coletiva* 16(6): 2817–28.

Ecuador: Social security health coverage from Instituto Ecuatoriano de Seguridad Social (IESS) (iess.gov.ec accessed March 2014).

Peru: coverage of social security health from Instituto Nacional de Estadistica (INE) and Seguro Social de Salud del Peru (EsSalud), *Series Estadísticas* (www.essalud.gob.pe, accessed March 2014).

Uruguay: data from Pereira (2010).

Venezuela: data from Instituto Venezolano de los Seguros Sociales (IVSS) and Instituto Nacional de Estadística (INE) (accessed March 2014).

Welfare Effects of Social Programs for Outsiders

Many academic studies, as well as evaluations carried out by governments, multilateral agencies, and think tanks have pointed to the positive welfare effects of social programs. See for example, IPEA (2006), Delgado and Cardoso Jr (2000), and the findings and discussion in Ham, Andrés. 2014. "The Impact of Cash Transfers on Educational Inequality of Opportunity," *Latin American Research Review* 49 (3) 153–75.

Appendix 2

Measuring Social Mobilization

In the case of protests, I counted protest acts to gauge the intensity of mobilization and whether it is sustained. When protest is recurrent, national (coordinated and carried out in different localities), disruptive, and involves on average two protest acts per week with at least 1,000 participants on average, I consider that large-scale. It bears noticing that movements may need initially more protest activity to show their power. Once movements have been efficacious, their contentious activities may have impact more rapidly, requiring fewer acts to achieve their goals. Public officials already have expectations about the evolution of contention and may be willing to negotiate to prevent its spread.

Regarding pressure through institutional channels, I measure the presence of organizations (and numbers and/or resources they mobilize), meetings with public officials, popular consultations, and signature collection for petitions. Other ways of mobilizing and showing public support for demands are also taken into account, such as demonstrations (for which I measure number of participants), public opinion campaigns, data of public support for demands, or public opinion knowledge about the movement's demands. I view mobilization as high when these activities are carried out by a coalition of organizations with large membership and powerful allies (namely a powerful sector of the union movement), in a sustained way, and mobilizing in those activities high numbers of activists (in the hundreds), gathering hundreds of thousands of signatures (usually meeting a required threshold for petitions to be considered by Congress), and supporters of petitions. Institutional channels employed have to be national-level venues.

I measure the presence of pressure through a party ally by examining if stable alliances between SMCs and political parties exist and whether SMCs pressure for policy change through the party ally. I assess this alliance systematically by looking at appointments and participation of movement members in party lists. For this kind of mobilization to be high, the SMC has to be allied to a party that is in power and thus can influence decision making. I triangulate interview material from varied key respondents to find out that SMCs do exert pressure to demand policy changes.

SMCs may at some point reduce protest activity, gain access, or join a government coalition, and therefore exert pressure through various channels, or different components of a SMC may pursue different strategies. Movements using multiple strategies may resort less to protest activity and at first glance that may seem indicative of a decline in social mobilization.

DATA SET OF PROTEST 1996–2010 (ARGENTINA)

I built this data set using online editions of two national newspapers, *Clarín* and *La Nación*. For some years, I have also used paper and online editions of *Página 12*, and online editions of local newspapers *Río Negro* and *Diario El Día*. The latter sources served to check the reliability of the two national newspapers. The unit of analysis is the *act of protest*, from the point when a particular set of demands is made through mobilization, until mobilization finishes. Mobilizations include demonstrations, marches, occupation of buildings, and roadblocks. I gathered and analyzed data on several characteristics of those acts (type, sponsors, location, duration, number of participants, demands, targets, violence, victims, arrests, and policy deals). This is the most comprehensive dataset of unemployed/informal poor protest in Argentina that I know for that period. For the construction of datasets of mobilization, see Beissinger (2002: 460–87) and Silver (2003: 180–203).

DATABASE OF POLICY MAKING

I have analyzed newspaper articles from 1987 until 2006 in Brazil, from 1989 through 2010 in Argentina and Mexico, and from 2004 through 2010 in Chile. I especially surveyed one national newspaper in Mexico and Argentina, *La Jornada* and *Clarín*, respectively. In Brazil for years 1987 and 1988, and between 1990 and 2006, I worked with an index of newspaper clippings of different national newspapers built by the Library of the Brazilian Senate. For each country I also surveyed electronic archives including *Reforma* and *Universal* for the same period (Mexico); *La Nación* for the same period (Argentina); *La Nación* for the same period (Chile); and also used the historical archive of *Folha de São Paulo* (Brazil). For the sake of simplicity, the names of Brazilian newspapers are abbreviated when cited in the text of this book.

Newspaper Abbreviations:

Folha de São Paulo, FdSP
O Estado de São Paulo, OEdSP
Jornal do Brasil, JdoB
Jornal da Tarde, JdT
Jornal de Brasília, JdeB
Correio Brasiliense, CB
O Globo, OG
Gazetta Mercantil, GM

Appendix 3

Measuring Electoral Competition for Outsiders

To measure electoral competition for outsider voters, I analyze existing pre- or postelection surveys, as well as ecological electoral data of national-level election results across electoral districts (municipalities or *departamentos*) since re-democratization for all cases. For Mexico, I also analyze local elections since the 1980s throughout the democratic transition.

I have built two systematic indicators of electoral competition for the vote of outsiders. The first indicator is the *margin of victory between the first and second party among outsider voters*; the second is *challenger victory among outsider voters*. I measure these indicators with two types of data – existing polls and ecological data. Using reported votes cast by respondents I code as "outsiders" in existing survey data, I measure the vote margin of the first and second parties, and whether the challenger wins among outsider voters. I consider elections to have electoral competition when this margin is less than ten percentage points or when a challenger that previously had not mobilized outsider voters wins the most votes.

I complement these measures based on poll data with data sets of ecological data, in which I work with national election results at the lowest level of aggregation for which I could construct sound measures of the "outsider" population and of electoral results at the municipal or district level. I classify each district according to the proportion of the outsider population and measure the margin of victory between the two parties receiving the most votes as well as challenger victories for every presidential election since re-democratization. To score elections on

348

having electoral competition for outsiders or not, I specifically focus on districts in which outsider voters represent the majority of the population (> = 55%), and call these districts "outsider." I consider elections to have electoral competition for outsiders if in at least 50 percent of the outsider districts (a) the margin of victory between the first and second parties is below ten percentage points, and/or a challenger wins, or (b) if 50 percent of the outsider population in outsider districts experiences electoral competition.

ECOLOGICAL DATA

Electoral Data

Argentina
I constructed a data set with the vote share of each presidential candidate and political party in legislative elections at the municipal level (all municipalities or electoral *departamentos*) since re-democratization. For 1995–2011, data were obtained from the Ministry of Interior. For 1999, I used the data set in Abal Medina, Juan Manuel, and Ernesto Calvo (2001) *El federalismo electoral argentino: sobrerrepresentación, reforma política y gobierno dividido en la Argentina*. Buenos Aires: Eudeba & Instituto Nacional de Administración Pública. For 1983 and 1989, I copied electoral results from the Electoral Acts available at the Ministry of Interior.

Brazil
I employ the vote share of presidential candidates at the municipal level from Cesar Zucco (2007). "Data: The President's New Constituency: Lula and the Pragmatic Vote in Brazil's 2006 Presidential Election," http://hdl.handle.net/1902.1/10701 Cesar Zucco [Distributor] V1 [Version] or Zucco (2009).

Chile
I employ the data set of presidential elections "Base histórica electoral de Chile" constructed by the Observatorio Político-Electoral, Universidad Diego Portales.

Mexico
I constructed a data set with the votes obtained by each presidential candidate at the municipal level for the 2000 and 2006 elections with data

compiled by CIDAC (www.cidac.org). I also built a data set of municipal-level elections for 1985–2007 with data compiled by CIDAC.

Outsider Districts

These are districts in which the majority of the population (at least 55 percent) is outsider.

I measure the outsider population with the best indicators for which I could obtain systematic data, as detailed next.

Argentina

Outsider districts are those in which the share of the population without social security health coverage from INDEC's 2001 census – the only census for which these data were available at the municipal level for the entire country – is 55 percent or more. The share of outsiders is particularly high in 2001 because of the financial collapse, representing approximately 11 and 7 percentage points more than the outsider populations in the 1991 and 2010 censuses, respectively. Knowing that outsiders grew during the 1990s and particularly spiked during the dramatic 2001 crisis, I use a stricter measure to code outsider districts for the 1983 and 1989 elections. For those two years, I consider outsider districts those in the outsider population in 2001 was at least 58 percent, instead of 55 percent, as I do for the remaining years. A smaller outsider population in the 2000s, especially after 2003, should not affect my measures of competition given that overall levels of electoral competition were low. In 1999, electoral competition grew, and there was high electoral competition for outsiders for the only time in this period. For that election I am confident that my coding of outsider districts is correct. In fact using different cutpoints to code outsider districts I reach similar assessments of the level of competition for outsiders.

Brazil

I measure the share of outsiders at the municipal level with data obtained from the United Nations Development Program (UNDP)'s Human Development Index (HDI). Because the exact number of people outside the formal labor market is not available at the municipal level, I employ the income variable of the HDI, which is available at the municipal level and scores each municipality according to its level of per capita income, which allows me to identify the poorest municipalities where outsiders constitute a larger share of the population. I code a municipality "outsider" if it scores below 0.65 in the *renda* (income) HDI. These scores correspond to municipalities with low or very low income per capita and to the poorest municipalities among those with moderate levels of income per capita.

Chile

I measure the share of outsiders at the municipal (*comuna*) level with data on the percentage of people with FONASA A and B (which are users of the health care system in extreme poverty or with earnings below 1.4 times the minimum wage, respectively). The data broken up at the municipal level corresponds to 2011. These data were accessed in 2011 from the government's *Observatorio Social*.

Mexico

The measure I use is the percentage of the population without social security health coverage from the 2000 census.

Individual-level Data

Argentina

I could find no national surveys to measure outsiders' vote choices.

Brazil

I employ Datafolha's pre-election surveys from 1989 to 2002. I consider low-income voters (with incomes below two and below five minimum wages) outsiders. For 1994 and 1998, I also employed the original databases of Datafolha surveys available from the Roper Archive.

Chile

I employ pre-election surveys from the Centro de Estudios Públicos (CEP) for all presidential elections between 1993 and 2005 (Encuestas N° 23, 38 and 51). Depending on the data available in each survey, I code outsiders in one of the following ways: unemployed, workers without income, and workers with part-time jobs, as well as respondents who report monthly household incomes below one minimum wage. Alternatively, I code as outsiders the following: independent workers, the unemployed, housewives, and students coded by the CEP as having the lowest socioeconomic levels (D y E in the CEP's survey).

Mexico

I use surveys carried out after elections in July 2000 and July and August 2006 by CIDE-CSES.

I classify respondents according to their economic activity, the type of institutions in which they work, whether they have part- or full-time employment, and the level of education they have attained. I code as outsiders the unemployed, part-time employees who do not work for the public sector, full-time employees, or the self-employed (e.g., store owners) who have completed at least secondary education (equivalent to ninth gradein the US), as well as people outside the economically active population (EAP) with similar levels of education.

Interviews

A total of 265 respondents was interviewed for this project. In this appendix, I list the interviews cited.

INTERVIEWS CITED

Argentina[1]

Amadeo, Eduardo. Secretary of Social Development, Menem administration. Presidential Spokesman, Duhalde administration. December 5, 2006.

Arrighi, Walter. Undersecretary of Social Security, Néstor Kirchner administration. March 20, 2007.

Arroyo, Daniel. Vice-Minister of Social Development, Néstor Kirchner administration. July 12, 2007.

Bullrich, Patricia. Minister of Labor, de la Rúa administration. March 28, 2007.

Cafiero, Juan Pablo. Minister of Social Development, de la Rúa administration. Chief of Staff, Duhalde administration. Minister of Social Development, province of Buenos Aires. December 18, 2006.

Caro Figueroa, Armando. Minister of Labor, Menem administration. July 4, 2007.

Castillo Marin, Luis. Director of Employment Programs, Ministry of Labor, March, 26 2007.

Crisis Committee of the Office of the President, Member #1, Néstor Kirchner administration. December 13, 2012.

---

[1] Interviews carried out in Buenos Aires unless noted.

Crisis Committee of the Office of the President, Member #2, Néstor Kirchner administration. December 17, 2012.

Deibe, Enrique. Secretary of Employment, Kirchner administration. December 12, 2007.

Duhalde, Eduardo. President of Argentina (2002–3), governor of the province of Buenos Aires (1991–9), presidential candidate PJ, 1999. April 19, 2014. Cambridge.

Duhalde administration. Top advisor. January 10, 2007.

Feijóo, María del Carmen. Social policy advisor, Duhalde administration, January 7, 2007.

Fernández Meijide, Graciela. Minister of Social Development (1999–2000). De la Rúa administration. July 11, 2007.

Isuani, Aldo. Secretary of Social Policy and Policies for the Elderly, de la Rúa administration. March 19, 2007.

Lozano, Claudio. Member of National Board, CTA. July 12, 2007.

Mastroccola, Vicente. Secretary General, Plastic Workers' Union. National Secretary of Education and Culture, CGT. July 11, 2007.

Ministry of Health Province of Buenos Aires. High Official. March 14, 2007. La Plata, Buenos Aires.

Ministry of Health. High official. March 12, 2007.

Ministry of Labor. High official. March 26, 2007.

Ministry of Social Development. High official, Menem administration. January 3, 2007.

Montoya, Santiago. Head of the Bank of the Province of Buenos Aires; Head of Buenos Aires Tax Agency (ARBA), October 31, 2012.

Neri, Aldo. Minister of Health, Alfonsín administration (1983–6). December 20, 2007.

PJ. High-ranking politician, province of Buenos Aires. November 2, 2012.

Pérez, Luis. Health policy expert, World Bank consultant. March 26, 2007.

Plan Nacer. High official. March 29, 2007.

Programa Alimentario Nacional (PAN). High official. December 20, 2007.

Remediar. High official #1, March 9, 2007.

Remediar. High official #2, March 12, 2007.

Rodriguez, Andrés. Secretary General, UPCN. National Secretary of International Relations, CGT. July 16, 2007.

Rosso, Graciela. Vice-Minister of Health (2002–5), Duhalde and Kirchner administrations. Legislator, Victory Front. March 15, 2007.

San Martino, Jorge. Secretary of Social Security, de la Rúa administration. March 12, 2007.

Social Security expert. July 7, 2007.

Tobar, Federico. Head of Remediar, Duhalde administration. March 12, 2007.

Unemployed workers' movement. Leader #1. July 10, 2007.

Unemployed workers' movement. Leader #2. July 4, 2007.

Unemployed workers' movement. Leader #3. July 10, 2007.

Unemployed workers' movement. Leader #4. December 12, 2012.

Unemployed workers' movement, CCC leader. January 5, 2012.

Unemployed workers' movement, Barrios de Pie leader. December 17, 2012.

Vinocur, Pablo. Secretary of Social Policy, de la Rúa administration. January 9, 2007.

World Bank, High official. December 22, 2006.

Brazil

Buarque, Cristovam. Senator. Minister of Education, Lula administration. Established Bolsa Escola while governor of Brasilia (1995–8). April 12, 2006. Brasília.

Brazilian Institute of Social and Economic Analysis. IBASE. High official. May 8, 2006. Rio de Janeiro.

Cardoso, Ruth. First Lady, Chair of Solidarity Community, Cardoso administration. July 30, 2007. São Paulo.

Cássia Tavares, Gisele. Chair of the National Social Assistance Fund, Lula administration. April 17, 2006. Brasília.

D'Agostini Jr., Angelo. Executive Director, SINDSAUDE (Sindicato dos Trabalhadores Públicos da Saúde no Estado de São Paulo). June 28, 2006. São Paulo.

Dau Motta, Denise. National Secretary of Organization, Unified Workers' Central (CUT). June 26, 2006. São Paulo.

De Oliveira, Eduardo. President of Federação Brasileira dos Hospitais (FBH). June 1, 2006. São Paulo.

Kayano, Jorge. Instituto Pólis. Member of the Health Reform Movement. June 26, 2006. São Paulo.

Landless Movement (MST). Member of national office. April 27, 2006. Brasília.

Ministry of Health. High official. April 27, 2006. Brasília.

Ministry of Social Development and Struggle against Hunger (MDS). High official #1. May 3, 2006. Brasília.

Ministry of Social Development and Struggle against Hunger (MDS). High official #2. May 3, 2006. Brasília.

Paes de Sousa, Rômulo. Secretary of Evaluation and Information, Ministry of Social Development and Struggle against Hunger (MDS), Lula administration. May 3, 2006. Brasília.

Partido dos Trabalhadores (PT). High official. August 3, 2007. São Paulo.

Peliano, Ana. Head of Social Studies, Institute for Applied Economic Research (IPEA). Executive Secretary of Comunidade Solidaria (CS), Cardoso administration. May 15, 2006. Brasília.

Rehem, Renislon. Secretary of Medical Assistance, Cardoso administration (1998–2002). May 5, 2006. Brasília.

Schwarzer, Helmut. Secretary of Social Security, Lula administration. May 4, 2006. Brasília.

Chile[2]

Alarcón Gómez, Roberto. President of CONFENATS (Confederación Nacional de Trabajadores de la Salud). September 13, 2007 and June 13, 2014.

Asociación AFPs [Association of Pension Funds]. High official. September 10, 2007.

Chile Solidario. High official, Bachelet administration, September 12, 2007.

Enriquez-Ominami, Marco. Campaign Manager for Ricardo Lagos (1999). Legislator from Socialist Party (2006–10). Presidential candidate for Progressive Party (2009). June 12, 2014.

FOSIS. High official, Bachelet administration. September 9, 2007.

Jiménez de la Jara, Jorge. Minister of Health, Patricio Aylwin administration. September 13, 2007.

Maturana, Esteban. President of CONFUSAM (Confederación Nacional de Funcionarios de Salud Municipalizada). June 14, 2014.

Ministry of Planning (MIDEPLAN). High Official, Direction of Subsidies, September 6, 2007.

Moraga, Etiel. Leader of Cooper Workers' Union. National Board of CUT. September 20, 2007 and June 12, 2014.

---

[2] Interviews carried out in Santiago de Chile unless noted.

Superintendecia de ISAPRES. High official. September 11, 2007.
Advisor on health reform of President Ricardo Lagos. September 5, 2007.

Mexico[3]

Araujo, Hugo Andrés. Head of UNORCA (Unión de Organizaciones Regionales Campesinas). President of the CNC (Confederación Nacional Campesina), Salinas administration. May 10, 2007.

Boltvinik, Julio. Academic, Legislator of PRD (2003–6). April 17, 2007.

Borrego, Genaro. Senator. President of PRI (1992), Director of IMSS, Salinas and Zedillo administrations (1993–2000). September 11, 2006.

Calderón, Felipe. President of Mexico (2006–12), President of PAN (1996–9). May 24, 2013. Cambridge.

Cárdenas, Cuathémoc. Founding member of the PRD. Presidential candidate in 1988, 1994, and 2000. Governor of Mexico City (1997–9). April 28, 2010. Berkeley.

Cordera Campos, Rolando. Academic, UNAM. Member of Advisory Committee of PRONASOL, Salinas administration. October 3, 2006.

Encinas, Alejandro. PRD politician. Head of Government. Mexico City (2005–6). May 11, 2007.

Escobedo-Zoletto, Salvador. Director of Oportunidades, Calderón administration. May 14, 2007.

Gómez-Hermosillo, Rogelio. Director of Oportunidades, Fox administration. May 17, 2007.

Herández Franco, Daniel. Director of Progresa, Zedillo administration. High official, Secretariat of Social Development SEDESOL, Fox administration (2000–6). September 29, 2006.

Hernández Juárez, Francisco. Secretary General, Telephone Workers' Union (STRM). Director of National Union of Workers (UNT). October 2, 2006.

Mexican Institute of Social Security (IMSS). High official. May 7, 2007.

IMSS-Oportunidades. Director, Fox administration. April 25, 2007.

Laurell, Asa Cristina. Secretary of Health. Government of Mexico City, López-Obrador administration. Secretary of Health, legitimate government (Gobierno Legítimo) of López-Obrador, 2007. May 8, 2007.

---

[3] Interviews carried out in Mexico City unless noted.

Marván, Ignacio. Academic from CIDE. Political consultant. May 15, 2007.

Oportunidades. High official. September 29, 2006.

Party of the Democratic Revolution (PRD). Social policy expert. May 5, 2007.

Pérez-Bejerano, Marta. PRD politician. Secretary of Welfare, Legitimate government of López-Obrador (Gobierno Legítimo). May 15, 2007.

PRONASOL. Program director. April 26, 2007.

PRONASOL. Program director. September 21, 2006.

Rojas, Carlos. Director of PRONASOL, Salinas administration. Secretary of social development, Salinas and Zedillo administrations. May 15, 2007.

Secretariat of Health. High official. October 4, 2006.

Secretariat of Social Development (SEDESOL). High official. September 26, 2007.

Székely, Miguel. Secretary of Evaluation, Secretariat of Social Development (SEDESOL), Fox administration. September 26, 2007.

Vega-Galina, Roberto. Secretary General of IMSS Workers' Union (SNTSS). Member of the national board of National Workers' Union (UNT). September 26, 2006.

Vélez, Félix. Secretary of Evaluation, Secretariat of Social Development (SEDESOL), Calderón administration. May 5, 2007.

Bibliography

Abrantes, Raquel Pêgo and Célia Almeida. 2002. "Ámbito y papel de los especialistas en las reformas de los sistemas de salud: Los casos de Brasil y México," Working Paper 299, Kellogg Institute. University of Notre Dame.

African National Congress. 1994. *The Reconstruction and Development Programme*. Johannesburg: African National Congress.

Alonso, Guillermo. 2000. *Política y seguridad social en la Argentina de los '90*. Buenos Aires: Miño y Dávila Editores.

Alves, Maria Helena Moreira. 1985. *State and Opposition in Military Brazil*. Austin: University of Texas Press.

Amenta, Edwin. 2006. *When Movements Matter: The Townsend Plan and the Rise of Social Security*. Princeton, NJ: Princeton University Press.

Ames, Barry. 2002. *The Deadlock of Democracy in Brazil*. Ann Arbor: University of Michigan Press.

Anderson, Karen. 2001. "The Politics of Retrenchment in a Social Democratic Welfare State," *Comparative Political Studies* 34, no. 9: 1063–91.

Angell, Alan. 2007. *Democracy after Pinochet: Politics, Parties and Elections in Chile*. London: Institute for the Study of the Americas.

Angell, Alan and Cristóbal Reig Salinas. 2007. "¿Cambios o continuidad? Las elecciones chilenas de 2005/6," in Carlos Huneeus, Fabiola Berríos, and Ricardo Gamboa, eds. *Las elecciones chilenas de 2005: partidos, coaliciones y votantes en transición*. Santiago de Chile: Catalonia.

Arce, Moisés. 2001. "The Politics of Pension Reform in Peru," *Studies in Comparative International Development* 36, no. 3: 88–113.

———. 2003. "Political Violence and Presidential Approval in Peru," *Journal of Politics* 65, no. 2: 572–83.

Arce, Moisés and Paul T. Bellinger Jr. 2007. "Low-Intensity Democracy Revisited: The Effects of Economic Liberalization on Political Activity in Latin America," *World Politics* 60, no. 1: 97–121.

Arellano, Juan Pablo. 2004. "Políticas para el crecimiento con equidad, Chile 1990–2002," *Serie Estudios Socio-económicos* no. 26. Santiago de Chile: CIEPLAN.

Arim, Rodrigo, Guillermo Cruces, and Andrea Vigorito. 2009. "Programas sociales y transferencias de ingreso en Uruguay: Los beneficios no contributivos y alternativas para su extensión," *Serie de Políticas Sociales* 146. Santiago de Chile: Comisión Económica para América Latina y el Caribe.

Arretche, Marta. 2005. "A política da política de saúde no Brasil," in Nísia Trindade Lima, Silvia Gerschman, Flavio Coelho Edler, and Julio Manuel Suárez, eds. *Saúde e democracia: história e perspectiva do SUS*. Rio de Janeiro: Fiocruz.

Asociación de AFP. 2006. "Presentación," in Gobierno de Chile. *Informe del Consejo Asesor Presidencial para la Reforma del Sistema Previsional*. Santiago de Chile.

Auyero, Javier. 2001. *Poor People's Politics: Peronist Survival Networks and the Legacy of Evita*. Durham, NC: Duke University Press.

Avritzer, Leonardo. 2009. *Participatory Institutions in Democratic Brazil*. Baltimore, MD: Johns Hopkins University Press.

Baiocchi, Gianpaolo. 2005. *Militants and Citizens: The Politics of Participatory Democracy in Porto Alegre*. Stanford, CA: Stanford University Press.

Barbosa, Rômulo Soares. 2008. "A previdência social rural na a Constituição de 1988: a perspectiva dualista da CONTAG," *Acta Scientiarum. Human and Social Sciences* 30, no. 2: 129–36.

Barozet, Emmanuelle. 2003. "Movilización de recursos y redes sociales en los Neopopulismos: hipótesis de trabajo para el caso chileno," *Revista de Ciencia Política* 13, no. 1: 39–54.

Beccaria, Luis and Roxana Maurizio. 2003. "Movilidad ocupacional en Argentina." San Miguel: Instituto de Ciencias, Universidad Nacional de General Sarmiento.

Beissinger, Mark R. 2002. *Nationalist Mobilization and the Collapse of the Soviet State*. Cambridge: Cambridge University Press.

Belmartino, Susana. 1995. "Transformaciones internas al sector salud: la ruptura del pacto corporativo," *Desarrollo Económico* 35, no. 137: 83–103.

———. 2005. *La atención médica argentina en el siglo XX: instituciones y procesos*. Buenos Aires: Siglo Veintiuno Editores Argentina.

Belmartino, Susana and Carlos Bloch. 1989. "Estado, clases sociales y salud," *Social Science & Medicine* 28, no. 5: 497–514.

Benitez Iturbe, Mauricio. 2009. "The Politics of Distribution. Subnational Policy Regimes in Mexico." PhD Dissertation, Department of Political Science, University of California, Berkeley.

Bennett, Andrew and Jeffrey Checkel. 2015. *Process Tracing: from Metaphor to Analytic Tool*. New York: Cambridge University Press.

Bensusán, Graciela. 2000. "El impacto de la reestructuración neoliberal: comparación de las estrategias neoliberales en Argentina, Brasil, México, Estados Unidos y Canadá." Unpublished manuscript.

Bensusán, Graciela and Maria Lorena Cook. 2003. "Political Transition and Labor Revitalization in Mexico," *Research in the Sociology of Work* 11: 229–67.

Boas, Taylor. 2005. "Neopopulism and Television in Latin America: Media Effects in Brazil and Peru," *Latin American Research Review* 40, no. 2: 27–49.

2010. "Varieties of Electioneering: Presidential Campaigns in Latin America." PhD Dissertation, Department of Political Science, University of California, Berkeley.

Boeninger, Edgardo. 2008. *Políticas Públicas en Democracia. Institucionalidad y Experiencia Chilena, 1990–2006*. Santiago de Chile: Uqbar.

Boix, Carles. 2003. *Democracy and Redistribution*. New York: Cambridge University Press.

Borges, Andre. 2011. "The Political Consequences of Center-Led Redistribution in Brazilian Federalism: The Fall of Subnational Party Machines," *Latin American Research Review* 46, no. 3: 21–45.

Borzutzky, Silvia. 2002. *Vital Connections Politics, Social Security, and Inequality in Chile*. Notre Dame: University of Notre Dame Press.

Briceño, Mercedes Pulido de. 1999. "El impacto de los programas sociales: balance y perspectivas," in Lourdes Alvarez, Helia Isabel del Rosario, and Jesús Robles, eds. *Política social: exclusión y equidad en Venezuela durante los años noventa*. Caracas: Nueva Sociedad.

Brooks, Sarah M. 2001. "Social Protection and the Market: The Political Economy of Pension Reform in an Era of Capital Mobility." PhD dissertation, Department of Political Science, Duke University.

2009. *Social Protection and the Market: The Transformation of Social Security Institutions in Latin America*. Cambridge: Cambridge University Press.

Brown, David S. and Wendy Hunter. 1999. "Democracy and Social Spending in Latin America, 1980–1992," *American Political Science Review* 93, no. 4: 779–90.

Bruhn, Kathleen. 1997. *Taking on Goliath: Emergence of a New Left Party and the Struggle for Democracy in Mexico*. University Park: Pennsylvania State University Press.

Bulmer-Thomas, Victor. 2010. *The Economic History of Latin America since Independence*. New York: Cambridge University Press.

Burgess, Katrina and Steven Levitsky. 2003. "Explaining Populist Party Adaptation in Latin America: Environmental and Organizational Determinants of Party Change in Argentina, Mexico, Peru, and Venezuela," *Comparative Political Studies* 36, no. 8: 881–911.

Calvo, Ernesto and Maria Victoria Murillo. 2004. "Who Delivers? Partisan Clients in the Argentine Electoral Market," *American Journal of Political Science* 48, no. 4: 742–57.

Cámara de Diputados. 1996. *Diario de los Debates*. Año III, Sesión 41 (11 de diciembre). Ciudad de México.

1997. *Diario de los Debates*. Año II, Sesión 42 (13 de diciembre). Ciudad de México.

2006. *Diario de los Debates*. Año I, Vol II, Sesión 38 (23 de diciembre). Ciudad de México.

Cameron, Maxwell. 2011. "Peru: The Left Turn that Wasn't," in Steven Levitsky and Kenneth Roberts, eds. *The Resurgence of the Latin American Left*. Baltimore, MD: Johns Hopkins University Press.

Camp, Roderic. 2004. "Citizen Attitudes toward Democracy and Vincente Fox's Victory," in Jorge Domínguez and Chapell Lawson, eds. *Mexico's Pivotal Democratic Election*. Stanford, CA: Stanford University Press.

Campello, Daniela. 2015. *The Politics of Market Discipline in Latin America: Globalization and Democracy*. Cambridge: Cambridge University Press.

Campos, Wagner de Sousa. 2005. "Romance de Formação de um Sanitarista: um estudo de caso," in Nísia Trindade Lima, Silvia Gerschman, Flavio Coelho Edler, and Julio Manuel Suárez, eds. *Saúde e democracia: história e perspectiva do SUS*. Rio de Janeiro: Fiocruz.

Cardoso, Fernando Henrique. 1998. *Avança Brasil: mais 4 anos de desenvolvimento para todos*. Brasília.

2006. *A arte da política: a história que vivi*. Rio de Janeiro: Civilização Brasileira.

Cardoso Jr., José Celso and Luciana Jaccoud. 2005. "Políticas Sociais No Brasil: Organização, Sbrangência E Tensões Da Ação Estatal," in *Questão Social E Políticas Sociais No Brasil Contemporâneo*. Brasilia: IPEA.

Cardoso, Ruth, Miguel Darcy de Oliveira, Augusto de Franco, and Thereza Lobo, eds. 2002. *Comunidade Solidária*. Rio de Janeiro: Comunitas.

Caristo, Anna. 2005. "Asignaciones familiares en el Uruguay," *Comentarios de Seguridad Social* 8 (julio). Montevideo.

2008. "Las estadísticas de beneficiarios de asignaciones familiares a julio de 2008," *Comentarios de Seguridad Social* 21 (octubre–diciembre). Montevideo.

n/d. "Evolucion de las asignaciones familiares 2007–2010," *Comentarios de Seguridad Social* 33. Montevideo.

Carnes, Matthew and Isabela Mares. 2009. "Deindustrialization and Social Policy Expansion. Theoretical Relationship and Empirical Test." Paper presented at the meetings of the American Political Science Association, Toronto, Canada, September 3–6.

2014. "Coalitional realignment and the adoption of non-contributory social insurance programs in Latin America," *Socioeconomic Review* 12: 695–752.

Carvallo, Moisés. 1999. "Los nuevos programas sociales: notas para un balance," in Lourdes Alvarez, Helia Isabel del Rosario, and Jesús Robles, eds. *Política social: exclusión y equidad en Venezuela durante los años noventa*. Caracas: Nueva Sociedad.

Castañeda, Jorge. 1999. *La Herencia: arqueología de la sucesión presidencial en México*. México: Aguilar, Altea, Taurus, Alfaguara.

Castiglioni, Rossana. 2002. "Retrenchment versus Maintenance: The Politics of Social Policy Change in Chile and Uruguay, 1973–1998." PhD dissertation, University of Notre Dame.

2005. *The Politics of Social Policy Change in Chile and Uruguay: Retrenchment versus Maintenance, 1973–1998*. New York: Routledge.

2010. "Las políticas sociales de la nueva (vieja) izquierda uruguaya," *Woodrow Wilson Center Update on the Americas* 6. Washington, DC: Woodrow Wilson Center Press.

Catterberg, Edgardo. 1991. *Argentina Confronts Politics: Political Culture and Public Opinion in the Argentine Transition to Democracy*. Boulder, CO: Lynne Rienner Publishers.

CENDA. 2006. "Algunos Principios Básicos a Considerar en el Diseño del Nuevo Sistema Previsional Chileno." Document submitted to the Consejo Asesor para la Reforma Previsional. Santiago de Chile.

Central de los Trabajadores Argentinos (CTA). 1991. "Debate para la organización de los trabajadores. Declaración de Burzaco." Buenos Aires. (Available at www.cta.org.ar).

Chilcote, Ronald. 1974. *The Brazilian Communist Party: Conflict and Integration 1922–1972*. New York: Oxford University Press.

Cipoletta, Graciela and Lilia Archaga. 1997. *Los nuevos sujetos de derecho en la seguridad social argentina: sistemas contributivo y no contributivo*. Buenos Aires: INAP.

Coelho, Vera Schattan. 2003. "Poder Excecutivo e Reforma da Previdência na América Latina," *Novos Estudos CEBRAP* 61: 93–108.

Coelho, Vera Schattan and Marcos Nobre. 2004. *Participação e deliberação. Teoria democrática e experiência institucional no Brasil contemporâneo*. São Paulo: Editora 34.

Coletti, Claudinei. 1998. *A estrutura sindical no campo: a propósito da organização dos assalariados rurais na região de Ribeirão Preto*. Campinas: Editora da Unicamp: Centro de Memória-Unicamp.

Collier, David and Richard E. Messik. 1975. "Prerequisites versus Diffusion: Testing Alternative Explanations of Social Security Adoption," *The American Political Science Review* 69, no. 4: 1299–1315.

Collier, Ruth Berins. 1992. *The Contradictory Alliance: State–Labor Relations and Regime Change in Mexico*. Berkeley: International and Area Studies, University of California at Berkeley.

1999. *Paths toward Democracy*. Cambridge: Cambridge University Press.

Collier, Ruth Berins and David Collier. 1991. *Shaping the Political Arena*. Princeton, NJ: Princeton University Press.

Collier, Ruth Berins and Samuel Handlin. 2009. *Reorganizing Popular Politics: Participation and the New Interest Regime in Latin America*. University Park: Pennsylvania State University Press.

Collier, Ruth Berins and James Mahoney. 1993. "Adding Collective Actors to Collective Outcomes: Democratic Transitions in South America and Southern Europe," *Comparative Politics* 29, no. 3: 285–303.

Comisión Económica para América Latina y el Caribe (CEPAL). 2009. *Anuario Estadístico de América Latina y el Caribe*. (Available at www.cepal.org).

Committee of Inquiry into a Comprehensive System of Social Security for South Africa (Taylor Committee). 2002. *Consolidated Report*. South Africa.

Comparato, Bruno Konder. 2001. "A Ação Política do MST," *São Paulo em Perspectiva* 15, no. 4: 105–18.

Conaghan, Catherine M. 2005. *Fujimori's Peru: Deception in the Public Sphere*. Pittsburgh: University of Pittsburgh Press.

CONEVAL. 2006. "El CONEVAL reporta cifras sobre la evolución de la pobreza en México," Mexico: CONEVAL.

2014. "Indicadores de acceso y uso efectivo de los servicios de salud de afiliados al Seguro Popular." México, DF: CONEVAL.

Consejo Asesor Presidencial para la Reforma Previsional. 2006. *Estado de avance.* Santiago de Chile.

Consejo Consultivo del Programa Nacional de Solidaridad. 1994. *El Programa Nacional de Solidaridad.* México: Fondo de Cultura Económica.

CONTAG. 2003. *40 Anos.* Brasília: CONTAG.

Coppedge, Michael. 1994. *Strong Parties and Lame Ducks.* Stanford, CA: Stanford University Press.

Cornelius, Wayne. 2004. "Mobilized Voting in the 2000 Elections: The Changing Efficacy of Vote Buying and Coercion in Mexican Electoral Politics," in Jorge Domínguez and Chapell Lawson, eds. *Mexico's Pivotal Democratic Election.* Stanford, CA: Stanford University Press.

Cornelius, Wayne, Ann Craig, and Jonathan Fox. 1994. *Transforming State–Society Relations in Mexico: The National Solidarity Strategy.* La Jolla: Center for U.S.-Mexican Studies, University of California, San Diego.

Cornwall, Andrea. 2008. "Deliberating Democracy: Scenes from a Brazilian Municipal Health Council," *Politics and Society* 36, no. 4: 508–31.

Cross, John C. 1998. *Informal Politics: Street Vendors and the State in Mexico City.* Stanford, CA: Stanford University Press.

Cruces, Guillermo and Helena Rovner. 2008. "Los programas sociales en la opinión pública. Resultados de la Encuesta de Percepción de planes Sociales en la Argentina," in Guillermo Cruces, Eduardo Amadeo, Dana Ringold, and Rafael Rofman, eds. *Los programas sociales en argentina hacia el bicentenario: visiones y perspectivas.* Buenos Aires: Banco Mundial.

Central Unitaria de Trabajadores de Chile (CUT). 2006. "Sistema de pensiones en Chile. Una propuesta de reforma a 25 años de su funcionamiento." Santiago de Chile.

Dahl, Robert A. 1971. *Polyarchy: Participation and Opposition.* New Haven, CT: Yale University Press.

Danani, Claudia, Magdalena Chiara, and Judith Filc. 1997. *El papel del fondo de reparación histórica del conurbano bonaerense en la reproducción de los sectores populares de la región metropolitana.* San Miguel: Universidad de General Sarmiento.

Dargent, Eduardo. 2011. "Agents or Actors? Assessing the Autonomy of Economic Technocrats in Colombia and Peru," *Comparative Politics* 43, no. 3: 313–32.

De La Rúa, Fernando. 2001. "El Mensaje Presidencial Completo," *La Nación*, November 1. Buenos Aires.

Delamata, Gabriela. 2004. *Los barrios desbordados: las organizaciones de desocupados del Gran Buenos Aires.* Buenos Aires: Editorial Universitaria de Buenos Aires, EUDEBA.

Delamaza, Gonzalo. 2010. "La Disputa por la Participación en la Democracia Elitista Chilena," *Latin American Research Review* 45: 274–97.

Del Frade, Carlos. 2012. *Crónica del FRENAPO: Un sueño colectivo inconcluso.* Buenos Aires: Ediciones CTA.

Delgado, Guilherme Costa and José Celso Cardoso Jr., eds. 2000. *A universalização de direitos sociais no Brasil: a previdência rural nos anos 90.* Brasília: IPEA.

D'Elia, Yolanda. 2006. "Las Misiones Sociales en Venezuela: una aproximación a su comprensión y análisis." Caracas: Instituto Latinoamericano de Investigaciones Sociales.

2008. "Las Misiones Sociales en Venezuela." Caracas: Instituto Latinoamericano de Investigaciones Sociales.

Della Cava, Ralph. 1989. "The 'People's Church,' the Vatican, and Abertura," in Alfred Stepan, ed. *Democratizing Brazil: Problems of Transition and Consolidation*. New York: Oxford University Press.

Di Tella, Guido. 1986. *Perón-Perón 1973–1976*. Buenos Aires: Sudamericana.

Diálogo Argentino. 2002. "Boletín Informativo No 1." Buenos Aires: Secretaría Técnica.

2002. "Mesa Sectorial de Salud." Buenos Aires: Secretaría Técnica.

Diani, Mario. 2003. "Social Movements, Contentious Actions, and Social Networks: from Metaphor to Substance? in Diani, Mario and Doug McAdam, eds. *Social Movements and Networks: Relational Approaches to Collective Action*. Oxford: Oxford University Press.

Díaz-Cayeros, Alberto, Federico Estévez, and Beatriz Magaloni. 2007. "Clientelism and Portfolio Diversification," in Herbert Kitschelt and Stephen Wilkinson, eds. *Patrons, Clients and Policies: Patterns of Democratic Accountability and Political Competition*. Cambridge: Cambridge University Press.

. *Strategies of Vote-Buying: Poverty, Democracy and Social Transfers in Mexico*. Cambridge: Cambridge University Press (forthcoming).

DIESSE & Ministério de Desenvolvimento Agrário. 2006. *Estatísticas do meio rural*. São Paulo: DIESSE.

2008. *Estatísticas do meio rural*. São Paulo: DIESSE.

Dion, Michelle L. 2010. *Workers and Welfare*. Pittsburgh: University of Pittsburgh Press.

Domínguez, Jorge and Chapell Lawson, eds. 2004. *Mexico's Pivotal Democratic Election*. Stanford, CA: Stanford University Press.

Draibe, Sônia. 2006. "Bolsa Escola e Bolsa Família," *Caderno 76*, Universidade Estadual de Campinas, UNICAMP.

Dresser, Denise. 1994. "Bringing the Poor Back In: National Solidarity as a Strategy of Regime Legitimation," in Wayne Cornelius, Ann Craig, and Jonathan Fox, eds. *Transforming State–Society Relations in Mexico: The National Solidarity Strategy*. La Jolla: Center for U.S.-Mexican Studies, University of California, San Diego.

DSD, SASSA, UNICEF. 2012. *South Africa's Child Support Grant: Impact Assessment*. Pretoria: UNICEF.

Dunning, Thad. 2008. *Crude Democracy: Natural Resource Wealth and Political Regimes*. New York: Cambridge University Press.

Eisenstadt, Todd A. 2009. "Agrarian Tenure Institution Conflict Frames, and Communitarian Identities: The Case of Indigenous Southern Mexico," *Comparative Political Studies* 42, no. 1: 82–113.

Escorel, Sarah. 1999. *Reviravolta na saúde: origem e articulação do Movimento Sanitário*. Rio de Janeiro: Fiocruz.

Escorel, Sarah and Renata Bloch. 2005. "As Conferências Nacionais de Saúde na construção do SUS," in Nísia Trindade Lima, Silvia Gerschman, Flavio

Coelho Edler, and Julio Manuel Suárez, eds. *Saúde e democracia: história e perspectiva do SUS.* Rio de Janeiro: Fiocruz.

Escorel, Sarah, Dilene Nascimento, and Flavio Elder. 2005. "As origens da Reforma Sanitária e do SUS," in Nísia Trindade Lima, Silvia Gerschman, Flavio Coelho Edler, and Julio Manuel Suárez, eds. *Saúde e democracia: história e perspectiva do SUS.* Rio de Janeiro: Fiocruz.

Esping-Andersen, Gøsta. 1990. *The Three Worlds of Welfare Capitalism.* Princeton, NJ: Princeton University Press.

1996. "Welfare without Work: The Impasse of Labor Shedding and Familialism in Continental European Social Policy," in Gøsta Esping-Andersen, ed. *Welfare States in Transition*, London: Sage Publications.

1999. *Social Foundations of Postindustrial Economies.* Oxford; New York: Oxford University Press.

Esping-Andersen, Gøsta and Walter Korpi. 1984. "Social Policy as Class Politics in Post-war Capitalism: Scandinavia, Austria, and Germany," in John Goldthorpe, ed. *Order and Conflict in Contemporary Capitalism.* Oxford: Oxford University Press.

Etchemendy, Sebastián. 2011. *Models of Economic Liberalization: Business, Workers, and Compensation in Latin America, Spain, and Portugal.* New York: Cambridge University Press.

Etchemendy, Sebastián and Ruth Berins Collier. 2007. "Down but Not Out: Union Resurgence and Segmented Neocorporatism in Argentina (2003–2007)," *Politics & Society* 35, no. 3: 363–401.

Etchemendy, Sebastián and Candelaria Garay. 2011. "Argentina's Left Populism in Comparative Perspective," in Steven Levitsky and Kenneth Roberts, eds. *The Resurgence of the Latin American Left.* Baltimore, MD: Johns Hopkins University Press.

Evans, Peter B. 1995. *Embedded Autonomy: States and Industrial Transformation.* Princeton, NJ: Princeton University Press.

Ewig, Christina. 2010. *Second-Wave Neoliberalism: Gender, Race, and Health Sector Reform in Peru.* Pennsylvania: Pennsylvania State University Press.

Fairfield, Tasha. 2010. "Business Power and Tax Reform: Taxing Income and Profits in Chile and Argentina," *Latin American Politics and Society* 52, no. 2: 37–71.

2011. "Business Power and Protest: Argentina's Agricultural Producers Protest in Comparative Context," *Studies in Comparative International Development* 46, no. 4: 424–53.

2015. *Private Wealth and Public Revenue in Latin America. Business Power and Tax Politics.* New York: Cambridge University Press.

Fairfield, Tasha and Candelaria Garay. 2013. "Redistribution under the Right in Latin America." Prepared for delivery at the Meetings of the American Political Science Association, Chicago, IL, August 29–September 1.

Feldman, Jorge, Laura Golbert, and Aldo Isuani. 1988. *Maduración y crisis del sistema previsional argentino.* Buenos Aires: Centro Editor América de Latina.

Ferioli, Néstor. 1990. *La Fundación Eva Perón.* Buenos Aires: Centro Editor América de Latina.

Fernández, María Eugenia. 2012. "La Protección Social frente a la vejez en Venezuela," *Anuario de Derecho* no. 29: 191–223.

Ferrara, Francisco. 1973. *Qué son las ligas agrarias: historia y documentos de las organizaciones campesinas del nordeste argentino.* Buenos Aires: Argentina Editores S. A.

Fleet, Michael. 1985. *The Rise and Fall of Chilean Christian Democracy.* Princeton, NJ: Princeton University Press.

Fleisher, David. 2002. "As eleições municipais no Brasil: uma análise comparativa (1982–2000)," *Opinião Pública* 8, no. 1: 80–100.

Fleury, Sônia, ed. 1997. *Saúde e democracia: A luta do CEBES.* São Paulo: Lemos Editorial & Gráficos.

Flynn, Peter. 1993. "Collor, Corruption and Crisis: Time for Reflection," *Journal of Latin American Studies* 25, no. 2: 351–71.

Fondo Solidario de Inversión Social (FOSIS). 2006. *Superar la Pobreza. Experiencia de Gestión del FOSIS 2000–2005.* Santiago de Chile: FOSIS.

Fox, Jonathan. 1994. "The Difficult Transition from Clientelism to Citizenship: Lessons from Mexico," *World Politics* 46, no. 2: 151–84.

Fung, Archon. 2006. "Varieties of Participation in Complex Governance," *Public Administration Review* 66, no. S1: 66–75.

Fung, Archon and Erik Olin Wright. 2003. "Thinking about Empowered Participatory Governance," in Archon Fung and Erik Olin Wright, eds. *Deepening Democracy: Institutional Innovations in Empowered Participatory Governance.* London; New York: Verso.

FUNSALUD. 2001. "Hacia un México más saludable." *Cuaderno 33.* México, DF: FUNSALUD.

Gamboa, Ricardo. 2007. "Renovación Nacional," in Carlos Huneeus, Fabiola Berríos, and Ricardo Gamboa, eds. *Las elecciones chilenas de 2005: partidos, coaliciones y votantes en transición.* Santiago de Chile: Catalonia.

Garay, Candelaria. 2000. "Los Hospitales sin Fines de Lucro," in Mario Roitter and Inés González Bombal, eds. *Estudios sobre el sector sin fines de lucro en Argentina.* Buenos Aires: Edipubli.

2003. "Policy Initiatives as a Trigger for Contention: Origins of the Unemployed Workers' Movement in Argentina." Master's Thesis, Department of Political Science, University of California, Berkeley.

2007. "Social Policy and Collective Action: Unemployed Workers, Community Associations, and Protest in Argentina," *Politics & Society* 35, no. 2: 301–28.

2016. "The Adoption of Cash Transfer Programs in Latin America." Prepared for delivery at the Latin American Studies Association, New York, NY, May 27–30.

Genoino, José. 2004. "Abertura," in Marlene da Rocha, ed. *Segurança alimentar: um desafio para acabar com a fome no Brasil.* São Paulo: Fundacão Perseu Abramo.

Gibson, Edward. 1996. *Class and Conservative Parties: Argentina in Comparative Perspective.* Baltimore, MD: Johns Hopkins University Press.

1997. "The Populist Road to Market Reform: Policy and Electoral Coalitions in Mexico and in Argentina," *World Politics* 49, no. 3: 339–370.

Gingrich, Jane. 2011. *Making Markets in the Welfare State: The Politics of Varying Market Reforms.* New York: Cambridge University Press.

Giraudy, Agustina. 2007. "The Distributive Politics of Emergency Employment Programs in Argentina (1993–2002)," *Latin American Research Review* 42, no. 2: 33–55.

Giugni, Marco C. and Florence Passy. 1998. "Contentious Politics in Complex Societies: New Social Movements between Conflict and Cooperation," in Marco Giugni, Doug McAdam, and Charles Tilly, eds. *From Contention to Democracy*. New York: Rowman and Littlefield Publishers.

Gobierno de Chile. 2006a. "Palabras de S.E. La Presidenta De La República, Michelle Bachelet," March 17. Santiago de Chile.

2006b. *Sistema de pensiones. Informe de diagnóstico para el Consejo Asesor para la Reforma Previsional*. Tomo 5. Santiago de Chile.

Godio, Julio. 2000. *Historia del movimiento obrero argentino: 1870–2000*. Buenos Aires: Corregidor.

Gohn, Maria da Glória. 2003. *História dos movimentos e lutas sociais: a construção da cidadania dos brasileiros*. São Paulo: Edições Loyola.

Golbert, Laura. 1998. "Los problemas del empleo y las políticas sociales," *Boletín Informativo Techint* 296. Buenos Aires.

2004. "Plan Jefes y Jefas, derecho de inclusión o paz social?" *Serie Políticas Sociales* 31. Santiago de Chile: Comisión Económica para América Latina y el Caribe.

Goldfrank, Benjamin. 2007. "The Politics of Deepening Local Democracy: Decentralization, Party Institutionalization, and Participation," *Comparative Politics* 39, no. 2: 147–68.

Gómez Dantés, Octavio, ed. 2005. *El Seguro Popular: siete perspectivas*. Cuernavaca: Instituto Nacional de Salud Pública.

Graham, Carol. 1991. *From Emergency Employment to Social Investment: Alleviating Poverty in Chile*. Washington, DC: The Brookings Institution.

1992. *Peru's Apra*. Boulder, CO: Lynne Rienner Publishers.

Grammont, Hubert and Horacio Mackinlay. 2006. "Las organizaciones sociales campesinas e indígenas frente a los partidos y al Estado, México 1938–2006," *Revista Mexicana de Sociología* 68, no. 4: 693–729.

Grassi, Estela, Susana Hintze, and María Rosa Neufeld. 1994. *Políticas sociales, crisis y ajuste estructural: un análisis del sistema educativo, de obras sociales y de las políticas alimentarias*. Buenos Aires: Espacio Editorial.

Graziano, José. 2004. "Abertura," in Marlene da Rocha, ed. *Segurança alimentar: um desafio para acabar com a fome no Brasil*. São Paulo: Fundacão Perseu Abramo.

Greene, Kenneth. 2007. *Why Dominant Parties Lose: Mexico's Democratization in Comparative Perspective*. Cambridge: Cambridge University Press.

Grinberg, Lucia. 2009. *Partido político ou bode expiatório: um estudo sobre a Aliança Renovadora Nacional, ARENA (1965–79)*. Rio de Janeiro: FAPERJ.

Grindle, Merilee. 1977. *Bureaucrats, Politicians, and Peasants in Mexico: A Case Study in Public Policy*. Berkeley: University of California Press.

Grzymala-Busse, Anna. 2002. *Redeeming the Communist Past: The Regeneration of Communist Parties in East Central Europe*. Cambridge: Cambridge University Press.

2007. *Rebuilding Leviathan: Party Competition and State Exploitation in Post-communist Democracies*. Cambridge: Cambridge University Press.

Hacker, Jacob S. 2002. *The Divided Welfare State: The Battle over Public and Private Social Benefits in the United States*. Cambridge: Cambridge University Press.

2010. "The Road to Somewhere: Why Health Reform Happened," *Perspectives on Politics* 8, no. 3: 861–76.

Haggard, Stephen and Robert Kaufman. 2008. *Development, Democracy, and Welfare States: Latin America, East Asia, and Eastern Europe*. Princeton, NJ: Princeton University Press.

2012. "Inequality and Regime Change: Democratic Transitions and the Stability of Democratic Rule," *American Political Science Review* 106, no. 3: 496–516.

Hagopian, Frances. 1996. *Traditional Politics and Regime Change in Brazil*. New York: Cambridge University Press.

2014. "Reorganizing Representation in Latin America in the Neo-liberal Age," in Peter A. Hall, Wade Jacoby, Jonah Levy, and Sophie Meunier, eds. *The Politics of Representation in the Global Age: Identification, Mobilization, and Adjudication*. New York: Cambridge University Press.

Hall, Peter A. 1993. "Policy Paradigms, Social Learning, and the State: The Case of Economic Policymaking in Britain," *Comparative Politics* 25, no. 3: 275–96.

1997. "The Role of Interests, Institutions, and Ideas in the Comparative Political Economy of the Industrialized Nations," in Mark Irving Lichbach and Alan S. Zuckerman, eds. *Comparative Politics: Rationality, Culture, and Structure*. Cambridge: Cambridge University Press.

Hall, Peter A. and Rosemary Taylor. 1996. "Political Science and the Three New Institutionalisms," *Political Studies* 44, no. 5: 936–57.

Hawkins, Kirk A. 2010. *Venezuela's Chavismo and Populism*. New York: Cambridge University Press.

Heclo, Hugh. 1974. *Modern Social Politics in Britain and Sweden: From Relief to Income Maintenance*. New Haven, CT: Yale University Press.

Hipsher, Patricia. 1998. "Democratic Transitions and Social Movement Outcomes: The Chilean Shantytown Dwellers' Movement in Comparative Perspective," in Marco Giugni, Doug McAdam, and Charles Tilly, eds. *From Contention to Democracy*. New York: Rowman and Littlefield Publishers.

Hochstetler, Kathryn. 2006. "Rethinking Presidentialism: Challenges and Presidential Falls in South America," *Comparative Politics* 38, no. 4: 401–18.

Holland, Alisha C. 2016. "Forbearance," *American Political Science Review* 110, no. 2: 232–46.

Holland, Alisha C. and Brian Palmer-Rubin. 2015. "Beyond the Machine: Clientelist Brokers and Interest Organizations in Latin America," *Comparative Political Studies* 48, no. 9: 1186–1223.

Houtzager, Peter P. 1997. "Caught between the State and Church: Rural Movements in the Brazilian Countryside, 1964–1989." PhD Dissertation, Department of Political Science, University of California, Berkeley.

1998. "State and Unions in the Transformation of the Brazilian Countryside, 1964–1979," *Latin American Research Review* 33, no. 2: 103–42.

Huber, Evelyne and John D. Stephens. 2000. "The Political Economy of Pension Reform: Latin America in Comparative Perspective." Prepared for delivery at the Meetings of the Latin American Studies Association, Miami, FL, March 16–18.

2012. *Democracy and the Left: Social Policy and Inequality in Latin America.* Chicago: University of Chicago Press.

Huber, Evelyne, Thomas Mustillo, and John D. Stephens. 2008. "Politics and Social Spending in Latin America," *The Journal of Politics* 70, no. 2: 420–36.

Huneeus, Carlos. 2000. *El régimen de Pinochet.* Santiago de Chile: Editorial Sudamericana.

2007a. *The Pinochet Regime.* Boulder, CO: Lynne Rienner Publishers.

2007b. "El Partido Demócrata Cristiano," in Carlos Huneeus, Fabiola Berríos, and Ricardo Gamboa, eds. *Las elecciones chilenas de 2005: Partidos, coaliciones y votantes en transición.* Santiago de Chile: Catalonia.

Huneeus, Carlos, Fabiola Berríos, and Ricardo Gamboa, eds. 2007. *Las elecciones chilenas de 2005: partidos, coaliciones y votantes en transición.* Santiago de Chile: Catalonia.

Hunter, Wendy. 2007. "The Normalization of an Anomaly: The Workers' Party in Brazil," *World Politics* 59, no. 3: 440–75.

2010. *The Transformation of the Workers' Party in Brazil, 1989–2009.* Cambridge: Cambridge University Press.

Hunter, Wendy and Timothy Power. 2007. "Executive Power, Social Policy and the Brazilian Elections of 2006," *Latin American Politics and Society* 49, no. 1: 1–30.

Hunter, Wendy and Natalia Borges Sugiyama. 2009. "Democracy and Social Policy in Brazil: Advancing Basic Needs, Preserving Privileged Interests," *Latin American Politics and Society* 51, no. 2: 29–58.

IBOPE. 2006. *Pesquisa de Opinião Publica sobre Assuntos Políticos/ Administrativos.* São Paulo: Julio. Opp 172.

Instituto Nacional de Estadística (INE). 1976. *Chile, XI censo de población (1940): recopilación de cifras publicadas por la Dirección de Estadística y Censos.* Chile, Centro Latinoamericano de Demografía.

International Labour Office (ILO). 1960. *Social Security in Agriculture.* Geneva: ILO.

IPEA. 2004. "Política Sociais." *Acompanhamento e Análise* 9. Brasília: IPEA.

2006. "A queda recente da desigualdade no Brasil." *Nota Tecnica* 8. Brasília: IPEA.

Instituto Brasileiro de Geografia e Estatística (IBGE). 2005. *Síntese de Indicadores Sociais. Estudos e Pesquisas* 17. Rio de Janeiro: IBGE.

2008. "Síntese de Indicadores Sociais." *Estudos e Pesquisas* 23. Rio de Janeiro: IBGE.

Instituto Nacional de Estadística y Geografía (INEGI). 2014. *Encuesta Nacional De Empleo y Seguridad Social 2013 (ENESS).* Mexico: INEGI.

Isuani, Ernesto A. 1985. *Los orígenes conflictivos de la seguridad social argentina.* Buenos Aires: Centro Editor de América Latina.

Isuani, Ernesto and Jorge San Martino. 1994. *La reforma provisional en Argentina, opciones y riesgos*. Buenos Aires: Miño y Dávila Editores.

Iversson, Lygia Busch. 1976. "Aspectos epidemiológicos da meningite meningocócica no município de São Paulo (Brasil) no período de 1968 a 1974," *Revista de Saúde pública*: 1–16.

Jaccoud, Luciana, Frederico Barbosa da Silva, Guilherme C. Delgado, Jorge Abrahão de Castro, José Celso Cardoso Jr., Mário Theodoro, and Nathalie Beghin, eds. 2005. *Questão social e políticas sociais no brasil contemporâneo*. Brasilia: IPEA.

James, Daniel. 1976. "The Peronist Left: 1955–1975," *Journal of Latin American Studies* 8, no. 2: 273–96.

1978. "Power and Politics in Peronist Trade Unions," *Journal of Interamerican Studies and World Affairs* 20, no. 1: 3–36.

Jenks, Margaret. 1979. "Political Parties in Authoritarian Brazil." PhD Dissertation, Department of Political Science, Duke University.

Joignant, Alfredo and Patricio Navia. 2003. "De la política del individuo a los hombres del partido," *Estudios Públicos* 89: 130–71.

Kalinsky, Beatriz, Wille Arrúe, and Diana Rossi. 1993. *La salud y los caminos de la participación social: marcas institucionales e históricas*. Centro Editor de América Latina.

Kaufman, Robert and Joan M. Nelson, eds. 2004. *Crucial Needs, Weak Incentives: Social Sector Reform, Democratization, and Globalization in Latin America*. Washington, DC: Woodrow Wilson Center Press.

Kaufman, Robert and Alex Segura-Ubiergo. 2001. "Globalization, Domestic Politics, and Social Spending in Latin America: A Time-Series Cross-Section Analysis, 1973–97," *World Politics* 53, no. 4: 553–87.

Kaufman, Robert and Guillermo Trejo. 1997. "Regionalism, Regime Transformation, and PRONASOL: The Politics of the National Solidarity Program in Four Mexican States," *Journal of Latin American Studies* 29: 717–45.

Kay, Stephen J. 1998. "Politics and Social Security Reform in the Southern Cone and Brazil." PhD dissertation, Department of Political Science, University of California, Los Angeles.

Keck, Margaret E. 1989. "The New Unionism in the Brazilian Transition," in Alfred Stepan, ed. *Democratizing Brazil: Problems of Transition and Consolidation*. New York: Oxford University Press.

1992. *The Workers' Party and Democratization in Brazil*. New Haven, CT: Yale University Press.

Keck, Margaret and Kathryn Sikkink. 1998. *Activists Beyond Borders: Advocacy Networks in International Politics*. Ithaca, NY: Cornell University Press.

Kessler, Timothy. 1998. "Political Capital. Mexican Financial Policy under Salinas," *World Politics* 51, no. 1: 36–66.

Kinzo, Maria D'Alva Gil. 1988. *Legal Opposition Politics under Authoritarian Rule in Brazil: the Case of the MDB, 1966-79*. New York: St Martin's.

Kitschelt, Herbert, Kirk Andrew Hawkins, Juan Pablo Luna, Guillermo Rosas, and Elizabeth J. Zechmeister, eds. 2010. *Latin American Party Systems*. Cambridge, New York: Cambridge University Press.

Kitschelt, Herbert and Stephen Wilkinson, eds. 2007. *Patrons, Clients and Policies: Patterns of Democratic Accountability and Political Competition.* Cambridge: Cambridge University Press.

Klesner, Joseph. 2005. "Electoral Competition and the New Party System in Mexico," *Latin American Politics and Society* 47, no. 2: 103–42.

Knight, Peter and Ricardo Moran. 1981. *Brazil: Poverty and Basic Needs Series.* Washington, DC: The World Bank.

Kowarick, Lúcio, ed. 1994. *As lutas sociais e a cidade.* São Paulo: Paz e Terra.

Kurtz, Marcus J. 2004a. "The Dilemmas of Democracy in the Open Economy," *World Politics* 56: 262–302.

2004b. *Free-Market Democracy and the Chilean and Mexican Countryside.* Cambridge: Cambridge University Press.

Labra, Maria Eliana. 2005. "Conselhos de saúde: dilemas, avanços e desafios," in Nísia Trindade Lima, Silvia Gerschman, Flavio Coelho Edler, and Julio Manuel Suárez, eds. *Saúde e democracia: história e perspectiva do SUS.* Rio de Janeiro: Fiocruz.

Lake, David A. and Matthew Baum. 2001. "The Invisible Hand of Democracy: Political Control and the Provision of Public Services," *Comparative Political Studies* 34 no. 6: 587–621.

Lakin, Jason M. 2010. "The End of Insurance? Mexico's Seguro Popular, 2001–2007," *Journal of Health Politics, Policy and Law* 35, no. 3: 313–52.

Lander, Edgardo. 1995. *Neoliberalismo, sociedad civil y democracia: ensayos sobre América Latina y Venezuela.* Caracas: Universidad Central de Venezuela.

Landim, Leilah, ed. 1998. *Ações em sociedade.* Rio de Janeiro: Nau Editora.

Lanzaro, Jorge. 2004. "Los uruguayos se acercan a la izquierda y la izquierda se acerca a los uruguayos. Claves del desarrollo del Frente Amplio," in Jorge Lanzaro, ed. *La izquierda uruguaya entre la oposición y el gobierno.* Montevideo: Editorial Fin de Siglo.

Lawson, Chappell H. 2004. "Introduction," in Jorge I. Domínguez and Chappell H. Lawson, eds. *Mexico's Pivotal Democratic Election: Candidates, Voters, and the Presidential Campaign of 2000.* Stanford, CA: Stanford University Press.

2009. "The Mexican 2006 Election in Context," in Jorge I. Domínguez, Chappell H. Lawson, and Alejandro Moreno, eds. *Consolidating Mexico's Democracy: The 2006 Presidential Campaign in Comparative Perspective.* Baltimore, MD: Johns Hopkins University Press.

Lenz, Rony. 2007. "Proceso Político de la reforma auge de salud en chile: algunas lecciones Para américa latina una mirada desde la economía Política," *Serie Estudios Socio-económicos* no. 38. Santiago de Chile: CIEPLAN.

Levitsky, Steven. 2003. *Transforming Labor-Based Parties in Latin America: Argentine Peronism in Comparative Perspective.* Cambridge: Cambridge University Press.

2013. "Peru: The Challenges of a Democracy without Parties," in Jorge Domínguez and Michael Shifter, eds. *Constructing Democratic Governance in Latin America.* Baltimore, MD: Johns Hopkins University Press.

Levitsky, Steven and Maxwell A. Cameron. 2003. "Democracy Without Parties? Political Parties and Regime Change in Fujimori's Peru," *Latin American Politics and Society* 45, no. 3: 1–33.

Levitsky, Steven and James Loxton. 2013. "Populism and Competitive Authoritarianism in the Andes," *Democratization* 20, no. 1: 107–36.

Levitsky, Steven, James Loxton, Brandon van Dyck, and Jorge I. Domínguez, eds. 2016. *Challenges of Party-Building in Latin America*. Cambridge; New York: Cambridge University Press.

Levitsky, Steven and María Victoria Murillo. 2003. "Argentina Weathers the Storm," *Journal of Democracy* 14, no. 4: 152–66.

2008. "Argentina: From Kirchner to Kirchner," *Journal of Democracy* 19, no. 2: 16–30.

2009. "Variation in Institutional Strength," *Annual Review of Political Science* 12: 115–33.

Levitsky, Steven and Kenneth Roberts. 2011. "Latin America's Left Turn: A Conceptual and Theoretical Overview," in *Latin America's Left Turn: Political Diversity and the Search for Alternatives*. Baltimore, MD: Johns Hopkins University Press.

Levitsky, Steven and Lucan A. Way. 2010. *Competitive Authoritarianism: Hybrid Regimes after the Cold War*. New York: Cambridge University Press.

Levcovitz, Eduardo, Luciana Dias de Lima, and Cristiani Vieira Machado. "Política de saúde nos anos 90: relações intergovernamentais e o papel das Normas Operacionais Básicas," *Ciência & Saúde Coletiva* 6, no. 2: 269–91.

Levy, Jonah D. 1999. "Vice into Virtue? Progressive Politics and Welfare Reform in Continental Europe," *Politics and Society* 27: 239–74.

Levy, Santiago. 2006. *Progress against Poverty: Sustaining Mexico's Progresa Oportunidades*. Washington, DC: Brookings Institution Press.

Lieberman, Evan. 2003. *Race and Regionalism in the Politics of Taxation in Brazil and South Africa*. New York: Cambridge University Press.

2009. *Boundaries of Contagion: How Ethnic Politics Have Shaped Government Responses to AIDS*. Princeton, NJ: Princeton University Press.

Lieberman, Robert. 1998. *Shifting the Color Line: Race and the American Welfare State*. Cambridge, MA: Harvard University Press.

Lima, Boris. 1995. "Focalización de programas masivos en Venezuela: la Beca Alimentaria," *Focalización y Pobreza*, Santiago de Chile: Cuadernos Comisión Económica para América Latina y el Caribe.

Lima, Nísia Trindade, Silvia Gerschman, Flavio Coelho Edler, and Julio Manuel Suárez, eds. 2005. *Saúde e democracia: história e perspectiva do SUS*. Rio de Janeiro: Fiocruz.

Lindvall, Johnnes and David Rueda. 2014. "The Insider-Outsider Dilemma," *British Journal of Political Science*, 44, no. 2: 460–75.

Lipsky, Michael. 1968. "Protest as a Political Resource," *American Political Science Review* 62, no. 4: 1144–58.

Lobato, Ana, ed. 1998. *Garantía de renda mínima*. Brasília: IPEA.

López Maya, Margarita. 2005. *Del viernes negro al referendo revocatorio*. Caracas: Alfa Grupo Editorial.

2011. "Venezuela: Hugo Chávez and the Populist Left," in Steven Levitsky and Kenneth. M. Roberts, eds. *The Resurgence of the Latin American Left.* Baltimore, MD: Johns Hopkins University Press.

Love, Joseph. 1970. "Political Participation in Brazil, 1881–1969," *Luso-Brazilian Review* 7, no. 2: 3–24.

Loveman, Brian. 1976. *Struggle in the Countryside: Politics and Rural Labor in Chile, 1919–1973.* Bloomington: Indiana University Press.

1979. *Chile: The Legacy of Hispanic Capitalism.* New York: Oxford University Press.

Lucchese, Patrícia. 1996. "Descentralização do financiamento e gestão da assistência à saúde no Brasil: a implementação do Sistema Único de Saúde—retrospectiva 1990/1995," *Planejamento e Políticas Públicas* 14. IPEA: Brasília.

Lujambio, Alonso. 2001. "Democratization through Federalism? The National Action Party Strategy, 1939–1995," in Kevin Middlebrook, ed. *Party Politics and the Struggle for Democracy in Mexico.* La Jolla: Center for U.S.-Mexican Studies, USDC.

Luna, Juan Pablo. 2007. "The Frente Amplio and the Crafting of a Social Democratic Alternative in Uruguay," *Latin American Politics and Society* 49, no. 4: 1–30.

2010. "Segmented Party-Voter Linkages in Latin America: The Case of the UDI," *Journal of Latin American Studies* 42, no. 2: 325–56.

2014. *Segmented Representation: Political Party Strategies in Unequal Democracies.* Oxford Studies in Democratization. Oxford: Oxford University Press.

Luna, Juan Pablo and Rodrigo Mardones. 2014. "Chile's Education Transfers, 2001–2009," in Diego Abente-Brun and Larry Diamond, eds. *Clientelism, Social Policy, and the Quality of Democracy.* Baltimore. MD: Johns Hopkins University Press.

Lund, Francie. 2008. *Changing Social Policy. The Child Support Grant in South Africa.* Cape Town: HSRC Press.

Lupu, Noam. 2014. "Brand Dilution and the Breakdown of Political Parties in Latin America," *World Politics* 66, no. 4: 561–602.

Lustig, Nora. 2015. "Most Unequal on Earth," *Finance and Development* 52, no. 3: 14-16.

Lvovich, Daniel. 2006. "Sindicatos y empresarios frente al problema de la seguridad social en los albores del peronismo," in Daniel Lvovich and Juan Suriano, eds. *Las políticas sociales en perspectiva histórica argentina, 1870–1952.* Buenos Aires: Prometeo Libros.

Lynch, Julia. 2006. *Age in the Welfare State: The Origins of Spending on Pensioners, Workers and Children.* Cambridge: Cambridge University Press.

Madrid, Raúl. 2002. "The Politics and Economics of Pension Privatization in Latin America," *Latin American Research Review* 37, no. 2: 159–82.

2003. *Retiring the State: The Politics of Pension Privatization in Latin America and Beyond.* Stanford, CA: Stanford University Press.

2012. *The Rise of Ethnic Politics in Latin America.* Cambridge: Cambridge University Press.

Magaloni, Beatriz. 2006. *Voting for Autocracy: Hegemonic Party Survival and Its Demise in Mexico*. Cambridge: Cambridge University Press.

Mahoney, James. 2000. "Strategies in Causal Inference in Small-n Research," *Sociological Methods and Research* 28, no. 4: 387–424.

Mahoney, James and Kathleen Thelen, eds. 2010. *Explaining Institutional Change: Ambiguity, Agency, and Power*. New York: Cambridge University Press.

Mainwaring, Scott. 1989. "Grassroots, Popular Movements, and the Struggle for Democracy: Nova Iguaçu," in Alfred Stepan, ed. *Democratizing Brazil: Problems of Transition and Consolidation*. New York: Oxford University Press.

1995. "Brazil: Weak Parties, Feckless Democracy," in Scott Mainwaring and Timothy R. Scully, eds. *Building Democratic Institutions: Party Systems in Latin America*. Stanford, CA: Stanford University Press.

1999. *Rethinking Party System Theory in the Third Wave of Democratization*. Princeton, NJ: Princeton University Press.

Mainwaring, Scott and Matthew S. Shugart. 1997. "Juan Linz, Presidentialism, and Democracy: A Critical Appraisal," *Comparative Politics* 29, no. 4: 449–71.

Makino, Kumiko. 2004. "Social Security Policy Reform in Post-Apartheid South Africa." Durban: Centre for Civil Society.

Malloy, James. 1979. *The Politics of Social Security in Brazil*. Pittsburgh: University of Pittsburgh Press.

Mares, Isabela. 2003. *The Politics of Social Risk: Business and Welfare State Development*. Cambridge: Cambridge University Press.

Marques, Rosa Maria and Áquilas Mendes. 2004. "O governo lula e a contra-reforma previdenciária," *São paulo em perspectiva* 18, no. 3: 3–15.

Marx, Anthony. 1998. *Making Race and Nation: A Comparison of South Africa, the United States and Brazil*. Cambridge: Cambridge University Press.

Masoud, Tarek. 2014. *Counting Islam: Religion, Class, and Elections in Egypt*. New York: Cambridge University Press.

Massa, Sergio Tomás and Miguel A. Fernández Pastor. 2007. *De la exclusión a la inclusión social: reformas de la reforma de la seguridad social en la República Argentina*. Ciudad de Buenos Aires, Argentina: TELAM: Prometeo Libros.

Mattini, Luis. 1990. *Hombres y mujeres del PRT-ERP: la pasión militante*. Buenos Aires: Editorial Contrapunto.

Maybury-Lewis, Biorn. 1994. *The Politics of the Possible: The Brazilian Rural Workers' Trade Union Movement, 1964–1985*. Philadelphia: Temple University Press.

Mayosi, Bongani and Solomon Benatar. 2014. "Health and Health Care in South Africa, 20 Years after Mandela," *The New England Journal of Medicine* 371, no. 14: 1344–53.

McAdam, Doug. 1999. *Political Process and the Development of Black Insurgency, 1930–1970*. Chicago: University of Chicago Press.

McAdam, Doug, John D. McCarthy, and Mayer N. Zald, eds. 1996. *Comparative Perspectives on Social Movements: Political Opportunities, Mobilizing Structures, and Cultural Framing*. New York: Cambridge University Press.

McCarthy, John D. 2005. "Persistence and Change among Nationally Federated Social Movements," in Gerald F. Davis, Doug McAdam, William Richard, Scott Mayer, and Nathan Zald, eds. *Social Movements and Organization Theory*. Cambridge: Cambridge University Press.

McGuire, James W. 1995. "Political Parties and Democracy in Argentina," in Scott Mainwaring and Timothy Scully, eds. *Building Democratic Institutions: Party Systems in Latin America*. Stanford, CA: Stanford University Press.

1997. *Peronism without Perón: Unions, Parties, and Democracy in Argentina*. Stanford, CA: Stanford University Press.

2010. *Wealth, Health, and Democracy in East Asia and Latin America*. New York: Cambridge University Press.

Medici, André Cezar. 1997. *A Dinâmica do setor saúde no Brasil. Transformações e tendências nas décadas de 80 e 90*. Santiago de Chile: Comisión Económica para América Latina y el Caribe.

Medlin, Carol Ann. 1999. "Limits to Social Reform: Neoliberal Social Policy in Chile 1973–1989." PhD Dissertation, Department of Political Science, University of California, Berkeley.

Melo, Marcus André. 2008. "Unexpected Successes, Unanticipated Failures: Social Policy from Cardoso to Lula," in Peter R. Kingstone and Timothy J. Power, eds. *Democratic Brazil Revisited*. Pittsburgh: University of Pittsburgh Press.

Meneguello, Rachel. 1989. *PT: a formação de um partido, 1979–1982*. São Paulo, SP: Paz e Terra.

Mercer, Hugo. 1990. "La atención de la salud infantil: un espacio para el cambio," in Eduardo S. Bustelo and Ernesto A. Isuani, eds. *Mucho, poquito o nada: Crisis y alternativas de política social en los 90*. Buenos Aires: Centro Interdisciplinario para el Estudio de Políticas Públicas: UNICEF: Siglo Veintiuno de España Editores: Distribuye Catálogos S.R.L.

Mesa-Lago, Carmelo. 1978. *Social Security in Latin America: Pressure Groups, Stratification and Inequality*. Pittsburgh: University of Pittsburgh Press.

1989. *Ascent to Bankruptcy: Financing Social Security in Latin America*. Pittsburgh: University of Pittsburgh Press.

1994. *Changing Social Security in Latin America: Toward Alleviating the Social Costs of Economic Reform*. Boulder, CO: Lynne Rienner Publishers.

Meyer, John W. and Brian Rowan. 1977. "Institutionalized Organizations: Formal Structure as Myth and Ceremony," *American Journal of Sociology* 83, no. 2: 340-63.

Michiles, Carlos, ed. 1989. *Cidadão constituinte: a saga das emendas populares*. Rio de Janeiro: Paz e Terra.

Middlebrook, Kevin J. 1995. *The Paradox of Revolution: Labor, the State, and Authoritarianism in Mexico*. Baltimore, MD: Johns Hopkins University Press.

Ministério da Previdência e Assistência Social. 2002. *Livro branco da Previdência Social*. Brasília-DF: MPAS.

Ministério da Saúde. 2009. *Mais saúde, direito de todos*. Brasilia DF: Ministério da Saúde.

Ministério das Relações Exteriores. 2008. "Discursos selecionados do Presidente Itamar Franco." www.funag.org.br.

Ministerio de Defensa Nacional 2014. *Ley-20735*. Santiago: Biblioteca del Congreso Nacional de Chile.

Ministerio de Desarrollo Social (MIDES). 2009. *Reporte social 2009*. Montevideo: MIDES.

Ministerio de Planificación y Cooperación (MIDEPLAN). 1994. *Integración al desarrollo. Balance de la política social: 1990–1993*. Santiago de Chile: MIDEPLAN.

    2001. *Caracterización de los sistemas de previsión social y de sus afiliados en Chile, Documento No. 21*, Santiago de Chile: MIDEPLAN.

Ministerio de Planificación (MIDEPLAN). 2005. *Informe de evaluación del estado de avance del Sistema Chile Solidario*. Santiago de Chile: MIDEPLAN.

    2006. *Resultados de la encuesta CASEN, adulto mayor*. Santiago de Chile: MIDEPLAN.

    2013. "Casen 2013: Adultos Mayores Síntesis de Resultados." Santiago de Chile: MIDEPLAN.

Ministerio de Planificación e Inversión Pública. 2008. "*Balance de gestión.*" Buenos Aires. www.minplan.gov.ar/html/publicaciones/doc/gestion2008.pdf

Ministerio de Salud. n/d. *Participacion Social en Salud. La Experiencia del Plan Remediar*. Buenos Aires: Ministerio de Salud. www.remediar.msal.gov.ar

    2004a. "Bases Del Plan Federal de Salud 2004–2007," Buenos Aires.

    2004b. *Boletin PROAPS-Remediar* 8, no. 2. Buenos Aires: Ministerio de Salud.

    2006. *El Programa Remediar: gestión y resultados de un modelo innovador de APS*. Buenos Aires: Ministerio de Salud.

Ministerio de Trabajo, Empleo y Seguridad Social (MTEySS). 2003. "Libro Blanco de La Prevision Social." Buenos Aires: MTEySS.

    2004. *Segunda evaluación del Programa Jefes de Hogar*. Buenos Aires: Subsecretaria de Programación Técnica y Estudios Laborales. MTEySS.

    2006. *Boletín Estadístico de la Seguridad Social*. Buenos Aires: MTEySS.

    2007. *Programa Jefes de Hogar. Informe Resumen*. Buenos Aires: Secretaría de Empleo. MTEySS.

    2009. *Boletín Estadístico de la Seguridad Social*. Buenos Aires: MTEySS.

Mizrahi, Yemile. 1994. "A New Conservative Opposition in Mexico: The Politics of Entrepreneurs in Chihuahua (1983–1992)." PhD Dissertation, Department of Political Science, University of California, Berkeley.

Moreira, Costanza. 2004. *Final de Juego*. Montevideo: Ediciones Trilce.

Mulligan, Casey B., Ricard Gil, and Xavier Sala-i-Martin. 2004. "Do Democracies Have Different Public Policies than Nondemocracies?" *Journal of Economic Perspectives* 18, no. 1: 51–74.

Murillo, M. Victoria. 2001. *Labor Unions, Partisan Coalitions, and Market Reforms in Latin America*. Cambridge: Cambridge University Press.

    2009. *Political Competition, Partisanship, and Policymaking in Latin American Public Utilities*. Cambridge: Cambridge University Press.

Murillo, M. Victoria and Cecilia Martínez Gallardo. 2007. "Political Competition and Reform Adoption: Market Reforms in Latin American Public Utilities," *American Journal of Political Science* 51, no. 1: 120–39.

Murillo, M. Victoria and Andrew Schrank. 2005. "With a Little Help from My Friends: Partisan Politics, Transnational Alliances, and Labor Rights in Latin America," *Comparative Political Studies* 38, no. 8: 971–99.

Nari, Marcela. 2004. *Políticas de maternidad y maternalismo político, Buenos Aires, 1890–1940*. Buenos Aires: Biblos.

Navia, Patricio. 2006. "Three Is Company: Old and New Alignments in Chile's Party System," in Silvia Borzutzky and Lois Oppenheim, eds. *Politics after Pinochet*. Gainesville: University Press of Florida.

Nelson, Joan M. 1992. "Poverty, Equity and the Politics of Adjustment," in Stephen Haggard and Robert Kaufman, eds. *The Politics of Economic Adjustment*. Princeton, NJ: Princeton University Press.

Neri, Aldo. 1982. *Salud y Política Social*. Buenos Aires: Librería Hachette.

Néri, Marcelo. 2004. "O Programa Fome Zero e a política social," in Marlene da Rocha, ed. *Segurança alimentar: um desafio para acabar com a fome no Brasil*. São Paulo: Fundacão Perseu Abramo.

Novaes, Regina. 1991. "CONTAG e CUT: Continuidades e rupturas na organização sindical no campo," in Armando Boitto Jr, ed. *O sindicalismo brasileiro nos anos 90*. São Paulo: Paz e Terra.

Novaro, Marcos and Vicente Palermo. 1998. *Los caminos de la centroizquierda*. Buenos Aires: Editorial Losada.

O'Donnell, Guillermo. 1979. *Modernization and Bureaucratic-Authoritarianism: Studies in South American Politics*. Berkeley: Institute of International Studies, University of California.

Oliveira, Jaime Araujo de, and Sonia Fleury de Teixeira. 1985. *(Im)previdência Social*. Petrópolis: Vozes.

Olson, Jr., Mancur. 1965. *The Logic of Collective Action: Public Goods and the Theory of Groups*. Cambridge, MA: Harvard University Press.

Ondetti, Gabriel. 2006. "Repression, Opportunity, and Protest: Explaining the Takeoff of Brazil's Landless Movement," *Latin American Politics & Society* 48, no. 2: 61–94.

———. 2008. *Land, Protest, and Politics: The Landless Movement and the Struggle for Agrarian Reform in Brazil*. University Park: Pennsylvania State University Press.

O'Neil, Shannon K. 2006. "Political Participation after Reform: Pensions Politics in Latin America." PhD Dissertation, Department of Government, Harvard University.

Ortiz, Mauricio. 2006. *El seguro popular: una crónica de la democracia mexicana*. Mexico: Fondo de Cultura Económica.

Ostiguy, Pierre. 1998. "Peronism and Anti-Peronism: Class-Cultural Cleavages and Political Identity in Argentina." PhD dissertation, Department of Political Science, University of California, Berkeley.

Oxhorn, Philip. 1995. *Organizing Civil Society: The Popular Sectors and the Struggle for Democracy in Chile*. University Park, PA: Pennsylvania State University Press.

———. 1998. "The Social Foundations of Latin America's Recurrent Populism," *Journal of Historical Sociology* 11, no. 2: 212–46.

Partido da Frente Liberal. 1998. *Política social para o Brasil*. Brasília: Diretório Nacional do PFL.

Partido dos Trabalhadores. 1994. *Os compromissos da Frente Brasil Popular com a saúde e a vida*. São Paulo: Fundação Perseu Abramo (CD-rom).

———. 1998a. *União do povo muda Brasil*. São Paulo: Fundação Perseu Abramo (CD-rom).

1998b. *Carta Compromisso*. São Paulo: Fundação Perseu Abramo (CD-rom).

Penfold-Becerra, Michael. 2007. "Clientelism and Social Funds: Evidence from Chavez's Missions," *Latin American Politics and Society* 49, no. 4: 63–84.

Pereira, Anthony. 1997. *The End of the Peasantry: The Rural Labor Movement in Northeast Brazil, 1961–1968*. Pittsburgh: University of Pittsburgh Press.

Pereira, Clara. 2010. "Análisis de cobertura del régimen previsional uruguayo 1996-2010," *Comentarios de Seguridad Social*, no 33. Montevideo.

Pérez-Liñán, Aníbal. 2007. *Presidential Impeachment and the New Political Instability in Latin America*. New York: Cambridge University Press.

Pérez-Liñán, Aníbal, and Scott Mainwaring. 2013. "Regime Legacies and Levels of Democracy: Evidence from Latin America," *Comparative Politics* 45, no. 4: 379–97.

Pierson, Paul. 1994. *Dismantling the Welfare State? Reagan, Thatcher and the Politics of Retrenchment*. Cambridge: Cambridge University Press.

1996. "The New Politics of the Welfare State," *World Politics* 48, no. 2: 143–79.

2004. *Politics in Time: History, Institutions, and Social Analysis*. Princeton, NJ: Princeton University Press.

Pinto, Carolina. 2006. *UDI: La Conquista de Corazones Populares (1983–1987)*. Santiago: Editorial A&V.

Pollack, Marcelo. 1999. *The New Right in Chile, 1972–97*. London: MacMillan Press.

Portes, Alejandro and Kelly Hoffman. 2003. "Latin American Class Structures: Their Composition and Change during the Neoliberal Era," *Latin American Research Review* 38, no. 1: 41–82.

Portugal Jr., José Geraldo, Fernando Azevedo de Arruda Sampaio, and Cristian Andrei, eds. 1998. *Gestão estatal no Brasil: o governo Itamar Franco, 1992–1994*. São Paulo: Edições Fundap.

Posner, Paul W. 2008. *State, Market, and Democracy in Chile: The Constraint of Popular Participation*. New York: Palgrave Macmillan.

Pozas Horcasitas, Ricardo. 1992. "El desarrollo de la Seguridad Social en México," *Revista Mexicana de Sociología* 54, no. 4: 27–63.

Pozzi, Pablo. 2004. *Por Las Sendas Argentinas: El PRT-ERP, La Guerrilla Marxista*. Buenos Aires: Imago Mundi.

Pribble, Jennifer. 2013. *Welfare and Party Politics in Latin America*. New York: Cambridge University Press.

Pribble, Jennifer and Evelyne Huber. 2011. "Social Policy and Redistribution: Chile and Uruguay," in Steven Levitsky and Kenneth M. Roberts, eds. *The Resurgence of the Latin American Left*. Baltimore, MD: Johns Hopkins University Press.

Raczynski, Dagmar. 1994. "Social Policies in Chile Origins, Transformations, and Perspectives," *Democracy and Social Policy Series Working Paper* 4. Kellogg Institute. University of Notre Dame.

2000. "Overcoming Poverty in Chile," in Joseph Tulchin and Alison Garland, eds. *Social Development in Latin America: The Politics of Reform*. Boulder, CO: Lynne Rienner Publishers.

2001. "The Crisis of the Old Models of Social Protection in Latin America," in Victor Tockman and Guillermo O'Donnell, eds. *Poverty and Inequality in Latin America: Issues and New Challenges*. Notre Dame: University of Notre Dame Press.

Ramacciotti, Karina Inés. 2006. "Las voces que cuestionaron la política sanitaria del peronismo (1946–1949)," in Daniel Lvovich and Juan Suriano, eds. *Las políticas sociales en perspectiva histórica argentina, 1870–1952*. Buenos Aires: Prometeo Libros.

Ramírez Sainz, Juan Manuel. 1994. "Aportaciones políticas del Movimiento Urbano Popular," *Revista Mexicana de Sociología* 56, no. 3: 89–112.

Rehem, Renilson. 2003. "Construindo o sus: a lógica do financiamento e o processo de divisão de responsibilidades entre as esferas de governo," in Cèlia Regina Pierantoni and Cid Manso M. Vianna, eds. *Gestão de Sistemas de Saúde*. Rio de Janeiro: UERJ, Instituto de Medicina Social.

Repetto, Fabián. 2001. *Gestión pública y desarrollo social en los noventa. Las trayectorias de Argentina y Chile*. Buenos Aires: Prometeo.

República de Chile. 2004. *Cámara de Diputados*. Legislatura 351, Sesión 26. August 10. Santiago de Chile.

——— 2007. *Cámara de Diputados*. Legislatura 355, Sesión 68. August 28. Santiago de Chile.

República Federativa do Brasil. 1997. *Diário da Câmara dos Deputados*. Ano LII (222), December 5. Brasília.

——— 2001. *Diário da Câmara dos Deputados*. Ano LVI (045), April 5. Brasília.

Cámara de Representantes. 2003. *Diario de Sesiones*. XLV Legislatura, December 30. Montevideo.

Roberts, Kenneth. 1995. "Neoliberalism and the Transformation of Populism in Latin America: The Peruvian Case," *World Politics* 48, no. 1: 82–116.

——— 1998. *Deepening Democracy? The Modern Left and Social Movements in Chile and Peru*. Stanford, CA: Stanford University Press.

——— 2002. "Social Inequalities without Class Cleavages in Latin America's Neoliberal Era," *Studies in Comparative International Development* 36, no. 4: 3–33.

——— 2006. "Populism, Political Conflict, and Grassroots Organization in Latin America," *Comparative Politics* 38, no. 2: 128–46.

——— 2014. *Changing Course in Latin America: Party Systems in the Neoliberal Era*. Cambridge: Cambridge University Press.

Rocha, Marlene da, ed. 2004. *Segurança alimentar: um desafio para acabar com a fome no Brasil*. São Paulo: Fundacão Perseu Abramo.

Rocha Andrade Silva, Enid. 2000. "Efeitos da previdência social rural sobre a questão de gênero," in Guilherme Costa Delgado, José Celso Cardoso Jr., and Enid Rocha Andrade Silva, eds. *A universalização de direitos sociais no Brasil : a previdência rural nos anos 90*. Brasília: IPEA.

Rock, David. 1993. *Authoritarian Argentina: The Nationalist Movement, Its History and Its Impact*. Berkeley: University of California Press.

Rodrigues, Marta A. and Eduardo Meira Zauli. 2002. "Presidentes e congresso nacional no processo decisório da política de saúde no Brasil democrático," *Dados* 45, no. 3: 387–431.

Rodrigues Neto, Eleutério. 1997. "A via do Parlamento," in Sônia Fleury, ed. *Saúde e democracia: a luta do CEBES*. São Paulo: Lemos Editorial & Gráficos.

Rodríguez, Victoria and Peter M. Ward, eds. 1995. *Opposition Government in Mexico*. Albuquerque: University of New Mexico Press.

Ross, Michael L. 2006. "Is Democracy Good for the Poor?" *American Journal of Political Science* 50, no. 4: 860–74.

Ross, Peter. 2007. "The Construction of the Public Health System in Argentina 1946–1955," *Electroneurobiología* 15, no. 5: 107–78.

Rothstein, Bo. 1992. "Labor Markets and Working Class Strength," in Sven Steinmo, Kathleen Thelen, and Frank Longhstreth, eds. *Structuring Politics: Historical Institutionalism in Comparative Analysis*. Cambridge: Cambridge University Press.

2011. *The Quality of Government: Corruption, Social Trust, and Inequality in International Perspective*. Chicago: University of Chicago Press.

Roze, Jorge Próspero. 1992. *Conflictos agrarios en la Argentina: el proceso liguista*. Vol. 2. Buenos Aires: Centro Editor de América Latina.

Rueda, David. 2005. "Insider-Outsider Politics in Industrialized Democracies: The Challenge to Social Democratic Parties," *American Political Science Review* 99, no. 7: 61–74.

Social Democracy Inside Out: Partisanship and Labor Market Policy in Industrialized Democracies. Oxford: Oxford University Press.

Rudra, Nita. 2002. "Globalization and the Decline of the Welfare State in Less Developed Countries," *International Organization* 56, no. 2: 411–45.

Rudra, Nita and Stephan Haggard. 2005. "Globalization, Democracy, and Effective Welfare Spending in the Developing World," *Comparative Political Studies* 38, no. 9: 1015–49.

Sader, Eder. 1988. *Quando novos personagens entraram em cena*. São Paulo: Paz e Terra.

Sagner, Andreas. 2000. "Ageing and Social Policy in South Africa: Historical Perspectives with Particular Reference to the Eastern Cape," *Journal of Southern African Studies* 26, no. 3: 523–53.

Samuels, David. 2004. "From Socialism to Social Democracy: Party Organization and the Transformation of the Workers' Party in Brazil," *Comparative Political Studies* 37, no. 9: 999–1024.

Samuels, David J. and Cesar Zucco. 2012. "Crafting Mass Partisanship at the Grass Roots, from the Top Down." American Political Science Association Annual Meeting Paper.

Schady, Norbert R. 2000. "The Political Economy of Expenditures by the Peruvian Social Fund (FONCODES), 1991–95," *American Political Science Review* 94, no. 2: 289–304.

Schamis, Hector. 1999. "Distributional Coalitions and the Politics of Economic Reform in Latin America," *World Politics* 51, no. 2: 236–68.

Schattschneider, E. E. 1975. *The Semisovereign People: A Realist's View of Democracy in America*. Chicago: Wadsworth Thomson Learning.

Schijman, Agustina and Guadalupe Dorna. 2012. "Clase media y clase media vulnerable. Evidencia empírica de la volatilidad intrageneracional de los sectores medios en Argentina (1966-mitad de 2007)," *Desarrollo económico* 52, no. 206: 179–204.

Schneider, Cathy. 1995. *Shantytown Protest in Pinochet's Chile*. Philadelphia. PA: Temple University Press.

Schwarzer, Helmut. 2000. "Impactos socioeconômicos do sistema de aposentadorias rurais no Brasil. Evidências empíricas de um estudo de caso no Pará," in *Texto para Discussão* 729. Rio de Janeiro: IPEA.

Schwarzer, Helmut and Ana Carolina Querino. 2002. *Non-contributory Pensions in Brazil: The Impact on Poverty Reduction*. International Labour Office.

Scully, Timothy. 1992. *Rethinking the Center: Party Politics in Nineteenth- and Twentieth-Century Chile*. Stanford, CA: Stanford University Press.

  1995. "Reconstituting Party Politics in Chile," in Scott Mainwaring and Timothy R. Scully, eds. *Building Democratic Institutions: Party Systems in Latin America*. Stanford, CA: Stanford University Press.

Seawright, Jason and David Collier. 2004. "Glossary," in Henry Brady and David Collier, eds. *Rethinking Social Inquiry: Diverse Tools, Shared Standards*. Boulder, CO: Rowman and Littlefield.

Secretaria de Comunicação Social. 2008. *Destaques. Ações e programas do governo federal*. Brasília.

Secretaría de Política Económica. 2003. "Informe sobre los programas de empleo de ejecución provincial 2002," *Documentos de Trabajo* 14. Buenos Aires: Ministerio de Economía y Producción.

Secretaría de Salud. 2002. *Seguro Popular de Salud. Documento Técnico*. México: Secretaría de Salud.

  2004. *Sistema de Protección Social en Salud. Informe de Resultados 2007*. México: Secretaría de Salud.

  2007. *Sistema de Protección Social en Salud. Informe de Resultados 2007*. México: Secretaría de Salud.

  2008. *Sistema de Protección Social en Salud. Informe de Resultados 2008*. México: Secretaría de Salud.

  2013. *Sistema de Protección Social en Salud. Informe de Resultados 2013*. México: Secretaría de Salud.

SEDESOL. 2005. *Ley General de Desarrollo Social*. Mexico: SEDESOL.

Seekings, Jeremy. 2000. "The Origins of Social Citizenship in Pre-Apartheid South Africa." *South African Journal of Philosophy* 19, no. 4: 386–404.

  2007. "Poverty and Inequality after Apartheid." Paper presented at the Second After Apartheid Conference, New Haven, April 27–28.

Seekings, Jeremy and Nicoli Nattrass. 2005. *Class, Race, and Inequality in South Africa*. New Haven, CT: Yale University Press.

Segura-Ubiergo, Alex. 2007. *The Political Economy of the Welfare State in Latin America*. Cambridge: Cambridge University Press.

Seidman, Gay W. 1994. *Manufacturing Militance: Workers' Movements in Brazil and South Africa, 1970–1985*. Berkeley: University of California Press.

Serra, Jose and Regina Faria. 2004. "Reforma de la salud en Brasil 1995–2002" in Clarisa Hardy, ed. *Equidad y protección social: desafíos de políticas sociales en América Latina*. Santiago, Chile: Fundación Chile 21.

Siavelis, Peter. 2000. *The President and Congress in Post-authoritarian Chile: Institutional Constraints to Democratic Consolidation*. University Park: Pennsylvania State University Press.

2005. "Electoral System, Coalitional Disintegration, and the Future of Chile's Concertacion," *Latin American Research Review* 40, no. 1: 56–82.

2006. "Accommodating Informal Institutions and Chilean Democracy," in Gretchen Helmke and Steven Levitsky, eds. *Informal Institutions and Democracy: Lessons from Latin America*. Baltimore, MD: Johns Hopkins University Press.

Silva, Eduardo. 1996. *The State and Capital in Chile: Business Elites, Technocrats, and Market Economics*. Boulder, CO: Westview Press.

2009. *Challenging Neoliberalism in Latin America*. Cambridge: Cambridge University Press.

Silva, Sidney Jard da. 2001. "Companheiros servidores: O avanço do sindicalismo do setor público na CUT," *Revista Brasileira de Ciências Sociais* 16, no. 46: 130–46.

Silver, Beverly J. 2003. *Forces of Labor. Workers' Movements and Globalization since 1870*. Cambridge: Cambridge University Press.

Singer, Paul. 1999. *O Brasil na crise: perigos e oportunidades*. São Paulo: Editora Contexto.

Skocpol, Theda. 1992. *Protecting Soldiers and Mothers: The Political Origins of Social Policy in the United States*. Cambridge, MA: Belknap Press of Harvard University Press.

Soberón, Guillermo. 2001. "Hacia un México más saludable," in *FUNSALUD Cuaderno* 33. México, DF: FUNSALUD.

Soifer, Hillel. 2015. *State Building in Latin America*. New York: Cambridge University Press.

Soss, Joe. 1999. "Lessons of Welfare: Policy Design, Political Learning, and Political Action," *The American Political Science Review* 93, no. 2: 363–80.

Sour, Laura, Sandra Robles, Irma Ortega, Omar Avelino, and Marina Peña. 2004. "Diagnóstico jurídico y presupuestario del ramo 33: una etapa del federalismo en México." México, DF, CIDE.

South African Social Security Agency (SASSA). 2009. *Annual Statistical Report on Social Grants*. Pretoria: SASSA. www.ssassa.gov.za.

Spalding, Rose. 1980. "Welfare Policymaking. Theoretical Implications of a Mexican Case Study," *Comparative Politics* 12, no. 4: 419–38.

Sposati, Aldaiza. 2003. "Governando a política estadual de assistência social do PT," in Jorge Bittar, ed. *Governos Estaduais: Desafios e Avanços*. São Paulo: Fundação Perseu Abramo.

Stallings, Barbara. 1978. *Class Conflict and Economic Development in Chile, 1958–1973*. Stanford, CA: Stanford University Press.

Stephanes, Reinhold. 1998. *Reforma da Previdência: sem segredos*. Rio de Janeiro: Editora Record.

Stephany, Keta. 2006. *Políticas de Ajuste y Protesta Popular en Venezuela: 1989 y 1996*. Caracas: Universidad Central de Venezuela, Vicerrectorado Académico Ediciones FACES/UCV.

Stokes, Susan. 2005. "Perverse Accountability: A Formal Model of Machine Politics with Data from Argentina," *American Political Science Review* 99, no. 3: 315–25.

Strooy, Luis Romero. 2011. "Modelos y Mecanismos de Financiamiento en Sistemas de Salud." Santiago, Chile: Superintendencia de Salud.

Stuckler, David, Sanjay Basu, and Martin McKee. 2011. "Health Care Capacity and Allocations among South Africa's Provinces: Infrastructure–Inequality Traps after the End of Apartheid," *American Journal of Public Health* 101, no. 1.

Suplicy, Eduardo Matarazzo. 2006. "Citizen's Basic Income." São Paulo.

Svampa, Maristella and Sebastián Pereyra. 2003. *Entre la ruta y el barrio: la experiencia de las organizaciones piqueteras.* Buenos Aires: Editorial Biblos.

　2005. "La política de las organizaciones piqueteras," in Federico Naishtat, ed. *Tomar la Palabra.* Buenos Aires: Prometeo.

Tarrow, Sidney. 1998. *Power in Movement: Social Movements and Contentious Politics.* Cambridge: Cambridge University Press.

Thelen, Kathleen. 1999. "Historical Institutionalism in Comparative Politics," *Annual Review of Political Science* 2, no. 1: 369–404.

　2004. *How Institutions Evolve. The Political Economy of Skills in Germany, Britain, the United States, and Japan.* Cambridge: Cambridge University Press.

Thompson, Andrés A. 1985. "Estado, sindicatos y salud: notas sobre las obras sociales en Argentina," *Cuadernos médico sociales* 33: 35–53.

Titelman, Daniel. 2000. "Reformas al sistema de salud en Chile: desafíos pendientes," *Serie financiamiento del desarrollo* 104. Santiago de Chile: Comisión Económica para América Latina y el Caribe.

Tobar, Federico, Graciela Ventura, Leticia Montiel, and Rodrigo Falbo. n.d. "El Gasto en Medicamentos en Argentina." Buenos Aires.

Torre, Juan Carlos. 1990. *La vieja guardia sindical y Perón: sobre los orígenes del peronismo.* Buenos Aires: Editorial Sudamericana: Instituto Torcuato di Tella.

　1995. *El 17 de octubre de 1945.* Buenos Aires: Ariel.

　1998. *El proceso político de las reformas económicas en América Latina.* Buenos Aires: Paidós.

Touchstone, Michael and Brian Wampler. 2014. "Improving Social Well-Being through New Democratic Institutions," *Comparative Political Studies* 47, no. 10: 1442–69.

Trejo, Guillermo. 2004. "Indigenous Insurgency: Protest, Rebellion, and the Politicization of Ethnicity in 20th Century Mexico." PhD dissertation, University of Chicago.

　2012. *Popular Movements in Autocracies: Religion, Repression, and Indigenous Collective Action in Mexico.* New York: Cambridge University Press.

Valenzuela, Julio Samuel and Arturo Valenzuela, eds. 1986. *Military Rule in Chile: Dictatorship and Oppositions.* Baltimore, MD: Johns Hopkins University Press.

Van Cott, Donna Lee. 2005. *From Movements to Parties in Latin America: The Evolution of Ethnic Politics.* Cambridge: Cambridge University Press.

　2008. *Radical Democracy in the Andes.* Cambridge: Cambridge University Press.

Vargas Côrtes, Soraya, ed. 2009. *Participação e saúde no Brasil.* Rio de Janeiro: Fiocruz.

Veronelli, Juan Carlos. 1975. *Medicina, gobierno y sociedad.* Buenos Aires: Editorial el Coloquio.

Weir, Margaret. 1992. *Politics and Jobs: The Boundaries of Employment Policy.* Princeton, NJ: Princeton University Press.

Weitz-Shapiro, Rebecca. 2014. *Curbing Clientelism in Argentina: Politics, Poverty and Social Policy.* Cambridge: Cambridge University Press.

Western, Bruce. 1997. *Between Class and Market: Postwar Unionization in the Capitalist Democracies.* Princeton, NJ: Princeton University Press.

Weyland, Kurt. 1993. "The Rise and Fall of President Collor and Its Impact on Brazilian Democracy," *Journal of Interamerican Studies and World Affairs* 35, no. 1: 1–37.

    1996a. *Democracy without Equity: Failures of Reform in Brazil.* Pittsburgh. University of Pittsburgh Press.

    1996b. "How Much Power Do Economic Forces Have? Conflict over Social Insurance Reform in Brazil," *Public Policy* 16, no. 1: 59–84.

    2002. *The Politics of Market Reform in Fragile Democracies: Argentina, Brazil, Peru, and Venezuela.* Princeton, NJ: Princeton University Press.

    2005. "Theories of Policy Diffusion: Lessons from Latin American Pension Reform," *World Politics* 57, no. 2: 264–98.

    2006. *Bounded Rationality and Policy Diffusion: Social Sector Reform in Latin America.* Princeton, NJ: Princeton University Press.

    2011. "The Left: Destroyer or Savior of the Market Model?" in Steven Levitsky and Kenneth M. Roberts, eds. *The Resurgence of the Latin American Left.* Baltimore, MD: Johns Hopkins University Press.

Weyland, Kurt, ed. 2004. *Learning from Foreign Models in Latin American Policy Reform.* Washington, DC: Woodrow Wilson Center Press.

Weyland, Kurt, Raúl L. Madrid, and Wendy Hunter. 2010. *Leftist Governments in Latin America: Successes and Shortcomings.* Cambridge: Cambridge University Press.

Wilson, Luis, Aníbal Velásquez, and Carlos Ponce. 2009. "La Ley Marco de Aseguramiento Universal en Salud en el Perú: Análisis de Beneficios y Sistematización del Proceso Desde su Concepción Hasta su Promulgación." *Revista Peruana de Medicina Experimental y Salud Pública* 26, no. 2.

Wise, Carol. 2003. "Mexico's Democratic Transition" in Carol Wise and Riordan Roett, eds. *Post-stabilization Politics in Latin America.* Washington, DC: Brookings Institution Press.

Wood, Elisabeth. 2000. *Forging Democracy from Below: Insurgent Transitions in South Africa and El Salvador.* Cambridge: Cambridge University Press.

Wuhs, Steven. 2008. *Savage Democracy: Institutional Change and Party Development in Mexico.* University Park: Pennsylvania State University Press.

Yashar, Deborah. 2005. *Contesting Citizenship in Latin America: The Rise of Indigenous Movements and the Postliberal Challenge.* New York: Cambridge University Press.

Zaramberg, Gisela. 2004. "Alpargatas y libros: estilos de gestión, género y política social en Argentina y Chile," *Serie Políticas Sociales* 90. Santiago de Chile: Comisión Económica para América Latina y el Caribe.

Zarazaga, Rodrigo. 2014. "Brokers beyond Clientelism: A New Perspective through the Argentine Case." *Latin American Politics and Society* 56, no. 3: 23–45.

Zorrilla Arena, Santiago. 1988. *50 años de política social en México: de Lázaro Cárdenas a Miguel de la Madrid*. México-DF: Editorial Limusa.

Zucco, Cesar. 2008. "The President's 'New' Constituency: Lula and the Pragmatic Vote in Brazil's 2006 Presidential Elections," *Journal of Latin American Studies* 40, no. 1: 29–49.

2009. "Data: The President's New Constituency: Lula and the Pragmatic Vote in Brazil's 2006 Presidential Election." Harvard Dataverse. http://hdl.handle.net/1902.1/10701.

Index